HUMANAE VITAE
and Catholic Sexual Morality

A Response to the Pontifical Academy for Life's
Etica Teologica della Vita

EDITED BY
Robert Fastiggi and
Matthew Levering

SAPIENTIA PRESS
OF AVE MARIA UNIVERSITY

Copyright © 2024 by Sapientia Press of
Ave Maria University, Ave Maria, Florida
All rights reserved.
No part of this publication may be reproduced or transmitted
in any form or means, electronic or mechanical, including photography,
recording, or any other information storage or retrieval system, without
permission in writing from the publisher. Requests for permission to make
copies of any part of the work should be directed to:

Sapientia Press
of Ave Maria University
5050 Ave Maria Blvd.
Ave Maria, FL 34142
800-537-5487

Distributed by:
The Catholic University of America Press
c/o HFS
P.O. Box 50370
Baltimore, MD 21211
800-537-5487

Text and Cover Design: Kachergis Book Design
Cover Image: "Maternal Admiration," painting by William-Adolphe
Bouguereau, oil on canvas, 1869. Private collection. Courtesy
Wikimedia Commons.
Printed in the United States of America.
Library of Congress Control Number: 2023946799
ISBN: 978-1-932589-90-0

HUMANAE VITAE
and Catholic Sexual Morality

CONTENTS

Introduction   1

PART I. FOUNDATIONAL ISSUES

1. The "New Paradigm" in Moral Theology: Moving Forward or Turning Back?   7
   MONSIGNOR LIVIO MELINA

2. "He Who Has My Commandments and Keeps Them, He It Is Who Loves Me" (Jn 14:21): The Relevance of Scripture for Normative Morality   20
   FR. LUIS SÁNCHEZ-NAVARRO

3. Boldness in Inversion: Reflections on the Encyclical *Veritatis Splendor*   38
   MONSIGNOR PIOTR MAZURKIEWICZ

4. From Preconciliar Conscience-Centered Manuals to Postconciliar Conscience-Centered Moral Theology   54
   MATTHEW LEVERING

5. The Development and Contestation of *Humanae Vitae*   83
   GRÉGOR PUPPINCK

PART II. THE DOCTRINAL DIMENSION

6. The Foundation of the Doctrine of Intrinsically Evil Acts   101
   FULVIO DI BLASI

7. The Infallibility of the Church's Teaching on Contraception   132
   JOHN FINNIS

8. Catholic Teaching on Sexual Morality and the Infallibility of the Ordinary Magisterium   151
   PETER RYAN, SJ

9. Catholic Sexual Morality and the Problem of Dissent   179
   ROBERT FASTIGGI

PART III. THE ANTHROPOLOGICAL DIMENSION

10. *Humanae Vitae* and the Unity of the Human Person   217
    MICHAEL WALDSTEIN
11. The Language of the Body and Intrinsically Evil Acts   231
    FR. JOSÉ GRANADOS
12. The Body Matters: Moral Implications of an Integrated versus Fragmented Anthropology   249
    PAUL GONDREAU
13. Disordered Desire and Contraception   262
    ANGELA FRANKS
14. St. John Paul II on Conscience   278
    ADRIAN J. REIMERS

PART IV. THE BEAUTY AND WISDOM OF CATHOLIC SEXUAL MORALITY

15. The Beauty of Chastity   295
    OANA GOTIA
16. Natural Family Planning versus Contraception   310
    THERESA NOTARE
17. Magisterial Teaching on Gender Ideology, the Person and Identity Project, and Catholic Schools   327
    THERESA FARNAN

List of Contributors   357

Index   361

HUMANAE VITAE
and Catholic Sexual Morality

Introduction

On December 8–10, 2022, a group of Catholic scholars gathered in Rome to take part in a conference titled "A Response to the Pontifical Academy for Life's Publication, *Etica Teologica della Vita. Scrittura, tradizione, sfide pratiche.*"[1] The present volume brings together a selection of the papers from this conference, with an added essay by Fr. Luis Sánchez-Navarro that addresses scriptural issues.

The purpose of this conference was to respond, in a spirit of respect and fraternity, to some of the issues raised in the recent publication of the Pontifical Academy for Life, *Etica Teologica della Vita: Scrittura, tradizione, sfide pratiche*. A number of the essays in that volume sharply contest the Church's moral teaching. Archbishop Vincenzo Paglia—in his presentation of *Etica Teologica*—rightly notes that "Today there is a deeply felt need to promote, safeguard and put into practice the service of theology, which is absolutely necessary for the Church and for the lives of all believers." Here we are in agreement with Archbishop Paglia. On July 29, 2022, during his return flight from Canada to Rome, Pope Francis stated that "the duty of theologians is research, theological reflection." He also noted that theologians are called to discuss various "hypotheses" among themselves while recognizing that it is up to the Magisterium to decide whether certain proposals go too far. It was in this spirit that our conference was convened.

The December 8–10, 2022, conference sought to respond to some of the important questions raised in *Etica Teologica*, especially those connected with sexual morality, objective moral norms, and conscience. The

---

1. The conference was sponsored by the International Catholic Jurists Forum with Ave Maria University, Ave Maria School of Law, and the Person and Identity Project of the Ethics and Public Policy Center serving as cosponsors.

INTRODUCTION

conference attempted to pursue certain questions touched on in *Etica Teologica* in more depth. Among these questions were the following:

1. What is meant by the "radical paradigm change" (*radicale cambio di paradigm*) mentioned by Archbishop Paglia in his presentation and by Pope Francis in his 2017 Apostolic Constitution, *Veritatis Gaudium* (no. 3)? Is this a change in educational orientation in light of cultural changes—as Pope Francis indicates—or is it a change in moral methodology and doctrine?

2. What is the doctrinal status of the Church's teaching against contraception? The foundational text (*testo base*) of *Etica Teologica* (no. 172) refers to *Humanae Vitae* (HV) 10–14. It rightly notes that the norm of HV 10–14 "always refers to a good that precedes and exceeds it" (*La norma rimanda sempre a un bene che la precede e la eccede*). Does the good of the norm ever allow for the use of "artificial methods" of regulating fertility in the act of sexual intercourse—methods that do not preserve the unity of the two ends, procreative and unitive? This raises the question of the irreformable status of the teaching of *Humanae Vitae*.

3. How is Catholic sexual morality related to the question of intrinsically evil acts, that is, actions that cannot be made good by intention or circumstances? In moral methodology, how are we to understand conscience and discernment in reference to actions that are intrinsically disordered, even if done with a good intention motivated by difficult circumstances?

4. How is Catholic teaching on contraception supported by Scripture, Christian anthropology, and the natural law? How is this teaching connected to the beauty of chastity, the dignity of the human person, and respect for nature?

5. How is Catholic moral theology related to gender ideology, including contemporary claims about homosexual unions and transgenderism? Would a change in Catholic teaching on contraception signal changes on these other issues? What are the legal challenges faced by Catholics who wish to uphold Catholic teachings on marriage, sexuality, and the right to life of the unborn?

The book is divided into four parts, reflecting different approaches to responding to these questions: (I) Foundational Issues, (II) The Doctrinal

Dimension, (III) The Anthropological Dimension, and (IV) The Beauty and Wisdom of Catholic Sexual Morality. All of the chapters seek to defend authentic Catholic sexual morality grounded in the natural law, Sacred Scripture, tradition, and the Magisterium. The authors seek to uphold the teachings of *Humanae Vitae* and *Veritatis Splendor,* an authentic Catholic understanding of the theology of the body and conscience, and the sacredness of marriage and human sexuality.

We should clarify at the outset that our conference did not aim to be comprehensive. The issues are vast, and it would not have been possible for the conference (let alone the volume) to cover them exhaustively or in the needed detail. Fortunately, there exists a large literature from the past five decades addressing the issues. The footnotes of the chapters in this volume tap into this literature. It is evident that the critiques and approaches found in *Etica Teologica* are nothing new. They represent perspectives that have been prevalent in academic circles since the late 1960s. The inadequacy of these perspectives for life in Christ has been taught by popes and demonstrated by scholars. Yet, owing to a range of factors, these perspectives have—sometimes in changed forms—seemingly gathered strength. Fundamentally, at issue is whether the teachings of Jesus Christ and his Apostles about marriage and sexual morality are true. For if sexual intercourse can licitly be disjoined from the procreative end (properly understood), and if intention and circumstances are determinative for the liceity of sexual acts, then the sexual revolution is correct.

In stark contrast to the sexual revolution, the Church's moral theology has always stood on the side of the vulnerable. In sexual matters, the Church sees things first from the perspective of the children who are harmed when they are not raised by their father and mother. The Church's moral theology perceives that sexuality is much more than a matter of consent between two adults. But we recognize that articulating the Church's moral teaching on these matters is not easy in the Western context, marked by the sexual revolution and by decades of weakened Catholic formation.

The present volume therefore should be seen simply as a beginning, a brief restatement of some of the insights needed to appreciate the Christian moral life in its integrity. Moreover, although the present volume originated in response to the publication of *Etica Teologica,* we intend to be speaking not solely to the current debate. Rather, this volume is a contribution to the debate that has been ongoing for decades and that, whatever happens in the short term, will continue for many decades to come—for as long as the sexual revolution lasts. The effects of the sexual revolution in the West are many, and their familial, ecological, psychological, and societal impacts are still unfolding. In the long term, the truth of the Church's consistent moral and marital theology—the truth of Scripture and Tradition—will be manifest. The purpose of this volume, then, is not only to contribute to the debates of the present day but also to strengthen future believers in reclaiming and living the Gospel of the family.

PART I

FOUNDATIONAL ISSUES

CHAPTER 1

The "New Paradigm" in Moral Theology
Moving Forward or Turning Back?

MONSIGNOR LIVIO MELINA

"We must return to our roots. It is from our roots that we draw inspiration, but only in order to move forward. Turning back is not Christian. Please, be wary of this turning back which is a real temptation for moral theologians too." These words were pronounced off the cuff, and in vibrant tones, by Pope Francis in his audience on May 13, 2022.[1] These words are now proudly displayed as a back cover aegis in the recent volume published by the Pontifical Academy for Life—edited by its president, Archbishop Vincenzo Paglia—with the title *Theological Ethics of Life: Scripture, Tradition, Practical Challenges*.[2] According to the pope, what hurts the Church the most today is that "turning back," either driven by fear, by lack of originality, or by absence of courage. Nonetheless, in the pope's words it is also understood that not every "moving forward" is true progress. There is a moving forward that goes far enough to detach itself from the very roots, thus cutting itself off from the source of life, so that one becomes like the branches that bear no fruit, which dry up and are thrown into the fire because they are no longer useful (cf. Jn 15:1–6). Jesus warns us against this "moving beyond": he invites

---

1. The same concepts were reaffirmed even more recently, on November 24, 2022, in the audience granted by Pope Francis to the members of the International Theological Commission.

2. *Etica Teologica della Vita: Scrittura, tradizione, sfide pratiche*, ed. Archbishop Vincenzo Paglia (Vatican City: Libreria Editrice Vaticana, 2022).

us to remain in him, to bear the true fruit that lasts. It is therefore necessary that every claim to novelty in theology be verified by its coherence with the origin, by that contact with the roots to which Pope Francis refers. Thus, in this essay, I propose to examine the cornerstones of the new paradigm put forward in the volume of the Pontifical Academy for Life.

A "New" Paradigm

The authors of the volume want to "move forward" following the pope's appeal and even wish to "move beyond" with respect to magisterial documents such as the encyclical *Humanae Vitae* of St. Paul VI, the encyclical *Evangelium Vitae* of St. John Paul II, and the Instruction *Donum Vitae*, published by the Congregation for the Doctrine of the Faith with the approval of the same pope. The novelty would be made possible by adopting an innovative theological model, a "radical paradigm shift," by virtue of which theological ethics assumes the hermeneutical task of reinterpreting the binding value of the norms taught by the Magisterium until now.

The "foundational text" (*testo base*, or TB) presented in the volume—together with many of the theological commentaries published in support of it—proposes as "theological progress" *the moving beyond the literal observance of the norm* (TB 172–73) heretofore enunciated by the Magisterium, which defines contraception and artificial procreation (even homologous) that prescinds from the conjugal act as "intrinsically evil" actions.[3] In explicit contradiction to St. John Paul II's encyclical, *Veritatis Splendor* (VS; compare no. 78), the authors affirm that it is not possible to specify an act morally only by its object; rather, it is also necessary to consider the singularity of the circumstances and the subjective intention of the acting person. They also apply this principle to intrinsically evil acts (TB 126–30).

Thus, according to this new model, one could no longer consider contraception or artificial procreation as acts that are always intrinsically evil and therefore to be avoided. Instead, a discernment in conscience based on the circumstances is called for. Negative moral norms no longer repre-

---

3. For a precise critique of the text, see Cardinal Gerhard Ludwig Müller and Stephan Kampowski, "Going Beyond the Letter of the Law: The Pontifical Academy for Life Challenges the Teachings of *Humanae Vitae* and *Donum Vitae*," *First Things* (August 2022).

sent absolutes, but only serve as a first and distant point of reference for the subjective judgment of conscience.

According to its proponents, such a paradigm would correspond to the "personalism" proposed by the Second Vatican Council, since it emphasizes the decisive role of conscience with respect to the norm in discerning the morality of an action. Those who reject this new paradigm for morality—particularly for the field of sexual morality and bioethics—are labeled rigorists and dangerous "backwardists" (a neologism coined to define and brand them as dangerous enemies of the Church's mission today). These are those who wish to turn back, rather than progress with courage and creativity.

The expression "new paradigm" was coined by Cardinal Walter Kasper in an essay in which he takes stock of the first reactions to the apostolic exhortation *Amoris Laetitia*. Faced with the accusation of attempting to change doctrine, the German cardinal replied that it is not a change of doctrine, but a change of paradigm (*Paradigmenwechsel*).[4] The doctrine remains intact and the moral norm remains the same: the teaching on the indissolubility of marriage does not change, but what changes is the overall model of application of the norm (Kasper refers to no. 300 of the apostolic exhortation *Amoris Laetitia*). This position supposes that we are moving from a fixed and ahistorical conception of the human being, with its deductive and rigorist interpretation of morality, to a dynamic, concrete, and historical conception of the person, with a morality of mercy that is not limited to proposing "abstract principles" but concerns itself with individual cases.

The term "paradigm shift" originates with the American philosopher of science Thomas Kuhn, who used it to denote those scientific revolutions that occur when new discoveries and new data require the setting aside of "models of problems and solutions" that are no longer suitable in a certain field of research.[5]

The notion of a paradigm shift, as proposed by Cardinal Kasper for

---

4. Walter Kasper, "*Amoris laetitia*: Bruch oder Aufbruch. Eine Nachlese," *Stimmen der Zeit* 234, no. 11 (2016): 723–32.
5. Thomas Kuhn, *La struttura delle rivoluzioni scientifiche* (Torino: Einaudi, 2000), 19–28. For the original English, see idem, *The Structure of Scientific Revolutions*, 2nd ed. (Chicago: University of Chicago Press, 1970), 23–34.

the hermeneutics of the Magisterium, was then taken on by Pope Francis himself in the apostolic constitution *Veritatis Gaudium*, where in no. 3 it is recommended as an instrument for a "courageous cultural revolution" in theological formation. The surprising recourse to this concept of Maoist and 1968 origins, however, is then tempered, reframing the paradigm shift within the Catholic tradition with a reference to St. Vincent of Lérins and the necessary development of the doctrine that *annis consolidetur, dilatetur tempore sublimetur aetate*.[6]

Yet if one considers the entire work of the fifth-century French monk, one can clearly see that he never speaks of ruptures, which for him are the distinctive sign of a heretic. In order to constitute an advancement of the faith, the authentic development of doctrine must correspond to two criteria: it must be organic and therefore take place through an internal maturation of the faith (*res amplificetur in se*); and it must reflect the same meaning and the same judgment (*in eodem sensu eademque sententia*). Otherwise, it does not constitute progress (*profectus fidei*) but a pernicious distortion of faith (*permutatio*).[7] A legitimate change of pastoral approach can never involve a corruption of doctrine.[8]

Another authoritative point of reference for verifying legitimate development, and one that is chronologically closer to us, is found in the work of St. John Henry Newman, *An Essay on the Development of Christian Doctrine* of 1845. Here, the great English theologian proposes a set of criteria for distinguishing development from corruption. The first two criteria are "permanence of type" and "continuity of principles." It is thus seen that a formal external reference to the same terms is not enough to ensure the stability of the faith: the internal form must be respected and safeguarded. Furthermore, there must be a logical continuity with the teachings of the past, which should be faithfully preserved (fourth and sixth criteria). This is where the crucial nucleus of the problem lies: how can it be said that the doctrine remains the same if its concrete meaning

---

[6]. St. Vincent of Lérins, *Commonitorium primum*, 23: PL 50, 668.

[7]. See the intervention by the St. Vincent of Lérins scholar Thomas G. Guarino, "Pope Francis and St. Vincent of Lérins," *First Things*, August 16, 2022.

[8]. See Cardinal Gerhard Ludwig Müller, "Non è cambiamento pastorale: è corruzione," *Nuova Bussola Quotidiana*, February 26, 2018. Along the same lines, see the study by J. A. Ureta, *Il "cambio di paradigma" di papa Francesco: Continuità o rottura nella missione della Chiesa?* (San Paolo: Instituto Plinio Corrêa de Olivera, 2018).

for life changes throughout history? And can it be changed to such an extent that what was previously forbidden, because it was judged to be evil, now becomes lawful and good? A paradigm shift that relegates dogmas to the abstract realm and opens up a radical change in the practice of life is one that calls into question the substantial identity of faith in history. Such a discordant moral practice will at first render the doctrine obsolete and at a later time necessarily claim to change it. The dogmas of the Catholic faith are not mere provisional, conceptual formulas, which can be interpreted according to the changing religious sentiment of the prevailing conscience in the Church.[9]

The Holy Spirit who accompanies the Church in history and nourishes the *sensus fidei* of the people of God allows a deepening of the enduring truth, but does not teach different and contradictory things. Such a notion of development contradicts the fullness of truth that is present in the historical person of Jesus Christ, the incarnate Word of God. In fact, "Jesus Christ is the same yesterday, today and forever! Do not be led astray by different and strange doctrines" (Heb 13:8–9). As St. Thomas Aquinas teaches, "the act of the believer does not stop at the proposition, but with the thing."[10]

This initial analysis of the paradigm shift allowed us to identify the criteria that enable us to verify an authentic progress of the faith. It is now necessary to examine the specific content of the "new paradigm." TB 109 offers two characteristics that concern firstly the primacy of hermeneutics in the inseparable link between anthropology and ethics, and secondly a new conception of conscience, as expressed in the link between norm, discernment, and conscience itself. We must therefore consider these two points critically.

---

9. In this regard, see the teaching of St. Pius X, *Pascendi Dominici Gregis*, against modernism, which St. Paul VI described as still fully relevant: General Audience of Wednesday 19 January 1972, in *Insegnamenti di Paolo VI*, vol. 10 (Vatican City: Poliglotta Vaticana, 1973), 56.

10. *Summa Theologiae* II-II, q. 1, a. 2, ad 2.

Primacy of Hermeneutics and the Dissolution of the Natural Law

To understand the implications of the new paradigm, we must turn our attention to a preliminary methodological concern; that is, the claim for the primacy of pastoral care over doctrine. This is the desired step in that "pastoral conversion" that should involve theology, and that aims overcome the dependence of pastoral care on doctrine in favor of a circularity between the two dimensions, or rather in favor of a participation of pastoral practice in the reformulation of the doctrine.[11]

At the theoretical level, this corresponds to the affirmation of the primacy of hermeneutics in accessing the truth and moral norms (cf. TB 104). Action is always and only based on a historical interpretation, which cannot but undergo continuous revision and therefore must be always provisional.[12] The inescapable historicity of the human condition and the relativity of cultural context make impossible any knowledge that defines itself in terms of "a metaphysical certainty of the truth about God and about man outside of history." Such knowledge is defined as "abstract" (*Etica Teologica della Vita*, 10).

The pragmatic character and existential nature of reason instead dictate that, rather than knowledge, one should speak of historical understanding, since no object of knowledge could exist without being at the same time shaped by the subject's own consciousness. Thus, the truth is not given in an absolute way but dissolves in the multiple hermeneutical situations and in the relativity of historically conditioned worldviews.

Therefore that characteristic of modernity is adopted which Cornelio Fabro called the "principle of immanence." This consists in the choice to think of being from within consciousness, that is, from experience and history, for which reason it is not possible to access the truth as such be-

---

11. See Pope Francis, *Evangelii Gaudium* 32, and the reflections of G. Angelini, "*Evangelii Gaudium*: La conversione pastorale e la teologia," *Teologia* 39 (2014): 493–507, esp. 495–96.

12. The reference in the field of moral theology is Klaus Demmer's *Deuten und Handeln: Grundlagen der Fundamentalmoral* (Freiburg: Herder, 1985), which is based on the theory of historical understanding by Hans-Georg Gadamer, *Wahrheit und Methode: Grundzüge einer philosophischen Hermeneutic* (Tübingen: Mohr, 1975). See also the work of one of the authors of the *testo base*: Alain Thomasset, SJ, *Interpreter et agir: Jalons pour une éthique chrétienne* (Paris: Cerf, 2011).

cause every truth is only known insofar as it is thought by the subject.[13] By virtue of this co-implication of the consciousness of the subject, the being that is known is not the being as such, but only the being of consciousness, which remains closed in on itself and does not touch on the reality of things.

The primacy of hermeneutics, which characterizes the new paradigm, not only affects the speculative level of ontology and anthropology, but also determines a new conception of practical rationality and, in particular, of natural law. In the foundational text of the Pontifical Academy for Life, a physicalist or biologist conception of the natural law is rightly rejected, as well as an intellectualist vision of it, as if moral precepts could be deduced from the physical nature of the human being or from his metaphysical essence. The scholastic precept *agere sequitur esse* is a valid principle in the speculative field, but it does not apply as a method for the practical knowledge of what is morally good or evil.[14] The Humean critique of the *naturalistic fallacy* remains entirely relevant against those deductivist conceptions that end up in a vicious circle.

An authentic Thomistic vision—as reproposed and recommended in the encyclical *Veritatis Splendor* (nn. 46–50)—does not fall into this error, and moreover recognizes the active role of the moral subject in the constitution of the natural law. This latter is, in fact, no more than the order that practical reason establishes in the sphere of human acts by virtue of participating in the eternal law.[15] Thus divine providence calls the rational creature to collaborate most excellently in its designs, becoming quasi providence to itself. This is made possible by the *ratio naturalis* that exists at the origin of moral knowledge, which offers fundamental principles on which to build the natural law, such as the first principle of practical reason and the principles of the virtues. Understood in the light of the

---

13. See Cornelio Fabro, *Introduzione all'ateismo moderno* (Segni: Edivi, 2013), 9–82. See also Stefano Fontana, *Ateismo cattolico: Quando le idee sono fuorvianti per la fede* (Verona: Fede e Cultura, 2022).

14. See the pertinent critical observations on the Foundational Text by Ángel Rodriguez Luño, "Superamento del soggetto come coscienza ed etica della virtù," in *Etica Teologica della vita*, 159. I refer to some of these in my analysis.

15. See *Summa Theologiae* I-II, q. 91, a. 2. On this point, see Martin Rhonheimer, *Legge naturale e ragione pratica: Una visione tomista dell'autonomia morale* (Rome: Armando, 2001).

good of the person, these principles allow us to grasp the specific moral value of certain goods to which the person is naturally inclined. Practical reason, in its direct exercise, is supported by the moral virtues, which are ontologically founded on natural inclinations.[16] The Thomistic perspective of the natural law is placed within the dynamism of action and of the virtues, and views the conscience and norms as belonging to a secondary level of reflective activity, rather than to the order of reason's operation in voluntary acts, which constitutes the natural law per se.

The "new paradigm" instead reinterprets natural law only as a hermeneutic—always historically and culturally conditioned—of general human experiences. Access to the experience of the "anthropological universal" (nature) would only be possible in the multiple and variable historical forms of culture.[17] Rejecting the idea that natural law constitutes a system of immutable and ahistorical principles, the "new paradigm" affirms its immanent historicity and therefore the need for its continuing hermeneutic. This must effect a twofold operation: firstly, a restructuring of the historical genesis of the law, as traced through the synthesis of individual experiences; secondly, to enable the insertion of the norm as currently comprehended into the present culture and situation. The understanding of the norm must indeed go beyond the literal meaning and consider its "practicability."

The natural law is therefore not only seen as internal to the conscience, but also as emerging from the continual hermeneutic of interpretation, which therefore collapses its function of providing an objective criterion for action. The assumption of the historical subject as an ultimate horizon of understanding leads to a dissolution of moral truth in the historical process by which it is mediated.

---

16. See *Summa Theologiae* I-II, q. 94, a. 2.

17. See the TB 112–14. See also M. Chiodi, P. D. Guenzi, and M. Martino, *Lex naturae: Storia del concetto, teologia biblica e questioni teoriche* (Sienna: Cantagalli, 2022).

Hypertrophy of Conscience and Denial of "Moral Absolutes"

The personalism claimed by this reinterpretation of the natural law, which rejects a conception of natural law as "given once and for all," ends up reducing the moral subject to his conscience (cf. TB 110–14). All prior data that could relate to truthful and normative knowledge is broken down as product of this conscience.

This constitutes a real hypertrophying of the conscience. Thus, while basically accepting the schema of the post-Tridentine manuals, which place law and conscience in a systemic dialectic, this interpretation pretends to resolve the opposition between law and conscience by absorbing the norm into the conscience itself. At first, "a virtuous circularity between the conscience and the law" is upheld, in order to overcome the rigid distinction between objectivity and subjectivity; but later the law is inevitably understood as having no ultimate meaning without the conscience, and therefore conscience always prevails over the norm because "only the conscience of the moral agent can formulate the concrete norm for action."[18]

The key word for interpreting the role of the conscience in the "new paradigm" is "discernment," defined as "a continuous back and forth between reasoning and experience" (TB 124) in which the moral norm—understood as the collective product of individual, lived-out discernments, and therefore always understood to be "abstract"—is interpreted by the conscience in the light of the present multiple and unique circumstances. Indeed, the appeal to discernment becomes the means for elaborating an ethics of intention and of circumstances, which nullifies the primacy of the object in the moral qualification of human acts (VS 78). To confirm the reduction of the moral subject to the conscience, to the latter is also attributed the function of "decision," in contrast with what is taught in VS 55.

The decision-making process is described in TB 68 and 127–28 according to the following triad: universal principles—particular norms—

---

18. This summarizes and expounds the theoretical proposal of the volume: Jorge José Ferrer, SJ, "Rileggere l'etica teologica della vita: Alla luce delle sollecitazioni di papa Francesco," *La Civiltà Cattolica* 4129 (July 2022): 60–71.

singular decisions of conscience. This differentiation accords with the views of the French moralist Xavier Thévenot, who has distinguished three dimensions of morality: the universal—the particular—the singular.[19] The first dimension concerns the first principles that are unchanging but formal and devoid of content; the particular concerns the more concrete normative indications, the elaboration of which are culturally and historically conditioned; finally, the third dimension, the singular, can only be determined by the subject in the concreteness of his circumstances. This approach aims to "harmonize as best as possible" the moral life, avoiding angelism, legalism, and individualism, all of which result from the unilateral absolutization of a single dimension. In this way, one could elaborate a moral decision "in situation," without falling into a "situation" morality.

Another key concept that characterizes the "new paradigm" is that of the "possible good" (TB 104, 129), a concept that was also used in *Amoris Laetitia* (no. 308). This is a highly problematic notion that needs clarification. On the one hand, it expresses the completely traditional idea that only what is possible can be an obligating good (*ad impossibilia nemo tenetur*). On the other hand, when it is used in reference to alleged conflicts of norms—as is the case in the foundational text—in order to affirm that a specific norm constitutes an impossible ideal, then, as Ángel Rodriguez Luño rightly observed, "one runs the risk of making the possible good the middle name of evil."[20] "There is no circumstance in which a little injustice, a little lust, a little cruelty can exceptionally be good things ... or fall into the category of the possible good."[21]

It is precisely here that the crux of the proposal for the "new paradigm" manifests itself. In the name of an equivocal personalism and a primacy of conscience, it denies the possibility that absolutes exist in the moral life, that is, negative moral norms that, because of their objective intentional content, are incompatible with the good of the person—namely moral virtue and charity. As VS 78 teaches, such acts are always and in every case excluded because they are contrary to God's commandments.

---

19. Xavier Thévenot, *Repères éthiques pour un monde nouveau* (Paris: Salvator, 1982), 14–17. This conception is also endorsed by Thomasset, *Interpréter et agir*, 281–83.

20. Rodriguez Luño, "Superamento del soggetto," 162–63.

21. Rodriguez Luño, "Superamento del soggetto," 162.

They cannot be subjected to a subjective discernment of conscience that exceptionally permits them as the only "possible good."

Thus we see how what is lost in the "new paradigm" is precisely the mystery of moral action itself; that is, the intimate link between the person and his act, by which the acting subject, through his free choices, not only effects changes exteriorly, but also changes himself interiorly, generating his own ethical identity. Moral norms are not the injunctions of an arbitrary authority or the synthesis of limited historical and cultural experiences, but expressions of a truth about the good. It is from here that they draw their imperative force. In this regard, the great words of Jesus sound forth a warning: "for what does it profit a man, to gain the whole world, and forfeit his life?" (Mk 8:36). It is at this level that the radical nature of moral value is understood, and the absoluteness of negative moral norms is justified. It is precisely here that one encounters the "seriousness of life," for which one can also be called to the supreme witness of martyrdom.[22]

The warning of Cardinal Joseph Ratzinger—in his homily at the Holy Mass *pro eligendo pontifice* on April 18, 2005, on the eve of his election to the Chair of Peter—remains timely: "Relativism, that is letting oneself be 'tossed here and there, carried about by every wind of doctrine' (Eph 4:14), seems the only attitude that can cope with modern times. We are building a dictatorship of relativism that does not recognize anything as definitive and whose ultimate goal consists solely of one's own ego and desires." It is precisely relativism, which does not recognize any moral absolute, that eliminates the possibility of martyrdom.

Going "Beyond" the Letter of the Law?

The foundational text proposed by the Pontifical Academy for Life underlines the "non-ultimate character of the normative formulation" (TB 104). In fact, "the norm always refers to a good that precedes and exceeds it" (TB 172); for this reason, we should always go "beyond a mere literal observance" and the "automatic application" of a norm, and entrust the subject's conscience with the task of discernment. Aware of the limits

---

22. In this regard, see Stephan Kampowski, *Il caso serio della vita: La morale cristiana tra autonomia e libertà del dono* (Siena: Cantagalli 2022).

of the norm, the conscience adopts a hermeneutical attitude to the norm, looking for exceptions, not only in the case of positive precepts but also of negative precepts. Within this perspective, norms are human formulas that require further clarification in order to correspond to the spirit of the law, beyond its letter. Neither do norms concern the practical principles of the virtues as such.

The normativist perspective, centered on the dialectic between norm and conscience, has the fundamental defect of describing the object of human actions in a physicalistic way (*genus naturae*), and therefore assuming that it is impossible to qualify human actions morally without considering the subjective intentions and the circumstances, as only the individual conscience can. The absolute character of negative moral norms is rejected.[23] In the Thomistic conception, *epikeia* is the virtuous principle of an excellent choice, not a logic of exceptions that does not admit the existence of intrinsically evil actions or, to put it differently, that does not admit the possibility of expressing through human language the demands of moral virtues that are both concrete and universally valid.[24]

Along the above lines, the foundational text of the Pontifical Academy for Life proposes a rereading of those moral norms concerning contraception and medically assisted procreation—as taught by the Magisterium in the encyclical *Humanae Vitae* and in the instruction *Donum Vitae*—by means of which a discernment of the conscience can lead to going beyond the letter of the prohibition, thus accepting that the conjugal sexual act can be intentionally separated from openness to procreation and that the desired procreation can be obtained from the technical act of doctors instead of from the conjugal act (TB 172–73).

We are dealing here not only with an interpretation that defines the moral norm itself, but also with a fundamental questioning of the entirety of the sexual morality and bioethics that the Catholic Church has taught for the past two millennia. In fact, moral norms are not merely expressions of a human legislative will or a historical synthesis of culturally marked experiences; rather, they express the demands of the truth about

---

23. See VS 78–79.
24. See Ángel Rodriguez Luño, "La virtù dell'epicheia: Teoria, storia e applicazione," in *Diffamazione, Epicheia, Divorziati: Tre saggi di Teologia Morale* (Rome: EDUSC, 2014), 73–147, here 140–45.

human love in the divine plan, which sees human sexuality as a call to love through respect for the language of the body, in the gift of self, and in the openness to the further gift of life that comes from God. When the moral norms that protect the self-giving meaning of sexuality and human generation are contradicted, in reality we are not only going beyond the letter of a particular norm, but we are also going against the spirit and meaning of the very law that God has written in our heart and revealed to us in the history of salvation.

Conclusion

In commenting on Jesus' proclamation, who in the Gospel of John defines himself as "the way, the truth and the life" (Jn 14:6), St. Thomas Aquinas observes that, "It is better to limp along the way than to walk briskly off the way. For one who limps along the way, even though he makes just a little progress, is approaching his destination; but if one walks off the way, the faster he goes the further he gets from his destination."[25] We could therefore say that when we are on the wrong road, every step back brings us closer to the goal. Sometimes, to move forward, you have to turn back off a wrong road. True progress is verified by getting closer to the goal and not simply by "moving forward."

Certainly, the truth that Christ proclaims must not only be guarded, but also followed as a path and deepened as a life. It is therefore important to go forward, as Pope Francis invites us to, and to grow in the understanding and practice of this truth, while being careful not to leave the road altogether and lose touch with the roots.

---

25. St. Thomas Aquinas, *Commento al Vangelo di San Giovanni /3*, XIV, lect. II, III, no. 1870, edited by T. S. Centi (Rome: Città Nuova, 1992), 96.

CHAPTER 2

"He Who Has My Commandments and Keeps Them, He It Is Who Loves Me" (Jn 14:21)
The Relevance of Scripture for Normative Morality

FR. LUIS SÁNCHEZ-NAVARRO

"He who has my commandments and keeps them, he it is who loves me" (Jn 14:21).[1] These words of Jesus in John's Gospel appear to us as a challenge because they make love for Christ dependent on keeping his commandments. Love subject to the law! But this, according to postmodern Christianity, is *the* sin. How can we understand these words of the Lord today, and even more, how can we show that they express the necessary condition for the "to be or not to be" of love? To do this, let us begin with the recent document of the Pontifical Academy for Life (PAL), *Theological Ethics of Life: Scripture, Tradition, Practical Challenges*. These are the proceedings of the seminar held by the same academy between October 30 and November 1, 2021; it was indeed the "test" or "basis" for the discussions.

Bible and Morality, Once Again

The question of the moral doctrine attested by Scripture, already largely resolved in recent decades, nevertheless continues to arise in the Church;

---

1. Unless otherwise indicated, biblical texts are taken from the *Revised Standard Version*, Catholic ed. (https://www.biblegateway.com/versions/Revised-Standard-Version-Catholic-Edition-RSVCE-Bible/#booklist).

it could be said to accompany her as a matter of fact, like other major theological issues. The underlying issue is the ability of Scripture to set the course of moral life today, millennia after its composition. And to set it with authority, that is, as the norm or canon of the Christian life.

A first observation: the approach to the question ("Bible and morality") is not perhaps the most adequate one, for it could imply a concept of revelation that removes and isolates Scripture from its vital context, the Church, as if it were *sola Scriptura*. But this would be an unreal abstraction, as Scripture has never existed outside the ecclesial community; the correct approach could be how the Bible bears witness to the anthropological and moral vision that flows from revelation and is preserved in tradition, which the then young theologian Joseph Ratzinger defined as *Scriptura in Ecclesia*.[2] Having made this basic clarification, however, I attempt to answer the question posed in order to show that the only valid reading of the biblical teaching on human life and happiness is the one that lives in the Catholic tradition. I also emphasize how the biblical witness manifests the greatness and depth of this doctrine: read in the Church, Sacred Scripture becomes an inexhaustible source of newness. John Paul II wrote:

Veritatis Splendor [VS] 28: "Sacred Scripture remains the living and fruitful source of the Church's moral doctrine; as the Second Vatican Council recalled, the Gospel is "the source of all saving truth and moral teaching" (DV 7). The Church has faithfully preserved what the word of God teaches, not only about truths which must be believed but also about moral action, action pleasing to God (cf. 1 Thes 4:1); she has achieved a doctrinal development analogous to that which has taken place in the realm of the truths of faith. Assisted by the Holy Spirit who leads her into all the truth (cf. Jn 16:13), the Church has not ceased, nor can she ever cease, to contemplate the "mystery of the Word Incarnate," in whom "light is shed on the mystery of man" (GS 22).

The Pontifical Academy for Life's Proposal

The PAL's document has the merit of bringing to light the question of the validity of Sacred Scripture to guide the lives of people today. It is a

2. "For [the Fathers], tradition is simply *scriptura in ecclesia*": Joseph Ratzinger to the German bishops (October 10, 1962), in Jared Wicks, SJ, "Six Texts by Prof. Joseph Ratzinger as Peritus before and during Vatican Council II," *Gregorianum* 89 (2008): 233–311, here 275.

subject of continuing interest in view of today's culture, which is so different from the biblical one. In addition to interesting and stimulating reflections, there are some elements in its approach that undermine the validity of its proposal.

Ambiguous Statements or Expressions

There are statements in this document that, for lack of explanation, are left at the reader's discretion:

- It criticizes, for example, "the instrumental use of Sacred Scripture" (§17). We agree that it is impoverishing to limit oneself to a merely "utilitarian" use of Scripture, since the Sacred Scripture shows all its fruitfulness when it inspires and generates theological reflection, as the Second Vatican Council rightly reminded us (*Sacrae Paginae studium sit veluti anima Sacrae Theologiae*, DV 24); certainly, its greatness is compromised when biblical quotation is intended only as a subsidiary argument. But I am reluctant to consider its use illegitimate as long as it serves to strengthen the Church's doctrine; recall what Paul said to Timothy in the only explicit affirmation of the dogma of divine inspiration in the New Testament: "All Scripture inspired by God is useful [ὠφέλιμος] for teaching, rebuking, correcting and training in righteousness" (2 Tm 3:16). Scripture is *useful*; it does not seem, therefore, that its "use" is in itself condemnable. For what is rejected—not without a certain self-sufficiency—namely, the use of Scripture as a "guarantee or proof for the subsequent application of doctrines or moral norms elaborated independently of it" (§16), seems in fact to call into question the Church's profession of faith and morals, written in her heart "more eminently than in material instruments" (i.e., Scripture) and firmly attested therein.[3] Moreover, could not the use

3. *Catechism of the Catholic Church*, §113: "According to a saying of the Fathers, '*Sacra Scriptura principalius est in corde Ecclesiae quam in materialibus instrumentis scripta*', Sacred Scripture is written principally in the Church's heart rather than in documents and records [references to St. Hilary and St. Jerome], for the Church carries in her Tradition the living memorial of God's Word, and it is the Holy Spirit who gives her the spiritual interpretation of the Scripture ('... *secundum spiritalem sensum, quem Spiritus donat Ecclesiae*, according to the spiritual meaning which the Spirit grants to the Church' [Origen])."

of a biblical passage to "homologate," at least in part, one of today's ideas (e.g., the biblical proof of infertility in the face of "surrogate motherhood," §17) be called an illegitimate "use" of Scripture?

- Second, man as *imago Dei* is treated in the PAL document in a way we could say is "original." Scripture testifies to a revealed anthropology: man, also in his sexual condition (male and female), is the image of God (Gn 1:27). But in the document the tables are sometimes turned, and God's face seems to be deduced from human behavior: "God makes himself known by starting from what is common to all human beings" (§19); that is, not only from what expresses genuine desires and hopes, but also—it is inferred—from what is contrary to his good, not excluding sin. Thus Scripture, defined as the "laboratory of the human condition" (§§19–20), that is, as a place for deepening the human condition and for verifying its fundamental experiences, can end up justifying a "laboratory" human life that does not correspond to its nature but turns out to be artificial.

- Moreover, the way we speak about the relationship with those who are different (we mean non-Christians) seems to discourage incorporation into the Church as an ordinary and excellent means of salvation; thus we read that "the hour has come to change our vision, to give it openness and generosity, recognizing that God has a people waiting for the Gospel that belongs to him beyond the boundaries of the visible body of the Church" (§34). But it is precisely from "Galilee of the nations" (cf. §34) that the Risen One sends the Eleven to baptize and teach the Gospel "to all the nations" (Mt 28:19). And a little later, it is said that at Pentecost the Spirit "raises up a community that celebrates with one heart the wonders of God, while preserving the diversity of memberships and languages of each one" (§35). What does "membership" here mean? If there is one thing the New Testament makes clear, it is the call to make all people, through sacraments and teaching (Mt 28:19–20), one body, that of Christ (1 Cor 12:27), with the same sentiments (Phil 2:14), with one heart and one soul (Acts 4:32). This unity not only preserves but also promotes the personal distinctiveness of each member, and Paul strongly emphasizes this (1 Cor 12:7–26).

"One Lord, one faith, one baptism" (Eph 4:5; cf. 4:13).[4] But from the developments described above, an ecclesiology of heterogeneity rather than an ecclesiology of communion seems to emerge. This is what we might call a "dogmatic transposition" of xenophobia: to fight the error of faith would be to close oneself to the stranger who knocks at the door. It implies that the concern to preserve the purity of the faith (an inalienable requirement for the Christian, according to the New Testament[5]) is tantamount to rejecting the stranger and the different (cf. §34, "hatred of all otherness"). But it is precisely the truth of faith that makes it possible to welcome the stranger and the different, without any discrimination, into the Body of Christ! On the contrary, it is "faith" distorted into ideology that fuels exclusionary hatred.

Scientific Truth and Truth of Faith

From the outset, the document presents an optimistic view of modern science, in the face of which the biblical way of thinking inevitably appears anachronistic (cf. §§15–16).[6] It thus fails to take into account the always precarious state of scientific discoveries and how not only human psychology but also neurology and even physics recognize the limitations of their findings, which are always open to new developments. In sharp contrast, it warns against the claim in current debates to "extract [from Scripture] immutable truths or models to be invoked out of context" (§16); it offers a distorted view of Scripture as a source of truth, a "caricature" that is obviously repugnant to any reasonable person. Thus biblical "truth" "develops progressively, at the cost of being corrected from one moment to the next" (§16), even the commandments of the Decalogue![7]

---

4. Eph 4:13: "until we all attain to the unity of the faith and of the knowledge of the Son of God, to mature manhood, to the measure of the stature of the fulness of Christ."

5. Cf. 1 Cor 15:14; 1 Thes 3:10; 2 Thes 3:2; 1 Tm 1:19, 3:9, 4:1; 2 Tm 2:17–18, 3:8; Ti 1:13; Heb 10:22; Jas 1:3; 1 Pt 1:7; Jude 3.

6. "Is there any point in claiming to find an aid to our discernment in a scriptural message structured by outdated representations of the cosmos, organized by a past social order, ignoring everything about the great revolutions of modern knowledge, and having no idea about technology and its means?" (§15).

7. "This also applies to the words solemnly placed under the authority of Moses, which convey the commandments of God" (§16).

Instead, in the fourth Gospel, Christ speaks several times of "*the* truth" with the definite article: "If you remain in my word, ... you will know the truth, and the truth will make you free" (Jn 8:31–32); "I am the way, the truth and the life" (14:6); "But when the Spirit of the truth comes, he will guide you into all the truth" (16:13). The claim to truth is consistent with Scripture: Jesus came "to bear witness to the truth" (Jn 18:37). And the Second Vatican Council speaks boldly of the "eternal" (i.e., unchanging) decrees of the divine will for the salvation of mankind, revealed by God (DV 6); indeed, the Gospel is "the source of all salutary truth and moral order" (DV 7). This truth, which is personal in nature, is inseparable from life, the moral category par excellence in the Bible. Thus, according to Ignace de la Potterie, "Jesus is the 'truth' because from now on he is the revelation of the Father; he is the 'life' because from now on he gives to believers the life of the Father."[8] The "music" that comes from the document we are commenting on is different; it seems that the Gospel did not reveal to us the truth about man, but the "truth" of today's fragile man.

In the Background: An "Idealistic" View of Biblical Morality

Reading our document leaves the reader with the feeling that the Gospel is elitist. It is not for everyone, not everyone can live up to it, so we must consider lowering its demands for those who cannot meet them. Otherwise, it would amount to imposing an unattainable ideal on the individual: a desperate cruelty, the result of an insufficient "spiritualization" (§19). In practice, then, there would be "A" Christianity (those who embrace the evangelical ideal) and "B" Christianity (those who cannot). This "idealistic" view of Christian perfection would lead to spiritualism, "that conception of man characteristic of Western thought which recognizes man as a thinking and willful being, independent and autonomous from sensible and material reality";[9] thus the choice of faith (moral ideal) could

---

8. Ignace de la Potterie, *La vérité dans Saint Jean, I: Le Christ et la vérité. L'Esprit et la vérité*, 2nd ed. (Rome: Pontifical Biblical Institute, 1999), 264–65.

9. Cornelio Fabro, "Espiritualismo," in *Diccionario de espiritualidad*, vol. 2, edited by Ermanno Ancilli (Barcelona: Herder, 1987), 32–36, here 32.

in certain cases be separated from concrete choices (failure to obey some commandment because of moral weakness).

But the Church's teaching, which expresses its millennial life experience, is different:

Only in the mystery of Christ's Redemption lie the "concrete" possibilities of man. It would be a most serious mistake to conclude ... that the norm taught by the Church is in itself only an "ideal" which must then be adapted, proportioned, graduated to, it is said, man's concrete possibilities according to a "balancing of the various goods in question." But what are the "concrete possibilities of man"? And which man are we talking about? Of man dominated by concupiscence or of man redeemed by Christ? For this is what it is all about: the reality of Christ's redemption. Christ has redeemed us! This means: He has given us the possibility of realizing the whole truth of our being; He has liberated our freedom from the dominion of concupiscence. And if the redeemed man still sins, it is not due to the imperfection of Christ's redeeming act, but to man's willingness to shirk the grace that flows from that act. God's commandment is certainly proportionate to man's abilities: but to the abilities of the man to whom the Holy Spirit is given; of the man who, if fallen in sin, can always obtain forgiveness and enjoy the presence of the Spirit. (VS 103b)

The "evangelical ideal" is therefore anti-evangelical. Idealism leads to the banality of action.

Reductive View of Revelation

The final element that draws our attention, in my opinion the most significant, is the concept of divine revelation that emanates from these pages. Six decades after the Second Vatican Council, its teaching on revelation (DV 2) seems to have fallen on deaf ears. We read in *Etica Teologica della Vita* (ETV): "The word that is adequate to this [evangelizing] mission must draw its nourishment from the source of Revelation, namely, Sacred Scripture" (§18). Sacred Scripture, source of revelation! It sounds too much like *sola Scriptura*, uprooted from the ecclesial faith. A little later, the document speaks of the "biblical Scriptures" as "bearers of revelation that comes to man from afar" (§19): revelation appears as the communication of a content, and not—as Vatican II insistently teaches—as a personal encounter; the Scriptures would be its means of communication. But as then Cardinal Ratzinger rightly reminded us,

In today's theological lingo, it is common to term the Bible "Revelation" without qualification. This usage would never have occurred to the ancients. Revelation is a dynamic event between God and man, which again and again becomes reality only in their encounter. The biblical Word attests to Revelation, but does not contain it in the sense of absorbing it and turning it into a sort of thing that one could stick in one's pocket. The Bible attests to Revelation, but the concept of Revelation as such is broader.[10]

To this is added another observation: the Church seems to be absent; it is as if the Scriptures came directly to man, like a meteorite, from the transcendence of God. This is the modern view of the relationship between man and God, from individual to individual. It is true that later on Tradition is cited as a source: "The Church must give voice to the word of wisdom which she receives from Sacred Scripture and Tradition" (§38), but this statement still seems to be placed in the perspective of the two sources of revelation, which was superseded by *Dei Verbum*. From a theological point of view, therefore, the document is surprisingly outdated and flawed.

The Christian View of the Bible

Still along these lines, the document reveals a conception of Scripture that, in some key elements, departs from the Christian view. We focus on two aspects.

The Bible: Testimony, Not Origin

The assumption that runs through the document is that the Church derives its *fides quae* from Sacred Scripture; therefore, in order to know her faith, she depends on professional interpreters, on exegetes. As an example, the document denounces what is considered a fundamental risk in the face of today's scientific knowledge: anachronism. It warns, for example, against the scholastic use of Sacred Scripture as a guarantee or proof of claims about faith or morals developed independently of it; "it should be

---

10. Joseph Ratzinger, "Biblical Interpretation in Conflict: On the Foundations and the Itinerary of Exegesis Today," in *Opening Up the Scriptures: Joseph Ratzinger and the Foundations of Biblical Interpretation,* edited by José Granados, Carlos Granados, and Luis Sánchez-Navarro (Grand Rapids, MI: Eerdmans, 2008), 1–29, here 26.

impossible for us today to treat Sacred Scripture as timeless propositions and norms, claiming to extract from it immutable truths or models to be invoked in the anthropological and ethical debates of the present" (§16). One gets the impression that the Church must always carry out an exercise of critical history in order to deduce the content of these writings.

But the Second Vatican Council, which recognized the necessity of historical methods for an adequate interpretation of the Bible, nevertheless strongly emphasized that in interpreting the sacred text, the exegete must take into account the unity of Scripture, the Tradition of the Church, and the analogy of faith (DV 12.3). This principle is so important that its emphasis and commentary constitute the most important contribution of the Apostolic Exhortation *Verbum Domini* (2010, §§34–35). Above all, however, the authors of this document seem to ignore the nature of Sacred Scripture. The Church has never derived her faith from Scripture; the Church's faith is her response to God's revelation, an event that precedes any Scripture.[11] In fact, Sacred Scripture originates in the Church, which is also—and therefore in its own right—the author of this Sacred Scripture.[12] The view of Sacred Scripture as the origin of the Church's faith is thus an intellectualism far removed from history. On the contrary, Sacred Scripture is a witness to this faith, a response to God's revelation.[13]

---

11. See Joseph Ratzinger, "Die Bedeutung der Väter für die Gegenwärtige Theologie," *Tübinger Theologische Quartalschrift* 148 (1968): 257–82.

12. "One could say that the books of Scripture involve three interacting subjects. First of all, there is the author or group of authors to whom we owe a particular scriptural text. But these authors are not autonomous writers in the modern sense; they form part of a collective subject, the 'People of God,' from within whose heart and to whom they speak. Hence, this subject is actually the deeper 'author' of the Scriptures. And yet likewise, this people does not exist alone; rather, it knows that it is led, and spoken to, by God himself, who—through men and their humanity—is at the deepest level the one speaking." Joseph Ratzinger/Benedict XVI, *Jesus of Nazareth: From the Baptism in the Jordan to the Transfiguration* (New York: Doubleday, 2007), xx–xxi. See also Aaron Pidel, SJ, "*Christi Opera Proficiunt:* Ratzinger's Neo-Bonaventurian Model of Social Inspiration," *Nova et Vetera* 13 (2015): 693–711.

13. See Luis Sánchez-Navarro, "The Testimonial Character of Sacred Scripture," in Carlos Granados and Luis Sánchez-Navarro, *In the School of the Word: Biblical Interpretation from the New to the Old Testament* (Saint Paul, MN: Saint Paul Seminary Press, 2021), 17–31.

Scripture That "Grows with the Reader"

The document cites Gregory the Great's classic formulation, *Divina eloquia cum legente crescunt* (§19), as a justification for doctrinal progress that could eventually lead to a renewed judgment on the morality of certain behaviors. According to this kind of interpretation, as the reader "grows" (through the acquisition of new knowledge: psychology, sociology, etc.), the text would also "grow," revealing something that was previously hidden. It would thus have a strange fruitfulness, not necessarily "organic." But in reality, Gregory presupposes a reader who participates in the faith of the Church. In fact, reading Scripture from other assumptions does not make it grow but diminishes it, because it trivializes or distorts its meaning. The saint's expression, as Pier Cesare Bori explains, has a mystical meaning: from the first vision of the Book of Ezekiel, Gregory speaks of how, as the reader mystically "rises," Scripture also "rises" and thus "grows."[14] He is referring to the application of the content of the sacred text to the reader, thus expressing the true fruitfulness of the Bible. This application to the reader is not external to the interpretation but constitutes its final moment, so that the reader, in a sense, "makes the text grow": "The text 'grows' or 'progresses' [...] until it reaches the reader where he is, until it embraces him with its prophecies, its warnings, its figures."[15] But a necessary condition for this growth is ecclesial belonging: "By identifying the Church with Christ and the believer with the Church, everything in the text speaks mysteriously of the believer."[16] It is therefore inappropriate to understand this expression—a true synthesis of the patristic view of Scripture—as the opening of Scripture to new meanings coming from a mentality alien to the Christian view, which may even contradict the explicit teachings of the sacred text; Bori, in a previous work, pointed out

---

14. Gregorio, *In Hiez.* I, VIII, 8: "When the living moved on the ground, the wheels also moved on the ground; and when the living rose, the wheels also rose" [Ezek 1:19], because divine words grow with those who read them (*quia divina eloquia cum legente crescent*), "for **the deeper** you look at them, **the deeper** you understand them" (*nam tanto illa quisque **altius** intellegit, quanto in eis **altius** intendit*), as quoted in Pier Cesare Bori, *L'interpretazione infinita: L'ermeneutica cristiana antica e le sue trasformazioni* (Bologna: Il Mulino, 1987), 44. See also the commentary on this text of Gregory in Bori, *L'interpretazione infinita*, 43–46.

15. Pier Cesare Bori, "Reflections on "L'interpretazione infinita: L'ermeneutica cristiana antica e le sue trasformazioni," in *Scienza & Politica: Per una storia del dottrine* 3 (1991): 110–13, here 111.

16. Bori, "L'interpretazione," 111.

how a misreading of Scripture can make this "growth of Scripture with the reader" impossible:

> Grave of consequences is a certain spiritual reading, where it is not a matter of that "growing of Scripture with the reader" of which Gregory the Great speaks, that is, of creative hermeneutics, but of loss of contact with what, from the point of view of religious anthropology, the doctrinal contents and the Judaic religious experience mean [...] To lose contact with these premises is to lose Christianity itself, to reduce it to intellectualism separated from any consideration of the material basis of existence.[17]

Moreover, as Bori also explains, "growth" is a way of speaking of spiritual "progress": "Growth and progress (*profectus*) [...] are equivalent in Gregory [...] In fact, they are two different metaphors: one of spatial advancement, the other of organic development or maturation."[18] In this way, the growth of the Christian benefits the Church: "It is precisely the body of Christ, that is, the body of which Christ is the head that grows and is articulated in time and space."[19] And so the growth of Scripture evokes an expression characteristic of the Acts of the Apostles, where "Word" and "Church" coincide, and which also conjugates "progress" and "growth": "The word of God *grew*, and the number of the disciples in Jerusalem multiplied greatly" (Acts 6:7; cf. 12:24, 19:20). This view is derived from the parable of the sower (Lk 8:4–15): "Thus, Luke expresses the dynamism of the Word, the apostolic testimony about Jesus, which like a seed 'grows.'"[20] In the reader, Scripture grows in the way of the seed.

This is why St. Gregory's formulation points to reading the Bible in the Spirit, as Ignace de la Potterie explains: "The Bible does not only contain the telling of a history; and it reveals to us the mystery of salvation because it is for us the book of Revelation. It is at this level, the level of the mystery, that it reveals its profound sense, 'the sense given by the Spirit,' which the whole Christian tradition has always sought to discover in

---

17. Pier Cesare Bori, *Il vitello d'oro: Le radici della controversia antigiudaica* (Torino: Boringhieri, 1983), 78–79.

18. Bori, *L'interpretazione infinita*, 45. Sometimes, Gregory understands the two metaphors in a complementary way: progress would be external, in good works, and growth an inner maturation.

19. Bori, *L'interpretazione infinita*, 49.

20. Joseph A. Fitzmyer, SJ, *The Acts of the Apostles* (New York: Doubleday, 1998), 493.

Scripture."[21] It is the Spirit—who may act outside the boundaries of the Church but always acts according to ecclesial grace—that promotes this "scriptural growth" until it reaches the whole world.

The Commandments in Scripture: Way of Life, Symbol of Love

The words of the Lord that give our study its title link commandment and love. Where there is no obedience to God's commandments, there is no love. But Jesus' words are fully embedded in biblical teaching; the Shema presents love as the fundamental object of the commandment and of the entire Torah. And it is so because it precedes it as a gift.

The Logic of the Gift

The study of biblical law and commandment introduces us to the logic of gift because, as Benedict XVI reminded us in his first encyclical, "love can be 'commanded' because it is first given" (*Deus Caritas Est* 4). Divine commandments are the expression of a love that precedes and thus belong to the structure of love. But they are not its foundation; as the Pontifical Biblical Commission stated in its 2008 document, "morality, without being secondary, is second."[22] Nor are they its fullness; "the law," says Paul Beauchamp, "is preceded by 'You are loved' and followed by 'You shall love.' 'You are loved': foundation of the law, and 'You shall love': its overcoming."[23] This is why "anyone who abstracts the law from this foundation and term will love the opposite of life, founding life on law instead of founding law on life."[24] This is the key to understanding Deuteronomy 30:11–14, a crucial passage:

---

21. Ignace de la Potterie, "Biblical Exegesis: A Science of Faith," in *Opening Up the Scriptures*, 30–64, here 48; he refers to Henri de Lubac, SJ, *L'Écriture dans la Tradition* (Paris: Aubier-Montaigne, 1966), 189–202, "The Sense Given by the Spirit."
22. "What is first and foundational is God's initiative, which we will express theologically in terms of gift." Pontifical Biblical Commission, *Bible and Morals: Biblical Roots of Christian Action* (2008), §4.
23. Paul Beauchamp, *La Legge di Dio* (Casale Monferrato: Piemme, 2000), 116.
24. Beauchamp, *La Legge di Dio*, 117.

11 For this commandment which I command you this day is not too hard for you, neither is it far off. 12 It is not in heaven, that you should say, "Who will go up for us to heaven, and bring it to us, that we may hear it and do it?" 13 Neither is it beyond the sea, that you should say, "Who will go over the sea for us, and bring it to us, that we may hear it and do it?" 14 But the word is very near you; it is in your mouth and in your heart, so that you can do it.

Moses expresses here the logic of the new covenant;[25] in it, the intimacy of the Word in the heart of the Israelite is a gift from God to be recognized as already fulfilled. In these words, St. Paul discovered the foreshadowing of the righteousness that comes from faith in Christ (Rom 10:6–10).

All this enables us to understand the nature and dignity of the biblical precept: it constitutes the *necessary path to life*. In fact, if the Old Testament is "a constant and indispensable condition for accessing the New,"[26] its commands—correctly interpreted according to their own nature, either ritual or moral—are a necessary part of this path; they belong to the "greater righteousness" (Mt 5:20) of the one who did not come to abolish the law and the prophets, but to give them the fullness they aimed at from their origin (cf. 5:17). "The law stands between a gift that precedes it and a reward that surpasses it. The law is in the path. And in this path it is the guide that enables us to advance toward the ultimate gift of life. How? By working on its maturation, that is, by teaching how to live."[27]

Commandment, Life, Goodness

To the young man who asked him what action would lead to eternal life, the Lord responded by recalling God's goodness and referring to the commandments, which thus appear as an expression and reflection of that goodness (Mt 19:16–17). And when asked what the commandments were, Jesus specified the most important ones in the Decalogue, which culminate in love for one's neighbor (19:18–19). Once again, commandments that culminate in love! The body of the Torah thus appears, in the totality

---

25. See Carlos Granados, *Deuteronomio* (Madrid: BAC, 2017), 405–8.
26. Carlos Granados, *El camino de la ley: Del Antiguo al Nuevo Testamento* (Salamanca: Sígueme, 2011), 10.
27. Granados, *El camino de la ley*, 12–13.

of its commandments—summarized in the main ones—as the way to participate in the life of God. The way of love.

Behaviors That Exclude from Divine Friendship

"You shall not kill, You shall not commit adultery, You shall not steal, You shall not bear false witness, Honor your father and mother, and, You shall love your neighbor as yourself" (Mt 19:18–19): in these commandments, Jesus concretizes the way of life. The enumeration is interesting because to the four negative commandments of the Decalogue (Dt 5:17–20) he adds another positive commandment, also from the Decalogue ("Honor your father and mother," Dt 5:16), culminating in the commandment of love for one's neighbor (Lv 19:18b). The two groups thus express, first negatively and then positively, the way of life. But they do so in different ways. The positive commandments give a clear direction, prescribing obligatory actions: honor your parents, love your neighbor. They are closed in terms of what is to be done, although they remain open in that they always point to something more, to going beyond; they thus constitute a constant challenge. In contrast, the first four, which are negative, only forbid certain behaviors: they may seem almost "repressive." But the reality is quite different; Paul Beauchamp rightly shows how, precisely because they are negative, they leave ample room for freedom; indeed, they make it possible:

"The Decalogue also impresses us by the importance it accords to *negative* commandments.... Not infrequently some readers of the Bible come out ill-prepared. More space given to the positive would have disconcerted them less. But everything changes if one understands that "saying what one ought to do" imprisons more than "saying what one ought not to do." Reading the Decalogue, one hears what God forbids. But the other side, related to the first, consists in the fact that God does not compel. What *not to* do? Those violations that are called murder, adultery, theft, perjury. Through them you deprive the other person and also deprive yourself of freedom. What prevents you from being free, that is what is forbidden. What to *do*? What you want."[28]

Thus we can understand why the Christian tradition attached so much importance to these negative commandments of the Decalogue, recognizing in them a decisive light for its moral teaching. Depriving man of his

---

28. Beauchamp, *La Legge di Dio*, 33–34.

freedom, the forbidden behaviors (murder, adultery, theft, perjury) make him a slave to sin, a slave to himself. They prevent him from accepting the gift; they exclude him from the kingdom of God (1 Cor 6:10; cf. Mt 5:20). Such actions can *never* be done lawfully because they contain the seeds of radical inhumanity. This is why James teaches in his letter that breaking one main commandment of the Torah makes one guilty of the whole law: the whole Torah subsists in each of these precepts.[29] The Church, speaking in its Magisterium of intrinsically evil acts (which can never be made honest), is prophetically faithful to this doctrine. According to John Paul II,

> By teaching the existence of inherently evil acts, the Church embraces the doctrine of Scripture. The apostle Paul states categorically, "Do not deceive yourselves: neither the immoral, nor idolaters, nor adulterers, nor effeminate, nor sodomites, nor thieves, nor drunkards, nor revilers, nor rapacious shall inherit the kingdom of God" (1 Cor 6:9–10) (VS 81).

The Practice of the Commandments, an Expression of Love

In contrast, fulfilling the commandments of God's law entails another inseparable dimension, this one of a symbolic order. Indeed, obeying the Torah's commands, creatively embracing its decisive impulse toward good, means accepting God's yoke, submitting to his kingdom. And this is tantamount to loving him above all else: not for nothing in rabbinic Judaism does "yoke" express the recitation of the *Shema* and thus the assumption of Torah.[30] Klemens Stock teaches in this regard:

> God's precepts are also perceived as signs of his grace: through them Israel can know what God desires and wills (cf. Ps 19; 119). The highest value for man, his deepest desire is not the emancipation of his will. The man who allows himself to be guided by this criterion feels God's precept as a burdensome prescription, as a limitation of free will; his attitude is centered on his own self and his own freedom. In contrast, when man accepts God's precept as a merciful gift, his greatest desire is union with God. He then reveals an attitude centered on his relationship with

---

29. Jas 2:10–11, "For whoever keeps the whole law but fails in one point has become guilty of all of it. For he who said, 'Do not commit adultery,' said also, 'Do not kill.' If you do not commit adultery but do kill, you have become a transgressor of the law."

30. "The yoke of the Torah" (*Misná Ab.* 3:5), "the yoke of the kingdom of heaven" (*Misná Ber.* 2:2), "the yoke of the commandments" (*Misná Ber.* 2:2).

God; he rejoices to know His will and would like, as it were, to read in His eyes what his desires are.[31]

Obedience or rejection of divine commands thus reveals the human heart: those who accept them as a gift seek God, those who feel them as a heavy burden close themselves off from him. This is why, by obeying the Torah, the Israelite expresses his allegiance to the covenant. This is the spirit of the enigmatic claim of "a single iota or a single superscript from the law" on the lips of the Lord, to the point that "whoever transgresses a single one of these precepts, even a minimal one [...] will be considered minimal in the kingdom of heaven" (Mt 5:18–19). In its recent document, the Pontifical Biblical Commission reminds us that "what counts is the great love that unfolds in the humble observance of even a small norm."[32] Thus, according to the summary offered by John Paul II's great encyclical,

> Through the morality of the commandments the belonging of the people of Israel to the Lord is manifested, for God alone is the One who is good. This is the testimony of Holy Scripture. (VS 11)

The Church that teaches this is not at all "a Church understood as a custom that rejects sinners" (§21). She is a loving mother who wants her children to be free and alive.

"He Who Has My Commandments and Keeps Them, He It Is Who Loves Me"

What has been said now enables us to turn our gaze to the Lord's words at the Last Supper: "He who has my commandments and keeps them, he it is who loves me" (Jn 14:21). It is a request repeated in this Gospel: "If you love me, you will keep my commandments" (14:15); "If a man loves me, he will keep my word" (14:23). Faithfulness to Jesus' love is expressed in the fulfillment of his commandments.[33] Indeed, what is at stake is radical

---

31. Klemens Stock, *Gesù il Figlio di Dio: Il messaggio di Giovanni* (Rome: Bibbia e Preghiera, 1993), 18.
32. Pontifical Biblical Commission, *"What Is Man?" (Ps 8:5) An Itinerary of Biblical Anthropology* (2019), §288.
33. Domingo Muñoz León, "Evangelio según san Juan," in *Comentario Bíblico Latinoamericano II: Nuevo Testamento*, edited by Armando J. Levoratti (Estella: Verbo Divino, 2003), 589–682, here 658.

fidelity to God, according to the biblical pattern that Jesus' words echo: God will love those who remain faithful to the covenant (Dt 7:12–13; cf. 23:6)[34]. The context of this statement is significant because it is framed by the earliest mentions of the Paraclete (Jn 14:16, 26); the observance of the commandments is inseparable from the influence of the Spirit of Truth. The commandments of Jesus and the Spirit of Jesus require each other; "keeping the commandments is an indispensable condition for experiencing and 'understanding' the post-Easter Jesus."[35] We notice that Jesus asks of his disciples only what he himself does: to keep the commandments of the Father (Jn 10:18, 12:49–50, 14:31, 15:14). In fact, it is his radical obedience to the Father that enables him to ask for similar obedience: "If you keep my commandments, you will abide in my love, just as I have kept my Father's commandments and abide in his love" (Jn 15:10); Jesus' authority (*exousia*) is obedience granted to him by the Father (Jn 17:2).

The formulation of John 14:21 is particularly rich. First, because, unlike 14:15, it is not limited to the disciples ("you") but its tenor is general ("he who ..."), and also because of its precise wording. It speaks first of "having" (Greek verb *ekhō*) the commandments of Jesus; in this case the verb does not indicate mere possession but careful "keeping," like someone who hides something precious (cf. Lk 19:20: the mine). And second, to "keep" (*tēreō*), a common verb in the New Testament (and especially in John) for observing the commandments. Jesus' commandments are "kept" and "observed." Because they belong to Jesus: the most important word in this sentence of the Lord (Jn 14:21) is undoubtedly the genitive *mou* "of mine," an enclitic monosyllable (τὰς ἐντολάς μου), but one with a powerful meaning. Thus his commandments are like the "treasure" of the parable (Mt 13:44): they are the most precious thing that fills the heart of those who find them with joy. They are the object of love: "Oh, how I love thy law! It is my meditation all the day" (Ps 119:97). For this reason, the language of the commandment and the language of love overlap on the lips of Jesus. Thus John can write:

---

34. Dt 7:12–13: "And because you hearken to these ordinances, and keep and do them, the Lord your God will keep with you the covenant and the steadfast love which he swore to your fathers to keep; **13** he will love you, bless you, and multiply you." Cf. Johannes Beutler, *Das Johannesevangelium: Kommentar* (Freiburg im Breisgau: Herder, 2013), 409.

35. Secundino Castro Sánchez, *Evangelio de Juan: Comprensión exegético-existencial* (Madrid: Universidad Pontificia Comillas, 2001).

2 By this we know that we love the children of God, when we love God and obey his commandments. 3 For this is the love of God, that we keep his commandments. And his commandments are not burdensome. 4 For whatever is born of God overcomes the world. (1 Jn 5:2–4)

In Conclusion

"Love subject to the law!" we exclaimed at first, almost shocked. No: what happens is that love is not abstract but exists only in concrete works, and so "a response to the revelation of God in Jesus through the observance of his commandments is simultaneously a loving commitment to Jesus."[36] The New Testament morality of love, precisely because it brings to fullness the revelation of the Old Covenant, does not renounce the commandments that, transmitted to Israel through Moses, illuminate man's life and reveal his vocation. On the contrary, these commandments, engraved in the Christian heart by the Paschal Mystery (cf. Jer 31:31), now appear as an integral part of love. Love for God and neighbor (Mt 22:37–40). Love "to the end" (Jn 13:1).

---

36. Francis J. Moloney, *The Gospel of John* (Collegeville, MN: Liturgical Press, 1998), 404 (*ad* Jn 14:21).

CHAPTER 3

Boldness in Inversion
Reflections on the Encyclical *Veritatis Splendor*

MONSIGNOR PIOTR MAZURKIEWICZ

When we say *Veritatis Splendor*, our thought naturally turns to the teaching of St. John Paul II the Great on intrinsically evil acts (*intrinsece malos*). The existence of acts that are ethically always evil—that is, always forbidden, regardless of the circumstances—was also recognized in the pagan world. On the one hand, we have the testimony of St. Paul, who states that pagans too are guided by conscience and have some basic, correct distinction between good and evil (Rm 2:14–15). On the other hand, we have Epictetus, whose moral indications are close to Christian morality, or the teaching of Aristotle, from which St. Thomas Aquinas drew abundantly. The main axis of Aristotle's ethics is the theory of virtue, together with the Pythagorean principle of the golden mean, which was transferred to moral considerations. Thus the good, we can say, lies in the middle, between the extremes resulting from excess or lack in terms of a certain trait. Courage, for example, is the right attitude toward fear. One should be afraid neither too much nor too little, but as much as necessary in a given situation. But Aristotle also raises the question of whether the principle of the golden mean applies to all human acts, and he gives a negative answer.

Not every action or emotion however admits of the observance of a due mean. Indeed the very names of some directly imply evil, for instance malice, shamelessness, envy, and, of actions, adultery, theft, murder. All these and similar actions and feelings are blamed as being bad in themselves; it is not the excess or deficiency of them that we blame.[1]

The belief that certain kinds of action are strictly prohibited or prescribed, notwithstanding the circumstances, is an essential and inalienable part of Aristotle's views. A breach of these principles or laws is an offense against natural and universal, not merely conventional, justice. Aristotle states: "Yet there seem to be some acts which a man cannot be compelled to do, and rather than do them he ought to submit to the most terrible death: for instance, we think it ridiculous that Alcmaeon in Euripides' play is compelled by certain threats to murder his mother!"[2] The awareness of the existence of intrinsically evil (*intrinsece mala*) deeds, which give rise to an unconditional moral obligation, is confirmed by the position of both Socrates and Hippocrates. The latter states: "I will use treatment to help the sick according to my ability and judgment, but never with a view to injury and wrong-doing. Neither will I administer a poison to anybody when asked to do so, nor will I suggest such a course. Similarly, I will not give to a woman a pessary to cause abortion."[3]

Reason itself, therefore, properly used, leads to the necessity of recognizing the existence of intrinsically evil acts. Josef Seifert points out the practical consequences of the opposite belief, that is, that intrinsically evil acts do not exist.

If, therefore, there are no acts that are *intrinsece mala*, it is permissible to murder Jews and other peoples in order to prevent even greater evils; it is permissible to kill children, rape women, etc., if in a particular situation taken together the effects of such an act seem better than their opposite.[4]

Appealing only to pure logic, Seifert chalks up the predictable consequences of recognizing that under certain circumstances and after proper "discernment" anything can be considered good and praiseworthy due to

---

1. Aristotle, *Nicomachean Ethics*, 1107a.
2. Aristotle, *Nicomachean Ethics*, 1110a.
3. Hippocrates, "Oath," in *Hippocrates*, translated by W. H. S. Jones (London: W. Heinemann, 1962), 299.
4. J. Seifert, "Blask prawdy jako fundament działania moralnego: O encyklice papieża Jana Pawła II *Veritatis splendor*," in Jan Paweł II, *Veritatis Splendor: Tekst i komentarze* (Lublin: Redakcja Wydawnictw KUL, 1995), 185.

the complexity of a given situation, lack of ethical knowledge or strength of will.

Can then not God also demand that a Sicilian, who feels obligated to extinguish the innocent family members of a family, whose head has murdered a member of his own family and whose brother would murder four families if he does not kill one, go ahead with his murder, because his act is, under his conditions, "what God himself is asking amid the concrete complexity of one's limits, while yet not fully the objective ideal"?[5]

In other words, any act ceases to be an abhorrent crime so long as we can find a suitable argument to justify it. But then the difference between vegetarianism and cannibalism boils down to a sense of taste.[6]

Regio Dissimilitudinis: The First Inversion

Despite the many correct intuitions of the ancient Greeks and Romans, Tacitus notes a fundamental difference between the morality of the highly civilized Romans—as he thought—and the rules handed down by Moses and practiced by the Jews who deserved—in his view—contempt. "Moyses, wishing to secure for the future his authority over the nation, gave them a novel form of worship, opposed to all that is practised by other men. Things sacred with us, with them have no sanctity, while they allow what with us is forbidden."[7] According to Tacitus, Moses, having led the Israelites out of Egypt, performed a kind of inversion of values. The Israelites, having come out of Egypt, did not re-create its political system based on slavery but adopted a free constitution in the form of the Decalogue. This implies an inversion of values in relation to those practiced not only in Egypt but also to a large extent in ancient Greece or Rome. For that civilization was marked by both freedom in the sexual sphere and the belief that slaves existed by nature, that women did not use reason,

---

5. Josef Seifert, "Does Pure Logic Threaten to Destroy the Entire Moral Doctrine of the Catholic Church?," One Peter Five, August 24, 2017, https://onepeterfive.com/josef-seifert-pure-logic-threaten-destroy-entire-moral-doctrine-catholic-church/.

6. See Leszek Kołakowski, *Modernity on Endless Trial* (Chicago: University of Chicago Press, 1997), 150–51.

7. Tacitus, *The History*, vol. 4, *The Complete Works of Tacitus* (New York: Random House, 1942).

and by the killing of handicapped children and "surplus" daughters.[8] The anthropological revolution wrought by the Jewish and Christian belief that every human being has unique value because he or she was created in the "image and likeness" of God turned the ancient world on its head. "Do not lie to one another, seeing you have put off the old nature with its practices, and you have put on the new nature, which is being renewed in knowledge after the image of its creator. Here there cannot be Greek and Jew, circumcised and uncircumcised, barbarian, Scythian, slave, free man, but Christ is all, and in all" (Col 3:9–11; see Gal 3:28).

Christianity fundamentally changes man's image of the world and self-understanding. In other words, paganism completely distorts the real vision of the world, the world as created by God. St. Augustine, trying to describe the state of his soul before his conversion, used the Platonic expression *regio dissimilitudinis*, the "zone of dissimilarity," the land where everything is backward (*et inveni longe me esse a te in regione dissimilitudinis*).[9] The world seen through the eyes of an unbeliever is a world seen backward, in which nothing is in its own place. "Hence the wise men of God and the wise men of the world are foolish in the eyes of each other, for the one group finds the wisdom and knowledge of God imperceptible, and the other finds the same of the knowledge of the world. Wherefore the knowledge of the world is ignorance to the knowledge of God, and the knowledge of God is ignorance to the knowledge of the world."[10] Perhaps a similar epistemic intuition is found in a phrase of Heraclitus: "'For the waking there is one common world ... the sleeping are turned to their separate worlds."[11]

---

8. Étienne Robert, "La conscience médicale antique et la vie des enfants," in *Annales de démographie historique: Enfant et Sociétés* (Paris: Société de Démographie Historique, 1973), 15–61.

9. St. Augustine, *Confessiones*, 7.11.16; cf. Benedict XVI, "Meeting with Representatives from the World of Culture, Collège des Bernardins, Paris," website of the Holy See, September 12, 2008, https://www.vatican.va/content/benedict-xvi/en/speeches/2008/september/documents/hf_ben-xvi_spe_20080912_parigi-cultura.html.

10. St. John of the Cross, *A Spiritual Canticle of the Soul*, 26:13.

11. "Heraclitus," in *A Presocratics Reader: Selected Fragments and Testimonia*, edited by Patricia Curd, translated by Richard D. McKirahan Jr. (Indianapolis, IN: Hackett, 1996), 32.

Do Not Take the Example of This World

When reading the encyclical *Veritatis Splendor*, it should be noted that it is not an apologetic lecture aimed at modern pagans; it is instead a strictly theological explanation for the needs of Catholics, that is, people who by definition live in an "inverted world" in relation to paganism. The reason why their hierarchy of values is "inverted" in relation to non-Christians is strictly religious. It is therefore about who the God of Christians is in relation to the various ancient and modern pagan deities.

What is the inversion when it comes to understanding God? Cardinal Joseph Ratzinger notes that not only Christians but also the Greeks called their god Zeus "father." "But for them this was not an expression of trust, but rather of the deep ambiguity of the god, the tragic ambiguity and of the terrifying nature of the world. When they said 'father,' it meant: he is like our fathers. Sometimes, when he is in a good mood, quite nice, but deep down he is selfish, incalculable, impenetrable and dangerous tyrant. Similarly, they experience the mysterious force that rules over the world: it chooses certain people as its favorites, towards others it is indifferent, allows them to starve to death, fall into slavery, perish. 'The Father' of the world, as life experiences us, is a reflection of human fathers: he is biased and ultimately awe-inspiring."[12] The biblical Father is not an enlarged image of the earthly father, but something entirely new, "God's critique of human fatherhood."[13]

The God of the Bible is the Father of Jesus Christ, whom he addresses by saying, "Abba" (Mk 14:36). The word encapsulates the cordiality with which a young child addresses his daddy, knowing that he is loved by him. It is into this relationship between the Father and the Son, as St. Paul states, that the Christian is introduced, who through baptism becomes an adopted child of God: "For all those who are led by the Spirit of God are sons of God. For you did not receive the spirit of bondage to fall back into fear, but you received the spirit of adoption as sons, in which we can cry out: 'Abba, Father!'" The Spirit himself supports with his witness our spirit that we are children of God (Rom 8:14–16). The Christian novelty is "a

---

12. J. Ratzinger, "Bóg jest w Trójcy jedyny," in *Opera omnia*, vol. 3.1, *Bóg wiary i Bóg filozofów* (Lublin: Wydawnictwo KUL, 2021), 109.

13. Ratzinger, "Bóg jest w Trójcy jedyny," 110.

radical reversal of the direction of the love relationship between God and man."[14] St. John the Apostle put it excellently: "In this is love, not that we have loved God, but that he loved us, and sent his Son to be the expiation for our sins... So we know and believe the love God has for us. God is love, and he who abides in love abides in God, and God abides in him" (1 Jn 4:10–16). So here we have God's "foolish love" (Nicholas Cabásilas: *manikós eros*) for man, to the point of offering his life for him on the cross. We have the overcoming through the Incarnation of the infinite distance between God and man. We have "the personal embodiment of the moral law in the Person whose imitation is the core of moral life."[15] When a Christian asks how he should believe, he finds the answer in the words of St. John: to believe is to discover that you are personally loved by God. To grow in faith is to understand this more and more deeply and to become more and more open to this love. When a Christian asks how he should arrange his life, in response he hears: look at Jesus and imitate him. Be like him. Nothing else is needed. Can you imagine a more daring change, a more radical reversal? We have come to know and believe the love that God has for us. We have become enthralled with the person of Jesus Christ and desire with all our hearts to be like him. In the context of this desire, one must ask, Are there not certain acts that make a person unlike Christ? In this context, one must also view the normative indications of Jesus, which are themselves a manifestation of his love for man, and not just a softening or reversal of them. "But he who does [these commandments] and teaches them shall be called great in the kingdom of heaven" (Mt 5:19).

In the Gospel, we have more surprising inversions: the knocking down of rulers from thrones and the lifting up of the poor, the birth in the Bethlehem crib, the washing of the Apostles' feet. They encourage us not to chase after what is great but what is humble. "Have this mind among yourselves, which was in Christ Jesus, who though he was in the form of God, did not count equality with God a thing to be grasped, but emptied himself, taking the form of a servant, being born in the likeness of men. And being found in human form he humbled himself and became obedient unto death, even death on a cross" (Phil 2:5–8).

---

14. Seifert, "Blask prawdy jako fundament działania moralnego," 176.
15. Seifert, "Blask prawdy jako fundament działania moralnego," 176.

Return Inversion

Paradoxically, this was well understood by Friedrich Nietzsche, who called for a "revaluation of all values," that is, a return inversion. He dreamed not only of the "death of God" but also of a return to the pagan civilization from before Moses and Socrates, in which strength, not human weakness, was valued. The postulate of destroying the Christian world and replacing it with another guided the French Revolution and later the Russian Revolution. In a slightly different way, it was promoted by the sexual revolution. Each time there was an attempt to reject Jesus as a model of man and to bring about anthropological palingenesis, that is, the creation of a new man in the likeness of a pagan idol.[16]

Rebellion against Christ and the hierarchy of values brought by him is not new. Rather, what is new is the fact that we are dealing with it today also inside the Catholic Church. In this context, Cardinal Joseph Ratzinger spoke on the victory of the *ecclesia pagana* over the Catholic Church;[17]

---

16. See Chantal Delsol, *La haine du monde: Totalitarismes et postmodernité* (Paris: Cerf, 2019).

17. Joseph Ratzinger, "The New Pagans and the Church," translated by Kenneth Baker, SJ, Catholic Culture, accessed June 24, 2023, https://www.catholicculture.org/culture/library/view.cfm?recnum=11509. This is well reflected in an anecdote quoted by St. Gregory of Nyssa in fourth century about a monkey, which he took from Lucian of Samosata: "They say that a certain showman in the city of Alexandria, having trained a monkey to dance with some grace, and having dressed him in a dancer's mask and a costume suitable for the occasion, and having surrounded him with a chorus, gained fame by the monkey's twisting himself in time with the music and concealing his nature in every way by what he was doing and what he appeared to be. While the audience was enthralled by the novelty of the spectacle, one of the clever persons present, by means of a trick, showed those watching the performance that the dancer was a monkey. When everyone was crying out and applauding the gesticulations of the monkey, who was moving rhythmically with the music, they say that he threw onto the dancing place some of the sweetmeats which arouse the greediness of such animals; whereupon the monkey, without a moment's delay, when he saw the almonds scattered in front of the chorus, forgetting the dancing and the applause and the elaborate costume, ran after them and grabbed what he found in the palms of his hands. And in order that the mask would not get in the way of his mouth, he energetically thrust aside the disguise with his nails and immediately evoked a laugh from the spectators in place of the praise and admiration, as he emerged ugly and ridiculous from the shreds of the mask. Therefore, just as the assumed form was not sufficient for that creature to be considered a man, once his nature was disclosed in the incident of the almonds, so those individuals not truly shaping their own natures by faith will easily be disclosed in the toils of the devil as being something other than what they are called. For, instead of a fig or an almond or some such thing, vanity and love of honor and love of gain and love of pleasure, and whatever else the evil assembly of the devil places before greedy men instead of sweetmeats, easily bring to light the ape-like souls who, through pretense and imitation, play the role of the Christian

others speak of an attempt to create a Brave New Church, and still others refer to the "Second Reformation."[18] What we have here is an outright rebellion against the moral teaching of the Catholic Church and a bold attempt to bring about a return inversion of values. The Christian ideal is considered unattainable and incompatible with life. What is at stake, however, is something much more serious than a mere deviation from the ideal. Cardinal Blase Cupich and Cardinal Pietro Parolin speak of "a New Paradigm of Catholicity."[19] This approach takes as its starting point an observation from the social sciences leading to the conclusion that societies are currently undergoing a phase of "the seismic shifts," which is associated with the phenomenon of secularization, technological development, globalization, and terrorism.[20] The new social context demands a new hermeneutic for reading the content of the Scripture and Tradition. Cardinal Cupich derives from these six new principles of interpretation, the application of which ultimately leads to a "paradigm shift." "These principles of interpretation, six in all, force a paradigm shift, allowing us to re-envision the Church's engagement with couples and families and open a pathway for doing so."[21]

I will not discuss in detail each of the "new principles" proposed by the Cardinal. I will only try to reproduce and analyze the underlying assumptions. First, as it seems, we are dealing here with an idealization of

---

and then remove the mask of moderation or meekness or some other virtue in a moment of personal crisis. It is necessary, therefore, for us to understand what the name 'Christian' means, for then, perhaps, we will become what the term implies and not be shown up by the one who perceives what is hidden, namely, that we have disguised ourselves by mere assent and by the pretense of the name alone when we are actually something contrary to what we appear to be." "The Dead Come to Life, or the Fisherman," in *Lucian in Eight Volumes*, vol. 3, translated by A. M. Harmon (Cambridge, MA: Harvard University Press, 1969), 54–55. See also St. Gregory of Nyssa, "On What It Means to Call Oneself a Christian," in *Ascetical Works*, translated by Virginia Woods Callahan (Washington, DC: Catholic University of America Press, 1967), 82–83.

18. See Nassim Nicholas Taleb, "On Christianity: An Essay as a Foreword for Tom Holland's *Dominion*," Medium, August 25, 2022, https://medium.com/incerto/on-christianity-b7fecde866ec.

19. Alessandro Gisotti, "Intervista con card. Card. Parolin: il 2018 di Francesco all'insegna di giovani e famiglia," Vatican News, January 11, 2018, https://www.vaticannews.va/it/vaticano/news/2018-01/card--parolin--il-2018-di-francesco-allinsegna-di-giovani-e-fami.html#play; Cardinal Blase Cupich, "Pope Francis' Revolution of Mercy: *Amoris Laetitia* as a New Paradigm of Catholicity," La Stampa, February 19, 2018, https://www.lastampa.it/vatican-insider/en/2018/02/09/news/pope-francis-revolution-of-mercy-amoris-laetitia-as-a-new-paradigm-of-catholicity-1.33978121.

20. See Cupich, "Pope Francis' Revolution of Mercy."

21. Cupich, "Pope Francis' Revolution of Mercy."

the past that is not fully realized, for marriage and the family were to face great challenges only in the current era, with which nothing in the past can compare. It seems that this outlook is ahistorical. The ancient institution of marriage and family found itself in an area of "seismic upheaval" due to Christianity. There followed a redefinition of marriage and family meaning, for example, the definitional separation of spouses and their children from slaves and equipment, the introduction of monogamy, the recognition of the equality of man and woman in marriage, the abolition of the principle of dual morality (different for women, different for men), the obligation of marital fidelity, the abolition of divorce, the prohibition of abortion, and the killing of "surplus" daughters, and so on. The family faced no less challenges in the era of industrialization, associated with mass migration from the countryside to the cities, or in the era of the first globalization and associated migration, for example, from Europe to the United States. No less challenging was the communist family model violently imposed in large areas of the world on Catholic families as well. Are the current challenges greater? I dare to doubt it. Conversely, they are certainly different from earlier ones and therefore demand new answers. But to apply to the present time the doctrine of "moral emergency" linked with the "temporary suspension of all moral norms" would be completely wrong.

Inversion of the Reference Point: The Victory of Statistics

A change that is crucial for the future of the Church is now taking place within the Church herself, related to the spread of defeatism. While in the past the Church generally assumed that its task was to transform the world, without negating the good that was in it, today there is often a bold reversal of Paul's postulate *nolite conformari quic saeculo* (Rom 12:2). The Church, therefore, wants to learn from the world and conform to the world. Not only to be in the world, but also to be of the world. She wishes not to arouse hostility toward herself even from the most ardent atheists. This is often accompanied by the temptation to horizontalize the church's mission, that is, to limit herself to administration of the faithful, just as the state administers the citizens. It is all about statistics, just as it was when David ordered the population of Israel to be counted (2 Sm 24:1–25; 1 Kgs 21:1–30). What matters, then, is the number of members here on earth, not in heaven. Instead of an instrument of salvation, the Church would become an instrument for "relieving" people from experiencing their various life situations.

The second issue of fundamental importance is the proposed bold inversion of the reference point. I think that it is mainly related to the subconscious recognition of the superiority of social science over theology. The social sciences are considered neutral yet infallible in their description of the world. What is forgotten is that the social sciences are not passive, like astronomy, for example. Describing the tracks on which the stars or planets move does not change their course. The suggestive description of social phenomena made on the ground of sociology changes the perception of the world and, consequently, the behavior of specific people and societies. And, as it turns out, also the teachings of the Church. Sometimes, therefore, we are dealing with the mechanism of "self-fulfilling prophecy" described by Robert Merton. Recognizing that the Church's teaching on marriage and family is "abstract," presenting only an unattainable ideal in the real world, useful only for hurling the "dead stones" at others,[22] consequently leads to the recognition of earthly reality, and especially families in various compositions as a special theological place. Cardinal Cupich states,

God has chosen the family as a privileged place to reveal how God acts and relates to humanity and the world. This insight has enormous consequences. If we are serious about fully appreciating that the concrete lives of families and couples are part of salvation history in which God continues to engage and redeem humanity, then at the least it will mean moving away from presenting an abstract and idealized presentation of marriage. Instead, we should begin with a view that married life is "a challenging mosaic made up of many different realities, with all their joys, hopes and problems" (AL 38). Likewise, if we accept that families are a privileged place of God's self-revelation and activity, then no family should be considered deprived of God's grace. Our ministerial approach should begin with the understanding that families are not problems to solve. Rather, they are opportunities for the Church to discern with the aid of the Spirit how God is active in our time and what God is calling us to do here and now.[23]

---

22. Pope Francis, *Conclusion of the Synod of Bishops*, website of the Holy See, October 24, 2015, https://www.vatican.va/content/francesco/en/speeches/2015/october/documents/papa-francesco_20151024_sinodo-conclusione-lavori.html.

23. Cupich, "Pope Francis' Revolution of Mercy."

From the above text, we learn that revelation is currently taking place in "various forms of the family," from which the bishops can learn "what the Spirit is saying to the Church" (Rv 3:22). And the Spirit (of today) is not teaching about sin and holiness, but about irregularity, diversity, complexity, "the necessity of living at some distance from the Church's understanding of the ideal" and on the "new stages of growth." At the same time, "in a genuinely synodal Church there is no hierarchical distinction between those with knowledge and those without."[24] For the process of forming the Church's teaching is a two-way street, and the deductive and inductive methods in determining the content of teaching are equated.[25] "There can be no better teacher for the Church than the faithful who actively walk this path of personal development," writes Cardinal Cupich.[26] These sentences raise many questions. What does "faithful" mean in this text? Faithful to whom or what? How does this "faithful" know what the Spirit is saying to the Church? I guess the proposed answer refers to the individual conscience, but individual conscience is sometimes fallible. We don't know whether the text refers to *synderesis* or *syneidesis*, for English uses the same term "conscience" in both cases. As John Finnis notes, even in the case of Cardinal John Henry Newman's well-known text, there is insufficient precision here.[27] Nevertheless, if individual conscience, however understood, says that the Church is wrong in proclaiming that there are intrinsically evil acts, can it even be right in arguing about such fundamental matters? If it says that there are no things that "poison human society [and] do more harm to those who practice them than those who suffer from the injury [and] are a supreme dishonor to the Creator" (*Gaudium et Spes* 27)? Is the individual conscience then trustworthy even in terms of individual life choices? Does it then still constitute a sanctuary and a privilege place of revelation?

---

24. Cupich, "Pope Francis' Revolution of Mercy."
25. See M. Gierycz, "On the 'New Paradigm of Catholicism' and Its Impact on Catholic Political Theory and Socio-Political Engagement of the Catholic Church," *Religiski-filozofiski raksti* 25 (2019): 46–75, https://www.researchgate.net/publication/335890723_On_the_New_Paradigm_of_Catholicism_and_Its_Impact_on_Catholic_Political_Theory_and_Socio-Political_Engagement_of_the_Catholic_Church.
26. Cupich, "Pope Francis' Revolution of Mercy."
27. See John Finnis, "Conscience in the Letter to the Duke of Norfolk," in *Religion and Public Reasons: Collected Essays*, vol. 5 (Oxford: Oxford University Press, 2013), 216.

There may also be a suspicion that the abolition of hierarchy in the teaching is the bold role reversal in education that Plato once wrote about in Book VIII of his *Republic*. Describing the breakdown of the democratic system, he points out that one of its manifestations is that there is a reversal of the master-student relationship. "The teacher in such case fears and fawns upon the pupils, and the pupils pay no heed to the teacher or to their overseers either.... while the old, accommodating themselves to the young, are full of pleasantry and graciousness, imitating the young for fear they may be thought disagreeable and authoritative."[28] Social acceptance becomes more important than the truth and the good of the students.

Growing Curiosity in Catholicism

The third chapter of the encyclical *Veritatis Splendor* is titled "So as Not to Nullify Christ's Cross" (1 Cor 1:17). Much of it is addressed directly to Catholic theologians and bishops. The Greek expression ἵνα μὴ κενωθῇ ὁ σταυρὸς τοῦ Χριστοῦ (hina mē kenōthē ho stauros tou Christou) (the word "kenosis" we know well) is translated as "would not be made void" (New American Standard Bible), "should be made of none effect" (King James Version), "[should] not be emptied of power" (New International Version). The cross through human action can be emptied of its meaning, made pointless.[29] Paul writes this in the context of a penchant for flashy debates in which the interlocutors display rhetorical prowess, but that bring no life-relevant knowledge to the listeners. Empty words. The Apostle makes a distinction in the Epistle between the wisdom of words (*sophia logou*; 1:17) and the word of wisdom (*logos sophias*; 12:8). The word of wisdom here means "the gift of giving practical advice of the kind recorded in the Book of Proverbs and the Wisdom of Sirach, but now purified and made complete by the light of the Holy Spirit. It might not seem wise from a purely human point of view—writes George T. Montague— to advise forgiving one's enemies, but that is what the supernatural gift of wisdom and the advice of wisdom would inspire."[30] Similarly, today,

---

28. Plato, *Republic*, VIII, 563a–b.
29. See George T. Montague, SM, *First Corinthians* (Grand Rapids, MI: Baker Academic, 2011), 41.
30. Montague, *First Corinthians*, 208–9.

advising a husband to return to the wife of his youth, or if he cannot or does not, to at least not take Holy Communion, or encouraging someone feeling same-sex sexual attraction to live a life of total abstinence, may not seem wise from the logic of the world. But "the wisdom of this world is folly with God," as we read again and again in the same Epistle to the Corinthians (1 Cor 3:19). Let's read the entire relevant passage:

For Christ did not send me to baptize but to preach the gospel, and not with eloquent wisdom, lest the cross of Christ be emptied of its power. For the word of the cross is folly to those who are perishing, but to us who are being saved it is the power of God. For it is written, "I will destroy the wisdom of the wise, and the cleverness of the clever I will thwart." Where is the wise man? Where is the scribe? Where is the debater of this age? Has not God made foolish the wisdom of the world? For since, in the wisdom of God, the world did not know God through wisdom, it pleased God through the folly of what we preach to save those who believe. For Jews demand signs and Greeks seek wisdom, but we preach Christ crucified, a stumbling block to Jews and folly to Gentiles, but to those who are called, both Jews and Greeks, Christ the power of God and the wisdom of God. For the foolishness of God is wiser than men, and the weakness of God is stronger than men. (1 Cor 1:17–25)

What fundamentally changes the perception of the world is the logic of the cross. The agreement to be crucified and for salvation to be accomplished precisely through what was previously a sign of damnation is the root cause of the Christian inversion of values. The sign of dishonor becomes the sign of love. "The Romans were befuddled to see members of that sect use for symbol the cross—punishment for slaves. It had to be some type of joke in their eyes," Nassim Nicholas Taleb writes aptly.[31] But such a possibility was intuited by the greatest minds of pagan antiquity. Plato, in the *Republic*, writes about the fate that would befall a fully righteous man, should one appear on earth:

such being his disposition the just man will have to endure the lash, the rack, chains, the branding-iron in his eyes, and finally, after every extremity of suffering, he will be crucified, and so will learn his lesson that not to be but to seem just is what we ought to desire.[32]

---

31. See Taleb, "On Christianity."
32. Plato, *Republic*, 361e–362a.

John Paul II names Christian martyrs as teachers of moral theology. "Martyrdom rejects as false and illusory whatever 'human meaning' one might claim to attribute, even in 'exceptional' conditions, to an act morally evil in itself. Indeed, it even more clearly unmasks the true face of such an act: *it is a violation of man's 'humanity,'* in the one perpetrating it even before the one enduring it" (VS 92). The last words are a quote from *Gaudium et Spes* (27), which is significant in that it makes us aware that those who question the existence of intrinsically evil acts are at the same time contesting the teaching of Vatican II.

Veritatis Splendor reminds us of the special responsibility of theologians: "They have the grave duty to instruct the faithful—especially future Pastors—about all those commandments and practical norms authoritatively declared by the Church. While recognizing the possible limitations of the human arguments employed by the Magisterium, moral theologians are called to develop a deeper understanding of the reasons underlying its teachings and to expound the validity and obligatory nature of the precepts it proposes, demonstrating their connection with one another and their relation with man's ultimate end. Moral theologians are to set forth the Church's teaching and to give, in the exercise of their ministry, the example of a loyal assent, both internal and external, to the Magisterium's teaching in the areas of both dogma and morality" (VS 110). Thus this is not moral theology understood as an intellectual training or a search for some "curious" ideas. Likewise in the case of the bishops, who are to recognize that a part of their pastoral ministry is to grant "that this moral teaching is faithfully handed down and to have recourse to appropriate measures to ensure that the faithful are guarded from every doctrine and theory contrary to it. In carrying out this task we are all assisted by theologians; even so, theological opinions constitute neither the rule nor the norm of our teaching. Its authority is derived, by the assistance of the Holy Spirit and in communion *cum Petro et sub Petro,* from our fidelity to the Catholic faith which comes from the Apostles. As Bishops, we have the grave obligation to be *personally* vigilant that the 'sound doctrine' (1 Tm 1:10) of faith and morals is taught in our Dioceses" (VS 116). For the faithful have the right "to receive Catholic doctrine in its purity and integrity" (VS 113). In the end, it is their salvation that is at stake, as well as the salvation of their children, for whom they accepted co-responsibility at the time of their own marriage and the baptism of their children.

Should the bishops and theologians fail in any particular case, however, the Church reminds the faithful that "[i]n the history of the people of God, it has often been not the majority but rather a minority which has truly lived and witnessed to the faith. The Old Testament knew the 'holy remnant' of believers, sometimes very few in number, over against the kings and priests and most of the Israelites.... it must be recalled that the experience of the Church shows that sometimes the truth of the faith has been conserved not by the efforts of theologians or the teaching of the majority of bishops but in the hearts of believers."[33] The same document "instructs" the faithful on how they should behave at certain critical moments in Church history, stating that "[f]or St Thomas, a believer, even without theological competence, can and even must resist, by virtue of the *sensus fidei*, his or her bishop if the latter preaches heterodoxy. In such a case, the believer does not treat himself or herself as the ultimate criterion of the truth of faith, but rather, faced with materially 'authorised' preaching which he or she finds troubling, without being able to explain exactly why, defers assent and appeals interiorly to the superior authority of the universal Church."[34] Even if they are not theologians, after all, they know the One who first loved them. But this sentence should not be interpreted as an encouragement to follow one's own subjective judgment. For at that point, his conduct would be no different in any significant way from those who follow their own "discernment." At the same time, they do not have to constitute a majority in the Church. As the document suggests, they may constitute the "remnant" of Israel.

St. John Henry Newman regarding the size of this "remnant" is skep-

---

33. International Theological Commission, *Sensus Fidei in the Life of the Church*, 118–19, website of the Holy See, accessed June 24, 2023, https://www.vatican.va/roman_curia/congregations/cfaith/cti_documents/rc_cti_20140610_sensus-fidei_en.html#_ftn78.

34. International Theological Commission, *Sensus Fidei in the Life of the Church*, 63. In note 78 one finds: "Thomas Aquinas, *Scriptum*, III, d.25, q.2, a.1, qla 4, ad 3: '[The believer] must not give assent to a prelate who preaches against the faith.... The subordinate is not totally excused by his ignorance. In fact, the habitus of faith inclines him against such preaching because that habitus necessarily teaches whatever leads to salvation. Also, because one must not give credence too easily to every spirit, one should not give assent to strange preaching but should seek further information or simply entrust oneself to God without seeking to venture into the secrets of God beyond one's capacities.'"

tical. "A few highly-endowed men will rescue the world for centuries to come. Before now even one man [Athanasius] has impressed an image on the Church, which, through God's mercy, shall not be effaced while time lasts. Such men, like the Prophet, are placed upon their watch-tower, and light their beacons on the heights. Each receives and transmits the sacred flame, trimming it in rivalry of his predecessor, and fully purposed to send it on as bright as it has reached him; and thus the self-same fire, once kindled on Moriah, though seeming at intervals to fail, has at length reached us in safety, and will in like manner, as we trust, be carried forward even to the end."[35]

The uncontaminated light of faith has reached all the way to us, and our hope that there will be even one who will carry it to the next generation, reversing the course of history and opposing the anthropological counterrevolution, is not unreasonable.

---

35. J. H. Newman, "Sermon 5: Personal Influence, the Means of Propagating the Truth," in *Oxford Sermons*, Newman Reader, accessed June 24, 2023, https://newmanreader.org/works/oxford/sermons5.html, 35.

CHAPTER 4

❊

From Preconciliar Conscience-Centered Manuals to Postconciliar Conscience-Centered Moral Theology

MATTHEW LEVERING

Introduction

How did it happen that the dominant stream of Catholic moral theology in the twentieth century shifted from a conscience-centered morality focused upon law and obligation, to a conscience-centered morality focused upon existential authenticity and acting in ways that feel right and that bring subjective peace, no longer joining conscience to universal moral norms? In this essay, which in part condenses the longer story that I tell in *The Abuse of Conscience: A Century of Moral Theology*,[1] I will trace this shift. Let me be clear at the outset that I think conscience-centered morality—both before and after the Council—to be a mistake. Christian moral theology should be Christ-centered, Spirit-centered, and virtue-centered along lines that give place to human nature and natural law; and conscience has its proper role within this broader framework. Understood as a judgment evaluating a particular action in light of the universal moral law, conscience is crucial—but it is not the driving center of the Christian moral life.

Furthermore, absent its grounding in law, conscience can only express

---

1. See my *The Abuse of Conscience: A Century of Catholic Moral Theology* (Grand Rapids, MI: Eerdmans, 2021).

one's personal intuitions, which would not have inviolable standing no matter how deep one's feelings might be. Tragically, the dominant academic stream of Catholic conscience-centered morality after the Council is marked by the separation of conscience from law. The result has been what Reinhard Hütter calls "subjective sovereignty," a distorted shell of conscience.[2]

Pope John Paul II's 1993 encyclical *Veritatis Splendor* well describes this postconciliar conscience: "This voice [of conscience], it is said, leads man not so much to a meticulous observance of universal norms as to a creative and responsible acceptance of the personal tasks entrusted to him by God."[3]

My goal in this essay is diagnostic. I will examine how the shift from one conscience-centered moral theology to another conscience-centered moral theology took place so quickly in mainstream Catholic moral theology after Vatican II, despite the Council's call for a more biblically grounded and virtue-centered moral theology. In *The Abuse of Conscience*, I show that the shift is related to the ethics of existential authenticity that one finds in the philosophers Martin Heidegger and Karl Jaspers before World War II, and also to in the "existential ethics" of Dietrich Bonhoeffer and Karl Barth, for whom there are no laws that govern all cases: we must instead hear Christ's personal and unrepeatable command in particular situations. These thinkers influenced Karl Rahner, who in turn influenced Josef Fuchs and Bernard Häring.

In what follows, I will first discuss Dominic Prümmer's moral manual as broadly representative of the moral manualist tradition of conscience-centered morality. Second, I will examine relevant arguments found in Erich Fromm's psychoanalytical 1941 book *Escape from Freedom* and in Karl Rahner's writings from the 1940s through the 1970s.[4] Third, I will compare Bernard Häring's preconciliar textbook *The Law*

---

2. See Reinhard Hütter, *Bound for Beatitude: A Thomistic Study in Eschatology and Ethics* (Washington, DC: Catholic University of America Press, 2019); Hütter, *John Henry Newman on Truth and Its Counterfeits: A Guide for Our Times* (Washington, DC: Catholic University of America Press, 2020).

3. Pope John Paul II, *Veritatis Splendor*, Vatican translation (Boston, MA: St. Paul Books and Media, 1993), §55.

4. I was alerted to Erich Fromm's importance by Peter Cajka, *Follow Your Conscience: The Catholic Church and the Spirit of the Sixties* (Chicago: University of Chicago Press, 2021).

of Christ with his postconciliar textbook *Free and Faithful in Christ*. In light of these authors, we will better understand the twentieth-century shift of the dominant stream of Catholic moral theology "from confessing sins" (before the Council) to "liberating consciences" (after the Council), no longer bound by universal moral precepts.[5] This shift has distorted the main line of Catholic moral theology, as found today in Fuchs's and Häring's disciples James Keenan and Charles Curran, among many others.

Dominic Prümmer, OP's *Handbook of Moral Theology*

Let me begin by providing an example of preconciliar Catholic conscience-centered moral theology. Dominic Prümmer's well-respected preconciliar moral manual begins with a short treatment of the ultimate end of human acts—namely, the end or goal that is desired for itself and not as an instrument toward something further. The ultimate end fulfills human desire and produces a lasting happiness. Prümmer argues that this ultimate end can only be God. Only God can satisfy human desire because only God is infinite goodness. Permanent sharing in God's goodness would make us happy. By contrast, no finite good can do this, since "there is no created good which is perfect in every respect and which endures for ever."[6] Jesus Christ, in dying to redeem all human beings, opened the way to the attainment of the ultimate end for which the human soul yearns. This ultimate end requires supernatural grace, which elevates us so that we can see God as he is.

After this three-page account of the ultimate end, Prümmer's next section is about human acts. In twenty pages, he covers various topics: what makes for a specifically *human* act, knowledge and ignorance (vincible and invincible), the effects of certain habits of sin, the voluntariness of actions, and so on. Prümmer explores in this section "indirectly" voluntary acts, and specifically the licitness of performing an act while anticipating that it will have an evil effect. He identifies four principles that, when they are all present, can justify such an act: "1. the act is good in itself or at least

---

5. See James F. Keenan, SJ, *A History of Catholic Moral Theology in the Twentieth Century: From Confessing Sins to Liberating Consciences* (New York: Continuum, 2010).

6. Dominic M. Prümmer, OP, *Handbook of Moral Theology*, translated by Gerald W. Shelton (Harrison, NY: Roman Catholic Books, n.d.), 7.

indifferent; 2. its immediate effect is good; 3. the intention of the agent is good; 4. the agent has a proportionately grave reason for acting."[7] In this section on human acts, therefore, Prümmer is already engaged in the kind of moral analysis that serves casuistic ethics. He adds that voluntariness can be compromised by such things as violence, fear, and concupiscence (or passion). With respect to actions performed under the influence of the passions, he explains, "Antecedent passion diminishes the voluntariness of acts performed under its influence; if it is sufficiently violent to prevent the use of reason, the acts are completely involuntary."[8] Yet, as he says, it may also be the case that the will urgently desires some particular good, and therefore the will itself causes the passions. Prümmer also attends to the impact of habits: some habits increase the freedom by which we perform acts, although "involuntary" habits diminish freedom. He adds that bodily and psychological disorders diminish knowledge and freedom in human acts, such as phobias and hysteria. The victims of such disorders "are almost incapable of committing mortal sin."[9]

In this same section on human acts, Prümmer reflects upon the source of moral standards. As he notes, there have been various candidates identified as the source: utility (individual or social), right reason or duty, God's arbitrary will, or whatever subjectively feels right. Prümmer deems "the *ultimate* objective standard" to be the eternal law, and "the *proximate* objective standard" to be human reason.[10] He explores the evaluation of a human action through analysis of the moral object of the action ("that to which the action tends of its very nature *primarily* and *necessarily*"), its circumstances, and its end as intended by the agent.[11]

The third section of Prümmer's manual focuses on law, which it treats in thirty pages. At the center is the eternal law, God's wisdom for the flourishing of his creatures; the natural law is our rational participation in the eternal law. Prümmer argues that the primary precepts (e.g., "good must be done") are always known and the secondary precepts (e.g., the Decalogue) of the natural law cannot be obscured for long. In this sec-

---

7. Prümmer, *Handbook of Moral Theology*, 13.
8. Prümmer, *Handbook of Moral Theology*, 18.
9. Prümmer, *Handbook of Moral Theology*, 19.
10. Prümmer, *Handbook of Moral Theology*, 20.
11. Prümmer, *Handbook of Moral Theology*, 21.

tion, he addresses difficult cases such as why all the baptized—including Protestants—are not subject to the Catholic Church's laws, for instance, the law that the baptized must regularly attend Mass. He explores such issues as whether children are answerable to the laws of Church and State. He inquires into legal interpretation, dispensations (particularly with regard to the Church's laws), privileges, the role of local custom, and so on.

Having studied human actions and law, Prümmer next turns to conscience because it is where the practical intellect makes a judgment about the goodness or wickedness of a particular act. Conscience is where human action and law determinatively intersect. Synderesis, which stands at the root of conscience, is "the habitual practical knowledge of the first principles" regarding good and evil.[12] Conscience takes the principles of moral reasoning, known to the mind through natural law, and applies them to particular acts. Conscience can be true or false, since conscience can reason incorrectly. Conscience can be scrupulous, perplexed, lax, hardened, or pharisaic. Worst of all is the hardened conscience, so called because repeated acts of the same sin have conditioned the person's conscience to regard the sinful act (or sinful acts in general) to be of minor import. Prümmer distinguishes between various degrees of certitude in conscience about the moral goodness or permissibility of an act. A person's decision in conscience may be certain, probable, or doubtful.

Since it is possible to possess a false conscience, and since one must obey the dictates of conscience, it is necessary to strive for a true conscience. This is done in four ways, says Prümmer: "a) a careful knowledge of the laws which govern our moral life; b) taking wise counsel; c) prayer to the Father of light; d) removal of obstacles to a true conscience, chief amongst which is the obscurity resulting from unforgiven sin."[13] Prümmer also devotes attention to how to deal with a lax, perplexed, or scrupulous conscience. He explains that a certain conscience alone is sufficient to guide human action, but he adds that it suffices that its certainty be imperfect. On the one hand, "the man who acts without being morally certain that his act is lawful commits sin by exposing himself unnecessarily to the proximate danger of formally offending God," but on the other

---

12. Prümmer, *Handbook of Moral Theology*, 59.
13. Prümmer, *Handbook of Moral Theology*, 60.

hand, "sometimes it is impossible to obtain anything more than *imperfect* certainty regarding to actions, and no one is bound to do the impossible."[14] Prümmer holds that it is safe to follow the most probable opinion (among the opinions of the eminent moral theologians) in cases where absolute certitude is not possible.

Prümmer distinguishes various kinds of doubt and emphasizes that in a case of positive practical doubt ("positive" here signifies the presence of grave reasons), one cannot rightly go forward with an action. He gives the example of "whether it is lawful to read this [particular] dangerous book."[15] If one has a serious doubt about it, then one would sin by reading the book. The question, then, is how to rid oneself of doubt and to arrive at certainty. In cases where the truth of the matter is not easily accessible to reason, doubts can be banished by keeping in view three principles: "1. A doubtful law has no binding force. 2. In doubt one must stand by presumption. 3. In doubt possession is nine-tenths of the law."[16] The first principle does not hold in all cases, as for instance when the case involves something necessary for salvation—in such a case "the safer opinion must be followed."[17]

Prümmer briefly lays out the moral systems known to the Catholic world. These systems envision conscience as evaluating courses of action in which the alternatives are "liberty" (the action is morally permissible) or "law" (one cannot rightly do the action). He begins with Rigorism or Absolute Tutiorism, which asserts that even if "the opinion in favour of liberty is most probable," one must always follow the *safest* course if there is any reasonable doubt whatsoever.[18] Rigorism, he notes, was condemned by the Church.

The system known as Moderate Tutiorism considers that if the opinion in favor of "liberty" is clearly the *most* probable opinion, then it can be followed even though it is less safe. Probabiliorism holds that one can follow the path of "liberty" so long as it is *more* probable than any opinion that advocates for "law." Equiprobabilism is the position of St. Alphonsus

---

14. Prümmer, *Handbook of Moral Theology*, 63.
15. Prümmer, *Handbook of Moral Theology*, 64.
16. Prümmer, *Handbook of Moral Theology*, 64.
17. Prümmer, *Handbook of Moral Theology*, 64.
18. Prümmer, *Handbook of Moral Theology*, 65.

de Liguori, and it holds that if "law" and "liberty" are almost equally or equally probable (according to the opinions of the great moral theologians), then it is permissible to follow the path of liberty, although one must "follow the opinion in favour of the law if this is certainly more probable."[19] Probabilism holds that even if the opinion favoring "law" is *much more* probable than the opinion favoring "liberty," it is acceptable to follow the latter so long as it too is "probable."

Clearly, much depends upon what "probability" entails. Prümmer explains, "Probability is said to be *intrinsic* when it is founded on reasons taken from the nature of the matter to prove its truth; it is *extrinsic* when based on the authority of learned men. An opinion is considered to be extrinsically probable when there are five or six noteworthy authorities in its favour or at least one outstanding doctor like St. Thomas or St. Alphonsus."[20] Of course, an intrinsically probable opinion will also be one held by erudite moral theologians. Prümmer introduces two other distinctions. First, one can have more or less probable opinions—including "doubtfully" or "slightly" probable ones. Second, there can be either an absolute probability or a relative one; in the latter situation, the strength of the argument for probability is seen only in comparison to the argument for the contrary.

The final two systems are Laxism (or Lax Probabilism) and Compensationism. Laxism, like Rigorism, has been condemned by the Church. The position of Laxism is that it is permissible to follow a doubtfully or slightly probable opinion when there are *certainly probable* opinions on the other side. The position of Compensationism is that "one may follow a certainly probable opinion in favour of liberty while abandoning a more probable opinion in favour of the law, but when there is a danger of sin there is required a sufficient reason (compensation) for acting in favour of liberty."[21] Prümmer concludes that other than Rigorism and Laxism, a moral theologian can advocate for any of these systems. The confessor may favor one or another system but cannot impose a system upon the penitent.

19. Prümmer, *Handbook of Moral Theology*, 65.
20. Prümmer, *Handbook of Moral Theology*, 66.
21. Prümmer, *Handbook of Moral Theology*, 66.

As a final note in his discussion of conscience, Prümmer attends to conscience's formation. Each person should educate his or her conscience by both natural and supernatural means. The person should examine his or her conscience with sincerity and diligence. The person should call upon the aid of God in prayer, should have regular recourse to the sacrament of penance, should obey his or her spiritual director, and should fight strenuously (aided by grace) against disordered passions.

Erich Fromm and Karl Rahner, SJ

It should be clear why I have termed Prümmer's moral theology conscience centered. His moral theology contains numerous other elements—I have only treated the early chapters of his work—but it is focused upon cases of conscience in which persons must choose between "law" and "liberty." Prümmer goes on to examine the theological virtues (faith, hope, and love) and the cardinal virtues, as well as their opposed vices. But even in this Dominican and therefore quite Thomistic manual, the virtues and gifts of the Holy Spirit receive a secondary place. In practice, the conscience-centered work of casuistry, with its competing opinions favoring "law" or "liberty" in diverse concrete moral situations, stands at the center of all the post-Tridentine moral manuals.

Today, the dominant stream of Catholic moral theology is much different. To describe the current situation of Catholic moral theology is beyond the scope of my essay, but I think it is safe to say that the dominant academic stream of contemporary Catholic moral theology (though certainly there are many exceptions) approaches moral problems in two related ways: through contextualist or existentialist analysis and through a new portrait of conscience, no longer firmly tied to the reception of a universal moral law whose source is God.

In this section, I will examine two notable authors who contributed to this shift: the existentialist psychoanalyst Erich Fromm and the Jesuit theologian Karl Rahner. Both of them were deeply affected by the experience of Nazism and by the existentialist ethics that Heidegger and Jaspers had pioneered in the 1930s. Fromm was a Jew who fled Germany when the Nazis took over and who taught at Columbia University from 1934 onward. Rahner spent the war in Germany working in pastoral ministry.[22]

Fromm

In 1941, Fromm published his most important work, *Escape from Freedom*. He declares himself in favor of all that enables human beings to be free from external domination—including freedom over nature (through technological advances), political freedom (through liberal democracy and voting rights), freedom to pursue one's chosen career, and religious freedom (as distinct from "the domination of the Church").[23] He perceives in the rise of Hitler a deliberately chosen flight from freedom on the part of the German people. People often do not want to be free; they would rather depend upon strong political and religious leaders enforcing as much uniformity as possible. As Fromm puts it, "Is there not also, perhaps, besides an innate desire for freedom, an instinctive wish for submission?"[24] Insofar as humans are individuals whose lives are directed by their own freedom, this produces insecurity and can make freedom into a burden.

Indeed, Fromm suggests that the freedoms promoted by modernity are experienced as intrinsically ambiguous. Having gained freedom of worship, people have ceased to believe in God. Having gained freedom of speech, people have had to recognize that they lack anything original

---

22. For background to the responses of German Catholic priests and bishops to Nazism (few were supporters of the Nazis), see Kevin P. Spicer, CSC, *Hitler's Priests: Catholic Clergy and National Socialism* (DeKalb: Northern Illinois University Press, 2008); Spicer, *Resisting the Third Reich: The Catholic Clergy in Hitler's Berlin* (DeKalb: Northern Illinois University Press, 2004); and Lauren Faulkner Rossi, *Wehrmacht Priests: Catholicism and the Nazi War of Annihilation* (Cambridge, MA: Harvard University Press, 2015).

23. Erich H. Fromm, *Escape from Freedom* (New York: Henry Holt, 1994), 2. While Fromm is a Freudian, he is also critical of Freud. Unlike Freud, Fromm holds that "[t]he most beautiful as well as the most ugly inclinations of man are not part of a fixed and biologically given human nature, but result from the social process which creates man. In other words, society has not only a suppressing function—although it has that too—but it has also a creative function. Man's nature, his passions, and anxieties are a cultural product; as a matter of fact, man himself is the most important creation and achievement of the continuous human effort, the record of which we call history" (10–11). Fromm "emphatically disagrees with his [Freud's] interpretation of history as the result of psychological forces that in themselves are not socially conditioned" (12).

24. Fromm, *Escape from Freedom*, 5.

to say and would not dare to say it even if they did think of something original. Capitalism has given economic freedom to many who previously would have lacked it. Yet, under capitalism, the individual is as a solitary and self-interested figure plugged into an all-encompassing economic system. The result is not so much a feeling of freedom but a feeling of serving as a cog in the machine, in which self-esteem depends upon being valued by others, not upon any intrinsic value of the self.

In response, the modern world has produced two main kinds of escape from freedom. The first is authoritarianism. This is where Fromm treats conscience. He asserts that in many instances, "conscience rules with a harshness as great as external authorities, and furthermore that frequently the content of the orders issued by man's conscience are ultimately not governed by demands which have assumed the dignity of ethical norms."[25] Whether one submits to conscience or submits to other powerful entities making commands, Fromm thinks that one has rejected true freedom, authentic self-love, and responsibility. What one loves instead is the powerful authority, and one will obey it in anything rather than exercise true freedom. One's "whole life becomes related and dependent" in such a way that one merely obeys and finds one's happiness in obedience.[26]

The complement to this first kind of escape from freedom is a second kind that Fromm identifies as "automaton conformity." People in modern societies imagine themselves to be free, but without daring to distinguish themselves in any way. People simply accept the authoritative opinions of others. People do not even *feel* for themselves. The great fear of being isolated leads to groupthink. Again, the result is a loss of self, a loss of real responsibility.

Turning to Nazism, Fromm observes that most Catholics in Germany were not enthusiastic about Nazism but did not seriously resist it either. Lacking an adequate sense of self, they went along with the authority of the Nazi regime. Authority and power, matched by sacrificial surrender to and dependence upon the powerful regime, carried the day. In Hitler's rise, Fromm identifies the embodiment of "the craving for power over

25. Fromm, *Escape from Freedom*, 165. See Claudia Koonz, *The Nazi Conscience* (Cambridge, MA: Harvard University Press, 2003).
26. Fromm, *Escape from Freedom*, 173; see also the summary on 252–53.

men and the longing for submission to an overwhelmingly strong outside power."[27] The implicit point is that had Catholics not resonated with this longing for submission, they would have resisted it more effectively. The problem ultimately is the isolated condition of modern individuals, their lack of a strong sense of self in relation to others, and their tendency to seek to escape from freedom. Fromm points out that modern democracies such as the United States have similar impulses toward authoritarian conditions.

According to Fromm, the solution is to recover the integrity of the self through authentic self-realization. When a person recognizes and accepts all aspects of himself (or herself), he or she acts spontaneously, rather than as an automaton awed by authority. Children are often spontaneous. At our happiest, we respond spontaneously to the beautiful, good, and true. A love that is spontaneous and authentic is not self-surrendering, but rather is self-realizing through a true "union of the individual with others."[28] Through creative action, the spontaneous person gains strength by becoming truly related to others. The spontaneous person dares to be himself or herself and thereby fosters a real integrity of self, able to withstand the authoritarian temptation. The spontaneous person finds meaning simply in the act of authentically living. Such a person attains to positive freedom, no longer marked by existential insecurity or alienation.[29] Such a person enjoys self-realization and integrity—against all forms of alienating submission or surrender.

In the face of Nazism, Fromm's goal is to help humanity finally to be free in a mature way. He calls for fostering all individuals' active and full participation in economic and political life. He seeks to build up a society in which a person's "conscience and ideals are not the internalization of external demands, but are really *his* and express the aims that result from the peculiarity of his self."[30]

---

27. Fromm, *Escape from Freedom*, 235.
28. Fromm, *Escape from Freedom*, 259.
29. Fromm adds, "Positive freedom also implies the principle that there is no higher power than this unique individual self, that man is the center and purpose of his life; that the growth and realization of man's individuality is an end that can never be subordinated to purposes which are supposed to have great dignity" (*Escape from Freedom*, 263).
30. Fromm, *Escape from Freedom*, 269.

Rahner

After World War II, a number of German Catholics thought that existentialist ethics provided the way forward. They believed that the ethics of the moral manuals, the weighing of probable opinions and authorities, had left German Catholics vulnerable to the authoritarian temptation. On this view, submission to the dictates of authorities had failed to produce existentially mature persons who could resist authoritarian commands.

Rahner does not make the above claim explicitly, but he does so implicitly. In 1946, for example, he remarked, "aren't we now seeing a failure of the individual good practicing Catholic in his duty to make decisions which is his precisely *as* an individual, while he looks inquiringly to the Church for directives ... ? And doesn't this force us to realize that in the Church too there is a sheep-like submissiveness and anti-individualistic self-effacement which ... should terrify us?"[31] In this 1946 essay, Rahner accepts that there are universal binding principles or laws, but he argues that these binding laws are not the real core of the moral life. The real core of the moral life is far more personal and existential: for each person, it is the will of God for him or her that matters. This personal domain of the moral life does not contradict the universal moral norms, but nevertheless it stands above them: it "has the decisive word over and above it and can no longer be contained within it."[32] This moral domain is not universalizable as a set of rules, and moral theologians—guardians of universal morality—cannot touch this domain. Here, one stands directly before God and his binding will. This moral domain is "conscience," but in a particular existential sense. Rahner remarks, "When we call it conscience we must distinguish between two functions of conscience; the one which tells a man's subjective self the *universal* norms of ethics and moral theology and applies them to his 'case,' and the one by which the individual hears God's call to him *alone*, which can never be fully deduced from universal norms."[33] Casuistry cannot approach the domain of God's unique call.

The Church, Rahner goes on to argue, must respect this domain of

---

31. Karl Rahner, SJ, "The Individual in the Church," in *Nature and Grace: Dilemmas in the Modern Church*, translated by Dinah Wharton (New York: Sheed and Ward, 1964), 9–38, at 11.
32. Rahner, "The Individual in the Church," 19.
33. Rahner, "The Individual in the Church," 20.

personal, unique moral life. After all, there is a sense in which only God, and not the Church, can pass judgment on a person's moral status. The Church has no "right to rule and command every part of a man."[34] Rahner describes in more detail what this means for conscience. Namely, the Church cannot directly govern a person's moral life. Individual conscience, ungovernable by the Church, universal principles or laws, or the opinions of expert casuists, must have the primary place.

Rahner's purpose at this stage is not to reject moral theology, universal laws, and casuistry. Instead, his purpose is to call Catholics to existential authenticity, away from "the sheeplike mob described in the story of the Grand Inquisitor, who think they are saved when they are freed *from* themselves—instead of to themselves—by the Church relieving them of the burden of having to take initiative and make decisions."[35] This is the flight from freedom Fromm describes. Rahner has taken Dostoevsky's anti-Jesuit tale as a fair description of Catholic reality under the moral manuals. Rahner underscores that "the Church may not and does not want ... to relieve the individual of the burden and the duty of having to be an individual," and as a result the Catholic "is not allowed at all times to take shelter behind the moral teachings of the Church.... Over and above the Commandments preached by the Church he still has to ask: Lord, what do you want *me* to do?"[36]

At this early stage of his career (1946–47), Rahner is striving simply to encourage the individual existential authenticity of believers, as an antidote to authoritarian collectivism. He insists, "Where universal norms are possible they cannot be appealed against in the name of individual conscience. If induced abortion or contraception can be universally recognized as morally wrong and are declared to be morally wrong by the Church, then there is no appeal against this in the name of individual conscience."[37] But the main point for Rahner is that individuals in the Church have fallen short not through a lack of obedience but through too much of it. Like the Nazi enablers portrayed by Fromm, such people lack existential authenticity and therefore flee from freedom. The prob-

---

34. Rahner, "The Individual in the Church," 25.
35. Rahner, "The Individual in the Church," 28–29.
36. Rahner, "The Individual in the Church," 28.
37. Rahner, "The Individual in the Church," 30.

lem consists in "the individual not being able to hold out and bear his responsibility any longer."[38]

In this same period, Rahner wrote an essay titled "The Appeal to Conscience" that argues against the extreme form of existentialist ethics (also called "situation ethics"). Nevertheless, in "The Appeal to Conscience" he also suggests that morality today is much more difficult than previously. In earlier times, when life was simpler, the basic moral situations had been lived through and tested, and the relevant moral norms were generally known. Today, no one agrees about what is the right thing to do; even having children has become a major problem for the future survival of the human race, given the threat posed by overpopulation. The discovery of cultural pluralism has demonstrated how much our ethics may be culturally specific rather than universal. People today recognize "the bewildering extent to which the fundamental principles of religion and morality and behaviour in economic, social, sexual and political life are relative to time and place."[39]

Rahner says that he wants to retain the universal moral law and to deny that a good subjective intention suffices to make an action morally good. At the same time, he describes with great vigor and sympathy the "extremely existentialist" mood of contemporary thought, which assumes that "where there is spirit, person and freedom, there is no 'essence,' no universal nature of man and his moral life, which can determine in advance, before he makes his free decision, the rightness or wrongness of his actions; hence there are no universal and universally binding norms."[40] Rahner argues against such a viewpoint. He denies that Christianity can accept that morality is reducible to a person's following his or her own conscience, as though there were no universal moral law. He urges that conscience is not the measure of moral truth, since conscience itself has a measure. He bemoans the fact that today "[t]he conscience is no longer the voice and the interpreter of a binding norm, about which an objective agreement among men is fundamentally possible, but is, as it were, itself the lawgiver, which issues its decrees from which there is no appeal,

---

38. Rahner, "The Individual in the Church," 31.
39. Karl Rahner, SJ, "The Appeal to Conscience," in *Nature and Grace*, 39–63, at 42.
40. Rahner, "Appeal to Conscience," 42.

unique and inscrutable, valid, always for the one individual case alone."[41]

Rahner makes clear that the adherents of the extreme existentialist ethics are influential. In their view, any appeal to a universally binding moral norm is "a relapse into Old Testament legalism, an exchange of outward forms for loving faith, a denial of the freedom of the children of God, [and] an exaggerated essence-philosophy, which postulates a definite human nature unchanged throughout all the changing course of history, whereas in fact man is an undetermined existence free ... to form himself anew."[42] Rahner stands in opposition to this viewpoint, even while articulating it powerfully.

Rahner affirms, of course, that conscience must be obeyed. But because conscience can be misinformed and can grievously err, conscience must also be instructed and refined. Rahner remarks, "man has a duty to do everything he can to conform his conscience to the objective moral law, to inform himself and let himself be taught and make himself prepared to accept (how difficult this often is!) instruction from the word of God, the magisterium of the Church and every just authority in its own sphere."[43] Thus his emphasis on the uniquely personal moral domain has everything to do with moral maturity on the part of the believer, but nothing to do with license to reject universal moral laws. The universal moral commandments of the Gospel and the Church are binding upon conscience.[44] As Rahner concludes, "if it is not to degenerate into a merely private subjective voice, the Christian conscience has the duty to order

---

41. Rahner, "Appeal to Conscience," 44.
42. Rahner, "Appeal to Conscience," 45.
43. Rahner, "Appeal to Conscience," 50.
44. Rahner adds the strong statement, "It is therefore quite untrue that only those moral norms for which there is a solemn definition (and those are criticized from all sides in the 'world') are binding in faith on the Christian as revealed by God, and must be accepted by him as the rule for his own behaviour.... When the whole Church in her everyday teaching [the "ordinary magisterium"] does in fact teach a moral rule everywhere in the world *as* a commandment of God, she is preserved from error by the assistance of the Holy Ghost, and this rule is therefore really the will of God and is binding on the faithful in conscience, even before it has been expressly confirmed by a solemn decision.... When, for example, the Church teaches that *every* directly induced abortion is morally wrong, that every sacramentally contracted and consummated marriage between two baptized persons is indissoluble, then this applies to every individual case quite regardless of the circumstances" (Rahner, "Appeal to Conscience," 52–53). As Rahner rightly perceives, "A situation-ethic carried to its logical conclusion would become an ethical and metaphysical nominalism in which the universal could never actually bear upon the concrete with binding force" (52).

itself by the objective moral norms" as found in the Church's teaching.[45]

In "On the Question of a Formal Existential Ethics," published in 1955, Rahner's thought is clearly beginning to shift. On the one hand, he continues to reject extreme existentialist or situation ethics on the grounds that "it basically denies the possibility of any universal knowledge which has objective significance and truly applies to concrete reality. It turns the human person into an individual who is absolutely and in every respect unique."[46] On the other hand, he raises difficult questions to which he does not offer answers, and he suggests they may not be answerable. These questions have to do with how we can identify the truly unchanging elements of human nature. A universal moral law, after all, requires that there be a universal human nature. Rahner raises the possibility that human beings, even if up until now they have had one kind of existence, may be able

---

45. Rahner, "Appeal to Conscience," 53. Rahner adds still more strong words, including the following against what is today termed the "gradualness of the law": "It goes without saying that God's grace has secret ways which we cannot fathom, which are not our ways, of redeeming and saving men who in human eyes can only seem far from God. His grace is beyond our understanding and does not have to give an account of itself to us. He binds us, not himself, to the ways which he has shown us. But it is true as well that he who honestly says, I have sinned, must also say, I will arise and go to my Father. But in God's country there is no commerce between light and darkness, God and sin. It is a defined truth of the Faith that God's grace makes it possible for the man who has been justified to keep God's commandments, so that if he falls again into sin, he falls although he could have stood firm and he himself is the really responsible, guilty cause of this fall. And so a conscience which tries to comfort the sinner with the thought that he could not avoid sinning, and that this sin was in fact no danger to his salvation, as long as even in his sin he went on trusting in God's forgiveness, is not the voice of grace, but the voice of the man's own self-delusion, which wants an easy compromise between sin and God. 'Felix culpa' can only be said by those who through God's grace have overcome sin. That God writes straight on crooked lines gives the creature no right to draw crooked lines in his book of life. Such an act which actually plans and calculates to make sin a stage in his development is a creature's most hateful *hubris*, which is prepared to outwit God's mercy, which tries to see and calculate human life from God's standpoint, and is arrogance and self-delusion of such a serious nature that God threatens to answer it not with his grace but with his justice. Precisely because sin can be committed not only immediately and expressly in the sphere of faith and trust, but also in the moral sphere in the narrower sense, in the sphere of the Commandments, and because from the creature's point of view there is no way of getting rid of it, no way out, man never has the right to surrender himself 'in faith' into this position merely because he imagines he can still hope for forgiveness and that even while he sins God's grace will not abandon him. If God gives his grace to a man who *has* sinned, this is always a new action of God's grace which is in no way due to the man, and cannot be calculatingly relied on before the sin is committed" (60–61).

46. Karl Rahner, SJ, "On the Question of a Formal Existential Ethics," in *Theological Investigations*, vol. 2, *Man in the Church*, translated by Karl-H. Kruger (Baltimore: Helicon Press, 1963), 217–34, at 219.

to change this existence through a deeper self-realization, with the result that the "universal" moral norms befitting the human person will likewise change. Rahner also raises a second problem: whether a universal moral norm can really be applied in an easy and certain way to particular cases. The conscience-centered moral manuals were built upon the assumption that the task of conscience, instructed by the experts, was to apply the universal rule in concrete cases. This moral theology was "a syllogistic, deductive ethics."[47]

Without proposing to reject casuistic ethics as such, Rahner now argues that we cannot assume that what we are morally obligated to do is "identical with what can be deduced from the universal norms" in light of the concrete situation.[48] Indeed, he thinks that such a view is a mistake built (in part) upon the false idea that a concrete situation can be reduced to a set of general propositions. No syllogism can capture a concrete situation in all its complexity; therefore, neither can a necessary imperative be provided.

In his 1955 essay, Rahner does not press this argument further. Instead, he proposes in a much more limited manner that there is often more than one thing that a person in a concrete situation may do in order to remain in accord with the universal moral law.[49] Again, Rahner continues to uphold the reality of universal moral norms, but he has begun to undermine an ethics based upon them and therefore to shift in a more fully existentialist direction. He maintains that the existential function of conscience is not to "apply the universal norms to each of my particular situations" (though this may certainly be a function of conscience), but rather to apprehend "what has not yet been made absolutely clear by the situation and the universal norms, and which is precisely and as such what has to be done by me individually."[50]

In the same 1955 essay, Rahner makes a third move that undermines

---

47. Rahner, "On the Question of a Formal Existential Ethics," 222.
48. Rahner, "On the Question of a Formal Existential Ethics," 222.
49. Rahner puts it this way: "In so far as the same man subsists in his own spirituality, his actions are also always more than mere applications of the universal law to the *casus* in space and time; they have a substantial positive property and uniqueness which can no longer be translated into a universal idea and norm expressible in propositions constructed of universal notions" ("On the Question of a Formal Existential Ethics," 226).
50. Rahner, "On the Question of a Formal Existential Ethics," 229.

the moral manuals. He introduces the notion of the "fundamental option." A person's fundamental option is the person's total or basic decision that grounds the person's self-understanding. It is the person's "non-reflective, non-propositional self-presence," in which the "existential quality" and personal uniqueness of our actions are manifest.[51] Rahner does not here explain what he means by the fundamental option in much detail. Nor, again, does he reject traditional casuistry—on the contrary, he suggests that it should not be rejected, but instead should be combined with existential ethics. He points to St. Ignatius of Loyola's view of moral choice as a uniquely personal "existential-ethical action" that embodies concrete obedience to God's will.[52]

In a 1964 essay, "Guilt—Responsibility—Punishment within the View of Catholic Theology," Rahner exhibits a further alteration. On the one hand, Rahner holds that there is "a permanent nature in man which is preserved throughout the whole history of mankind."[53] Yet humans are spiritual and realize themselves creatively through freedom. Therefore, on the other hand, Rahner emphasizes that "[man is] the being which always has a relationship to itself, which is a subject and never merely a nature, which is always already a person.... Man, by his freedom of being, is always the incomparable who cannot be pigeon-holed in any system or completely subsumed under any idea."[54] The core of ethics, therefore, is not about obedience to universal moral laws applicable to universal human nature. Rather, the core of ethics consists in the fundamental option, in which the unique and incomparable human person disposes himself or herself existentially to God—or refuses to do so. Rahner describes the fundamental option as the "basic act of freedom which embraces and moulds the whole of existence."[55] It is a total decision about the whole of one's reality. It is not a decision that one can take and reflect upon. Rather, although it has an impact upon our particular ethical acts, it occurs on the "transcendental" level of one's being. No particular ethical act, moreover,

51. Rahner, "On the Question of a Formal Existential Ethics," 230.
52. See Rahner, "On the Question of a Formal Existential Ethics," 232, 234.
53. Karl Rahner, SJ, "Guilt—Responsibility—Punishment within the View of Catholic Theology," in *Theological Investigations*, vol. 6, *Concerning Vatican Council II*, translated by Karl-H. Kruger and Boniface Kruger (London: Darton, Longman & Todd, 1969), 197–217, at 199.
54. Rahner, "Guilt—Responsibility—Punishment," 202.
55. Rahner, "Guilt—Responsibility—Punishment," 203.

can bear the weight of the total decision or fundamental option. The only sin that can be truly mortal is a deliberate exercise of one's fundamental option against God. But it is difficult to do this, and it cannot be done solely at the level of a mere particular action in the world, although it is inseparable from particular actions in the world. Also, it is impossible to know with assurance, no matter what sins one has committed, that one actually *has* ever chosen against God in one's fundamental option.

In the depths of conscience, then, what matters is the radical freedom with which it is possible either to give oneself to God and to close oneself off from God. Rahner holds in 1964 that it is this existential freedom that constitutes human nature in its permanent spiritual form. The true sin (and true guilt) is found on this deepest level. The violation of God's law that Rahner deems to be of eternal significance is solely the transcendental rejection of God, a rejection that God himself, however, embraces within his "eschatologically victorious grace ... in Christ."[56]

As a final step, let me mention Rahner's 1972 book *The Shape of the Church to Come*, in which Rahner says goodbye to the old conscience-centered moral theology that he had once accepted. He does not say goodbye to the absolute centrality of conscience for Catholic ethics. The new centrality of conscience, however, is broadly separable from universal moral law. Rahner urges that "consciences must be formed, not primarily by way of a casuistic instruction, going into more and more concrete details, but by being roused and trained for autonomous and responsible decisions in the concrete, complex situations of human life which are no longer completely soluble down to the last detail, in fields never considered by the older morality."[57]

Today, says Rahner in 1972, we know that human spiritual nature, and thus human moral consciousness, is constantly evolving, both in the concrete individual and in societies. Human nature is a historical nature. Some moral precepts were rightly binding in the past, given the stage of historical development in which human nature then was, that can no longer be accepted as binding today. Every believer must "remain open to a further evolution of his own reality and to a higher actualization of his

---

56. Rahner, "Guilt—Responsibility—Punishment," 211.
57. Karl Rahner, SJ, *The Shape of the Church to Come*, translated by Edward Quinn (New York: Seabury, 1974), 68.

moral consciousness."[58] The task of conscience today is to be attuned to this evolving human reality. No doubt the moral life will continue to involve moral principles, although generally one cannot say with certitude whether the principles are true only for a time or are universally true. The overall purpose of ethics remains the same: perfect love of God and neighbor, so that we experience the Holy Spirit encountering us with God's gracious love, redeeming us from fear and self-alienation at the core of our moral being, our conscience.

The way in which Fromm urges that humans must move away from authoritarian ethics to existential responsibility, where authentic freedom is truly embraced, has a strong echo in Rahner's movement from the (divine) law-based work of conscience in the manuals to the autonomous and evolving conscience opening itself to God as its fundamental option.

Bernard Häring, CSsR

As a final step toward illuminating the twentieth-century Catholic shift, let me briefly compare Bernhard Häring's preconciliar *The Law of Christ* with his postconciliar *Free and Faithful in Christ*. Häring, of course, was deeply influenced by Rahner, especially with respect to the fundamental option, but also in envisioning the new place for conscience. Along with Rahner's close friend Josef Fuchs, Häring was the most influential ethicist of his era. Servais Pinckaers influenced *Veritatis Splendor* and argued against conscience-centered morality as such, but Häring's postconciliar voice was unfortunately more decisive in most Catholic academic circles, which largely resisted Pope John Paul II's moral teaching.

In *The Law of Christ*, Häring devotes more than fifty dense pages near the outset of his work to the topic of conscience. For St. Paul, says Häring, "moral conscience is the instructor of the Gentiles, in so far as it binds them to the law of God as manifested in creation, in so far as it reproaches them if they act against their reason."[59] Conscience hears the call of Christ, who desires us to be configured to him. Christ illuminates conscience. Confronted with a value that prompts an "ought," conscience

---

58. Rahner, *Shape of the Church to Come*, 65.
59. Bernard Häring, CSsR, *The Law of Christ*, vol. 1, *General Moral Theology*, translated by Edwin G. Kaiser, CPpS (Westminster, MD: Newman Press, 1963), 138.

responds to this moral imperative. Conscience points us to the divine and personal source of all value. Conscience stands at "the inmost center of the soul."[60] In the supernatural order, conscience is open to the word and example of Christ, and conscience is docile to the Spirit's guidance.

Conscience's relation to law is crucial for the preconciliar Häring. He states that "the natural function of conscience is to make us partakers of the eternal law of God through the created nature around us and through our own rational nature. Our bond with the natural moral law is an exalted participation in the eternal law of God manifested by our conscience whose natural function it is to reveal our likeness to God."[61] Conscience's relation to law is not a drawback, as though law were non-evangelical. On the contrary, conscience, law, and truth are inseparable. As Häring puts it, "conscience and objective truth, and ultimately also conscience and the authority of God teaching us, essentially belong together. By its very nature conscience seeks illumination and guidance, which it finds naturally in the order and harmony of creation, in the supernatural order with the wonderful fulness in Christ, and through Christ and the Holy Spirit in the teaching Church."[62]

The preconciliar Häring is aware that some people try to set up conscience as though it were a domain of autonomous freedom. Häring replies that conscience responds to and communicates the law of the good. Conscience receives and communicates universal moral principles. Although people are obligated morally to follow their conscience, conscience can err, and it can err culpably owing to a deliberate failure to form conscience. When it does err—as for instance regarding pornography or abortion—the state should not condone such error.

Like all preconciliar moral textbooks, *The Law of Christ* spends a good bit of time on the varieties of conscience: invincibly erroneous, culpably erroneous, perplexed, scrupulous, lax. After a number of pages addressing scrupulosity, Häring admits that an uncertain conscience is no rare thing: "in the multitudinous situations of real life the Christian is constantly confronted with new uncertainty and unanticipated moral risk."[63]

60. Häring, *Law of Christ*, 1:140.
61. Häring, *Law of Christ*, 1:147.
62. Häring, *Law of Christ*, 1:148.
63. Häring, *Law of Christ*, 1:169.

Häring's view of the various moral systems and controversies within casuistry—probabilism, equiprobabilism, and so on—is not uncritical. His textbook does not intend to be a work of casuistry; he wants instead to reconceptualize the moral life within the domain of discipleship to Christ. At the same time, he considers that the sacrament of penance required casuistic reasoning in some form. In his view, it is impossible to get around the basic question that prompts casuistry at its best: "how shall I take law and obedience seriously without excessively taxing human liberty or unduly narrowing the scope of personal initiative through a multiplicity of doubtful laws and obligations?"[64]

Therefore, he treats with seriousness and respect the "reflex principles" that come into play in cases of uncertain conscience (stuck between "law" and "liberty"), as for instance the reflex principle "in case of doubt the presumption of law favors the possessor."[65] He notes that the domain of liberty, in which prudence is exercised, "may not be extended so far beyond the sphere of legal obligation as to jeopardize any good essential for salvation."[66] At some length, he defends the reasonableness and fruitfulness of equiprobabilism, long the foundation of Redemptorist ethics. But he also accepts probabiliorism (classically the standpoint of Dominicans, such as Prümmer) and moderate probabilism.

Häring's section on conscience in *The Law of Christ* precedes his section on human actions and law. By contrast, we saw that Prümmer followed the order beatitude, human actions, law, conscience. Häring begins his book with a short history of moral theology from Scripture through the present day, followed by a section on "Essential Concepts of Moral Theology" (such as responsibility and fellowship—inclusive of divine commandments), followed by theological anthropology, freedom, and knowledge of the good and value. Conscience then appears as the linchpin, in the section I have described above.

The postconciliar Häring largely restructures his moral theology. Just like *The Law of Christ*, his *Free and Faithful in Christ* opens with a historical section grounding moral theology in Scripture and investigating

---

64. Häring, *Law of Christ*, 1:176.
65. Häring, *Law of Christ*, 1:179.
66. Häring, *Law of Christ*, 1:183.

the history of moral theology. There then follow four lengthy, crucial chapters. The first focuses on theological anthropology, arguing that creative freedom and creative co-responsibility are the characteristics of the moral life of the Christian. The second chapter explores how Christ and the Holy Spirit liberate humans. These two paired chapters lead into two further paired chapters: "Fundamental Option" and "Conscience: The Sanctuary of Creative Fidelity and Liberty." After these chapters comes a chapter on "Traditions, Laws, Norms, and Context," followed by a final chapter in volume one on "Sin and Conversion."

What *Free and Faithful in Christ* offers is a revamped moral manual. Freedom and spontaneity receive emphasis. Moral decision-making no longer requires much consulting of authorities or weighing probable opinions. Häring states, "The fundamental option brings forth a great spontaneity in individual ethical decisions. A person who has firmly dedicated himself to that freedom for truth and final meaning does not need long reflection and pain before making decisions coherent with his dedication. Rather, the choice arises spontaneously and creatively from the inner depth where the unseen God is present."[67] As we saw in Rahner, the fundamental option names the existential decision to commit oneself to God that is made at the core of the self. So long as the person does not close off himself or herself, such a person has a good fundamental option that will result in authenticity and self-realization (understood as self-transcendence). When we commit ourselves to the Other in our fundamental option, we deepen this decision through further fundamental decisions, above all faith in Jesus Christ. Other fundamental decisions include marriage, entering the priesthood or religious life, choice of career, and so on. The fundamental option will also become "embodied in fundamental attitudes," such as the virtues that respond to human values.[68] If we are to flourish, everything in our daily life must come to bear the imprint of our fundamental option.

In Häring's view, "it should not be denied that there are moments in a person's history when a concrete act may reverse the fundamental

---

67. Bernard Häring, *Free and Faithful in Christ: Moral Theology for Clergy and Laity*, vol. 1, *General Moral Theology* (New York: Crossroad, 1984), 181.

68. Häring, *Free and Faithful in Christ*, 1:195.

option."[69] Of course, such moments are rare, or at least cannot be judged from the outside. Unless a person has a fundamental option against God, such a person cannot be in a state of mortal sin. The fundamental option is a dynamism toward "the total transfiguration of our life for the love of God and of fellowmen."[70]

Regarding conscience, Häring first treats the biblical understanding of it and then traces the history of the development of theories of conscience, from the Church Fathers to contemporary psychoanalysts. For my purposes, the central point is how exalted and all-encompassing his postconciliar view of conscience is. He deems that conscience is neither an intellectual nor a volitional power; rather, it involves both intellect and will and brings them together in our deepest psychic domain. In his view, "Conscience has to do with man's total selfhood as a moral agent."[71] Conscience reflects our inner wholeness and openness to God and others. Conscience is a creative force, especially when working in conjunction with other consciences. Häring maintains, "It is conscience itself that teaches the person to overcome the present stage of development and to integrate it into a higher one."[72]

Häring treats the perplexed conscience, but only briefly. He simply notes, "A moral theology that has multiplied the absolutes that can conflict with each other in concrete situations has produced many cases of 'perplexed conscience.' A moral education that helps to discern both the urgency and the priority of values will greatly alleviate such pain for conscientious people."[73] At some length, he explores the development of conscience and the nature of Christian conscience. He focuses on relationship with Christ as the key to faith, rather than conceiving faith as an assent to doctrines. The person and grace of Christ must be at the center of the moral life, against legalistic thinking. Christ's teaching of the beatitudes should have a decisive place in moral theology: the beatitudes may be an ideal, but they are a "*normative* ideal."[74] He argues, "As the strength of

---

69. Häring, *Free and Faithful in Christ*, 1:213.
70. Häring, *Free and Faithful in Christ*, 1:217.
71. Häring, *Free and Faithful in Christ*, 1:235.
72. Häring, *Free and Faithful in Christ*, 1:239.
73. Häring, *Free and Faithful in Christ*, 1:243.
74. Häring, *Free and Faithful in Christ*, 1:253.

our fundamental option grows, we accept in the depths of our conscience the still remaining need to put to death our selfish self and to take up every day our burden and a part of the burden of our fellowmen."[75]

Häring reflects briefly on the relationship of conscience and prudence, in light of the gifts of the Holy Spirit. As in Rahner, it is discernment of spirits that receives most attention in this respect. In conjunction with other consciences, we can make progress. Our conscience can be both creative and critical as we seek to improve ourselves and our societies. At the same time, we must take care to repent and ask for forgiveness after sinning. Häring gives an important role to the reciprocity of consciences, in which two people meet "in each one's singularity and identity, in mutual respect for each other's conscience," with the result being "a process of reciprocal liberation."[76] This respect for consciences awakens believers to the need to respect other persons' religious freedom. There needs to be a similar freedom of conscience in the Church, or else the Church will lack self-criticism and will stultify, as Häring believes took place in the post-Tridentine period. Prophetic dissenting voices are needed in the Church in every age.

Turning as a last step to evaluate the conscience-centered moral tradition of probabilism, the postconciliar Häring makes clear that the way forward is more conscience, not less. He urges that "we must have and can have more hope and courage than the old probabilists when we examine these problems [i.e., tensions between law and Church authority on the one hand, and individuals' desire for freedom and respect for personal conscience on the other hand] with a sharper awareness of the primacy of conscience and, at the same time, in a perspective of a covenant morality in which the reciprocity of consciences is fundamental."[77] He contends that innovators and traditionalists have always lived in tension. The Church of the past reflected the authoritarian political cultures in which it lived. In Häring's view, his perspective is a moderate one; he keeps his eyes upon Christ's grace and mercy as the core of ethics, while rigorist moral theologians focus negatively on controls and "thou-shalt-not." He respects the creative consciences of those who disagree with papal teach-

---

75. Häring, *Free and Faithful in Christ*, 1:254.
76. Häring, *Free and Faithful in Christ*, 1:266.
77. Häring, *Free and Faithful in Christ*, 1:285.

ings on morality. Against rigorists who seek to control others, he wants the Church to be able "to respond to new needs and opportunities in a creative way," and he hopes that every Christian will be encouraged "to respond to his concrete situation by a creative conscience, in genuine responsibility."[78]

Häring looks back to the great founder of the Redemptorists, St. Alphonsus, as a model for the present day, even if many particulars of St. Alphonsus's approach need now to be adjusted. For St. Alphonsus, says Häring, the key thing is "the dignity of the individual conscience that must never be manipulated."[79] Häring thinks that St. Alphonsus would have agreed that today "[t]he Church can build itself up only in a genuine reciprocity of consciences."[80] In Häring's view, great probabilists such as St. Alphonsus recognized that the Church's morality was in a process of ongoing revision, as the consciences of believers engaged in reciprocal dialogue. The great probabilists recognized the importance of historical context. The great probabilists also, unlike the rigorists, valued freedom. Theirs was not an authoritarian ethics. Like Fromm, Häring bemoans the fact that "[s]ome people do not want to be allowed to live according to their own conscience; they want to be guided by others, to be told what to do. They do not want to take the risk inherent in living one's own life in creative liberty and fidelity."[81] Authoritarians in the Church take advantage of insecure people and their need to flee from their own freedom into the embrace of laws and conformity. Häring states, "St. Alphonsus and all great probabilists did not aim at legal security but at a covenant morality by which everyone lives according to his own conscience and in full co-responsibility."[82]

Thus, although Häring shifts his position significantly, he certainly does not take leave of conscience-centered morality or of the basic impulse of probabilism in seeking responses to cases of conscience. His view of law is quite different after the Council, since he now (like Rahner) sees human nature as fully historical nature, progressively evolving to higher

---

78. Häring, *Free and Faithful in Christ*, 1:288.
79. Häring, *Free and Faithful in Christ*, 1:289.
80. Häring, *Free and Faithful in Christ*, 1:289.
81. Häring, *Free and Faithful in Christ*, 1:290.
82. Häring, *Free and Faithful in Christ*, 1:290.

levels of historical consciousness and humanness. He finds that at every point of history, human nature is relational, open to others through knowing and loving; and "[i]n this openness and reciprocity of consciences man is on the wavelength of the order of revelation and salvation."[83] The Church's universal moral laws often have proven timebound and revisable—with the exception of basic points such as the commandment to love God and neighbor and therefore to refrain from using and exploiting one another. No doubt, the prohibitions of slavery, torture, rape, and other such things are universal moral absolutes. But even these examples show the moral progress of the Church, since Catholics even in the nineteenth century thought it acceptable to participate in slavery and in certain forms of torture (and perhaps even, within marriage, what we would now call rape). In Christ and through the Holy Spirit, believers are called in freedom and dialogue—in true reciprocity of consciences—to advance ever more toward the fullness of the kingdom of God.

Conclusion

My argument in the present essay has been a simple one. I have given some examples of how and why the dominant stream of academic Catholic moral theology in the twentieth century went from one form of conscience-centered moral theology to another form of conscience-centered moral theology, even while radically changing its understanding of conscience in its relation to law. The shift largely jettisoned eternal law, divine law, and natural law (whose first principles are mediated to conscience by synderesis). The shift ended the preconciliar focus upon cases of conscience adjudicated by experts in moral theology. Instead, what came to be emphasized was evolving human consciousness, the reciprocity of consciences by which the community evolves upward in Christ and the Spirit, the fundamental option at the core of one's being where one directly decides for or against God, and conscience as a place where we encounter one another with respect and dialogue and where we are open to the love and mercy of God. The authoritarian ethics that emphasized law (while allowing "liberty" in casuistically delimited cases) was replaced by existentialist ethics.

83. Häring, *Free and Faithful in Christ*, 1:326.

Many Catholic moral theologians see nothing wrong with the situation that I have sketched. In accordance with the cultural trends, they go along gladly with new forms of existentialist and contextualist ethics—today focused on ecology, race, sexual identity, and so on. They generally offer not universal moral precepts, but (in James Keenan's phrase) "tools more for thinking than resolving questions," such as the broad principles of "no unjust harm, free consent, mutuality, equality, commitment, fruitfulness, and social justice."[84] Accommodating themselves to cultural norms, they emphasize that we should listen for "God's call to discipleship" and strive "to hear the will of God in the sanctuary of our consciences calling us to just love."[85]

By contrast, I see the twentieth century as a missed opportunity, and in certain ways a disaster, for the dominant strand of academic Catholic ethics. Both in the academy and at the parish level, the Catholic world at present is rapidly losing touch with core revealed elements in Scripture and Tradition of personal and social morality. The degrading of Catholic morality has gone hand in hand with a sharp loss of faith.

The effort to develop a more biblical, Christ-centered, Spirit-centered, virtue-centered, hylomorphic ethics (in which law, too, receives its due) gained some important traction in the mid-twentieth century. It was taken up by Pope John Paul II in *Veritatis Splendor* and elsewhere. In his broadly Thomistic moral theology, conscience has a significant but limited place, certainly not the central place. But this retrieval does not appear to have succeeded in the global Church, in large part because it never became popular in most academic contexts and thus was only rarely taught. The mainstream academic schools of Catholic moral theology, including those led by Jesuits and Redemptorists, firmly resisted John Paul II's approach to moral theology. They did so in part owing to rejection of *Humanae Vitae* and other traditional Catholic sexual teachings, but they likely would have rejected John Paul II's vision anyway. They preferred the

---

84. Keenan, *A History of Catholic Moral Theology in the Twentieth Century*, 222. Here, Keenan appreciatively has in view the sexual ethics of Margaret Farley, RSM.

85. Keenan, *A History of Catholic Moral Theology in the Twentieth Century*, 222. See also James F. Keenan, SJ, "Redeeming Conscience," *Theological Studies* 76 (2015): 129–47; and idem, "To Follow and to Form over Time: A Phenomenology of Conscience," in *Conscience and Catholicism: Rights, Responsibilities, and Institutional Responses*, edited by David E. DeCosse and Kristin E. Heyer (Maryknoll, NY: Orbis, 2015), 1–15.

new conscience-centered moral theology as more aligned with contemporary culture.

The new understanding of conscience, however, is too subjective to bear much moral weight. It lacks the solidity of being rooted in the communication of God's law and in a broader hylomorphic account of human nature. The result is that moral teachings that have consistently been present in Catholic Tradition no longer seem intelligible. For many Catholic moral theologians today, there is no longer in any serious way a revealed deposit of moral teaching that constitutes the basis for ongoing development. Increasingly, moral theology has become the domain of what has been aptly termed ecclesial "presentism," marked by ideological conformity to the cultural Zeitgeist.[86]

In my view, the solution involves reassessing the path taken in beginning in the 1940s with Catholic versions of existentialist ethics, such as we saw in Rahner. While understandable in certain ways after World War II, this path turned out to be inadequate for sustaining the moral vision of Scripture and Tradition. I suggest that instead the Church should retrieve and deepen, as many thinkers prior to the Council were striving to do, a broadly Thomistic vision of moral theology. The key will be enabling young people to experience this moral vision as viable and livable. Given that sexuality is generally separated today from procreation—and given that procreation is often seen as an economic and ecological evil—this will be a difficult task, one that will require revitalizing a sense of the Christian marital vocation of child-raising, complementing celibate Christian vocations. In this task, it will be crucial to remember that Christian ethics has never really been popular. Jesus commanded forgiveness and love of enemy, but Christians have never exactly rushed to comply. The precepts of the Decalogue and the Sermon on the Mount have often been observed more in the breach than in practice. But this is why the Church's discipline of moral theology is needed. Its purpose is to invite believers afresh to take up their crosses and, in the joy of the Gospel, to journey with Jesus Christ through the Spirit's power.

86. See the works of Reinhard Hütter cited above.

CHAPTER 5

The Development and Contestation of *Humanae Vitae*

GRÉGOR PUPPINCK

To understand the new challenge to the Church posed by birth control, it is necessary to recall briefly the traditional Magisterium of the Catholic Church in matters of procreation. In response to a resolution adopted in August 1930 by the Anglican bishops meeting in Lambeth, admitting the use of contraceptive means,[1] Pope Pius XI published the encyclical *Casti Connubii*.[2] This encyclical is a collection of Christian principles on the nature and ends of marriage, with regard to the intrusion of the state into the family and the influence of eugenics. Pius XI reminds us that "no reason, however grave, can make what is intrinsically unnatural conform to nature and become honest. Since the act of marriage is, by its very nature, destined for the generation of children, those who, in performing it, deliberately endeavor to deprive it of its strength and efficacy, act against nature; they do a shameful and intrinsically dishonest thing.... As St. Augustine reminds us: 'Even with a legitimate woman, the conjugal act becomes illicit and shameful as soon as the conception of a child is avoid-

---

1. According to the Lambeth Conference, contraception is admitted "in cases where this moral obligation to limit or avoid fatherhood is clearly apparent, and where a morally sound reason opposes complete continence..., provided that this is done in the light of the same Christian principles." Quoted by J. F. Chiron, *L'infaillibilité et son objet: L'autorité du magisterium infaillible de l'Eglise s'étend-elle aux vérités non révélées* (Paris: Cerf, 1999), 322–23.

2. Pius XI, December 31, 1930, Encyclical *Casti Connubii*; French translation: *Le Mariage* (*Les Enseignements Pontificaux*) (Bruges-Tournai: Desclée, 1954).

ed.'" Pius XI concludes by affirming that "this is the unshakeable truth of the pure Christian faith, expressed by the magisterium of the Council of Trent."[3]

In 1936, a Roman Dicastery consulted on the Ogino method (periodic abstinence). While admitting its licitness, it warned that "the system must be proposed not as an encouragement to act in this way, but as a remedy, a means, to withdraw from sin."[4] It is not a good, but a lesser evil. Pius XII, in his speech to midwives on October 29, 1951, confirms the encyclical *Casti Connubii* by affirming the definitive and irreformable character of this doctrine: "This prescription is in full force today as it was yesterday, and it will be so tomorrow and always, because it is not a simple precept of human law, but the expression of a natural and divine law."[5] Nevertheless, he encourages and recognizes the heroic nature of periodic continence. John XXIII, in the encyclical *Mater et Magistra*[6] of 1961, refers to the problem of artificial insemination and recalls that human procreation is essentially different from animal procreation. As such, it has a particular dignity because of its effect: the generation of human beings.

The Difficult Work of the Pontifical Commission for the Study of Population, Family, and Birth Problems

A potential weakening of the doctrine appeared in March 1963, when because of the demographic problem and the marketing of the Pill, John XXIII established a "Pontifical Commission for the Study of Problems of Population, Family and Births."[7] The question was precisely whether

---

3. Pius XI, *Casti Connubii*, §61.

4. *Final Report of the Pontifical Commission of June 27, 1966*, Wijngaards Institute for Catholic Research, https://www.wijngaardsinstitute.com/papal-report-contraception-1966/, 6. Page numbers refer to the French version, available at http://www.twotlj.org/Final-Report.pdf.

5. Pius XII, *Address to the Congress of the Italian Catholic Union of Midwives*, October 29, 1951, *La Documentation catholique* [DC] 1951, 1473–94, §613.

6. John XXIII, *Mater et Magistra*, *Acta Apostolicae Sedis* (AAS) 53 (1961): 447; DC 1961, §1357, col. 978.

7. In Latin: *Commissio pro studio populationis, familiae et natalitatis*. On the history of this commission, see P. de Locht, *Les Couples et l'Eglise: Chroniques d'un témoin* (Paris: Centurion, 1979), 122–250 (a member of the commission, a supporter of the majority position, gives a detailed account of the debates, with supporting documents); M. Rouche, "La Préparation de l'encyclique

the Pincus Pill—the birth control pill developed by Dr. Gregory Pincus—was a contraceptive method compatible with the Catholic Magisterium. Initially composed of eight members, Cardinal Cicognani—John XXIII's secretary of state—stated that the objective of this commission was to bring together "a small group of experts to continue the examination of the demographic problem in its multiple aspects (medical, moral, social, economic and statistical) and to propose effective means of action for the maintenance of the seriously threatened ethical order."[8] These experts are doctors, demographers, economists, and sociologists, secular and religious.[9]

The work of this commission continued during the Second Vatican Council, where a chapter dedicated to marriage and the family, *"De dignitate matrimonii et familiae fovendae,"* was under discussion.[10] Paul VI, succeeding John XXIII, confirmed the Pontifical Commission, and while calls for a change in conjugal morality were multiplying in the press, he informed the Council Fathers that he reserved the final decision on this topic to himself with the help of the commission.[11] The Council Fathers then asked that the commission be enlarged. Paul VI increased the number of members to fifty-six, then to seventy-one,[12] and he opened it to the

---

'Humanae vitae': La commission sur la population, la famille et la natalité," in *Colloque de l'Ecole française de Rome, Paul VI et la modernité dans l'Eglise, 2–4 June 1983* (Rome: École française de Rome, 1984), 361–83; B. Häring, *Quelle morale pour l'Eglise* (Paris: Cerf, 1989); R. Blair Kaiser, *The Encyclical That Never Was: The Story of the Pontifical Commission on Population, Family and Birth, 1964–1966* (London: Sheed & Ward, 1987); R. McClory, *Rome et la contraception: Histoire secrète de l'encyclique "Humanae vitae"* (Paris: Editions de l'Atelier, 1998); J. Grootaers, "Éléments d'information pour une histoire de la Commission pontificale," in H. and L. Buellens-Gusen and J. Grootaers, *Mariage catholique et contraception* (Paris: Éditions de l'Épi, 1968), 193–272 (prior to *Humanae Vitae*).

8. Locht, *Les Couples et l'Eglise*, 122. Stanislas de Lestapis, SJ, received a similar letter on May 22, 1963, which spoke of a "careful examination of the 'demographic question' under its various aspects (medical, moral, social, economic, statistical), in order to provide the Holy See with the suggestions it deems opportune in this so important and delicate field." See Martine Sevegrand, *Les Enfants du Bon Dieu: Les catholiques français et la procréation au XXe siècle* (Paris: Albin Michel, 2016), 2:44.

9. Rouche, "La Préparation de l'encyclique 'Humanae vitae.'"

10. Future nos. 47–52 of scheme XIII.

11. For a synthesis on this question, see the complete dossier edited by J. Grootaers and J. Jans: *La régulation des naissances à Vatican II: Une semaine de crise* (Leuven: Peeters, 2002).

12. On this commission, see *Documentation Catholique*, 1965, 673–76, 1632; 1966, 320, 669, 1440; 1967, 1043, 1051. On the whole preparation of *Humanae Vitae* (HV) and related problems, see *Catholic Documentation*, 1961, 978–79; 1962, 781–83; 1964, 19, 99, 817, 1561–62, 1601–16; 1965,

laity, who became the majority. In addition to theologians, the commission was composed of demographers, sociologists, physicians, economists, and couples from Canada, France, and the United States. In this new configuration, the opponents of the traditional doctrine, including twelve theologians, became the majority.[13] The work, carried out in specialized subcommittees, was of a scientific, moral, and theological nature. From the moral and theological point of view, the hierarchy of the ends of marriage, the meaning of human sexuality, the relationship between fertility, love and responsibility, the moral difference between natural and artificial methods of controlling fertility, and more were at issue. From a scientific point of view, the methods of birth control, demographic changes, and the impact on natural resources were studied.

During the work of this commission, the whole Church was subject to internal and external pressure to accept contraception. In 1965, for example, a joint statement signed by leading American Catholics was sent to the pope to this effect. The statement was adopted at the 1965 session of a series of confidential annual conferences on "population problems" held between 1963 and 1967—that is, during the term of the Pontifical Commission—at the prestigious University of Notre Dame. These conferences, organized by the president of the university (Fr. Theodore Hesburgh), his assistant (George Shuster), the Population Council, the Planned Parenthood Federation of America, and the Ford and Rockefeller Foundations, brought together the big names in birth control (Alan Guttmacher, Frank Noteststein, Oskar Harkavy, etc.) and liberal Catholic intellectuals, with the aim of formulating a liberal Catholic position compatible with artificial birth control.[14] Father Hesburgh,[15] who would become a member of the Rockefeller Foundation's Executive Council in 1966, intervened in July 1965 before Paul VI so that he would agree to

---

1155, 1736; 1966, 237–39, 275, 405–12, 923; 1967, 687; 1968, 1441–57 (HV); Commentaries by Paul VI, *Catholic Documentation*, 1968, 1457–61, 1569, 1648, 1688; and by the episcopates, *Catholic Documentation*, 1968 and 1969.

13. Rouche, "La Préparation de l'encyclique 'Humanae vitae,'" 365.

14. Donald T. Critchlow, *Intended Consequences: Birth Control, Abortion, and the Federal Government in Modern America* (Oxford: Oxford University Press, 1999), 64.

15. In 1966, Fr. Theodore Hesburgh, president of the University of Notre Dame, was appointed to the Executive Board of the Rockefeller Foundation, which supported various projects of the university. See Critchlow, *Intended Consequences*, 64.

receive John Rockefeller III in audience.[16] The University of Notre Dame subsequently received further funding from the Ford and Rockefeller Foundations to continue its work on sexual morality and fertility, particularly in the Catholic countries of Latin America.[17]

On March 27, 1965, Pope Paul VI received the commission in audience and told it of "the urgency of a situation which requires unambiguous indications from the Church and its supreme authority," since it was "a problem which impassions world opinion, just as it preoccupies spouses and their pastors." The Holy Father summarizes the problem as follows: "In what form and according to what norms should spouses, in the exercise of their mutual love, perform that service of life to which their vocation calls them?" He immediately clarifies: "As guardian of God's natural and positive law, the Church will not allow the price of life to be minimized, nor the sublime originality of love, which is capable of surpassing itself in the gift of the spouses to each other, and then in the even more selfless gift of each of them to a new being."[18]

From March 1965 onward, the meetings of the enlarged commission took place. The commission came to see itself as a magisterial body capable of changing the doctrine.[19] If at the beginning of its work a majority of its theologians considered the Church's Magisterium on the subject to be irreformable, opinions quickly evolved in the direction of the licitability of birth control. This sudden change in the position of many of the theologians raised questions among the bishops and cardinals who had to give their opinion at the end of the work.

The work of the Pontifical Commission was in fact studied by a small commission of sixteen bishops, under the presidency of Cardinal Ottaviani. On June 24, the commission decided, by a majority of nine votes, in favor of the Magisterium's recognition of the licitness of contraceptive intervention "in the terms used by the majority of the expert theologians of the commission, "and it considered it urgent for the Supreme Magiste-

---

16. Charles E. Rice, *What Happened to Notre Dame?* (South Bend, IN: St. Augustine's Press, 2009).

17. Critchlow, *Intended Consequences*, 64.

18. Paul VI, *Allocution of H.H. Paul VI to the Commission for the Study of Population, Family and Birth Problems*, website of the Holy See, March 27, 1965, https://www.vatican.va/content/paul-vi/fr/speeches/1965/documents/hf_p-vi_spe_19650327_demographic-commission.html.

19. Chiron, *L'infaillibilité et son objet*, 332.

rium to pronounce itself.[20] The majority of the members of the restricted commission thus followed the opinion of the majority of the members, especially theologians, of the enlarged commission. The Pontifical Commission completed its work on June 25, 1966.

Two reports were submitted to the pope: Cardinal Julius Doepffner submitted the majority text, and a few days later, Cardinal Ottaviani submitted the minority text. The first, which should have remained confidential, was improperly leaked to the press to spread the rumor of a probable change in the Church's position on contraception.

This report, written for the most part in French and Latin, deserves attention because it sets out the details of the majority thesis. If the argumentation of the minority is presented summarily, that of the majority is much more developed. It deserves to be exposed because it contains the elements of the later philosophical and bioethical debates. After a lengthy presentation of the arguments involved, the report proposes to the pope a doctrinal document titled *De Responsabili Paternitate* (On Responsible Paternity), which synthesizes what would be the (new) Catholic doctrine on marriage, sexuality, and procreation.

On the main question submitted to him, the final report submitted to the pope states that the use of artificial contraception is not intrinsically evil, and "it is up to them [the spouses] to decide together—without allowing themselves to be arbitrary—but always with the objective criteria of morality in mind and conscience." The praise for periodic continence was removed from the text. For the fifteen majority members of the theology section of the enlarged commission, it is possible to affirm that "the use of a contraceptive procedure for the purpose of depriving a conjugal act or series of acts of their procreative force is not intrinsically evil." For them, this use "takes its morality from the totality of the human act in which they are integrated, without bringing to bear one element of morality in itself."[21] Morality is in the subjective intention that guides the action, not in each of the actions. In contrast, the four minority members reaffirm the intrinsic evil of contraception.

This change, based on a disruption of the hierarchy of the purposes

20. Chiron, *L'infaillibilité et son objet*, 333.
21. Final report of June 27, 1966, 10.

of marriage that had been affirmed until then, places on an equal footing the subjective purpose of the *affective bond between the spouses* and the objective purpose of *procreation*. Such a change makes it possible to subordinate the natural course of procreation to the search for the quality of the relationship between the spouses, and thus, *in fine,* makes contraception lawful if it improves the conjugal relationship. The majority believes that it is sufficient that the relationship between the spouses be generally open to fertility to guarantee the morality of contraception. *Responsible paternity* by means of contraception is therefore considered moral and compatible with the Magisterium.

The minority position is based on three arguments. First is an argument of authority, based on the traditional Magisterium of the Church, in particular the encyclical *Casti Connubii*. Second is an argument of reason, based on the "inviolability of the sources of life," according to which "it is not for man to distort voluntarily and skillfully the mechanism of the act which transmits life or which structures it with a view to transmitting it."[22] Finally, a third argument completes the two previous ones by drawing absurd consequences from the contrary position: if one renounces the procreative order (finality) inscribed in the very structure, even physiological, of the conjugal act in order to judge its morality, then one abandons at the same time the criterion that allows one to condemn other sexual excesses in and out of marriage, consisting of sexual practices not ordered to procreation (sodomy and others). This third argument has been summarized in the statement: "Today contraception, tomorrow sterilization and abortion."[23]

The majority of theologians believe that the condemnation contained in the encyclical *Casti Connubii* is not infallible, especially since it deals with natural law and not directly with revelation.[24] The questioning of infallibility goes hand in hand with that of natural law. They take as an example the modification of the Magisterium on the question of usury and religious freedom (15). The majority claims to deepen and develop the

---

22. Final report of June 27, 1966, 11.
23. Final report of June 27, 1966, 12.
24. The questioning of the authority of *Casti Connubii* will facilitate the later questioning of *Humanae Vitae*.

Magisterium in a personalist approach,[25] to advance it in the light of new knowledge and the evolution of society. With this personalist approach, the conception of the natural law is modified: "It is not so much a question of respecting the 'givens' of nature, but of administering them for the good of the whole human person" (52). According to the majority, the natural ordination of every conjugal act to procreation must be thought of in the light of the requirement of "responsible parenthood,"[26] which "forces parents in conscience not to procreate, without reasonable prospects of being able to bring up children in a harmonious home." Recognizing a conflict between procreation and the good of the home, the good of procreation (*bonum prolis*) is thus subjected to the educational capacity and good of the home. According to this conception, it is not the physical act itself that is ordered to the child, but the whole conjugal community, because "the end of marriage is the child, not only to procreate but to educate" (42). The responsibility of the spouses cannot be centered on the sole duty to procreate; it is much more complex.

For the majority, the sexual act, in spite of original sin, is good in itself, and procreation has "become for itself the object of a decision and a human act." The assessment of the morality of the act is not based primarily on biological requirements, but on the "good of the procreative and responsible conjugal community." The majority opposes the approach based on the intrinsic malice of contraception in favor of an approach based on "the principle of totality, which has been used more and more in connection with the skillful interventions on the organs and even on the psyche of man."[27] For the majority of theologians, and the unanimity of the doctors consulted by the commission, the good of the conjugal community can take precedence over "the physiological integrity of the act," that is to say, its procreative capacity. The principle of totality, classical in moral philosophy, means that one can sacrifice a part for the good of the whole. Thus one can amputate a person's limb to save his or her life, even if it is wrong in itself to cut off a limb. A physical evil can be ordered to the

---

25. "It is always clearer, that the purpose which dominates everything in marriage is the person, that of the spouses, that of the children." Final Report of June 27, 1966, 43.

26. This notion of "responsible parenthood" is borrowed from Pope Pius XII.

27. Final report of June 27, 1966, 8.

greater good of the person; the morality of the act is then derived from its ultimate, global purpose.

More fundamentally, the commission is thus marked by the question of the existence or not of intrinsically bad acts, the relationship between objective and subjective morality. Is the morality of an act determined first in the nature of the act itself, or in that of the intention of its author?[28]

For the majority—while abortion attacks the life of a third party, and sterilization, because of its irreversibility, prejudges the future of the entire conjugal life—contraception does not call into question any "absolute value." For the majority, in sum, the Church preaches a "duty of conjugal responsibility" and cannot deny couples the means to exercise this duty in practice in the name of respect for life, which is nonexistent before fertilization. Moreover, it would be inconsistent to admit the liceity of periodic continence and to refuse that of biochemical contraception, since there is only a difference in means.

Finally, there is the question of the evolution of the Magisterium as a result of scientific knowledge. The Magisterium, according to the majority, was opposed to contraception in the past because it was "repugnant to nature," and it was on the basis of a dated knowledge of nature upon which affirmations of natural law were formulated. Current medical knowledge, however, especially concerning the cyclical infertility of women, calls into question the existence of a procreative intention in nature (*intentio naturae*). Therefore it would not be against nature (*contra naturam*) to bring about the infertility of the woman. For the majority, it would now be established that the conjugal act is not "always and of itself ordered to procreation" (15), that it participates of a "complex reality, still formless, morally indifferent of itself." This reality is "like so many others, given to the man so that, good administrator of his body and his organic functions, he makes them serve the human good of the whole person. His own, that of his spouse, that of the children born or to be born."[29] Contraception would only be an imitation of nature (47).

---

28. See on this question Servais Pinckaers, OP, "La question des actes intrinsèquement mauvais et le 'proportionnalisme,'" *Revue Thomiste* 82 (1982): 181–212.

29. Final report of June 27, 1966, 14.

Finally, the majority refuted the argument that the acceptance of contraception would lead to the acceptance of other sexual practices that are immoral because they lack a procreative purpose. Affirming that the "moral norm of the human act in which a contraceptive intervention is integrated is the good of the procreative conjugal community," the majority concluded that "it goes without saying that attitudes which contradict the reciprocal dignity of the spouses and the unitive scope of their carnal intimacy are excluded." This argument suffers from the very ambiguity of the notions of "dignity" and "carnal intimacy," the appreciation of which, once distinguished from procreative purpose, becomes entirely subjective. (Who is the judge of the dignity and quality of the carnal unity of a relationship, when it is devoid of procreative purpose?)

As for the doctors consulted, it seems obvious to them that "the biological responsibility of procreation cannot be left to chance" (25), both in its quantitative aspects (as regards the number of children) and in its qualitative aspects (as regards the risk of generating children with genetic anomalies). The doctors were unanimous in rejecting sterilization, in that it is irreversible. They also rejected abortion, which "can never constitute a form of responsible fatherhood" (26) because it consists of "killing a human life" as soon as the ovum is fertilized. As a result, the intrauterine device (IUD) cannot be tolerated.

The commission's report, in its section on scientific facts, also justifies its perspective in light of the psychological dimension of the question. It holds that "what is really in question is the new meaning of sexuality": it can no longer be considered "as a simple physiological need," but must be understood "as a fundamental and specifically human dimension of existence" that "reaches the totality of the human being." Sexuality should be made less guilty and given a new meaning (33), a higher relational quality that rejects both eroticism and puritanism. Sexuality and procreation should no longer be a form of biological fatality, but on the contrary become the means of a stronger expression of love. For the report: "it is love that gives meaning to procreation and not the other way around. It is the love of the parents that makes the child a human being" (31). The report continues: "reduced to simple natural fertility, procreation ceases to be a value. In order to be the language of love, sexuality cannot be assumed without a reasonable regulation of births." Thus it would be the voluntary regulation of births that would give its value to sexuality by allowing it to be a more authentic form of expression of conjugal love: contraception makes it possible to humanize sexuality where the weight of "*instinctive impulses*" naturally tends to predominate. This approach implies a conception of human nature that opposes the body to the mind, according to which the body would be humanized by being subjected to reason. A sexuality that is not reasonable, that is to say, not controlled in its various aspects, would not be finally human. The report goes so far as to oppose the legitimacy of the refusal of birth control: "[r]esistance to a necessary regulation of fertility goes hand in hand with immaturity, guilt, a poor acceptance of sexuality, an insufficiency of love" (32). In other words, to refuse the regulation of fertility would be to remain at a subhuman, bestial degree of sexuality.

Man would thus humanize nature by extending his technical control; he would perfect the work of God by artificially suppressing a conflict between sexuality and procreation. One perceives here the echo of the libertarian discourse of Robin and his successors, who have seen in "responsible and conscious motherhood" a humanization allowing true love to express itself by escaping bestiality. A question arises: What is the nature of this conflict, made more and more significant by the fall in infant mortality? If it exists, does it result from original sin or from God's intention? As for periodic continence, as a means of overcoming this conflict, it is considered "dangerous for the stability of the conjugal bond" (32). For the majority, it is up to the spouses alone, in dialogue, to determine in an adult way the method of contraception they wish to use. If morality is thus subjective, then it is important to give the best possible education to individuals. The report proposes criteria for discernment for couples.

There is a reversal of the perspective of sexuality: unregulated sexuality is not fully humanized; it "becomes an object and people become things" (33). The report notes, however, that, with regard to human action: "The more [man] increases his chances of humanizing his nature, the more he runs the risk of distorting it. Never has moral effort, the duty to discern values and responsibility been so promising or so demanding" (33).

The report also looks at the demographic and sociological effect. It notes that "uncontrolled fertility is proving to be ... completely impractical in the modern world," both at the societal and family level, owing to the decline in infant mortality. The report describes birth control programs in both developed and developing countries, and hopes that the Catholic Church can humanize these programs, especially with regard to the fight against abortion and the widespread use of the IUD. The report concludes that there is "a very strong push to get major international organizations of the United Nations to include effective birth control measures in their regional or global programs."

The report also notes the transformation of traditional society and the "growing conviction among all" that "effective planning is required in all areas of life, not only in the nation but also in the family. There is less reliance on tradition, chance or fate" (36) to ensure social justice. What the report refers to as responsible procreation is part of the movement to change values, especially the autonomy of women.

In the reduced Commission of Bishops, presided over by Cardinal Ottaviani, only two members actively took a position in favor of maintaining the intrinsic illegality of contraception: Cardinal Gracias and Bishop Colombo. The latter noted that accepting contraception was tantamount to conforming to the spirit of the world, to satisfying "those who advocate governmental policies of 'birth control,' and all those who would rejoice to see the Magisterium of the Church contradict itself for the first time in its history". On the substance, Cardinal Gracias objects that the question is not so much whether the sexual act is really procreative, "but whether or not its non-procreativity is attributable to the fault of the person concerned, as a result of the voluntary intervention." As for Bishop Colombo, he particularly objects that conjugal chastity requires openness to life, which is opposed to the complete dissociation between the sexual act and procreation; he also notes that the ultimate ordination of marriage is the service of God, which is accomplished essentially through the transmission of life.

The Encyclical *Humanae Vitae*

Paul VI waited two years before publishing his decision on July 25, 1968: the encyclical *Humanae Vitae*.[30] During these two years, he had to endure a considerable campaign of pressure[31] while a Western consensus in favor of birth control was already being formed. At that time, Julian Huxley publicly argued, aimed at the Catholic Church, that "it has become fundamentally immoral for any individual, group or organization to obstruct birth control or to oppose any policy tending to reduce population growth."[32]

In spite of the pressure, Paul VI could not accept the conclusions of the Pontifical Commission, even though they were adopted by a large majority, because they "departed from the moral doctrine on marriage which has been proposed with a constant firmness by the Magisterium of the Church."[33]

The encyclical *Humanae Vitae* reformulates the doctrine of the Catholic Church in the face of three developments:

1. Rapid population growth: "Many people fear that the world's population is growing faster than the resources at its disposal; this is causing increasing concern for many developing families and peoples, and there is a great temptation for the authorities to take radical measures to counter this danger" (§2).

2. The situation of women and the meaning of marriage: "There is also a change in the way of considering the person of the woman and her place in society, as well as in the value to be attributed to conjugal love in marriage, as well as in the way of appreciating the meaning of conjugal acts in relation to this love" (§2).

3. Scientific knowledge: "Man has made astonishing progress in the

---

30. Official text: *AAS* 60 (1968): 481–503; French translation: *Documentation Catholique* 1968, no. 1523: 1442–58.

31. Cardinal Edouard Gagnon, president of the Pontifical Council for the Family from 1974 to 1990, confided to me during an interview in Louisville, Kentucky, a few months before his death, that he had been the object of bribery attempts by American institutes (from New York) to convince the pope to accept contraception.

32. Julian Huxley, *The Human Crisis* (Seattle: University of Washington Press, 1963), 80.

33. *Humanae Vitae*, §6.

mastery and rational organization of the forces of nature, to the point that he tends to extend this mastery to his own being taken as a whole: to the body, to physical life, to social life, and even to the laws which regulate the transmission of life" (§2).

Based on "a global vision of man" that requires "respect for the nature and purpose of the matrimonial act" in "fidelity to God's plan," the encyclical exposes the "necessary" link between conjugal union and procreation. "To use this divine gift [sexuality] in such a way as to destroy, even partially, its meaning and purpose, is to contradict the nature of both man and woman and their most intimate relationship, and thus to contradict God's plan and will" (*§13*). The encyclical rejects "the direct interruption of the process of generation already begun" (abortion), "direct sterilization, whether perpetual or temporary" (*§12*), and "any action which, either in anticipation of the conjugal act, or in its course, or in the development of its natural consequences, is intended to make procreation impossible" (contraception) (§14).

The encyclical redefines the concept of "responsible fatherhood" by indicating that it implies "that spouses fully recognize their duties to God, to themselves, to the family and to society, in a just hierarchy of values." The pope adds, referring to the Pastoral Constitution *Gaudium et Spes*, that "[i]n the task of transmitting life, therefore, they are not free to proceed as they please, as if they could determine in an entirely autonomous way the honest paths to be followed, but they must conform their conduct to God's creative intention, expressed in the very nature of marriage and its acts, and manifested by the constant teaching of the Church" (§10). If the concept of "responsible paternity" is retained, it is no longer the guiding value, in the light of which contraception could become licit, but a simple ordinary duty of responsibility.

The Challenge to the Encyclical

As soon as it was published, the opposition to this encyclical was organized, particularly within liberal Catholic circles that were distressed that their position, although a majority one, had been contradicted, especially in the binding form of an encyclical. Thus, the day after the publication of the encyclical (July 31, 1968), an article was published in the *New York Times* signed by several hundred theologians, led by Father Charles Curran. The op-ed echoed some of the majority arguments of the commission and explicitly stated that "the encyclical is not an infallible teaching" and that therefore "spouses can responsibly decide in accordance with their conscience" that artificial contraception is permissible in certain circumstances. The main argument of the opponents was, as in the commission, the idea that the morality of the sexual act depends less on "biological" considerations than on the intention of the couple; the contraceptive intention being as if absorbed into the unitive intention. The immediate publication of this statement and its wide support among Catholic scholars testifies to the influence and coordination of the reformist and protest movement within the Church, especially in the United States. In 1986, Rome declared Fr. Curran unfit to teach Catholic theology because of his public disagreement with the ordinary Magisterium regarding "the indissolubility of consummated marriage, abortion, euthanasia, masturbation, artificial contraception, premarital relations, and acts of homosexuality."[34] Fr. Curran's positions illustrate the accuracy of the warning of the minority theologians on the Pontifical Commission about the inevitable "slide" to abortion that would result from an acceptance of contraception.[35]

A good number of bishops, including the French and Canadian episcopal conferences, led the rebellion by directly contesting or disseminating erroneous interpretations of the encyclical, according to which contraception could be licit in certain circumstances, as determined by those concerned themselves.[36] Thus, on November 8, 1968, the majority of French bishops adopted a "pastoral note" on *Humanae Vitae* in which they indicated that "Contraception can never be a good. It is always a disorder, but this disorder is not always guilty." According to this note,

---

34. Congregation for the Doctrine of the Faith, *Letter to Fr. Charles Curran,* July 25, 1986.

35. This shift can be explained not only because, through artificial contraception, the person chooses to extend his or her control over life, but also because the acceptance of contraception results from a displacement of the locus of morality. Reformers no longer place morality in the act itself but exclusively in the person, so that no action would be wrong in itself, and in any case, respect for the internal forum of the person would make it impossible to fully appreciate the morality of his action.

36. See the Winnipeg Statement, adopted by the Plenary Assembly of the Canadian Conference of Catholic Bishops on September 27, 1968, in St. Boniface-Winnipeg, Canada.

spouses can decide in conscience to have recourse to contraception in order to preserve the "stability of their home" that would be shaken by the incompatibility of a double "duty" to avoid a new birth and to express their love physically.[37] Similarly, the Canadian Bishops' Conference believes that "many spouses find it difficult to reconcile the need to express their conjugal love with responsible fatherhood," and that they "find themselves in the presence of what seems to them to be a conflict of duties." The Canadian bishops conclude that "insofar as these persons have made a sincere effort to conform to the directives given, but have not succeeded, they can be certain that they are not cut off from God's love [i.e., that they have not sinned], as long as they honestly choose the path that seems best to them."

Let me sum up the early reception of the encyclical in the West by quoting a statement Cardinal Joseph Ratzinger made in 1995: "Rarely in the recent history of the Magisterium has a text become such a sign of contradiction as this encyclical, which Paul VI wrote after a decision that was deeply painful for him."[38] Among the principal defenders of Paul VI at this time emerged Cardinals Karol Wojtyla and Joseph Ratzinger. Cardinal Karol Wojtyla, the future Pope John Paul II, a member of the pontifical commission, was prevented from participating by the refusal of the Soviet authorities to issue him a visa.

---

37. Pastoral note of November 8, 1968: "On the one hand, they are aware of the duty to respect the openness to life of every conjugal act; they also feel in conscience that they must avoid or postpone a new birth, and are deprived of the resource of relying on biological rhythms. On the other hand, they do not see, as far as they are concerned, how they can renounce the physical expression of their love at the present time without the stability of their home being threatened (G.S., 51, §1). In this regard, we will simply recall the constant teaching of morality: when one is faced with an alternative of duties where, whatever decision one makes, one cannot avoid an evil, traditional wisdom foresees that one should seek before God which duty, in this case, is greater. The spouses will make their decision at the end of a common reflection carried out with all the care that the greatness of their conjugal vocation requires."

38. "40th Anniversary of *Humanae Vitae*, A 'Sign of Contradiction': The Editor of *L'Osservatore Romano* Comments on the Encyclical of Paul VI," Zenit, July 25, 2008.

PART II

THE DOCTRINAL DIMENSION

CHAPTER 6

The Foundation of the Doctrine of Intrinsically Evil Acts

FULVIO DI BLASI

Introduction

There are legitimate philosophical and theological discussions regarding the so-called intrinsically evil actions. There is no doubt, however, that the truth about the existence of such actions belongs to the magisterial tradition of the Church. Hence, from a Catholic perspective, they must be studied in the light of the Magisterium, with sincere love for the Sacred Tradition, and with "the religious submission of will and intellect."[1]

In this chapter, I want to dwell on what we Catholic scholars have in common with respect to this topic, not on the differences and subtleties that we are so passionate about in academic contexts. The focus on different opinions sometimes makes us lose sight of the essential. I will not address specific intrinsically evil acts, but rather their common features and foundational traits. For reasons that I will explain later, I focus on John

---

1. Congregation for the Doctrine of the Faith, Instruction *Donum Veritatis* on the Ecclesial Vocation of the Theologian, Rome, May 24, 1990, no. 23. "The freedom proper to theological research is exercised within the Church's faith.... In theology this freedom of inquiry is the hallmark of a rational discipline whose object is given by Revelation, handed on and interpreted in the Church under the authority of the Magisterium, and received by faith. These givens have the force of principles. To eliminate them would mean to cease doing theology" (nos. 11–12). "The right conscience of the Catholic theologian presumes not only faith in the Word of God whose riches he must explore, but also love for the Church from whom he receives his mission, and respect for her divinely assisted Magisterium" (no. 38).

Paul II's encyclical *Veritatis Splendor*. But first, I want readers to get a taste of pre-Christian philosophy to put the subject in a broader and deeper ethical context. Intrinsically evil acts are not just out-of-time Catholic mannerism or a nostalgic medieval wreck. Rather, they embody, reveal, and protect some critical elements of Christian and Western morality of which we must never lose sight. I will offer this flavor through a short commentary of three quotations from Aristotle's *Ethics*.

Thus, in what follows, I will first focus on these quotations and on the connection between classical pre-Christian philosophy and the Catholic doctrine on intrinsically evil actions. Then, after briefly reviewing the reasons that make *Veritatis Splendor* so important, I will quickly review some crucial elements that form the background to *Veritatis Splendor*'s argument that leads to the truth about intrinsically evil acts and to the condemnation of theories that deny them. Finally, I will explain the central argument of Thomistic origin that the encyclical uses to explain the foundation of the doctrine of intrinsically evil acts. This argument, as is known, hinges on the analysis of the object of moral action.

Given that the basic meaning of this chapter is to invite Catholic scholars to reflect on the theme correctly in the light of the Magisterium and in fidelity to it, I will try to highlight not so much my personal reflections on the issue but the logical reasoning of *Veritatis Splendor*. I will therefore emphasize the concepts, the exact words, and the relevant passages of the encyclical. All emphases in this essay's quotations are mine. If I am successful, this writing will help honest readers to find and/or re-read in the Magisterium the beauty and simplicity of the basic elements on which legitimate differences of views within the Catholic tradition can only be based.

A Taste of Pre-Christian Ethics

In this introductory section, I will revisit some key features of classical and Christian morality drawing on famous quotes from Aristotle regarding intrinsically evil actions. This type of action is not a secondary or negligible element of ethical theory. In fact, the study of ethics itself may benefit at times from being approached or framed starting precisely from the profound and beautiful moral meaning of those acts.

Not Every Action Admits of a Mean

Aristotle's crucial passage on intrinsically evil acts is found in the context of the study of virtue as the measure of moral action, or as the mean between the excess and deficiency of human inclinations or passions.

> But not every action nor every passion admits of a mean; for some have names that already imply badness, e.g., spite, shamelessness, envy, and in the case of actions adultery, theft, murder; for all of these and suchlike things imply by their names that **they are themselves bad**, and not the excesses or deficiencies of them. **It is not possible, then, ever to be right with regard to them; one must always be wrong.** Nor does goodness or badness with regard to such things depend on committing adultery with the right woman, at the right time, and in the right way, but simply to do any of them is to go wrong.[2]

For Christian ethics, it is revealing and interesting that Aristotle, in his most defining passage of intrinsically evil acts, uses the example of adultery. Not only the assistance of the Spirit of Truth in the history of salvation, but also the assistance of natural reason in the common sense of human history reveals the key role of conjugal fidelity for human love and community.

I do not intend to dwell here on the logical question that vices cannot admit the mean because they have already names of the excesses or deficiencies. This logical question does not detract from the profound value of the anthropological and ethical analysis of virtuous action according to the mean. The important thing here, for our purposes, is that Aristotle's example is clearly based on the irrelevance of the circumstances. It is clear, in other words, that for Aristotle, the teaching on intrinsically evil actions is justified both with respect to the ethical interpretation of virtue and with respect to the analysis of the act according to the circumstances.[3]

---

2. Aristotle, *Nicomachean Ethics* (NE), from *The Complete Works of Aristotle: The Revised Oxford Translation,* edited by Jonathan Barnes (Princeton, NJ: Princeton University Press, 1984), II:1107a9–17.

3. Useful bibliographic indications to deepen Aristotle's ethics can be found in Richard Kraut, "Aristotle's Ethics," in *The Stanford Encyclopedia of Philosophy*, edited by Edward N. Zalta and Uri Nodelman, https://plato.stanford.edu/archives/fall2022/entries/aristotle-ethics/.

Ethics' Aesthetics

Another passage of Aristotelian ethics in favor of intrinsically evil acts is found in the treatise on courage and concerns the malice of suicide as a choice incompatible with virtue.

> As we have said, then, courage is a mean with respect to things that inspire confidence or fear, in the circumstances that have been stated; and it chooses or endures things because it is noble (*kalòn*) to do so, or because it is base not to do so. But to die to escape from poverty or love or anything painful is not the mark of a brave man, but rather of a coward; for it is softness to fly from what is troublesome, and such a man endures death not because it is noble (*kalòn*) but to fly from evil (*kakón*).[4]

The focus here is on moral beauty (*kalòn*), and it is surprising that the Oxford revised translation translates *kalòn* with noble instead of beautiful. In this way, it misses a key trait of classical and Christian ethics. For Aristotle, there is no way to portray suicide as a beautiful action because, however we look at it, it implies fleeing (from the ugly, *kakón*).

The constant and intrinsic link between beautiful and the good (*kalòs kai agathòs*) in Aristotle's ethics is too often overlooked. The good is always attractive, as is the *phronimos*,[5] that is, the good, exemplary person, the proximate rule of moral action. The good man's virtue attracts us, excites us, which is why the hero of the movie gives us goosebumps or makes us cry. We want to be like him or her. We want our life to be as beautiful as the one of that hero, of that saint. We are never aesthetically indifferent to the moral good, which is why the exemplarity of the *phronimos* is so important in classical ethics. The best way to understand what is right or wrong is to ask what the Aristotelian *phronimos* would do in our place, or, for Christians, what Jesus would do. We don't want to do what he would not do. Would Aristotle's *phronimos* or Jesus commit suicide, use contraceptives, engage in oral or anal sex, or in sex with fake organs or toys, as is done in homosexual relationships? Are these things beautiful or ugly?

---

4. NE, III:1116a10–15.

5. Although in the specific ethical and epistemological context of the pandemic, I explain the essential features of classical virtue ethics in my book *The Death of the Phronimos: Faith and Truth about Anti Covid Vaccines* (Palermo: Edizioni *Phronesis*, 2021).

Does the perspective of such actions appeal to the ethical hero, make him proud, give him goosebumps? These are concrete, crucial questions that a classical ethicist and a Christian person should always address first.

The above passage from Aristotle invites us to analyze our moral actions from the aesthetic point of view of the moral good. Some people get lost in abstract reasoning when they only focus on the rationale of the *agathòs*, but they can be easily brought back down to earth by helping them focus correctly on its *kalòs*.

Forgiveness and Moral Firmness

In doing ethics, we must always consider human weakness and forgiveness. In the context of his analysis of the voluntary and involuntary in moral action, Aristotle suggests that some bad, ugly actions can be forgiven when they are done in some way against our will—when we are forced in a direction we do not like by pressures that exceed the normal human capacity to resist.

"On some actions praise indeed is not bestowed, but **forgiveness** is, when one does what he ought not under *pressure which overstrains human nature* and which no one could withstand."[6]

Think of killing someone to save our lives or to avoid unbearable torture. The Italian (Aristotelian) legal system, in these cases, while recognizing the malice of the act, allows not punishing the guilty party.[7] The state forgives on the assumption that justice (at least the earthly one) cannot require heroism and must accept human weakness. After all, why put a

---

6. NE, III:1110a23–28.

7. See Italian Criminal Law Code: "Those who committed the act by chance or force majeure are not punishable" (art. 45); "Those who committed the crime due to having been forced by others, through physical violence to which they could not resist or in any case escape, are not punishable. In this case, the perpetrator of the violence is liable for the act committed by the forced person" (art. 46); "Those who committed the crime because they were forced to do so by the need to save themselves or others from the current danger of serious personal injury, a danger they did not voluntarily cause or otherwise avoidable, are not punishable, provided that the crime is proportionate to the danger. This provision does not apply to anyone who has a particular legal duty to expose themselves to danger. The provision of the first part of this article also applies if the state of necessity is brought about by the threat of another; but, in this case, the person who forced him to commit it is liable for the act committed by the threatened person" (art. 54).

person in prison who did what he did only in exceptional circumstances to save his life? Regardless of the reasons for forgiveness, there would be no reasons for deterrence.

Still, Aristotle adds to the passage just quoted that sometimes we must accept death, even the most terrible one, in order to avoid carrying out certain acts.

"But some acts, perhaps, we cannot be forced to do, but ought rather to face death after the most fearful sufferings; for the things that forced Euripides' Alcmaeon to slay his mother seem absurd."[8]

Apparently,[9] Alcmaeon killed his mother in revenge or to avoid his father's curse, and this does not seem sufficient to forgive such an ugly act.

In the same section of his ethics, Aristotle explains that pleasures and beauty cannot make the action involuntary. The general point is that forgiveness, even when applicable, does not turn an ugly action into a beautiful one and does not affect the concept of intrinsically evil acts. This passage from Aristotle tells us about courage and moral strength, but there is more to it than that. It contains a defining feature of moral life, which requires heroism, men of principles, truths that cannot be bargained or compromised.

We have to ask ourselves if a moral account of human existence would still be beautiful or good in which there were no questions of principle, in which people did not set themselves any insurmountable limit beyond which they would lose themselves, their dignity, their beauty and attractiveness, their self-respect, love of neighbor, love of God. Intrinsically evil acts are the theoretical sign of a moral theory in which men of integrity and principle, as well as ultimate moral beauty, exist.[10]

Veritatis Splendor in Defense of the Human Being and the Moral Order

Indeed, there are many reasons for affirming that without intrinsically evil acts there is truly no ethics, no moral person, or a moral order worthy

---

8. NE, III:1110a23–28.
9. The work of Euripides cited by Aristotle has been lost, except for a few fragments.
10. John Finnis makes a similar point in his book *Moral Absolutes: Tradition, Revision and Truth* (Washington, DC: Catholic University of America Press, 1991).

of the name. No wonder, then, to find, at the end of *Veritatis Splendor*'s treatment of intrinsically evil actions, the following statement in defense of the human being:

> As is evident, in the question of the morality of human acts, and in particular the question of whether there exist intrinsically evil acts, we find ourselves faced with the question of man himself, of his truth and of the moral consequences flowing from that truth. By acknowledging and teaching the existence of intrinsic evil in given human acts, the Church remains faithful to the integral truth about man; she thus respects and promotes man in his dignity and vocation. Consequently, she must reject the theories set forth above, which contradict this truth.[11]

And this one in defense of an objective moral order:

> "Without the rational determination of the morality of human acting as stated above, it would be impossible to affirm the existence of an "objective moral order" and to establish any particular norm the content of which would be binding without exception. This would be to the detriment of human fraternity and the truth about the good, and would be injurious to ecclesial communion as well."[12]

The Importance of *Veritatis Splendor*

Veritatis Splendor is not like a magisterial document among many. It is the highest Magisterium of the Church systematically addressing and explaining the very foundation of moral theology. It contains the basic truths of Catholic doctrine that must be put at the foundation of moral theology. As such, it must be taken as the *starting point* of any sound and faithful Catholic moral theology.

To be clear, this is not an encyclical that among other things, perhaps accidentally, contains some important teachings for moral theology. It is an encyclical whose specific object is precisely to clarify the foundations of Catholic moral theology.

> Given these circumstances, which still exist, I came to the decision [...] to write an Encyclical with the aim of treating "more fully and more deeply the issues regarding the very foundations of moral theology," foundations which are being undermined by certain present day tendencies.[13]

---

11. Pope John Paul II, Encyclical letter *Veritatis Splendor* (VS), 1993, no. 83.
12. VS, no. 82.
13. VS, no. 5.

This document is also a true *ecclesiastical* achievement, in the sense that its draft has been reviewed by all bishops and countless theologians in the whole world and edited by trying to consider all comments and suggestions. It would be a mistake to see it only as the document of a single pope. Understanding its strategic and doctrinal importance, John Paul II wanted it to somehow express the voice of the whole Church. Moreover, it was drafted together with the Catechism, which went through the same process, with reviews and editing by all bishops and experts all around the world. Indeed, *Veritatis Splendor* could have been promulgated at the same time as the Catechism, but it was decided that it was convenient that the truths of the Church, before being *explained*, were clearly *stated*.

If this Encyclical, so long awaited, is being published only now, one of the reasons is that it seemed fitting for it to be preceded by the Catechism of the Catholic Church, which contains a complete and systematic exposition of Christian moral teaching [...] Consequently, while referring back to the Catechism "as a sure and authentic reference text for teaching Catholic doctrine," the Encyclical will limit itself to dealing with certain fundamental questions regarding the Church's moral teaching, taking the form of a necessary discernment about issues being debated by ethicists and moral theologians. The specific purpose of the present Encyclical is this: to set forth, with regard to the problems being discussed, the principles of a moral teaching based upon Sacred Scripture and the living Apostolic Tradition, and at the same time to shed light on the presuppositions and consequences of the dissent which that teaching has met.[14]

As is obvious, its intention and purpose are not extraneous to the value of a magisterial document. Therefore, since this is the first document in history that systematically and by the highest authority aims at clarifying the foundations of moral theology, the interpreter can only take note of it with the due "religious submission of will and intellect." The history of Catholic moral theology is divided by now between *before* and *after Veritatis Splendor*.

Furthermore, in the context of this purpose, the encyclical's more specific objective is to affirm the truth of the doctrine of intrinsically evil acts by condemning theories that seek to deny it both in theory and in practice. As we shall see better shortly, this is truly an encyclical on intrinsical-

---

14. VS, no. 5.

ly evil acts, and this too is something that the Catholic interpreter cannot fail to perceive with the greatest attention and respect.

Key Conceptual Background

Unfortunately, this is not the place to undertake a systematic interpretation or explanation of *Veritatis Splendor*, which is an inspired text of unique richness and depth. A fair overall approach to it should follow and savor the rhythm that moves from the first theological part, centered on the dialogue with the rich young man, to the more philosophical part of Thomistic inspiration, centered on the relationship between freedom and truth, to the final pastoral part, concerned with how to help a world victim of cultural and moral relativism. Here I will limit myself to recalling some essential conceptual elements that can help us address the question of intrinsically evil acts in the correct hermeneutical context of the encyclical, without reductionisms and without neglecting what the text, from its own viewpoint, presents to us as important.

Ethics versus Ethics? The Pastoral Challenge and the Creative Hermeneutic

First, I would like to mention an aspect that connects well the encyclical both to the Aristotelian beginning of this chapter and to the problems raised by those who today would like to question the teaching on intrinsically evil acts.[15] This aspect takes us from pastoral questions to the very heart of classical ethics as a practical science and to the only correct and sensible way to approach moral questions.

Veritatis Splendor warns us against the challenge to the human being and to the objective moral order that can come from ethical theories that try to allow in practice what is prohibited in theory. It addresses this challenge in terms of "pastoral solutions" and "creative hermeneutics":

In order to justify these positions, some authors have proposed a kind of double status of moral truth. Beyond the doctrinal and abstract level, one would have to

---

15. I am referring above all to the Pontifical Academy for Life, *Etica Teologica della Vita* (Vatican City: Libreria Editrice Vaticana, 2022).

acknowledge **the priority of a certain more concrete existential consideration.** The latter, by taking account of circumstances and the situation, could legitimately be the basis of certain **exceptions to the general rule** and thus **permit one to do in practice and in good conscience what is qualified as intrinsically evil by the moral law.** A separation, or even an opposition, is thus established in some cases between the teaching of the precept, which is valid in general, and the norm of the individual conscience, which would in fact make the final decision about what is good and what is evil. On this basis, an attempt is made to legitimize so-called "pastoral" solutions contrary to the teaching of the Magisterium, and to justify a **"creative" hermeneutic** according to which the moral conscience is in no way obliged, in every case, by a particular negative precept.[16]

This passage from the encyclical fits perfectly with the logic of today's attempts to counter the doctrine of intrinsically evil acts, which do not seek direct confrontation but precisely an alleged continuity between the theoretical affirmation of the doctrine and the practical exceptions to be allowed for "ethical" reasons, that is, for reasons related to the importance of the concrete reality of the moral agent. Today's strategy is precisely that of "creative hermeneutics" and the development of doctrine. The goal is to allow in practice what the moral law forbids in theory. The theoretical context is an apparent contrast between the *abstractness* of the norm and the *concreteness* of the moral choice. It is surprising that this strategy moves exactly along the line condemned by the encyclical.

This attempt, this strategy, besides being directly unfaithful to the Magisterium of *Veritatis Splendor*, has the defect of radically misunderstanding the meaning of ethics. In fact, the first thing a student of Aristotle or Thomas Aquinas must understand is that ethics is a practical science.[17] This means that its truths are not supposed to be merely theoretical. They are ethical truths if and only if they are supposed to be lived by real people and inform the objective order of morality in the actual human world. An ethical truth that was merely abstract would simply be ethically false. There is no alternative: if the doctrine of intrinsically evil acts makes sense, it is only and solely because performing these acts makes beauty and moral goodness impossible in the concrete life of human beings. The very idea of saving both the abstract absolute norm and the con-

---

16. VS, no. 56.

17. On ethics as a practical science, let me refer to my book *From Aristotle to Thomas Aquinas: Natural Law, Practical Knowledge, and the Person* (South Bend, IN: St. Augustine's Press, 2021).

crete exception is naive to say the least. The Church must decide whether these alleged exceptions that some authors today so ardently desire are worth the dissolution and ruin of the truth-value and logical consistency of the Magisterium.

The Contradictory Accusation of Abstractness

But is it true, as they claim, that the ethics of intrinsically evil acts is abstract? As a matter of fact, it is quite the opposite. If anything, the reasoning of the critics who make this accusation are abstract.

As we have just seen through Aristotle, and as we shall see better shortly through Thomas Aquinas and John Paul II, classical ethics starts from the concreteness of action—from asking ourselves, even graphically, what specific actions look like and are about. For example, what does the action of using a contraceptive involve and/or look like? What do sexual acts in homosexual relationships involve and look like (anal sex, fake penis, etc.)? What meaning do they have? Are they beautiful? Do they imply a raising or lowering of the dignity of the person? Would Jesus take part in the concrete and existential reality of these human actions?

Critics of intrinsically evil acts do the opposite. They shift from the concrete action to the abstractness of presumed good intentions. As if we could evaluate a movie solely on the producer's intention to make a love story. The end comes first in the order of intention, but moral life begins and exists in the execution. These critics go in the exact direction of eliminating the concreteness of existence in favor of a single alleged *abstract* intention. One way or another, their method consists in sacrificing the richness of any human action on the altar of a (often merely presumed) generic act of fundamental love. Unfortunately, in this way anything can ultimately be justified (even an atomic bomb on innocent civilians) when (supposedly) done for a good purpose or in an abstractly and hypothetically good context. Sadly, this approach favors today's technocratic and eugenic society, which does not want any a priori limit, even human dignity, in the pursuit of its presumed higher ends.

Ultimately, criticisms that classical morality or magisterial doctrine on intrinsically evil acts is abstract are sophistic. They subtly attribute their own methodology and mistakes to their opponents.

On *Veritatis Splendor*'s Response to the Accusation of Abstractness:
The Condemnation of Fundamental Option

One theoretical justification of the "pastoral solutions" is the so-called fundamental option, which is likewise condemned by *Veritatis Splendor* precisely on the account that ethics cannot be reduced to the abstractness of intention.

It is easy to see the connection and analogy between these two topics addressed by the encyclical—as well as with the concept of practical science. If the pastoral solution wants to create an exception to the "abstract" norm by looking at the "true moral reality" of the agent, the fundamental option tries to justify this *solution* by claiming that ethics is truly about the basic intention of the agent, and not about his specific actions (as *abstractedly* condemned by absolute norms). Both (pastoral and theoretical) strategies remove ethics from the concrete life of the agent in favor of a purely abstract approach to the good.

Indeed, the fundamental option should be seen more as a practical and theoretical trend than as a specific theory. For this reason, its condemnation is particularly significant in the current debate, which is highly characterized by it. *Veritatis Splendor*'s methodology goes in the exact opposite direction of this trend: namely, in the direction of bringing ethics back to the concrete. The encyclical clarifies that concrete acts can be sinful regardless of the underlying intention of the agent and they affect it. As virtue ethics has taught since Aristotle, the agent is really involved in his choices and becomes good or bad on the basis of them. This is what virtues and vices are about.

Even so, "care will have to be taken not to reduce mortal sin to an act of 'fundamental option'—as is commonly said today—against God," seen either as an explicit and formal rejection of God and neighbour or as an implicit and unconscious rejection of love. "For mortal sin exists also when a person knowingly and willingly, for whatever reason, chooses something gravely disordered. In fact, such a choice already includes contempt for the divine law, a rejection of God's love for humanity and the whole of creation: the person turns away from God and loses charity. Consequently, the fundamental orientation can be radically changed by particular acts. Clearly, situations can occur which are very complex and obscure from a psychological viewpoint, and which influence the sinner's subjective imputability. But from a consideration of the psychological sphere one cannot proceed to create a theological category, which is precisely what the "fundamental option" is, understanding it in such a way that it objectively changes or casts doubt upon the traditional concept of mortal sin.[18]

Foundation of the Moral Order in God

The main point of the theological part of the encyclical is to emphasize, through the dialogue with the rich young man, that the entire moral life is founded in God as man's ultimate end. This is apparent from the very beginning of the dialogue, with the question about morality, which serves the purpose of making us raise our mind and heart to God as the meaning of our entire existence and of the law.[19]

Acknowledging the Lord as God is the very core, the heart of the Law, from which the particular precepts flow and towards which they are ordered.[20]

For the interpreter, this means, among other things, that the explanation of the intrinsically evil acts rests ultimately on the love of God. Yet this ultimate foundation of the moral order makes its observance impossible by human forces alone.

But if God alone is the Good, **no human effort**, not even the most rigorous observance of the commandments, **succeeds in "fulfilling" the Law**, that is, acknowledging the Lord as God and rendering him the worship due to him alone (cf. Mt 4:10).[21]

This is why the encyclical focuses particularly on the relationship between law and grace (the new law).

"Then who can be saved?" ... To imitate and live out the love of Christ **is not possible for man by his own strength alone**. He becomes capable of this love only by virtue of a gift received. As the Lord Jesus receives the love of his Father, so he in

---

18. VS, no. 70.

19. I deepen the meaning of the question about morality and the theological foundation of the natural moral law in the seventh chapter of *From Aristotle to Thomas Aquinas*.

20. VS, no. 11.

21. VS, no. 11. The passage continues as follows: "This 'fulfilment' can come only from a gift of God: the offer of a share in the divine Goodness revealed and communicated in Jesus, the one whom the rich young man addresses with the words 'Good Teacher' (Mk 10:17; Lk 18:18). What the young man now perhaps only dimly perceives will in the end be fully revealed by Jesus himself in the invitation: 'Come, follow me' (Mt 19:21)."

turn freely communicates that love to his disciples: "As the Father has loved me, so have I loved you; abide in my love" (Jn 15:9). Christ's gift is his Spirit, whose first "fruit" (cf. Gal 5:22) is charity: "God's love has been poured into our hearts through the Holy Spirit which has been given to us" (Rom 5:5). Saint Augustine asks: "Does love bring about the keeping of the commandments, or does the keeping of the commandments bring about love?" And he answers: "But who can doubt that **love comes first? For the one who does not love has no reason for keeping the commandments.**"[22]

Love is the foundation and primary energy of moral life, and it is a love that passes from the Father to the Son and from the Son to us creatures. This love is the new law, which alone makes obedience and fidelity to the moral law possible. "The law of the Spirit of life in Christ Jesus has set me free from the law of sin and death" (Rom 8:2). With these words the Apostle Paul invites us to consider in the perspective of the history of salvation, which reaches its fulfilment in Christ, **the relationship between the (Old) Law and grace (the New Law)**. He recognizes the pedagogic function of the Law, which, by enabling sinful man to take stock of his own powerlessness and by stripping him of the presumption of his self-sufficiency, leads him to ask for and to receive "life in the Spirit." **Only in this new life is it possible to carry out God's commandments.** Indeed, it is through faith in Christ that we have been made righteous (cf. Rom 3:28): the "righteousness" which the Law demands, but is unable to give, is found by every believer to be revealed and granted by the Lord Jesus. Once again, it is **St. Augustine** who admirably sums up this Pauline dialectic of law and grace: "**The law was given that grace might be sought; and grace was given, that the law might be fulfilled.**"[23]

An Atheistic Objection?

One point I want to highlight here is that moral life on this earth—even if it ultimately meets the true beauty and fulfillment of the person—is supposed to be tough, but it is also supposed to be with God, with his grace.

I believe that many of the critics of intrinsically evil acts, such as those

---

22. VS, no. 22.
23. VS, no. 23.

who would like to reform contraceptive teaching (or create *practical* or *pastoral* exceptions to it), feel in good faith that they have to take into account human weakness—the fact that so many people cannot help but have certain sexual relationships or that some marriages die and cannot be, so to speak, *resurrected*. Love, compassion, an understanding of the human condition, require allowing for exceptions. Anyone who does not understand this is therefore a *legalist*, one who remains in his *abstract* world instead of understanding the sufferings and struggles of men of flesh and blood.

This attitude, in addition to undervaluing or sometimes even denigrating the ethical reasons of others, reveals a dangerous practical atheism with respect to the authentic Christian faith. As John Paul II has often stressed,[24] this world is not left alone, like the world of Enlightenment deism, but is a world in which the natural and the supernatural coexist, in which God is Emmanuel, God with us. It's not like the supernatural spiritual reality belongs to a different dimension. Angels and grace are here with us. Human nature, the entire world even, is supposed to function properly with their help, in a loving and faith-based beautiful relationship.[25]

This is why God can call us to be heroes, saints, because he not only shows us the truth but also walks with us on our path toward it. He gives us his angels to support us and takes us by his own hand. In showing us and making us understand the full truth of the moral life and its ultimate beauty, he also gives us the strength to reach it with him. Those who focus on human weaknesses to dilute the value and truth of moral standards erase de facto God from human history and from our ethical life. They turn people away from God, replacing him with a misconceived human pleasure-based eschatology.

Truth, Moral Conscience, and Participated Theonomy

As I mentioned, it is not my intention to undertake here a systematic interpretation of *Veritatis Splendor*, but only to highlight its concepts and

---

24. See, e.g., *Crossing the Threshold of Hope* (New York: Knopf, 1995), chap. 10.
25. See Fulvio Di Blasi, "The Role of God in the New Natural Law Theory," *National Catholic Bioethics Quarterly* 13, no. 1 (2013): 35–45.

language that lead to the truth about intrinsically evil actions. I need to show the logic of the document through its own words. Thus there are many key aspects that I cannot but take for granted, referring readers to deepen them by rereading the encyclical directly.

This is the case, for example, with moral conscience and the autonomous and heteronomous character of the law.[26] The nature of moral conscience and its relationship with the truth constitute central and fascinating points of the encyclical that must be read and meditated upon in depth. Conscience is reasoning. Our practical reason does not create the law, the truth.[27] We recognize the truth and serve it. Our conscience is a witness of a higher law that obligates man. The dignity of the moral conscience lies in not being a place of solitude.[28] There is no conflict between nature and freedom,[29] especially because the duty that our conscience experiences reveal a love for God and the truth that runs way deeper than our inclinations toward pleasures.[30]

This having been said, let me briefly recall two specific points of the encyclical's treatment of moral conscience that directly relate to my present discussion. One relates to the way in which it reconciles what critics may consider "an abstract norm" with the concrete life of the agent.

The universality of the law and its obligation are acknowledged, **not suppressed**, once reason has established the law's application **in concrete present circumstances**. The judgment of conscience states "in an ultimate way" whether a certain particular kind of behaviour is in conformity with the law; it formulates **the proximate norm of the morality** of a voluntary act, "applying the objective law to a particular case."[31]

The other relates to erroneous conscience and the good of the person. Here the encyclical poses a slightly different problem from the one we had

---

26. To deepen the autonomous and heteronomous nature of the moral law, see Fulvio Di Blasi, *God and the Natural Law: A Rereading of Thomas Aquinas* (South Bend, IN: St. Augustine's Press, 2003).

27. VS, nos. 40–41.

28. VS, nos. 54, 58.

29. VS, no. 46.

30. See Di Blasi, *God and the Natural Law*, chap. 2, sec. 4.2, "The Meaning of Moral Experience"; Robert Spaemann, *Basic Moral Concepts*, translated by T. J. Armstrong (London: Routledge, 1989).

31. VS, no. 59.

just seen in Aristotle. The question is not only that of the voluntary and of forgiveness but that of the effects of the objectively bad action on the person. Even those who commit an evil act without fault suffer damage. Helping them to form their conscience well and to understand their mistakes is therefore a way to help them fulfill themselves better and reach the love of God. To put it differently: erroneous conscience still hurts.

It is possible that the evil done as the result of invincible ignorance or a **non-culpable error** of judgment **may not be imputable to the agent**; but even in this case **it does not cease to be an evil**, a disorder in relation to the truth about the good. Furthermore, a good act which is not recognized as such **does not contribute to the moral growth of the person** who performs it; it does not perfect him and it does not help to dispose him for the supreme good. Thus, before feeling easily justified in the name of our conscience, we should reflect on the words of the Psalm: "Who can discern his errors? *Clear me from hidden faults*" (Ps 19:12). There are faults which we fail to see but which nevertheless remain faults, because we have refused to walk towards the light (cf. Jn 9:39–41).[32]

The Importance of the Body and the Unity of the Human Person

More important to my present strategy is the way in which *Veritatis Splendor* addresses and frames the significance of the body and the unity of the human person (body and spirit).

A doctrine which dissociates the moral act from the bodily dimensions of its exercise is **contrary to the teaching of Scripture and Tradition**.[33]

At this point the **true meaning of the natural law** can be understood: it refers to man's proper and primordial nature, the "nature of the human person," which is the person himself **in the unity of soul and body**, in the unity of his **spiritual** and **biological** inclinations and of all the other specific characteristics necessary for the pursuit of his end.[34]

The document lays down a crucial two-step methodology for ethicists, who (1) need to look at natural inclinations (both spiritual and biolog-

---

32. VS, no. 63.
33. VS, no. 49.
34. VS, no. 50.

ical) (2) in light of the overall good of the person (plurality in light of unity).

This is the path necessary to move from the authentic good of the person (true love) to the authentic ultimate end in God (true God). This following passage shows the moral relevance of our inclinations as well as the correct moral methodology we should follow from (1) the true human love to (2) the true love of God.

"The natural moral law expresses and lays down the purposes, rights and duties which are based upon the bodily and spiritual nature of the human person. Therefore this law cannot be thought of as simply a set of norms on the biological level; rather it must be defined as the rational order whereby man is called by the Creator to direct and regulate his life and actions and in particular to make use of his own body." To give an example, the origin and the foundation of the duty of absolute respect for human life are to be found in the dignity proper to the person and not simply in the natural inclination to preserve one's own physical life. Human life, even though it is a fundamental good of man, thus acquires a moral significance in reference to the good of the person, who must always be affirmed for his own sake. While it is always morally illicit to kill an innocent human being, it can be licit, praiseworthy or even imperative to give up one's own life (cf. Jn 15:13) out of love of neighbour or as a witness to the truth. Only in reference to the human person in his "unified totality," that is, as "a soul which expresses itself in a body and a body informed by an immortal spirit," can the specifically human meaning of the body be grasped. Indeed, natural inclinations take on moral relevance only insofar as they refer to the human person and his authentic fulfilment, a fulfilment which for that matter can take place always and only in human nature. By rejecting all manipulations of corporeity which alter its human meaning, the Church serves man and shows him the path of true love, the only path on which he can find the true God."[35]

---

35. VS, no. 50.

Negative Precepts Protect Love of God and Human Dignity

With regard to the treatment of positive and negative precepts, I want to recall the way in which the negative ones are ethically justified precisely on the basis of the same methodology we have just seen that aims at the love of God and at full respect for the dignity of the person. Acting against an intrinsically evil act is not compatible with a good will. Doing something intrinsically evil violates the dignity of the human person and our "vocation to life with God."

The negative precepts of the natural law are universally valid. They oblige each and every individual, always and in every circumstance. It is a matter of prohibitions which forbid a given action semper et pro semper, without exception, because the choice of this kind of behaviour is **in no case compatible with the goodness of the will** of the acting person, with his **vocation to life with God** and to **communion with his neighbour**. It is prohibited—to everyone and in every case—to violate these precepts. They oblige everyone, regardless of the cost, never to offend in anyone, beginning with oneself, the **personal dignity** common to all.[36]

The Morality of Human Acts

Having recalled these basic concepts and terms of *Veritatis Splendor*, let me address now the central question concerning the morality of human acts and the rational justification of intrinsically evil acts. In what follows, by using some exemplifying passages from the encyclical, I want readers to focus on the following three-step conceptualization:

1. Objective Aspect: Orderability of the Action
   - Based on **conformity** with the **good of the person** or, in other words, based on the **rational ordering of specific goods of natural inclinations** to the **good of the person in its totality**.
   - This rational ordering cannot just depend on the agent's intention and needs to consider the bodily dimension. Compared to the Sources of Morality and the Doctrine of the Object,[37] this

---

36. VS, no. 52.
37. See the *Catechism of the Catholic Church* (CCC), §1750ff.

step depends on the analysis of the act according to its object[38] (and on circumstances when relevant).

2. Intention-Based Aspect Regarding the Action: **Voluntary Pursuit**
   • Accepting and fostering the objective good of the action.
   • Based on a rationality that looks at the action's capability of being ordered (see first step above).
   • Sources of Morality: object (and circumstances when relevant) + intention.

3. Intention-Based Aspect Regarding God: **Deliberate Ordering**
   • Of the human act to God as the **ultimate end**.
   • Sources of Morality: object (and circumstances when relevant) + intention.

This conceptualization corresponds to an ethical methodology of action analysis that starts from the objective element and moves toward the intention, which in turn from a human level (horizontal) reaches a higher level of perfection (vertical). Let's see how this emerges from the encyclical's own wording.

Freedom and law.
The relationship between man's freedom and God's law, which has its intimate and living centre in the moral conscience, is manifested and realized in human acts.[39]

Relationship of freedom with the authentic good and the ultimate end.
The morality of acts is defined by the relationship of man's freedom with the **authentic good**. This good is established, as the eternal law, by Divine Wisdom which orders every being towards its **end**: this eternal law is known both by man's natural reason (hence it is "natural law"), and—in an integral and perfect way—by God's supernatural Revelation (hence it is called "divine law"). Acting is morally good when the choices of freedom are in conformity with **man's true good** and thus express the **voluntary ordering** of the person towards his **ultimate end**: God himself, the supreme good in whom man finds his full and perfect happiness.[40]

---

38. See VS, no. 78.
39. VS, no. 71.
40. VS, no. 72.

Rational ordering to good/truth as different from its voluntary pursuit.

At the level of intention, note here the explicit difference between the intentional ordination to the complete good of the person (the voluntary pursuit of the good) and intentional ordination to the ultimate end in God (the voluntary ordering to the ultimate end).[41]

The rational ordering of the human act to the good in its truth and the voluntary pursuit of that good, known by reason, constitute morality. Hence human activity cannot be judged as morally good merely because it is a means for attaining one or another of its goals, or simply because the subject's intention is good. Activity is morally good when it attests to and expresses the voluntary ordering of the person to his ultimate end and the conformity of a concrete action with the human good as it is acknowledged in its truth by reason. If the object of the concrete action is not in harmony with the true good of the person, the choice of that action makes our will and ourselves morally evil, thus putting us in conflict with our ultimate end, the supreme good, God himself.[42]

Deliberate ordering to the ultimate end as a teleological character of moral life.

The moral life has an essential "teleological" character, since it consists in the **deliberate ordering of human acts to God**, the supreme good and **ultimate end** (telos) of man.[43]

Capable of being ordered (*ordinabilità*):

But this ordering to one's ultimate end is **not** something **subjective**, dependent solely upon one's intention. It presupposes that such acts are in themselves capable of being ordered to this end, insofar as they are in conformity with the **authentic moral good of man**, safeguarded by the commandments.[44]

The reason why a good intention is not itself sufficient, but a correct choice of actions is also needed, is that the human act depends on its **object**, whether that object is **capable or not of being ordered** to God, to the One who "alone is good," and thus brings about the perfection of the person. An act is therefore good if its

---

41. This distinction resembles the classical concepts of imperfect and perfect happiness: see Thomas Aquinas, *Summa Theologiae* (*ST*) I-II, q. 5. As we are about to see in the quotations below, the moral life's teleology is referred to both concepts.
42. VS, no. 72.
43. VS, no. 73.
44. VS, no. 73.

object is **in conformity with the good of the person with respect for the goods morally relevant for him**. Christian ethics, which pays particular attention to the moral object, does not refuse to consider the inner "teleology" of acting, inasmuch as it is directed to promoting the **true good of the person**;[45] but it recognizes that it is really pursued only **when the essential elements of human nature are respected**. The human act, **good** according to its object, is also **capable** of being ordered to its ultimate end. That same act then attains its ultimate and decisive perfection when the will actually does order it to God through charity.[46]

Needless to say, this methodology is completely extraneous to the possibility of depriving concrete acts of the possibility of an ethical evaluation independent of the intentionality of the agent.

Sources of Morality and the Object of the Moral Action

The crucial element of the doctrine of intrinsically evil acts depends on the analysis of the so-called sources of morality (object, intention, circumstances) and, in particular, on the "doctrine of the object as a source of morality."[47] Let's now address directly this doctrine.

First, I need to focus on two basic conceptual elements related to the will and to the correct angle to be used. *Veritatis Splendor* wants us to keep in mind that the will is always involved in the action and that we need to always assume the perspective of the acting agent. This is how it expresses these two points.

The will is involved in its choices:

Some authors do not take into sufficient consideration the fact that *the will is involved in the concrete choices* which it makes: these choices are a condition of its moral goodness and its being ordered to the ultimate end of the person.[48]

The perspective of the acting person:

The morality of the human act depends primarily and fundamentally on the "**object**" rationally chosen by the deliberate will, as is borne out by the insightful analysis, still valid today, made by Saint Thomas [I-II, q. 18, a. 6] In order to be able to

---

45. Here the teleological character of moral life is seen in relation to imperfect happiness.
46. VS, no. 78.
47. VS, no. 82.
48. VS, no. 75.

grasp the object of an act which specifies that act morally, it is therefore necessary to **place oneself in the perspective of the acting person**.[49]

These points represent at the same time the strength of the argument and its greater exposure to criticism. Indeed, the object is supposed to be the technical element that allows us to consider an act good or evil independently from the other sources of morality (intention and circumstances). But the will's involvement and the "perspective of the acting person" seem to have those elements back in through the back door.[50] Can or cannot the object be described or identified independently of the specific intention and circumstances of the moral agent?

We Do It All the Time in Court Trials

As difficult as this problem may appear, we solved it long time ago in our legal systems. In fact, in courts of justice, we always evaluate human acts as objectively good or evil before evaluating the intention of the agent.

Imagine that you have to deal with a criminal law case, perhaps a murder. The defendant's crime analysis takes place through a three-step process.

1. First, we need to evaluate whether there is a **material cause/effect connection** between the death event and the presumed technical/material cause (gun, stone, drug, etc.). It is in fact possible that the defendant wanted to kill but used tools unable to do so (candy instead of poison) and that the victim died from a different cause, perhaps a stroke. This analysis concerns the "event" that took place in the world, which could hypothetically be the object of the criminal action of the defendant. This event has a material cause/effect structure—external to the defendant—that needs to be studied and understood before shifting the focus to the "human" element.

2. Second, we need to evaluate whether the material event (cause/

---

49. VS, no. 78.
50. To further study these aspects of the theory of action from the Thomistic point of view used by *Veritatis Splendor*, useful bibliography includes Stephen Brock, *Action and Conduct* (Edinburgh: T&T Clark, 1998); Steven A. Long, *The Teleological Grammar of the Moral Act* (Naples, FL: Sapientia Press, 2007); and Steven J. Jensen, *Good and Evil Actions* (Washington, DC: Catholic University of America Press, 2010).

effect: the administration of the poison that killed the victim) is attributable to a voluntary act by the accused. It is possible, for example, that the defendant can only be connected to the event *materially* because he was sleepwalking or drunk or thought the poison was a candy. In such a case, the material event that occurred in the world cannot be interpreted as part of a *human* action.

3. The Italian penal code treats this analysis under the label "causality relationship" as part of the study of the "objective" element of the crime:

> No one can be punished for a fact envisaged by law as a crime, if the damaging or dangerous event on which the existence of the crime depends is not a consequence of his act or omission. Not preventing an event, which one has a legal obligation to prevent, is equivalent to causing it.[51]

If the causality relationship exists, numbers 1 and 2 allow the material event to be qualified as a homicide precisely by placing it in the "perspective of the acting person," and independently of the specific purpose for which the defendant wanted to kill.

The crime is therefore qualified based on a chosen event, which as "chosen" becomes the "object" of the act, and which coincides with the *material structure* of the *external event*. The reason for this qualification is that the free agent, by accepting the cause/effect event, and by making that event his own in terms of the proximate end of his action, turns it into a human action. In other words, the material cause/effect event becomes "murder" (or contraception, or adultery, etc.) when number 1 and number 2 match.[52]

The will is involved. Again, "Some authors do not take into sufficient consideration the fact that **the will is involved** in the concrete choices which it makes: these choices are a condition of its moral goodness and its being ordered to the ultimate end of the person."[53]

---

51. Italian penal code, art. 40 (*causality relationship*).

52. Of course, the causality connection—and the analysis according to the *chosen* event—exists also in case of faulty or negligent behavior. For example, anyone who kills by violating traffic laws has essentially chosen the possibility of murder by their dangerous conduct. It is a less evil action than willful homicide, but it is still a human action responsible for someone's death.

53. VS, no. 75.

1. Third, we need to evaluate the "subjective" element of the crime,[54] which includes the specific purpose for which the accused wanted to kill, and which could imply excuses, aggravating or mitigating circumstances, and the like. This analysis reveals the *internal act* of the defendant's will, which defines him more as a person but does not alter the qualification and nature of the *external* act he has agreed to perform (or to possibly cause in terms of negligence).

2. In Aquinas's words:

Now that which is on the part of the will is formal in regard to that which is on the part of the **external action**: because the will uses the limbs to act as instruments; nor have external actions any measure of morality, save in so far as they are voluntary. Consequently the species of a human act is considered **formally** with regard to the end, but **materially** with regard to the object of the external action. Hence the Philosopher says (Ethic. v, 2) that "he who steals that he may commit adultery, is strictly speaking, more adulterer than thief."[55]

This passage by Aquinas is the very one used by *Veritatis Splendor*. Its key meaning should now be obvious. Whatever the reason for stealing, it is qualified as theft because it can be traced back to a human agent, who is "more adulterer" but who is also a thief. The internal action (the true intention, if you like) tells us more about the agent, but the external qualifies him too because theft is part of his action.

The external action, in contrast, is not qualified by the internal if not accidentally. Imagine a murderer who wants to kill and is convinced that he has killed, but the victim was already dead. Shame on her, but case dismissed. Incidentally, the moral relevance of external action should never be underestimated. In an episode of the television show *House*,[56] a woman was tormented by the thought that she had caused the death of her son, who died in a car accident after she had allowed him to try driving the car. Her guilt is finally relieved when House (lying) tells her that the accident was a mere coincidence because her son had died instantly, before the accident, from a rare dis-

---

54. Clearly, "subjective" here does not involve relativism. It only relates to the crime's elements that belong to the agent as such.
55. *ST* I-II, q. 18, a. 6 c.
56. *House,* season 7, episode 3, "Unwritten."

ease. This episode shows well how moral intention (and/or the internal action) is never indifferent to reality. A person who really wanted to kill but didn't kill is not a murderer in the same way as the one who actually killed, and moral conscience feels the difference very well.

Describing the Action May Be Difficult

Anyone who has faced concrete legal cases in a court of law knows how difficult it can sometimes be to describe human action. Similar difficulties exist in all sciences. In biology, there are cases in which it is not even clear whether we are dealing with a marine plant or an animal species. These difficulties do not undermine the difference between vegetative life and animal life—they only reveal the magnificent complexity of reality. Similarly, the difficulties of describing some human actions do not imply that it is impossible to do so. The underlying logic still stands strong.

Sometimes, for example, the external (material) reality to describe involves already a human reality. Think of stealing. The objective description of this crime:

1. presupposes a principle that determines who is the owner of something and
2. requires an assessment of the state of need of the alleged thief—a state that affects his intention (does he want to steal or save his life?).

Determining who owns what implies an objective interpretation of human reality. For example, in many legal systems since ancient Rome, a recognized way of acquiring property is having found something (*invenio*) or having taken possession of a piece of land (*occupatio*). Under certain conditions accepted by law, these forms of acquiring property are protected and recognized as objective facts of human reality from which consequences of intersubjective justice derive. Another generally recognized principle is that movable objects are presumed to be the property of whoever possesses them. Therefore, as an example interpretation of an event as theft, it may initially be sufficient to note that someone has taken a fruit from the tree in someone else's garden without being authorized. This is an objective interpretation of human reality. Yet human reality of private property also implies the (deeper than *invenio* or *occupatio*) principle of the universal destination of goods, according to which the goods of the earth must serve the needs of all. Therefore, if a person were so hungry as to need food immediately, taking fruit from any tree would not imply theft because that fruit would be his more than anyone else's. This too is an objective interpretation of human action that, however, requires the interpretation of the alleged thief's state of need. The state of need could make it impossible to objectively qualify the action in terms of theft.[57]

This interpretation (concerning both the state of need and the principles of private property) does not imply the analysis of the agent's intention. In order to possibly define the action as theft, the internal action of the agent does not matter. Perhaps he wanted to stay strong or alive so he could help his son or commit murder. Whether he is an ugly or beautiful person, the action he has performed will be characterized as theft or not based solely on the objective features of the external action (which involves the will).

It should also come as no surprise that the objective description of the action requires certain circumstances, such as the fact that the stolen thing belongs to someone else. "Circumstance" is an analogical term that, in the theory of action (in the sources of morality), indicates relevant elements as distinct from the end and the object. It is the same logical procedure that is used in other disciplines. The circumstance that insects have "jointed feet" classifies them as arthropods. The fact that some insects have hard wings (elytra) classifies them as beetles. The classification of species logically requires understanding which circumstances are essential and which are accidental. The essential ones define (are part of the object). Law does the same with crimes and torts, and Thomas Aquinas did the same to explain, in general terms, the theory of human action.

Let's briefly shift our focus to other examples to better understand the possible complexity of the objective description. Imagine having to materially describe a context of murder. What if the alleged murderer is rather a victim who was trying to defend himself? Should the person killed be described as a victim or as an aggressor? These doubts pertain to the

---

57. Today's legal systems do not need to explicitly understand the principle of the universal destination of goods in this specific context. They just need to include in their rules a way not to punish crimes based on the state of necessity. The Italian system does it, for example. with article 54 of the penal code mentioned above, which is labeled precisely as "State of necessity."

objective description of the action, not to subjective elements. Materially speaking, the aggressor is not such because of his intentions but because of how he appears in the picture, so to speak. Even the case of error, in which the aggressor was not really an aggressor, normally results in favor of the defendant only if the objective circumstances were such as to lead to error. The material, objective context, in other words, had to be such that a person of ordinary diligence would have mistaken the victim for an aggressor.

Again, is the material context a sexual intercourse or a rape? Is it violence or mere shared pursuit of sexual pleasure? Was there a "pressure which overstrains human nature and which no one could withstand," which for Aristotle would make the action involuntary? Did the defendant kill the rapist in self-defense or kill a sexual partner without legitimacy? These doubts, too, need to be addressed at the objective level of the action before wondering about real or possible intentions.

This analysis affects every scenario. Think of contraception. Is this specific device both a contraceptive and a medicine? What is the context of its specific use, sexual or medical? This context is not merely the external reality as such (like in the first step of the analysis described in the previous section); it is the external cause/effect reality as traced back to a human action. Yet was the will "involved" in a sexual act or in a medical act? This too is a question that pertains to the objective description of the action even if it requires the perspective of the acting person.

Condemnation of Those Who Deny Intrinsically Evil Acts

Let us now quickly read how *Veritatis Splendor* condemns theories that deny intrinsically evil acts using both Aquinas's analysis of the moral act according to species and object, and consistently using the logical elements that we have distinguished in the previous sections.

First condemnation:

One must therefore reject the thesis, characteristic of teleological and proportionalist theories, which holds that it is impossible to qualify as morally evil according to its **species**—its **"object"**—the deliberate choice of certain kinds of behaviour or specific acts, apart from a consideration of the intention for which the choice is made or the totality of the foreseeable consequences of that act for all persons concerned.[58]

Based on the doctrine of the object and the non-orderability:

The primary and decisive element for moral judgment is the object of the human act, which establishes whether it is capable of being ordered to the good and to the ultimate end, which is God.[59]

Based on the overall good of the person:

This capability is grasped by reason in the very being of man, considered in his **integral truth**, and therefore in his natural inclinations, his motivations and his finalities, which always have a spiritual dimension as well. It is precisely these which are the contents of the **natural law** and hence that ordered complex of "personal goods" which serve the "**good of the person**": the good which is the person himself and his perfection. These are the goods safeguarded by the commandments, which, according to Saint Thomas, contain the whole natural law.[60]

Reason attests that there are objects of the human act which are by their nature "incapable of being ordered" to God, because they radically contradict the good of the person made in his image.[61]

Example of contraception and quotation from Paul VI:

With regard to intrinsically evil acts, and **in reference to contraceptive practices** whereby the conjugal act is intentionally rendered infertile, **Pope Paul VI teaches**: Though it is true that sometimes it is lawful to tolerate a lesser moral evil in order to avoid a greater evil or in order to promote a greater good, it is never lawful, even for the gravest reasons, to do evil that good may come of it (cf. Rom 3:8)—in other words, to intend directly something which of its very nature contradicts the moral order, and which must therefore be judged unworthy of man, even though the intention is to protect or promote the welfare of an individual, of a family or of society in general.[62]

---

58. VS, no. 79.
59. VS, no. 79.
60. VS, no. 79.
61. VS, no. 80.
62. VS, no. 80.

Reiteration of the condemnation in relation to the doctrine of the object:

The doctrine of the object as a source of morality represents an authentic explicitation of the Biblical morality of the Covenant and of the commandments, of charity and of the virtues. The moral quality of human acting is dependent on this fidelity to the commandments, as an expression of obedience and of love. For this reason—we repeat—the opinion must be rejected as erroneous which maintains that it is impossible to qualify as morally evil according to its species the deliberate choice of certain kinds of behaviour or specific acts, without taking into account the intention for which the choice was made or the totality of the foreseeable consequences of that act for all persons concerned.[63]

Conclusion

In this chapter, I explained the essential conceptual elements that, in the mind of *Veritatis Splendor* (and not of individual authors who may legitimately express their specific points of view on the matter), underlie the doctrine of intrinsically evil acts and justify the condemnation of anyone who tries to undermine its meaning both in theory and in practice.

I began from some crucial aspects that express the depth and beauty of Greek moral thought from which the Fathers of the Church and the entire Christian tradition drew. The goal was to show (as *Veritatis Splendor* itself does) that the doctrine of intrinsically evil acts is neither dry nor abstract but expresses and defends the true dignity and beauty of the human being. The connection between moral good and beauty is one of the aspects that was most important to me to recover and express.

From *Veritatis Splendor*, in the second structural phase of my discussion (see the Key Conceptual Background section), I tried to draw and summarize the concepts essential to the argument. In this phase, reconnecting with the practical sense of moral science, I highlighted the relevance of the argument compared to the current attempts to change or criticize the doctrine. These attempts (besides a certain ethical ugliness) show a profound misunderstanding of the very foundations of the moral order and of the human condition. In spite of their words, they express an abstract, dry, and lowly view of human existence, especially compared

---

63. VS, no. 82.

to the higher perspective of the new law and grace, to our call to be God's friends and walk with Him.

Finally, in the central part of the chapter (see The Morality of Human Acts section), I showed, in the most descriptive and simplest way possible, the logical steps of *Veritatis Splendor*'s argument, and the way these steps make use of the key concepts of the encyclical. My main goal here was to show both the meaning and reasonableness of the analysis of the action according to its object or species. To do this, I mainly used legal science and the typical way of dealing with crimes in the courts of justice.

Just as happens in trial cases, the simplicity and reasonableness of the doctrine of the moral object does not imply that it is equally easy to analyze and understand concrete cases and individual evil actions. Yet as difficult as it may be for philosophers and theologians to explain why some acts are intrinsically evil, the commitment to do so is praiseworthy and necessary if we want to preserve the dignity of the person and the possibility of an objective moral order. Fortunately, we Catholics are not blind in this search because the Magisterium shows us the way.

CHAPTER 7

The Infallibility of the Church's Teaching on Contraception

JOHN FINNIS

That the Church, protected by divine assistance from error, has taught a number of specific moral precepts of the natural and revealed moral law, such as the wrongness of contracepting conjugal intercourse, is a truth stated straightforwardly by Karl Rahner SJ in 1950, in his little German book *Gefahren im heutigen Katholizismus* (*Dangers in Catholicism Today*). Originally one of the first three or four books put out by Hans Urs von Balthasar's new publishing house (Johannes-Verlag, Einselden), it had a second edition in 1954 and a third in 1955, and was translated in New York and London as *Nature and Grace*, with an imprimatur dated January 1963, just after the end of the Second Vatican Council's first session.[1] The most relevant pages, in the section "Appeal to Conscience," are in the subsection "Situation-Ethics." There, on pages 98–100, Rahner firmly says:

First of all, it goes without saying for Catholics ... that ... [t]he fulfilment of the Commandments is an essential part of Christianity as such ... Furthermore, the Church teaches these commandments with divine authority exactly as she teaches the other "truths of the Faith," either through her "ordinary" magisterium or through an act of her "extraordinary" magisterium in definitions of the Pope [*ex cathedra*] or [of] a general council. But also through her ordinary magisterium, that

---

1. Karl Rahner, SJ, "Dangers in Catholicism Today: The Appeal to Conscience," in *Nature and Grace: Dilemmas in the Modern Church* (New York: Sheed & Ward, 1964). The original German of the essay is in vol. 10 (1995) of his thirty-two-volume *Sämtliche Werke*, edited by Karl Lehmann (Freiburg-im-Breisgau: Herder, 1995).

is in the normal teaching of the Faith to the faithful in schools, sermons and all the other kinds of instruction. In the nature of the case this will be the normal way in which moral norms are taught, and definitions of Pope or general council [will be] the exception; but it [the teaching of the ordinary magisterium] is binding on the faithful in conscience just as the teaching through the extraordinary magisterium is. It is therefore quite untrue that only those moral norms for which there is a solemn definition (and these are criticised from all sides in the "world") are binding in faith on the Christian as revealed by God, and must be accepted by him as the rule for his own behaviour ... When the whole Church in her everyday teaching does in fact teach a moral rule everywhere in the world as a commandment of God, she is preserved from error by the assistance of the Holy Ghost, [i.e., her teaching of this moral rule is infallible] and this rule is therefore really the will of God and is binding on the faithful in conscience, even before it has been expressly confirmed by a solemn definition.

... And so when it is fully grasped and rightly understood and interpreted (that is, understood as the magisterium means it, not just as an individual thinks fit to interpret it), and bears on an individual case, then this unique individual concrete case is bound by the norm and obliged to abide by it. When, for example, the Church teaches that *every* directly induced abortion is morally wrong ... then this applies to *every* individual case quite regardless of the circumstances [the German says: whatever the concrete circumstances as they exist and are experienced].[2]

On page 74 of the same little book, in a section called "The Individual in the Church," Rahner gives another example:

Where universal norms are possible they cannot be appealed against in the name of individual conscience. If induced abortion or contraception [*Misbrauch der Ehe*, abuse of marriage] can be universally recognized as morally wrong and are declared to be morally wrong by the Church, then there is no appeal against this in the name of individual conscience.

My topic in this essay is not the extensive criticisms that Rahner leveled in these preconciliar writings against attempts to find warrant in such "appeals to individual conscience," or in the alleged impossibility of compliance, for doing acts—such as direct abortion or contraception (to take his examples)—that are exceptionlessly excluded by precepts. My topic is Rahner's affirmation of the infallibility of the Church's teaching that identifies such kinds of act as always wrong. He articulated that affirmation

---

2. The emphases are Rahner's.

of infallibility well, as we saw above: "When the whole Church in her everyday teaching does in fact teach a moral rule everywhere in the world as a commandment of God, she is preserved from error by the assistance of the Holy Ghost." That is, these teachings are certainly true.

Rahner took it to be obvious—or obviously taught by the Church[3]—that there are some specific moral norms that have been defined by a pope or Council. His remark that *these* defined norms are "criticised from all sides in the 'world'" suggests that he had in mind the teaching of Pius XI, in the encyclical *Casti Connubii* in 1931, that every act of conjugal intercourse [*quilibet matrimonii usus*] done "in such a way that it is intentionally deprived of its natural power to generate life contravenes the law of God and of nature." For the centerpiece of *Casti Connubii*'s paragraphs against contracepting conjugal intercourse certainly *could* be called a solemn definition. Referring unmistakably to the resolution of the Anglican Lambeth Conference in 1930, cautiously departing from a teaching that Conference of Anglican bishops worldwide had reaffirmed without equivocation twice in the preceding twenty-one years, Pius XI declared:

Since, therefore, some—openly departing from a Christian doctrine handed on from the beginning, without any break—have recently thought to preach another doctrine about the kind of act in question, the Catholic Church, mandated by God to teach and defend moral integrity and rightness, raises its voice in the midst of this moral ruin in token of this divine ambassadorship, and—to keep the chastity of the conjugal bond undefiled by this guilt and dishonour—through Our mouth proclaims again: any and every act of conjugal intercourse [*quemlibet matrimonii usum*] done in such a way that it is intentionally [*de industria hominum*] deprived of its [that act's] natural power to generate life contravenes the law of God and of nature, and those who so act incur the guilt of serious wrongdoing.[4]

---

3. He says on page 95 of *Nature and Grace* that the following pages will try to give the Church's teaching, in its basic principles, from which he gives no hint of dissenting.

4. The English translation still to be found on the Vatican website and elsewhere is rhetorical and inexact. Here are the Latin and the Italian:

Cum igitur quidam, a christiana doctrina iam inde ab initio tradita neque umquam intermissa manifesto recedentes, aliam nuper de hoc agendi modo doctrinam sollemniter praedicandam censuerint, Ecclesia Catholica, cui ipse Deus morum integritatem honestatemque docendam et defendendam commisit, in media hac morum ruina posita, ut nuptialis foederis castimoniam a turpi hac labe immunem servet, in signum legationis suae divinae, altam per os Nostrum extollit vocem atque denuo promulgat: quemlibet matrimonii usum, in quo exercendo, actus, de industria hominum, naturali sua vitae procreandae vi destituatur, Dei et naturae legem infringere, et eos qui tale quid commiserint gravis noxae labe commaculari.

But we cannot be completely sure that the specific moral norm exceptionlessly excluding contraception was what Rahner had in mind when he referred to moral norms defined by the extraordinary Magisterium despite the world's opposition; for alongside direct abortion and contraception, he mentioned the attempted dissolution of any "sacramentally contracted and consummated marriage between two baptized persons."[5] But no matter: Rahner's purpose at this point, like mine, is to set aside the question whether such moral *definitions, ex cathedra*, by pope or Council, are to be found and are few or many, and to go directly to the main point.

Which is this: there are a considerable number of moral teachings, by the *ordinary* Magisterium, that have been protected by God from error. For, as we have just seen Rahner say: "it is ... quite untrue that only those moral norms for which there is a solemn definition ... are binding in faith on the Christian as revealed by God.... When the whole Church in her everyday teaching does in fact teach a moral rule everywhere in the world as a commandment of God, she is preserved from error ... and this rule is therefore really the will of God and is binding on the faithful in conscience, even before it has been expressly confirmed by a solemn definition."

The point Rahner was making in those sentences about *this* category of teaching preserved from error was sound, but his description of this category or mode or kind of infallible teaching was a bit vague. It is a category and mode identified and affirmed by Vatican I as one of the three modes/categories/kinds of infallible teaching, and was well articulated in then-classic theological textbooks, some of them by experts involved in the drafting of the relevant teaching documents promulgated by Vatican II (as indeed Rahner too was involved). In 1964, the Dogmatic

---

Pertanto, essendovi alcuni che, abbandonando manifestamente la cristiana dottrina, insegnata fin dalle origini, né mai modificata, hanno ai giorni nostri, in questa materia, preteso pubblicamente proclamarne un'altra, la Chiesa Cattolica, cui lo stesso Dio affidò il mandato di insegnare e difendere la purità e la onestà dei costumi, considerando l'esistenza di tanta corruttela di costumi, al fine di preservare la castità del consorzio nuziale da tanta turpitudine, proclama altamente, per mezzo della Nostra parola, in segno della sua divina missione, e nuovamente sentenzia che qualsivoglia uso del matrimonio, in cui per la umana malizia l'atto sia destituito della sua naturale virtù procreatrice, va contro la legge di Dio e della natura, e che coloro che osino commettere tali azioni, si rendono rei di colpa grave.

5. *Nature and Grace*, 100.

Constitution on the Church, *Lumen Gentium*, set out in section 25 the category's four necessary and sufficient elements: bishops, even if they are scattered throughout the world (provided they maintain communion with each other and the pope), "infallibly proclaim the teaching of Christ" when "[i] authoritatively teaching [ii] matters of faith and morals, they [iii] agree in one judgment [iv] as that to be held definitively." But just as Vatican I's definition of the necessary and sufficient conditions for an infallible papal definition is accompanied by the statement of an assumption or axiom, so Vatican II's statement of the necessary and sufficient conditions for the bishops to teach infallibly while scattered throughout the world is accompanied (two sentences later) by a statement of that same axiom or assumption, applicable to all three categories/kinds/modes of infallible teaching. The axiom is this: where a doctrine of faith or morals has been infallibly taught, it is because it pertains to revelation, *either* by being more or less directly or expressly revealed, *or* (though not as such revealed) simply by being important for the articulating and expounding (*exponendum*) and the safeguarding (*custodiendum*) of what is revealed in a strict sense. Writing recently with Christian Brugger, I counted that as a fifth criterion, a fifth necessary condition. But that was mistaken. To be entitled and required to conclude that a particular proposition has been taught by the infallible ordinary Magisterium, one need only find that the four conditions specified by *Lumen Gentium* 25 are satisfied. LG 25 then, two sentences later, tells us the axiom, which applies like this: *any* doctrine that can rightly be judged to have been infallibly taught (by papal definition, conciliar definition, or the bishops scattered through the world) *will certainly belong* to the class of all those doctrines and only those doctrines that, in the words of the drafting committee's final explanation, "either directly belong to the revealed deposit itself, or are required to guard as inviolable and expound with fidelity this same deposit."

I will show how the four conditions and their accompanying axiom apply to the teaching about contraception. But first we should not overlook the preliminary phrase about the subjects, the bishops doing this teaching: they can do it "even if—*etiam*, also when—they are scattered throughout the world." The half-hidden point of the "even" or "also" is that bishops in communion with the pope and with each other *can* when meeting in Council (and there agreeing teaching declarations) *give witness and evidence* about how they *have been* exercising this ordinary Magisterium while scattered throughout the world. Their conciliar deliberation and teaching can provide good evidence of the fact that, before assembling in Council, they were, throughout the world, teaching a proposition in a way that satisfies the four conditions. For example, the bishops in Vatican II *evidenced* their long-standing and continuing exercise of this infallible ordinary (nonconciliar) Magisterium when they issued (as a Council) the teaching contained in section 51 of the Pastoral Constitution on the Church in the Modern World, *Gaudium et Spes* (GS).

That section begins with a frank recognition of the difficulties of periodic or indefinitely prolonged abstinence, difficulties that can sometimes imperil faithfulness and endanger the upbringing of the children and the courage to accept new ones. The passage has latterly been quoted out of context, with a *suggestio falsi* that the Council was putting in place a premise for consequentialist/proportionalist/situationist reasoning toward an amending or abandoning of the teaching against contraception. But the bishops at Vatican II were not proportionalists or situationists, and this was in reality their preface, their preliminary, first to saying that there are immoral ways (*viae inhonestae*) of trying to surmount these difficulties and their genuine bad consequences, and second to restating their common teaching that contraception is one of those immoral ways—and to restating it in a way that shows that (as they had been teaching everywhere) this is a Catholic doctrine that the faithful must hold and adhere to, in judgment and practice, in a manner that can be summed up with the word "definitively." The bishops in Council do not use that word, but what they say about contraception is this:

When there is a question of harmonizing marital love with the responsible transmission of life, the moral aspect of whatever is done ... must be determined by objective standards [*obiectivis criteriis*] that, based on the nature of the human person and of his or her acts, *preserve the full sense* [= full meaning] [or preserve unimpaired, *integrum*, the meaning, the signifying] *of mutual self-giving and human procreation* in the context of true love.

To make clear the *demanding* character of that moral standard, they immediately add: "This [preservation of the full sense ...] cannot be achieved unless the virtue of conjugal chastity is sincerely practised." And the following sentence states the conclusion: "Relying on these principles, [the faithful] may not [*non* licet, it is not morally permissible to] undertake methods of birth control that are found to be immoral [*improbantur*, condemned] by the teaching authority of the Church in its expounding of [*explicanda*] the divine law."

GS 50 had already said that, in considering responsible transmission of human life, one must always by ruled by a conscience that is "in conformity with the divine law" and with the Magisterium's authoritative *interpretation* "in the light of the gospel" *of that law*—a law that displays conjugal/marital love's full meaning or full sense [*plenam significationem*]. Section 49 set out the bishops' understanding of this love, "true love between husband and wife," a mutual commitment that pervades their whole life but is "in a unique way *expressed* [*exprimitur*] and fulfilled in the activity that properly belongs to marriage ... acts by which the spouses are intimately and chastely united ... and which *signify* [*significant*] and nourish their mutual self-giving," acts that as "*expressions* [*expressiones*] of body and mind" are "elements and special *signs* [*signa*] of conjugal friendship." And now, in section 51, the Council in a long footnote recalls some magisterial identifications of ways of regulating procreation that violate—do not conform to—divine law. First up for citation are the passages I quoted and summarized from *Casti Connubii*. Second was Pius XII's famous address to the Italian Association of Midwives, in 1951:

Pius XI, in ... *Casti Connubii* ... solemnly proclaimed anew the fundamental law governing the marital act and conjugal relations; he said that any attempt on the part of the husband and wife to deprive this act of its inherent force or to impede the procreation of a new life, either in the performance of the act itself, or in the course of the development of its natural consequences, is immoral, and furthermore, no alleged "indication" or need can convert an intrinsically immoral act into a moral and lawful one.

This precept is as valid today as it was yesterday, and it will be the same tomorrow and always, because it does not involve a precept of human law but is the expression of a law which is natural and divine.

Singly and together, these statements and citations by Vatican II amount to saying that that precept (norm), as distinct from explanations and expositions of it such as GS 51 sketches, has been set out to the faithful by their bishops throughout the world as a precept (norm) that any

Catholic must definitively hold—that is, as an inseparable and on the evidence irreversible element in adhering to the Catholic faith as true.

And as a matter of historical fact, and of sound theological analysis, all four conditions for infallible teaching by the ordinary Magisterium of bishops throughout the world are certainly fulfilled, as John C. Ford, SJ, and Germain Grisez demonstrated with precision in their 1978 essay "Contraception and the Infallibility of the Ordinary Magisterium" in *Theological Studies*, vindicated in detail by Grisez in his responses to various Jesuit critics in *The Thomist* in 1985 and *Theological Studies* in 1986, and in his 1994 *Theological Studies* reply to further criticism (again by the Gregorian's specialist on ecclesiology and the Magisterium, Francis Sullivan SJ)—all available to everyone today with a few keystrokes on Grisez's posthumously maintained website, twotlj.org.

When we take up the first four conditions in LG 25, it is obvious that the first three are all easily satisfied, fulfilled, met in relation to the teaching against contracepting conjugal intercourse: "[i] authoritatively teaching [ii] matters of faith and morals, they [iii] agree in one judgment." Ford and Grisez point to six kinds of evidence confirming the conclusion reached in 1964 by John T. Noonan in his 600-page study of the history of Catholic teaching on contraception (despite his own keen hope that he might find evidence giving support for substantial change, abandoning the exceptionlessness of the moral condemnation). In Noonan's words,

> [from the fourth century] the teachers of the Church have taught without hesitation or variation that certain acts preventing procreation are gravely sinful. No Catholic theologian has ever taught, "Contraception is a good act." The teaching on contraception is clear and apparently fixed forever.[6]

The six heads of evidence summarized by Ford and Grisez are, first, Western and Eastern Fathers; second, many bishops, some of them saints, some doctors of the Church; third, canon law's penalization, from the thirteenth century to 1917, of the moral crime of giving or taking drugs of sterility, whether abortifacient or simply to prevent conception, defining this kind of contraception in terms replicated in the moral teaching of the *Catechism of the Council of Trent*; fourth, the constant consensus of the nineteenth- and twentieth-century moral theology textbooks approved

---

6. John T. Noonan, *Contraception* (Cambridge, MA: Harvard University Press, 1965), 6.

by bishops for use in their seminaries "for the training of confessors who communicated Catholic moral teaching to the faithful in the confessional, in premarital instructions, in the preaching of missions, and so on," and so made these approved authors a mediated form of exercise of the bishops' teaching authority; fifth, from say 1816 to 1962, many statements by bishops, by national groups of bishops, and by organs of the Holy See; and sixth, the absence of any significant negative reaction within the Catholic Church to the statements in which Pius XI and Pius XII summed up and reaffirmed this existing consensus, and the many manifestations of support for those statements in episcopal public statements, organizing or supporting of family life programs, and so forth.

What about LG 25's condition or criterion [iv], that the position is proposed as to be held definitively? Ford and Grisez point first to the fact that the teaching always was proposed as a received and certain part of the obligatory moral teaching of the Church; second, that the teaching always has been that acts intended to render intercourse sterile are the matter of mortal sin endangering salvation; third, that when challenged by other Christians, it was insisted upon as true, certain, and integral to Catholic belief; and fourth, that it was often proposed as not only required by human reason ("nature") but also as revealed, a thesis that, regardless of its correctness, implied that the teaching was to be held definitively. All these elements in the transmission of the teaching were repeated, articulated, shared in, and contributed to by the great papal statements of Pius XI and Pius XII—and, in a cooler linguistic register but firmly and insistently, by Paul VI in *Humanae Vitae*. And in sum, as Ford and Grisez say:

> A point of teaching surely is proposed as one to be held definitively if a bishop proposes it in the following way: not at his option but as part of his duty to hand on the teaching he has received; not as doubtful or even as very probable but as certainly true; and not as one which the faithful are free to accept or to reject but as one which every Catholic must accept.

None of the first set of seven points made by Ford and Grisez, concerning the first three conditions, has been seriously challenged. There were some attempts, notably by Francis Sullivan, to contest the effectiveness of the five arguments to show the fulfilling of condition [iv], that the teaching against contraception was proposed as *to be held definitively* (*definitive tenenda*). These attempts were rebutted easily enough, it seems to me, by Grisez.

The weight of the theological pushback against the Ford-Grisez thesis and against the infallible status of the teaching against contraception came from a sudden, unapologetically radical shifting of ground by a good many theologians, to a theological position unheard of in 1962, or 1966, or even in 1968, a new paradigm fully developed between 1968 and 1975: the position that *no* specific moral norm, about any kind of action whatever, can be infallibly taught by the ordinary Magisterium because no such norm could be infallibly taught at all, even by conciliar definition or papal definition *ex cathedra*; and revelation includes no such norm, whether against contraception, abortion, suicide, killing the innocent, sodomy, bestiality, self-abuse, or adultery. Statements in sources of revelation about, say, adultery do no more (on this view) than invite and orient a theological inquiry into the goods and values beyond the norm—beyond because both deeper and higher than the norm, which therefore can and should be surpassed and set aside whenever adherence to it would, in the circumstances actual and foreseeable, be—or be judged or opined to be—prejudicial on balance and in the long run to those values, that is, would in the circumstances be disproportionate. And this new paradigm (perhaps without the flattery of that phrase) was blandly declared by those concerned to be—now, in the mid-1970s—the consensus of the majority of moral theologians, or of theologians generally (it was said).

So this new paradigm was the crisis that elicited from John Paul II the carefully considered response that is the primary purpose and teaching of his 1993 encyclical *Veritatis Splendor*, by far his most notable act of teaching and one that, precisely because it responds in a Catholic and apostolic way to this defection of Catholic theologians, is too often not acknowledged by those whom it most concerns—all who have or mediate or oversee the episcopal responsibility of handing on the faith. *Veritatis Splendor* unambiguously reaffirmed the existence of kinds of acts that, by reason of their object (i.e., by reason of the precise content of the choice that adopts the proposal-for-action that the choosing person shaped in deliberation as a proposed means), are intrinsically wrong whatever the circumstances or the good intentions of the acting person. Equally unambiguously, the encyclical pointed to the error in various ways of attempting to evade the binding applicability of those specific exceptionless moral norms or precepts that identify actions of those kinds—and direct us unconditionally to exclude such proposals from our deliberations—never to choose them.

Veritatis Splendor, regrettably I think, does not address the infallibility of the Church's identification of instances of such norms or precepts. It treated that matter as sufficiently addressed in the Congregation for the Doctrine of the Faith's *Instruction on the Ecclesial Vocation of the Theologian*, adopted by the plenary congregation, signed by its Prefect Cardinal Ratzinger and approved and ordered to be published by John Paul II on Ascension Day 1990. Here we find it affirmed that:

[16] By its nature, the task of religiously guarding and loyally expounding the deposit of divine Revelation (in all its integrity and purity), implies that the Magisterium can make a pronouncement "in a definitive way" on propositions which, even if not contained among the truths of faith, are nonetheless intimately connected with them, in such a way, that the definitive character of such affirmations derives in the final analysis from revelation itself.

What concerns morality can also be the object of the authentic Magisterium because the Gospel, being the Word of Life, inspires and guides the whole sphere of human behavior. The Magisterium, therefore, has the task of discerning, by means of judgments normative for the consciences of believers, those acts which in themselves conform to the demands of faith and foster their expression in life and those which, on the contrary, **because intrinsically evil**, are incompatible with such demands. By reason of the connection between the orders of creation and redemption and by reason of the necessity, in view of salvation, of knowing and observing the whole moral law, the competence of the Magisterium also extends to that which concerns the natural law.

Revelation also contains moral teachings which *per se* could be known by natural reason.... It is a doctrine of faith that **these moral norms can be infallibly taught by the Magisterium.**

I would add that, on the question of the infallibility of the teaching on contraception by the ordinary Magisterium (a mode or way of teaching infallibly that is neither reaffirmed explicitly nor in any way put in doubt by the 1990 instruction), the across-the-board "mainstream" theological abandonment of the Catholic teaching on specific exceptionless moral norms, taught from the Church's very beginning in Galilee and Jerusalem, is evidence, in its backhanded way, of the strength of Ford and Grisez's argument that contraception has been dealt with irreversibly under that mode of infallibility. They had made that case to Paul VI—in a less academically articulated and buttressed way, and without mention of LG 25, but soundly and strongly—in the early weeks after the pope had received the report of the majority of his "Birth Control Commission" in June 1966. My point is this: the case was so strong that these new majority theologians could only really meet it by pulling down the pillars holding up the whole temple of moral doctrine, so far as any set of theologians can do so.

In the years before the episcopal and Petrine response in *Veritatis Splendor*, the main tracks and strategies of this error-strewn theological effort to evade the true status of the teaching against contraception were analyzed and responded to in the last chapter of my book *Moral Absolutes: Tradition, Revision and Truth* (1991) and later—again with particular focus on the use and abuse of Thomas Aquinas—in my book *Aquinas* (1998), in chapter 5, section 6, "'Prudence,' 'Virtues' and Exceptionless Specific Norms." That section leads off on pages 163–65 with an anticipatory statement of and response to precisely the striking, fallacious appeal to Aquinas that in 2016 would be made in section 304 of *Amoris Laetitia*.

But here I shall leave these swaths of a moral theology and pastoral praxis and preaching that has set aside the entire Christian and humanist tradition of specific exceptionless negative precepts; I again suggest that it constitutes a kind of testimony to or evidence of the inclusion of the precept against contraception among the specific precepts infallibly taught by the ordinary Magisterium. The majority of Paul VI's Birth Control Commission attempted to deny its inclusion by claiming that a reversal of the teaching against contraception would leave standing rationally unimpaired the many other notable specific precepts in the tradition, such as that which excludes homosexual sex acts (a kind of act that this majority claimed was against human dignity—a claim made for the occasion, for a season).

I want instead to go back to that so-called fifth condition, better understood as the doctrinal axiom that whatever is infallibly taught, in any of the three modes, is either directly revealed or important for the expounding and safeguarding of what is directly revealed. I am tempted to put back on the table what Ford and Grisez—in 1966 (in and in relation to the commission's discussions) and in 1978—took off the table when they granted (though not conceded) *both* that the teaching against contraception was not defined in *Casti Connubii and* that it is not directly revealed. I'm not saying that they should not have made these "grants for the sake of discussion," and I'm not going to try to show here that the teaching definitely *is* directly revealed or *has been* explicitly defined. The good case for thinking it was defined is developed over almost a thousand pages by Ermenegildo Lio in his 1986 Editrice Vaticana book *Humanae Vitae e Infallibilità*.

What I want to argue for now is the thought that what *has* been both directly revealed and explicitly defined in this zone—for instance, some teachings of Trent against polygamy and (as we saw Rahner mentioning) divorce—requires for its adequate exposition and defense the affirmation of the teaching that contracepting is intrinsically wrong and grave matter.

About the time that Karl Rahner in Germany was republishing his affirmation of the infallibility/irreversibility and exceptionless applicability of the precepts against direct abortion and contraception, two scholarly English priests wrote short popular explanations of just why Christian teaching judges contraception to be contrary to natural reason. D. J. B. Hawkins had written half a dozen excellent short books in the interface between Thomist and English and Scottish commonsense and analytical philosophy. In his last book, *Christian Morality*, published in 1963 shortly before his death (a real loss to English Catholicism), the relevant chapter begins its engagement with the basis of Christian sexual ethics with the "elementary observation" that

> although sexual intercourse does not always result in procreation, its adaptation to this purpose indicates its most obvious significance in human life. Hence, in harmony with the ordinary opinion of mankind, we [Catholics] condemn solitary and homosexual activity as contrary to the manifest nature of sex.... no reasonable person has any doubt that they ought to be avoided.

Then, going back to the point he had earlier made, that to prima facie generalizations—such as that killing is wrong or telling falsehoods is wrong—there are reasonable *exceptions*, he remarks that "no plausible exception can be supposed in the cases of solitary and homosexual activity; hence we may there legitimately convert our *prima facie* generalizations into strictly universal condemnations." It is after these preliminaries that he turns to consider whether the prima facie generalization that "interrupted or obstructed intercourse" is wrong is subject to plausible exceptions. I will not follow his argumentation further here, except to note that at an important point it deploys the premise that "promiscuity"—that is, intercourse to express affection between an unmarried man and woman—is obviously wrong.

And in the collective work *The Catholic Faith* published in 1958, the chapter by E. J. Mahoney on Christian marriage had begun its treatment of "birth prevention" not very differently, with the premise that "with regard to the nature and purpose of the faculty of generation, there can be no two opinions.... [it is:] supporting the [human] race," and then the prompt conclusion that "the frustration of the natural purpose of the act of generation is immoral; the immorality consists in gratifying sexual pleasure while frustrating the object of the act. Grossly unnatural vice is punished by every civil code, and between actions of this kind punishable by law, and actions which frustrate the purpose of natural sexual relations, there is only a difference of degree."

Each of these two highly unsatisfactory sets of passages belongs to the range of bad arguments relentlessly criticized in Grisez's first book, *Contraception and the Natural Law* (1964). Each of them also manifests the great gulf between today's cultural assumptions and those still operative in the deliberations of Paul VI's Birth Control Commission. Each of the two arguments is a kind of witness to the existence of an unbroken Christian teaching, understood as certainly true and therefore irreversible, that every one of the ways of choosing sexual satisfaction other than between a husband and wife acting together in a marital way is always wrong.

And each of the authors probably thought his key premise about the object of the generative faculty and its exercise could be found in St. Thomas's *Summa contra Gentiles* III, c. 122 in the opening paragraphs. If so, each was mistaken. Aquinas laid out his argument in that chapter in *much* too compressed a form, but even without the interpretative aids provided by his other works (as I show in detail in my *Aquinas*, chap. 5, sec. 4), it is clear, given sufficient reflection and analysis, that the key ethical premise to which and from which the chapter is working is not about preservation or frustration of the sexual or generative faculty or its physiological object. It is more like this: the form of association we call marriage (*matrimonium*) is rational, a human good or constitutive element in the human good (*bonum hominis*), in the morally significant sense that any kind of act is morally wrong which, by reason of *its* object (the chosen act's proximate and thus defining intent), is opposed to either of the two defining goods of natural marriage. The kinds of act that Aquinas is dealing with in that short chapter are not only the act mentioned in the title question, intercourse between unmarried man and unmarried woman, but also, explicitly, homosexual sex acts, solitary sex acts, sex acts with subhuman animals, adultery, and contraception.

Analyzing Aquinas's sex ethics at proper textual and critical depth in the late 1970s or early 80s, Germain Grisez, Joseph Boyle, and I found that what is providing Aquinas with his conclusions (which are the theses of the unbroken and irreversible apostolic tradition) is the two-sided good of marriage. This—marriage—he affirms to be one of the primary human goods, picked out and directed to in and by one of the shortish lists of practical reason's first, self-evident principles:[7] it appears as marriage, *conjunctio maris et feminae*, in Aquinas's frequently mistranslated and misunderstood article 2 of question 94 of the *Prima Secundae*. And his specific discussions display it as irreducibly two sided. It comprises not only the good of transmission of human life by procreation of offspring (*bonum prolis*), but also the good which *that* good inherently calls for and is uniquely befitted by, the good of *fides*, of the mutual committed *amicitia* of husband and wife. This *fides* is not merely their abstaining from the infidelity of adultery in deed or thought, but more importantly it is the positive commitment of each to be maritally united to each other, sharing in and actualizing the human good of marriage instantiated as their marriage. Thus—I may mention in passing—across St. Thomas's many discussions of sex and marriage, the thesis is affirmed and never is doubted that

---

7. ST I-II, q. 94, a. 2c. That the vice of all extra- and nonmarital sex is its opposition to the principles of practical reasonableness (i.e., to the intelligible human goods picked out and directed to by those principles) is put at the forefront of Aquinas's accounts of sex ethics, e.g., ST II-II, q. 153, a. 2c and a. 3c; q. 154, a. 1c and a. 2, ad 2 and a. 11c; ScG III, c. 122, n. 2 [2948]; IV Sent. d. 26 (= Supp. q. 49) q. 1, a. 1c. (Aquinas's moral arguments never run from "natural" to "therefore reasonable and right," but always from "reasonable and right" to "therefore natural.") All extramarital sex (and even conditional assent [*consensus*] to it) is contrary to nature inasmuch as it is contrary to reason's requirements, e.g., Mal. q. 15, a. 1, ad 7; In Rom. 1.8, ad v. 26 [149]. Some extra- or nonmarital sex is also unnatural in a narrower sense, viz. every act in which sexual satisfaction is sought and which is not an act of the generative type; ST II-II, q. 154, a. 11c.

marital *fides*, even alone and independently of any generative purpose or possibility, is a morally unflawed and authentically good reason for conjugal intercourse—a thesis that Noonan in his book, profoundly influential in Paul VI's commission, quite falsely claims Aquinas did *not accept* and indeed denied.

Back to the main point. Aquinas's position, in effect though never clearly articulated or summarized in some one place, is that whether one is married or unmarried, any chosen exercise of sexual capacities must respect the good of marriage, a chosen way of life systematically favorable to the well-being of the offspring who can supervene upon the conjugal intercourse of wife and husband and be helped by them to grow as befits these infants' human dignity and serves their flourishing.

A disposition of judgment and will is prejudicial to marriage, *contra bonum matrimonii*, if it involves approving by thought or action the gaining of sexual satisfaction in a way or context such that it does not express the goods of marriage. Here I shall put his underlying thought more in the *language* of *Gaudium et Spes* 49 and 51: assent to the precept or norm reserving sexual activity and satisfaction to marriage, and within a marriage to the marital kind of intercourse, makes it possible for spouses to understand their conjugal intercourse as an expressing, actualizing, and experiencing of their relationship as authentically marriage in both its essential elements. This enabling of them—this elevating of their sexual acts together—is *essential* to real-world actualizing of the good of children, spouses, and their communities; indeed, it is *so* essential that choosing *or approving* any kind of sex act other than the authentically marital (as just explained) is immoral.

This wrongness is serious and grave because marriage as a lived reality is so vital to justice and human flourishing, that is, to justly promoting and respecting the good of children and of the society on which parents and children and everyone else depend. And as St. Thomas says in the *Summa Theologiae*, the many behavioral kinds of sexual immorality or perversion are, similarly, more and less serious by being more and less distant from marital intercourse,[8] intercourse generative in kind (even when known to

---

8. John Finnis, *Aquinas* (Oxford: Oxford University Press, 1998), 153: "But the specifically sexual vice in morally bad sex is in every case measured by the chosen act's deviation—and the extent of its deviance—from truly marital intercourse (*secundum quod magis distat a matrimoniali concubitu*:

be unable to generate) and expressive of the commitment of husband and wife to each other *as* conjoined I to thee in our marriage of mind, heart, choice, and flesh.

All this goes to show why the apostolic tradition conveying the teachings of Christ about sex and marriage, together with the apostolic articulations of their rationale and implications, constitute a revealed unity of developing and developed doctrine, beginning from the summary lists of kind of sexual wrongdoing (sins) and the affirmations of virtues that bear more or less closely on the upholding of marriage as a form of life less exalted, to be sure, in dedication and intended fruits, than celibacy for the kingdom but essential in its own indispensable way to the sustaining of both Church and state and building up of the kingdom. The unified doctrine centers on the propositions that sex is exclusively for marriage, and that within marriage it is reserved to acts that in their culmination are authentically *expressive of—signify*, without willed separation—each of marriage's two defining goods of marriage: *proles* and *fides*, offspring and marital commitment.

So, in even the earliest evidences—the Christian tradition of the Two Ways, of life or light and of death or darkness, evidences that convey the teaching of the Apostles in Jerusalem in the Church's first decade—we find references, in close conjunction with adultery and fornication, to *mala medicamenta, pharmakeia* (distinguished from magic), probably alluding to drugs for inducing sterility (temporary or lasting). Augustine, in one of the two passages quoted in *Casti Connubii*'s teaching about contraception, will distinguish between but associate with each other contraceptive drugs and abortifacient drugs, a distinction and association that will go into canon law, as I mentioned, in the thirteenth century.

Unlike abstention from marital intercourse at times thought to be fertile—an abstention that might be unjustified if insufficiently attentive, in all a particular marriage's circumstances, to the good of procreating—the chosen impeding of the possible and unwanted procreativeness of an actual act of conjugal intercourse (whether the impeding is before, during, or after that act) negates, so far forth, the marital character of the act. Those

---

IV Sent. d. 41 a. 4 sol. 3c; see also Mal. q. 15 a. 1c), intercourse which is wholly uncoerced on both sides, generative in type in its chosen behaviour, and genuinely motivated by that *fides* which in its central case is a true friendship."

who approve such impeding set their mind and heart willy-nilly on the way to approving many other kinds of nonmarital sex act. In the late 1960s and early 70s, I was the one Catholic in an otherwise Anglican group of Oxford Christian philosophers and theologians known as the Metaphysicals. Though sex and marriage were far from being its primary topic of discussion, I was able to observe, close up, how leading theologians in the group were thinking their way *from* the acceptance of contraception—acceptance that in 1930 had been hedged by moral cautions[9] but by 1968 had become for Anglicans completely unproblematic—*to* the acceptance of the moral permissibility of homosexual sex acts. This acceptance was in those days cautious and reluctant. But, and here's the point, it was reached explicitly on the basis that acceptance of contraception as permissible blocks and nullifies moral objection to many other kinds of sex acts. As we know, Paul VI's commission majority denied the validity of that progression and, when challenged, bluntly asserted the wrongness of all homosexual sex because it is contrary to human dignity. But like the same majority's short-lived theory that contraception is justifiable if and only

---

9. Resolution 15:
Where there is clearly felt moral obligation to limit or avoid parenthood, the method must be decided on Christian principles. The primary and obvious method is complete abstinence from intercourse (as far as may be necessary) in a life of discipline and self-control lived in the power of the Holy Spirit. Nevertheless in those cases where there is such a clearly felt moral obligation to limit or avoid parenthood, and where there is a morally sound reason for avoiding complete abstinence, the Conference agrees that other methods may be used, provided that this is done in the light of the same Christian principles. The Conference records its strong condemnation of the use of any methods of conception control from motives of selfishness, luxury, or mere convenience.

The Lambeth Conferences (1867–1948) (London: SPCK: 1948), 165–66. In 1920, the conference had passed Resolution 68:

The Conference, while declining to lay down rules which will meet the needs of every abnormal case, regards with grave concern the spread in modern society of theories and practices hostile to the family. We utter an emphatic warning against the use of unnatural means for the avoidance of conception, together with the grave dangers—physical, moral, religious—thereby incurred, and against the evils with which the extension of such use threatens the race. In opposition to the teaching which, under the name of science and religion, encourages married people in the deliberate cultivation of sexual union as an end in itself, we steadfastly uphold what must always be regarded as the governing considerations of Christian marriage. One is the primary purpose for which marriage exists, namely the continuance of the race through the gift and heritage of children; the other is the paramount importance in married life of deliberate and thoughtful self-control.

Lambeth Conferences (1867–1948), 50–51.

if within a marriage sufficiently open to procreation as a whole, this theory about homosexual sex's wrongness within the frame of transformed (imaginary) Catholic sex ethics accepting of contraception has in practice not survived. Indeed, as Cardinal Ladaria observed to the German bishops *ad limina* not long ago, really nothing in the *Catechism*'s teaching on sex survives in their thinking. And that cannot surprise us, given that they all or mostly treat as axiomatic the falsity and reversibility of the central propositions in *Humanae Vitae*, *Casti Connubii*, and *Gaudium et Spes* 51 and all the teaching of fathers, doctors, bishops, and theologians with moral unanimity of judgment in so many periods. They take for granted, too, the falsity of all that Karl Rahner wrote in the years before the Council about the infallibility of the ordinary Magisterium in teaching specific moral norms applicable in every case, regardless of conscientious objections. Yet it was not false but true, and—as I and others have argued—Rahner's later attempts to justify denying the definability or infallible proposing of any specific moral norm, attempts relying upon an alleged and unexplained changeability of human nature, fail comprehensively.[10]

So we are left with the conclusion that because it was everywhere taught as *to be held definitively*, it should be regarded by all Catholics as certainly true, now as always, even though the episcopal unity that guaranteed that judgment as irreversible has subsequently shattered. That loss of unity in judgment is a problem for them and for the sees they govern, not for the truth of a teaching which predecessors of theirs, dispersed about the world at some ascertainable period, had by their unity in a certain kind of judgment taught infallibly.

---

10. See Finnis, "Historical Consciousness and Theological Foundations," in *Collected Essays of John Finnis*, vol. 5, *Religion and Public Reasons* (Oxford: Oxford University Press, 2011), 139–62, esp. 148, 154–62; see also 270, 272; Karl Rahner, "Basic Observations on the Subject of Changeable and Unchangeable Factors in the Church," in *Theological Investigations*, vol. 14 (New York: Crossroad, 1976), 15.

CHAPTER 8

Catholic Teaching on Sexual Morality and the Infallibility of the Ordinary Magisterium

PETER RYAN, SJ

In his essay in this volume, Professor Finnis showed that the Church's teaching on the intrinsic evil of contraception has been proposed infallibly by the ordinary and universal Magisterium. He did this by explaining that the conditions set out in *Lumen Gentium* (LG) 25 for that sort of teaching have been met in the case of the Church's teaching on contraception. To argue that *any* particular teaching meets the conditions for infallibility of the ordinary Magisterium, one must follow the same procedure. Before I ask whether the Church's teaching that the choice to engage in nonmarital sexual acts is gravely wrong meets those conditions, I would like to explain why we should expect a positive answer.

In their article "Contraception and Infallibility,"[1] Christian Brugger and John Finnis explain that the teaching that contraception is intrinsically wrong "has two distinct but overlapping foundations: that human life be respected in its transmission; and that sex acts always be marital (conjugal)."[2] They follow *Humanae Vitae* in focusing primarily on the latter. According to this second foundation, then, the choice to contracept is

---

1. Brugger and Finnis, "Contraception and Infallibility: Part 1," *National Catholic Register*, August 21, 2022, https://www.ncregister.com/commentaries/contraception-and-infallibility-part-1; "Part 2," *National Catholic Register*, August 21, 2022, https://www.ncregister.com/commentaries/contraception-and-infallibility-part-2.

2. Brugger and Finnis, "Contraception and Infallibility," Part 1.

intrinsically wrong precisely because it inevitably renders a couple's sexual intercourse *nonmarital.* Brugger and Finnis explain: sexual intercourse is morally good only when it enables a married couple "to express, actualize, and experience *their marriage*"—their freely chosen, procreative, one-body relationship. And they note that a married couple's sexual intercourse cannot do that when certain conditions obtain:

when either of them is having—or even willing to have—sex alone, or outside their marriage, or in a way that is non-marital because it coerces the other, or fantasizes sex with another person or creature, or intends to impede any procreativity it (this particular act of intercourse) is feared to have.

In fact, they point out, even the failure of either spouse to *repent* such acts renders that spouse incapable of "expressing, actualizing and experiencing his or her marriage"[3] through their sexual intercourse.

I mention this because if the ordinary Magisterium infallibly teaches that contraception is inherently immoral precisely because it renders a married couple's sexual intercourse nonmarital, it should come as no surprise that the ordinary Magisterium also infallibly teaches that nonmarital sexual acts are themselves inherently immoral.

Conditions for Infallible Teaching by the Ordinary and Universal Magisterium

For centuries, the Church has taught that intentional nonmarital sexual acts—including *incomplete* sexual acts and deliberately arousing sexual *thoughts*—are intrinsically and gravely wrong. This teaching shaped the Church's sacramental practice and the pastoral advice dispensed by her ministers, and faithful Catholics universally believed the teaching, cooperated with the practice, and took the pastoral advice seriously. Let's take a closer look.

Vatican I includes in its discussion of teachings that must be believed by divine and Catholic faith those that are proposed infallibly by the ordinary and universal Magisterium.[4] Vatican II explicates that mode of teach-

---

3. Brugger and Finnis, "Contraception and Infallibility," Part 1; emphasis original.

4. *Dei filius,* chap. 3. "Further, by divine and Catholic faith, all those things must be believed which are contained in the written word of God and in tradition, and those which are proposed by

ing in LG 25, which affirms that the bishops "proclaim the doctrine of Christ infallibly, although they are dispersed throughout the world, when they [1] maintain communion with one another and with Peter's successor, [2] authoritatively teach on a matter of faith and morals, and [3] agree in one judgment [4] as something to be held definitively."[5] For a teaching to be proposed infallibly by the ordinary and universal Magisterium, then, those four conditions must be met. I shall consider them in turn.

First: those bishops proclaiming the teaching are in unity with one another and the pope. This does not mean they act formally as a body, but only that they are not separated from collegial communion. Thus, for bishops separated from collegial communion to deny the intrinsic immorality of nonmarital sexual acts does not prevent the consensus required for the ordinary Magisterium to teach that truth infallibly.

Second: the bishops teach authoritatively on a matter of faith and morals. This means they teach not as private individuals but as bishops, on a matter that falls within the ambit of their authority. While there is controversy about what faith and morals includes, it surely includes any matter explicitly dealt with in Scripture that gravely affects Christian life.[6]

Third: the bishops agree in one judgment. This means that the bishops as a whole teach the same thing, even if some never mention the matter and a few dissent. As I will explain below, once this condition is met, the necessary universality is not nullified by a later lack of consensus.

---

the Church, either in a solemn pronouncement or in her ordinary and universal teaching power, to be believed as divinely revealed."

5. *Lumen Gentium*, 25, Grisez's and my translation. My explication of these conditions closely follows our treatment in "Indissoluble Marriage: A Reply to Kenneth Himes and James Coriden," *Theological Studies* 72, no. 2 (2011): 369–415, at 410–12.

6. Here I include what Brugger and Finnis list as a fifth condition, namely, that the matter must be either a revealed truth or necessary to set out what has been revealed. *CIC*, canon 750, articulates this requirement: "§1. A person must believe with divine and Catholic faith all those things contained in the word of God, written or handed on, that is, in the one deposit of faith entrusted to the Church, and at the same time proposed as divinely revealed either by the solemn magisterium of the Church or by its ordinary and universal magisterium which is manifested by the common adherence of the Christian faithful under the leadership of the sacred magisterium; therefore all are bound to avoid any doctrines whatsoever contrary to them. §2. Each and every thing which is proposed definitively by the magisterium of the Church concerning the doctrine of faith and morals, that is, each and every thing which is required to safeguard reverently and to expound faithfully the same deposit of faith, is also to be firmly embraced and retained; therefore, one who rejects those propositions which are to be held definitively is opposed to the doctrine of the Catholic Church."

Fourth: the bishops propose the teaching as a truth to be held definitively. This condition does not refer to the formulation necessary for a solemn definition, because what is at stake is the bishops' ordinary teaching.[7] Rather, the condition means the teaching is not proposed as optional or merely probable, but as something Catholics have an obligation to accept as certainly true. To propose something as a *truth of faith*—as a truth to be held as *divinely revealed*—is a fortiori to propose it as a truth to be held definitively.

Is It Possible to Determine Whether These Conditions Are Met?

Before considering how these conditions apply to the teaching that intentional nonmarital sexual acts are intrinsically and gravely wrong, it is important to respond to the claims of those who doubt that *any* teaching can be identified as having that kind of infallibility. Peter Phan, for example, says that "although the existence of an infallible ordinary universal magisterium is generally accepted by Catholics, in practice it is an extremely complicated affair to determine which particular teaching is infallibly taught in this way." He alleges "the near-impossibility of this enterprise" because of a lack of clarity about three matters.[8]

Phan first wonders how it is possible "to ascertain whether there is in fact an 'agreement' in the worldwide episcopate about a particular teaching in matters of faith and morals."[9] He quotes the preface of the Order of the Synod of Bishop, which affirms that "the *consensus ecclesiae* is not determined by the tallying of votes, but is the outcome of the working of the Spirit, the soul of the one Church of Christ." Phan immediately objects: "Nevertheless, there is no way to determine whether there is an

---

7. Lawrence J. Welch distinguishes the formulation required for formal definitions from that required for statements of the ordinary Magisterium in "On Recognizing Infallible Teachings of the Ordinary Universal Magisterium: A Rejoinder to Francis Sullivan," *New Blackfriars* 86 (November 2005): 591–97, at 596n13. He observes: "It is all too easy to think that the infallible teachings of the ordinary universal magisterium should look like the infallible teachings of the extra-ordinary magisterium and thus conclude that therefore there must be very few of them."

8. Peter Phan, "From Magisterium to Magisteria: Recent Theologies of the Learning and Teaching Functions of the Church," *Theological Studies* 80 (2019): 393–413, at 404.

9. Phan, "From Magisterium to Magisteria," 403.

agreement concerning a doctrine of faith and morals except through some kind of 'tallying of votes.'" Counting votes is what makes it possible, he says, "to determine whether and to what extent the Holy Spirit is actually working in shaping the church's belief in and teaching of a particular doctrine."[10] Phan's second concern is closely related to his first: "how to decide what the extent of this agreement must be."[11] He asks whether the Synod of Bishops' rule for deliberation should be followed, namely, "To arrive at the majority of votes, if the vote for the approval of some item, two-thirds of the votes of the Members casting ballots is required; if for the rejection of some item, the absolute majority of the same Members is necessary."[12] His third concern, which he considers the most important, is the difficulty of establishing whether the teaching in question is proposed to be held definitively. Referring to the Church's teaching that only males are eligible for priestly ordination, Phan says "it is extremely rash to assume that a majority of current and future bishops maintain this doctrine 'to be held definitively,' especially if no poll has been taken on this precise point."[13] (He does not consider the question of whether the agreement of future bishops is necessary for the body of bishops to teach something infallibly at an earlier point in history.) Since he uses that issue as an example, he apparently means it would be rash to conclude to a consensus of bishops on any particular issue without a poll on that specific issue.

Is it true that the only way to ascertain whether a consensus has been reached about a particular teaching is by tallying votes? If so, the teaching of LG 25, on the conditions for establishing that a teaching is infallible by the ordinary Magisterium, is essentially meaningless because systematic tallying is virtually impossible. Bear in mind, however, that if Phan's claim about what is necessary to ascertain consensus were true, it also would render meaningless Trent's decree "that no one may dare to interpret the Scripture in a way contrary to the unanimous consensus of the Fathers."[14]

---

10. Phan, "From Magisterium to Magisteria," 404.
11. Phan, "From Magisterium to Magisteria," 403.
12. Phan, "From Magisterium to Magisteria," 404, quoting the Order of the Synod of Bishops, 8, art. 26 §1.
13. Phan, "From Magisterium to Magisteria," 404.
14. Council of Trent, *Decree Concerning the Edition and Use of the Sacred Books* (Denz. 1507).

The alternative to making claims that render nugatory the teachings of Vatican II and Trent on these matters is to acknowledge that in both instances, the Council Fathers had a view of what constitutes consensus that they saw no need to explain exhaustively, a view we can understand well enough to apply with confidence to particular doctrines.

There were significant disagreements among Church Fathers about the interpretation of some biblical passages, but their agreement about the interpretation of other passages is so overwhelming that one cannot reasonably deny that their agreement is indeed a unanimous consensus and therefore infallible. What precisely does *unanimous* mean? Etymologically, it means that the bishops are of one (*unus*) mind (*anima*). Although *unanimous* often means without any exception, unanimous consent in Church documents has always referred to moral unanimity, which explains why the Church has not spelled out a mathematical formula for determining consensus. This does not mean that numbers are irrelevant, but that determining consensus is not reducible to math.[15] One reason why determining whether there is a consensus of the Fathers cannot be reduced to counting votes is that different Fathers have different weight. An effort to make such a determination has to take into account who is expressing a particular view. For example, for St. Augustine to hold a view that contradicts a majority is far more significant than for a relatively obscure Father, and particularly for one not clearly acknowledged as orthodox, to do the same.

Although identifying unanimous consent is not as simple as tallying votes, it is simple enough. The Fathers need not agree about every detail of an issue or explain it with the same language. The fact that a few Fathers might not be as clear as others, or that that there might be outliers, is not a concern. There is a unanimous consensus when the Fathers or bishops hold, as a whole, the same basic view. This means they hold it overwhelmingly and despite the possible contrary view of a small minority.[16]

---

15. To support this point, John C. Ford, SJ, and Germain Grisez in "Contraception and the Infallibility of the Ordinary Magisterium," *Theological Studies* 39 (1978): 258–312, at 273, use the example of the doctrine of the divinity of Christ before the Council of Nicaea. Although mathematical unity of bishops on the divinity of Christ was never achieved before or even at the Council, the ordinary and universal Magisterium taught the doctrine infallibly before the Council defined it.

16. St. Vincent of Lérins puts the point well: "Moreover, in the Catholic Church itself, all possible care must be taken, that we hold that faith which has been believed everywhere, always, by

INFALLIBILITY OF THE ORDINARY MAGISTERIUM

In some cases, the infallibility of the Fathers' teaching about the interpretation of some scriptural passages was later confirmed by definitive Church teaching that excluded contradictory interpretations. By paying attention to such cases, we can learn something about what constitutes a consensus. For example, no Church Father I am aware of thought that Jesus' statement "The Father is greater than I" in John 14:28 means that Jesus is any less than the Father in terms of his ontological status. They all read the text as concordant with his unsubordinated divinity, and the truth to which their consensus bears infallible witness was later confirmed by definitive Church teaching.[17] We can be sure that we are mistaken if we regard the Son as less divine than the Father, not only because of the specific definitions that came later, but also because the consensus itself bears infallible witness to the truth of the Fathers' interpretation.

So, too, none of the Fathers take a merely symbolic reading of Jesus' Bread-of-Life statements, as in John 6:55–56: "For my flesh is food indeed, and my blood is drink indeed. He who eats my flesh and drinks my blood abides in me, and I in him." Here, too, definitive Church teaching later confirmed the truth to which the Fathers' consensus bears infallible witness.[18] We can be sure that if we take a merely symbolic reading of such passages, as in fact in the sixteenth century some Protestant reformers being addressed by Trent were doing, we are mistaken, because none of the Fathers read John 6 in that way, and the Church teaches that we must never interpret Scripture in opposition to their consensus.[19] Again, we can be sure about this and other matters not only because of the specific definitions that came later, but because the consensus itself bears infallible witness. This is by no means to suggest that the later definitions are super-

---

all. For that is truly and in the strictest sense Catholic, which, as the name itself and the reason of the thing declare, comprehends all universally. This rule we shall observe if we follow universality, antiquity, consent. We shall follow universality if we confess that one faith to be true, which the whole Church throughout the world confesses; antiquity, if we in no wise depart from those interpretations which it is manifest were notoriously held by our holy ancestors and Fathers; consent, in like manner, if in antiquity itself we adhere to the consentient definitions and determinations of all, *or at the least of almost all* priests and doctors." *Commonitorium*, chap. 2, no. 6; emphasis mine; https://www.newadvent.org/fathers/3506.htm.

17. *Denz.* 73–76. The author is grateful to R. J. Matava for bringing this point to my attention and proposing these two examples.

18. *Denz.* 847, 1637–38, 1649, 1651.

19. *Denz.* 1507.

fluous. Such definitions clarify matters about which theologians disagree and provide important confirmation of the view of those theologians who recognized a teaching as infallible even before it was formally defined.

As noted above, Phan considers his third concern—the difficulty of establishing whether a teaching is proposed to be held definitively—to be the most important. As Ford and Grisez point out, a bishop plainly proposes a teaching in that way when he does so "not at his option but as part of his duty to hand on the teaching he has received; not as doubtful or even as very probable but as certainly true; and not as one which the faithful are free to accept or to reject but as one which every Catholic must accept."[20] Such a teaching need not be expressed explicitly as a doctrine calling for assent; indeed, infallible moral teachings are likely to be proposed as pertaining to the requirements of living a faithful Christian life.[21] A moral teaching has the infallibility of the ordinary Magisterium when it has always been proposed as a certain part of the Church's teaching about acts that must be avoided because, being the matter of mortal sin, they endanger salvation, and when in the face of a challenge by Christians to the teaching, the Church insists on the need to live up to it.

Phan raises concerns about what he and many others have referred to as "creeping infallibility," and this is hardly surprising given his conviction about the near impossibility of showing that a teaching meets *Lumen Gentium*'s conditions for infallibility of the ordinary and universal Magisterium.[22] But his view gives rise to other concerns. The assumption that infallible teachings can be recognized only when they are formally defined by a conciliar or papal statement—through acts not of the ordinary but only of the extraordinary Magisterium—suggests that infallibility itself is something extraordinary, a bolt out of the blue, rather than simply the guarantee of the integrity or verity of the Church's faith. This guarantee is by the gift

---

20. Ford and Grisez, "Contraception and the Infallibility of the Ordinary Magisterium," 276.

21. Congregation for the Doctrine of the Faith, *Doctrinal Commentary on the Concluding Formula of the* Professio fidei (1998), n. 17: "It should be noted that the infallible teaching of the ordinary and universal Magisterium is not only set forth with an explicit declaration of a doctrine to be believed or held definitively, but is also expressed by a doctrine implicitly contained in a practice of the Church's faith, derived from revelation or, in any case, necessary for eternal salvation, and attested to by the uninterrupted Tradition: such an infallible teaching is thus objectively set forth by the whole episcopal body, understood in a diachronic and not necessarily merely synchronic sense."

22. Phan, "From Magisterium to Magisteria," 403n32.

of the Holy Spirit and the fact that Jesus acts in the Church through those ordained to act in his person. The guarantee covers everything essential that God offers us in and through Christ: revealed true propositions, the sacraments, and the Church's basic constitution. The point of the guarantee is that these gifts are meant for everyone until the end of the world and can be available to them only if the offered gifts are kept intact and neither diminished nor adulterated. The guarantee is of the faith of the Church as a whole, and so of those acts of bishops that per se articulate and shape that faith. Such acts include solemn definitions by a council or by a pope acting as the Church's head, and the bishops' ordinary teaching proposing something to be held definitively. To eliminate the latter gives the impression that most of what Catholics have for centuries held about the faith and what it means to live it out is not entirely reliable.[23]

Application of Those Conditions to the Teaching That Intentional Nonmarital Sexual Acts Are Intrinsically and Gravely Wrong

Since the 1960s, many Catholic theologians have argued that nonmarital sexual acts—masturbation, homosexual acts by people so oriented, and fornication (and the incomplete sexual acts that correspond to them)—can be morally acceptable. Bishops and even cardinals have suggested as much, and some have asserted that the Church's teaching in this area should be changed. These views have had a significant impact on many Catholics.

The New Testament teaches the contrary in many places. Two examples: Jesus warns, "Everyone who looks at a woman with lustful intent has already committed adultery with her in his heart" (Mt 5:28).[24] And Paul proclaims, "Do you not know that the unrighteous will not inherit the kingdom of God? Do not be deceived." On his list of those whose inheritance is forfeit, Paul includes "the sexually immoral," "adulterers," and "men who practice homosexuality" (1 Cor 6:9–10).[25] Indeed, Scripture

---

23. Much of this paragraph is drawn from the notes I worked on with Grisez for his *Clerical and Consecrated Life and Service*. See chaps. 8 and 13, http://www.twotlj.org/OW-4-8-Notes.pdf.

24. All Scripture quotations are from the Revised Standard Version, second Catholic edition, unless otherwise indicated.

25. English Standard Version.

as a whole—notably the beginning of Genesis and certain dominical and Pauline passages—emphasizes that the body is integral to the person and that its personal meaning, including the bodily complementarity of man and woman, has important implications for sexual morality. St. John Paul II famously explicates and applies this anthropology in his Theology of the Body, making it clear that sexual activity is morally good only between a man and a woman committed to each other in the permanent and exclusive relationship of marriage. That teaching has been reiterated many times in magisterial documents.

For centuries, there was unanimous agreement among approved Catholic theologians that intentionally seeking sexual pleasure outside of marriage is always grave matter, and that even within marriage, intentionally engaging in complete sexual acts other than marital intercourse is always grave matter. These theologians were called *approved* authors because their works were authorized by bishops and popes for the teaching of seminarians. Germain Grisez notes:

> This theological consensus both reflected and shaped the belief of the whole Catholic Church. All the faithful, from the bishops to the least of the laity, held the same sexual morality. Moreover, they accepted it as part of the faith, for it was taken to be implicit in the sixth and ninth commandments and to be illustrated by various other texts of sacred Scripture.[26]

Grisez recalls the teaching of LG 12 that "the faithful as a whole cannot err when they all agree on what they take to be God's revealed word about a matter of faith and morals." He continues:

> Therefore, this teaching on sexual morality, although never solemnly defined, cannot be mistaken. It is guaranteed by the Holy Spirit's gift to the Church of infallibility.... This universal, constant, and most firm teaching of the popes and the bishops in communion with them around the world meets the conditions which Vatican II articulated for the infallibility of the ordinary magisterium. Although the Church has not solemnly defined the teaching excluding parvity of matter with respect to all intentional sexual sins against the good of marriage, that teaching has been infallibly taught.[27]

---

26. Germain Grisez, *The Way of the Lord Jesus*, vol. 2, *Living a Christian Life* (Quincy, IL: Franciscan Press, 1993), 659 (chap. 9, q. E, 6, a), http://twotlj.org/G-2-9-E.html#Note199Return.
27. Grisez, *The Way of the Lord Jesus*, 2:659.

Unfortunately, in *Etica Theologica,* the Pontifical Academy for Life never considers whether the teachings it questions meet the conditions set out in LG 25 for infallibility of the ordinary and universal Magisterium. Indeed, authors who deny that a particular teaching can be identified as having the infallibility of the ordinary Magisterium tend not to do so on the basis of a lack of evidence that the teaching in question meets the conditions but because, like Phan, they doubt that *any* teaching can be identified as having that kind of infallibility. This general doubt warrants further consideration. I will first consider the question of whether a consensus of theologians is necessary for one to recognize an infallible teaching of the ordinary Magisterium, and then the question of whether the agreement of future bishops is necessary for the body of bishops to teach something infallibly now or for us to recognize their teaching as infallible.

Is a Consensus of Theologians a Necessary Condition for Establishing That a Teaching Has Been Infallibly Taught by the Ordinary Universal Magisterium?

Richard Gaillardetz denies that "currently disputed issues" can be resolved by "appeals to the teaching of the ordinary universal Magisterium"[28] and tries to refute arguments that were offered against that view by Lawrence Welch.[29] In particular, Gaillardetz argued that the lack of a current consensus among theologians that a proposition has been infallibly taught by the ordinary Magisterium entails that it has not been.[30] Welch responded to that argument.[31] Gaillardetz and Welch had discussed the views of Francis Sullivan, who then replied to Welch.[32]

Although Sullivan says that without a consensus of theologians, "it

---

28. Richard R. Gaillardetz, "The Ordinary Universal Magisterium: Unresolved Questions," *Theological Studies* 63 (2002): 447–71, at 466.

29. See Lawrence J. Welch, "The Infallibility of the Ordinary Universal Magisterium: A Critique of Some Recent Observations," *Heythrop Journal* 39 (1998): 18–36.

30. See Gaillardetz, "Ordinary Universal Magisterium," 466–67.

31. See Lawrence J. Welch, "Quaestio Disputata: Reply to Richard Gaillardetz on the Ordinary Universal Magisterium and to Francis Sullivan," *Theological Studies* 64 (2003): 598–609. Welch also better explained why subsequent dissent cannot count against a truth of faith once it has been identified and held by the Christian community as a whole.

32. Francis A. Sullivan, SJ, "Reply to Lawrence J. Welch," *Theological Studies* 64 (2003): 610–15.

would be difficult *to be certain* that the conditions for infallible teaching had been fulfilled," he clearly denies holding "that the absence of the consensus of theologians would mean that *there has not been* a definitive teaching of the ordinary universal magisterium."[33] Sullivan explains:

> In other words, I hold that because Catholic theologians are professionally qualified to make informed judgments about the degree of authority with which doctrines have been taught by the magisterium, a lack of consensus among them as to whether a doctrine had been taught infallibly would make it questionable whether that fact was "manifestly established." It is possible that it might subsequently become evident that the conditions for the infallible teaching of the ordinary universal magisterium had in fact been fulfilled.[34]

Is a consensus of theologians a necessary condition for establishing that a teaching has been infallibly taught by the ordinary universal Magisterium? Certainly, a consensus of faithful theologians can help to establish that, but a distinction must be made. Although such a consensus can help people who lack theological training see that a particular teaching is infallible, theologians should be able to come to a sound judgment about whether a teaching meets the conditions of LG 25 without such a consensus. After all, it is precisely the judgment of theologians about whether the conditions have been fulfilled based on a consideration of the relevant facts, and apart from a consideration of the percentage of theologians who have judged one way or the other (but not necessarily apart from a consideration of their arguments), that makes it possible even to ask what theologians think and whether they have reached a consensus in one direction or the other. It is not enough for theologians to rely on the conclusions of other theologians; they must argue for their own conclusions according to the merits of the case at hand. Indeed, if theologians required a consensus of theologians before they could judge soundly, a consensus would be impossible in principle, with the result that it would be impossible for any of them to reach a sound judgment about the status of a teaching.

Of course, theologians should be concerned not only with premises and arguments, but also with what people thought and who they were, for awareness of such historical realities equips theologians to consider

---

33. Sullivan, "Reply," 614–15; emphasis original.
34. Sullivan, "Reply," 615.

the important matter of authoritative consensuses. Theologians should attend to the question of whether there is or has been a consensus of bishops on particular issues of faith and morals, a matter we will soon discuss, because that sort of consensus is guaranteed to have the Holy Spirit. So, too, theologians should ask whether there is a consensus of Church Fathers (most of whom are also bishops) on particular issues, because the Church recognizes that they have a privileged voice.[35] Theologians also should take note when there is a consensus of believers, because insofar as they hold the faith of the Church, they share in her gift of infallibility.[36] It is essential to distinguish between sources that are authoritative because they have the guarantee of the Holy Spirit and sources that are only as authoritative as the reasons they adduce for their views. This latter is the case with theologians as theologians. No one guarantees that theologians have the gift of the Holy Spirit any more than any other believer, but bishops by virtue of their office, Fathers by virtue of their magisterially recognized authority, and believers by virtue of their sharing in the Church's faith have authority that goes beyond the reasons they put forward for their views.[37]

In short, theology is not just an abstract enterprise; it is also historical. Theologians should be ecclesially minded and realize that embedded,

---

35. *Denz.* 1507 (see text at n. 14 above).

36. LG 12: "The entire body of the faithful, anointed as they are by the Holy One (cf. 1 Jn 2:20, 2:27), cannot err in matters of belief. They manifest this special property by means of the whole peoples' supernatural discernment in matters of faith when 'from the Bishops down to the last of the lay faithful' they show universal agreement in matters of faith and morals."

37. After discussing the different ways in which the Magisterium can teach infallibly, LG 25 says, "To these definitions the assent of the Church can never be wanting, on account of the activity of that same Holy Spirit, by which the whole flock of Christ is preserved and progresses in unity of faith." In *Teaching with Authority: A Theology of the Magisterium in the Church* (Collegeville, MN: Liturgical Press, 1997), 220, Richard Gaillardetz treats that statement as support for his claim that "the infallibility of the college of bishops, in turn, depends on the infallibility of the people of God." But LG plainly does not mean that the Magisterium cannot teach infallibly unless the faithful assent to the teaching; rather, LG is affirming that the faithful are obliged to assent to teaching that is already infallible and that in so doing they share in the Church's charism of infallibility. The Congregation for the Doctrine of the Faith explicitly rejected the view that the Magisterium's infallible teachings depend on the *consensus fidelium* in its declaration *Mysterium ecclesi*ae (June 24, 1973), §2: "Thus, however much the Sacred Magisterium avails itself of the contemplation, life and study of the faithful, its office is not reduced merely to ratifying the assent already expressed by the latter; indeed, in the interpretation and explanation of the written or transmitted Word of God, the Magisterium can anticipate or demand their assent."

historical, contextualized consensuses do matter for theology when they have ecclesial authority. They should also realize that important as the theologian's service to the Church is, the guild of theologians does not as such have authority, but, rather, the authority of theologians is limited to the sound and convincing exercise of their expertise.

Welch affirms "that there are other ways [than a consensus of theologians] to recognize and know that a doctrine has been infallibly taught."[38] He gives the example of *Evangelium Vitae*, in which Pope St. John Paul II "identifies as infallibly taught by the ordinary universal magisterium" the grave immorality of the intentional killing of innocent human beings (no. 57), and the grave immorality, specifically, of intentional abortion (no. 62) and intentional euthanasia (no. 65). Welch's affirmation is well founded, for each instance includes a reference to LG 25; moreover, as Welch notes, Sullivan himself "admits that there are good reasons for thinking that the Pope meant to invoke the infallibility of the ordinary universal magisterium in EV, nos. 57, 62, 65," even if Sullivan holds that "questions remain."[39]

To Sullivan's claim, "It is too soon to know whether there will be the consensus of theologians that would show that it is 'clearly established' that the immorality of murder, abortion and euthanasia are infallibly taught,"[40] Welch replies with a rhetorical question: Does this position "not make the consensus of theologians more important than the judgment of the head of the apostolic college about *what is* an infallible teaching of the ordinary universal magisterium?"[41]

Sullivan also observes: "What this would mean is that the Church has taken an irreversible stand on these issues."[42] He apparently intends those words as a caution against prematurely claiming that a teaching is infalli-

---

38. Welch, "On Recognizing," 592.

39. Welch, "On Recognizing," 592n7, citing Sullivan, *Creative Fidelity: Weighing and Interpreting Documents of the Magisterium* (New York: Paulist Press, 1996), 159. I would say *identify* rather than *invoke,* since the latter could be taken to mean extraordinary authority, which is precisely what is not at stake here. The pope's act of referring to the ordinary and universal Magisterium is not what guarantees the infallibility. Rather, infallibility adheres to or characterizes certain papal teachings that meet the four conditions. John Paul II simply identifies the teachings in question as meeting those conditions and therefore pertaining to the infallibility of the ordinary and universal Magisterium. His doing so gives us good reason for thinking that the teachings do indeed have that status.

40. Welch, "On Recognizing," 593, citing Sullivan, *Creative Fidelity,* 160.

41. Welch, "On Recognizing," 593; emphasis original.

42. Welch, "On Recognizing," 593, citing Sullivan, *Creative Fidelity,* 160.

ble. Of course, we should not hastily claim that the Church has made an irreversible affirmation; indeed, it is important to realize that if *Lumen Gentium*'s conditions have *not* been met, then a common supposition of bishops can be reversed, and even an authoritative teaching of bishops can be reversed. But if those conditions have been met, the teaching is irreversible. And it is not reasonable to regard it as all but impossible to show that a particular teaching has met the conditions for infallibility of the ordinary universal Magisterium. The Church, after all, sometimes has the pastoral responsibility to take irreversible stands, for by doing so she clarifies essential elements of Christian faith and life, and promotes (or restores) communion. It is hardly incautious for the Church to take the irreversible stand that the intentional killing of the innocent, whether through abortion, euthanasia, or any other means, is always gravely wrong. Nor, after noting how often and solemnly those teachings have been repeated, and after taking into consideration John Paul II's confirmation of those teachings in *Evangelium Vitae,* with its references to LG 25, is it premature to judge that the conditions for infallibility of the ordinary Magisterium have been met in their regard.

A statement from the pope asserting that he, as head of the apostolic college, confirms the truth of a particular teaching and identifies it as having the infallibility of the ordinary universal Magisterium is very significant.[43] Still, some object that unless such a papal statement is itself clearly infallible, it cannot show in an absolutely reliable way that the teaching to which it refers really does have the infallibility of the ordinary Magisterium.[44] While there is a certain logic to the objection, one must bear in mind that the point of the pope's confirmatory statement is not that it confers the infallibility of the teaching at stake; rather, the statement recognizes and announces that infallibility, which one can discover firsthand by recognizing what the pope himself recognized, namely, that the teaching meets the conditions set out in LG 25. Ultimately, the only sure way

---

43. Some such papal statements go beyond *Evangelium Vitae* 57, 62, and 65, and explicitly assert that a teaching has the infallibility of the ordinary Magisterium. See, e.g., the apostolic letter *Ordinatio sacerdotalis* (May 22, 1994), 4, and the corresponding papally approved *Responsum ad dubium* by the Congregation for the Doctrine of the Faith (October 28, 1995). For examples of appeals to the infallibility of the ordinary universal Magisterium in ecclesiastical documents, see Gaillardetz, "Ordinary Universal Magisterium," 448–55.

44. See Phan, "From Magisterium to Magisteria," 405.

for the Church to recognize and affirm that something has been taught infallibly by the ordinary and universal Magisterium is by asserting the fact through some authoritative noninfallible statement, for to require an infallible proclamation of the teaching is effectively to require that the corresponding truth be taught through an extraordinary act before it is accepted as infallible. Such a requirement would render pointless the four conditions specified in LG 25, and indeed the whole category of the infallibility of the ordinary and universal Magisterium.

Is the Agreement of Future Bishops Necessary for the Body of Bishops to Teach Something Infallibly Now or for Us to Recognize Their Teaching as Infallible?

What about the question of a consensus of bishops? Sullivan says, "I do not believe that one can appeal to a past consensus of bishops as infallible if they are no longer agreed in teaching that doctrine."[45] Is the agreement of future bishops necessary for the body of bishops to teach something infallibly now or for us to recognize their teaching as infallible?[46] Welch acknowledges that "if one could show that there was an interruption in the consensus of bishops on a particular teaching then it might be an indication that there is not the kind of episcopal consensus that would alert us to a definitive and infallible teaching." But he nevertheless affirms "that there could be a breakdown in consensus among bishops about a particular point of doctrine that has in fact been taught infallibly prior to a later lack of consensus,"[47] and he points out that "Sullivan himself seems to

---

45. Sullivan, "Reply to Lawrence J. Welch," 611. Sullivan continues, "To take one example: the bishops at the Council of Florence taught that all pagans and Jews would go to hell if they did not become Catholics before they died." This example, however, concerns a conciliar teaching, not a teaching of the ordinary Magisterium. Moreover, Sullivan's "if they did not become Catholics before they died" misstates Florence's necessary condition: "unless they are joined [*aggregati*] to the catholic church before the end of their lives" (Tanner 1:578). LG 16 explains how people can be related to the Church in ways adequate for salvation without becoming Catholics by making an act of faith and receiving sacramental baptism.

46. Suppose all the bishops of the world currently agreed in teaching as a truth to be held definitively that it is always gravely wrong to sell a human being, and suppose Sullivan acknowledged that state of affairs. Unless he gave up his position, he would have to insist that the wrongness of ever selling a human being had not been infallibly taught by the ordinary Magisterium because future bishops might no longer be agreed in teaching that doctrine.

47. Welch, "On Recognizing," 594.

recognize there can be times that a prior consensus has been lost but is still binding and needs to be restored and received again."[48]

Welch finds a telling example in the eighth-century iconoclast controversy:

> The use and veneration of images which was common at least since the 5th century came to be rejected not only by numerous bishops but several patriarchs of Constantinople as well.[12] Prior to the solemn proclamation of the Church's faith regarding holy images at the Seventh Ecumenical Council in 787, the teaching of the Church on this point of doctrine was taught by what we would call the ordinary universal magisterium. This doctrine of the Church was taught most especially in and through the Church's liturgical tradition and practice as well as in the common teaching of bishops. The popes (Gregory I and Gregory II) and other bishops who defended the holy images taught quite clearly that the Church's teaching was permanent and irreversible. In other words, the popes and bishops appealed to a prior consensus. They did not think that because there was no longer the kind of consensus among bishops in their own time that it was not possible to appeal to the long standing prior consensus of former times *and that such a consensus was binding on all bishops for all times.*

It certainly seems sound to say that the Church's teaching on holy images prior to the Seventh Ecumenical Council was taught infallibly by the ordinary universal magisterium despite the fact that there was not the consensus among bishops in the 8th century that existed in former centuries.[49]

---

48. Welch, "On Recognizing," 594n11. He refers to Sullivan's observation that "papal definitions (extra-ordinary magisterium) can sometimes be '... needed to overcome a threat to the Church's unity in the faith and bring about a consensus, or restore one that had been lost.'" The internal quotation is from Sullivan's article "Magisterium," in *Dictionary of Fundamental Theology* (New York: Crossroads, 1994), 619. Welch points out ("On Recognizing," 594n10), however, that Sullivan seems to have changed his mind about this in his "Reply to Lawrence J. Welch," 611. CDF, *Doctrinal Commentary on the Concluding Formula of the* Professio fidei, provides magisterial support for Welch's point: "Such an infallible teaching is thus objectively set forth by the whole episcopal body, understood in a diachronic and not necessarily merely synchronic sense" (see n. 21 above). As Archbishop Tarcisio Bertone, SDB, then Secretary of the Congregation for the Doctrine of the Faith, observes in *Magisterial Documents and Public Dissent,* in *L'Osservatore Romano,* weekly English ed. January 29, 1997, sec. I, 3, b, "When speaking of the need to verify the actual consent of all the Bishops dispersed throughout the world or even of the whole Christian people in matters of faith and morals, it should not be forgotten that this consent cannot be understood only *synchronically,* but also *diachronically.* This means that a morally *unanimous* consent embraces every era of the Church, and only if this totality is heard does one remain faithful to the Apostles. 'If in some quarter,' the wise Cardinal Ratzinger observes, 'a majority were to be formed in opposition to the faith of the Church in other times, it would not be a majority at all.'" Emphasis original; for the internal quotation, Bertone cites J. Ratzinger, *La Chiesa: Una comunità sempre in cammino* (Milan: San Paolo Edizioni, 2008), 71.

49. Welch, "On Recognizing," emphasis original. 595n12 mentions several such patriarchs of

Finally, there is no mention in LG 25 of a requirement that the agreement of future bishops is necessary for the body of bishops to teach something infallibly now or for us to recognize their teaching as infallible. The reason is obvious. If the agreement of future bishops were necessary, it would follow that because it is always possible for future bishops to disagree, it would be impossible ever to know that a teaching has met that criterion, in which case the very category of the infallibility of the ordinary and universal Magisterium would be pointless.

Given what I have argued is the essential simplicity of identifying unanimous consent, it is hard to avoid the impression that those who insist that such consent is virtually impossible to identify are motivated by the desire to avoid what they regard as an unacceptable outcome. In the matter with which we are concerned, those who are so motivated have adopted the cultural assumption that the idea that nonmarital sexual acts are intrinsically and gravely immoral is simply unthinkable, and they can therefore only hold that the claim of infallibility for the Church's teaching affirming that truth is a bridge too far.

Pastoral Implications

The infallibility of the Church's teaching on the grave immorality of nonmarital sexual activity has profound pastoral implications, for very many people rationalize such activity and in doing so seriously jeopardize their salvation. How can we know that those who rationalize nonmarital sexual activity risk their salvation? By bearing in mind two clear Church teachings. The first is that everyone who dies in unrepented mortal sin ends in hell, which is a truth defined in *Benedictus Deus* by Pope Benedict XII in 1336.[50] The second teaching, which is guaranteed by the infallibility of the ordinary Magisterium, is that nonmarital sexual acts—even incomplete ones—are grave matter. Of course, those who through no fault of their own are unaware of this fact do not incur the guilt of a mortal sin when they engage in such acts, but many are well aware that such acts are gravely

---

Constantinople who endorsed iconoclasm after the prior consensus: "Anastasius (730–54) Constantine II, (754–66), Nicetas I (766–80) and 12 Paul IV (780–84). The latter later recanted his iconoclasm."

50. *Denz.* 1000; cf. LG 49 and *Catechism of the Catholic Church*, §1023.

wrong and freely choose to engage in them anyway. This includes those who have dulled their consciences and rationalize such choices. That is, they realize that such acts are gravely wrong, but they suppress that truth to give themselves permission to engage in those acts anyway.

If people risk their salvation by rationalizing sexual sin, pastoral ministers plainly have the responsibility to help them stay chaste, and to offer that help, ministers need to communicate the truth about sexual sin clearly. Pope Francis insists that doctrine and pastoral care should not be treated as disparate realities,[51] and his point is verified here, since communicating Church teaching about sexual morality is an essential element of proper pastoral care.

Mortal sin has that name because it is indeed deadly; by sinning mortally, people cause serious harm to themselves that remains forever unless one repents of the sin before death. Mortal sin destroys the life of grace and sets a person on the path to hell, which should be conceived not as an externally imposed punishment, but as the continuation of the condition of alienation from God brought about by one's unrepented choice to sin. Hell is a fearful destiny. St. John Paul II calls it the "state of definitive self-exclusion from communion with God and the blessed." He says Scripture's images of hell "show the complete frustration and emptiness of life without God.... hell indicates the state of those who freely and definitively separate themselves from God, the source of all life and joy."[52]

When people bear that the Church's teaching on hell steadily in mind and clearly understand what is and is not mortal sin—and the forthright proclamation of Catholic teaching on sexual morality greatly helps them in this—it becomes much harder to rationalize sexual sin. Of course, it can sometimes seem impossible *not* to sin, especially to the many people enslaved by sexual sin, people who repeatedly give in to sexual temptation—

---

51. "Not infrequently an opposition between theology and pastoral ministry emerges, as if they were two opposite, separate realities that had nothing to do with each other.... False opposition is generated between theology and pastoral ministry, between Christian reflection and Christian life." Video message of September 3, 2015, to the International Theological Congress, Buenos Aires' Pontifical Catholic University of Argentina. Elise Harris, "Doctrine and Pastoral Care Go Hand-in-Hand, Pope Francis Reminds Theologians," Catholic News Agency, September 4, 2015, https://www.catholicnewsagency.com/news/32573/doctrine-and-pastoral-care-go-hand-in-hand-pope-francis-reminds-theologians.

52. John Paul II, General Audience, July 28, 1999, 3.

for example, the temptation to look at Internet pornography, which is pervasive and easily accessible. Some such people want to avoid sexual sin, but they face repeated and often intense temptation. They resist at first because they are aware that grave matter is at stake, and that to give in would be mortally sinful. But they find that temptation keeps returning, and the only alternative to giving in *seems* to be the experience of endless, and ever more intense, temptation.

Often, when they do give in, they plan to repent of the sin. Anyone who doubts the power of sexual temptation need only consider the plight of such a person—call him George—who gives in, but with the intention of going to confession later. George is so desperate that he both *consents* to doing the sinful act and at the same time plans to *regret* having consented! Soon after, George goes to confession, but despite efforts to stay chaste, he finds himself caught in a cycle that begins with renewed temptation that seems all but impossible to resist. George's plight is quite common and clearly reveals the seemingly hopeless spiritual struggle many people face. Of course, sinning with the intention to repent later is better than sinning *without* planning to repent—but it does not compare with refusing to consent to the sin in the first place. It does not compare with consistently refusing to commit mortal sin. Living a life that is regularly punctuated by the spiritual death of mortal sin—spiritual death that remains until it is repented in the Sacrament of Penance—does not compare with living a life of consistent cooperation with God's grace and always remaining alive in him.

But how can a person who is tempted so powerfully and repeatedly consistently resist? Despite the seeming impossibility of such a situation, it is by no means hopeless. Those who are tempted and persistently cry out to the Lord with faith experience the strength they need to conquer temptation by the power of the Holy Spirit. St. Paul repeatedly affirms that by the Spirit's power, the compulsion of sin can be defeated: "I say, then: live by the Spirit and you will certainly not gratify the desire of the flesh" (Gal 5:16;[53] cf. 5:25); "For the law of the Spirit of life in Christ Jesus has set me free from the law of sin and death" (Rom 8:2; cf. 8:5–6); "So then, brethren, we are debtors, not to the flesh, to live according to the flesh—

---

53. New American Bible.

for if you live according to the flesh you will die, but if by the Spirit you put to death the deeds of the body you will live" (Rom 8:12–13). Theologians, pastors, teachers, and parents have the responsibility to bring hope by proclaiming the truth about sexual sin, but always along with the far greater truth that Jesus Christ is Lord, that he is infinitely stronger than any temptation, no matter how overwhelming it may seem, and that he fervently desires to communicate that strength to us by sending us the Holy Spirit from the Father.

Now let's consider the alternative scenario. When those responsible for communicating the truth about the harm mortal sin does to people, and about what is and is not mortally sinful, *fail* to communicate that truth, it is much easier for the people entrusted to their care to rationalize. We would consider it gross malpractice if those responsible for helping us stay physically healthy failed to warn us about behaviors that could cause us serious bodily harm and even kill us. We would consider it even worse malpractice if medical professionals not only failed to warn us, but also gave us the impression that such behaviors are not harmful and can even be appropriate and good for us. We should be concerned a fortiori if those responsible for people's *spiritual* health and *ultimate* welfare not only fail to make it clear how harmful to their spiritual health and how much of a risk to their ultimate welfare certain acts are, but even suggest that those acts are not harmful and can even be appropriate and good for them.

One reason this seductively bad advice is given by so many pastors and theologians is that they assume that it is virtually impossible for people *not* to give in to such strong temptation, and conclude that the Lord cannot possibly be asking people to resist it. So, they reason that these behaviors must not be wrong after all, or must at most be only light matter and not anything that could endanger one's salvation. Or these pastors and theologians may have convinced themselves that in some situations these behaviors can be good. For example, they may reason as follows. If someone experiences strong same-sex attraction and little if any attraction to members of the opposite sex, would it not be good for that person to settle into a committed sexual relationship with a same-sex friend? Should not the Church be happy about those kinds of relationships? And should we not want priests to bless them?

People who are tempted to sexual sin are hardly likely to turn to God and wholeheartedly beseech him for the grace they need to resist temptation if theologians and pastoral ministers entrusted with their spiritual welfare give them the impression that nonmarital sexual activity is not gravely wrong, poses no real risk to their salvation, and can even be appropriate and good. The Lord's own words—"You are wrong because you know neither the scriptures nor the power of God" (Mt 22:29)—seem directly addressed to those who let such skewed thinking shape their pastoral care. So, too, does the Lord's proclamation through the prophet Isaiah: "Woe to those who call evil good and good evil, who put darkness for light and light for darkness" (Is 5:20).

It is a terrible thing to help people rationalize sin, but the failure to recognize the power of God can incline theologians and pastoral leaders to do just that. We must instead help people acknowledge their sin for what it is and call upon the Lord, who wishes to empower them to overcome it. And, of course, we ourselves must do the same. We would do well to bear in mind a scriptural theme that is proclaimed in various ways throughout the Bible: "With God all things are possible" (Mt 19:26). "If God is for us, who is against us?" (Rom 8:31). "I can do all things in him who strengthens me" (Phil 4:13).

I serve as chaplain for the Detroit chapter of the Courage apostolate, which helps people with same-sex attraction live chaste lives. The very first of the five goals of Courage, which members recite at the beginning of every meeting, is "To live chaste lives in accordance with the Roman Catholic Church's teaching on homosexuality." If they didn't begin with clarity about that point, they would be courting disaster. Courage members don't define themselves by their sexual attractions; they recognize their own dignity as created in God's image and likeness, redeemed by Christ, and invited to grace in this life and glory in the life to come. They realize that their same-sex attraction is not sinful in itself, but that it is disordered because it inclines them toward the use of sexuality not in harmony with God's plan for married love. And they understand that consenting to such acts would be mortally sinful because they cannot help them pursue any true human good, since unlike the sexual acts of even infertile married couples, homosexual acts lack the requisite bodily complementarity for one-flesh union and are inherently closed to the gift of life.

This understanding by Courage members in no way compromises

their awareness of their personal dignity as children of God. Most are doing remarkably well in the area of chastity, and as a spiritual father, I can only say that I am proud of them and find their witness humbling. They experience success in their pursuit of chastity insofar as they bear in mind the truth about sexual sin and rely on the power of God, with whom all things are possible. Courage members find it discouraging when people in positions of authority suggest that homosexual activity can sometimes be morally good, and when they endorse the blessing of same-sex unions.

We all know how strongly human beings are drawn to the experience of sexual pleasure. Unless they have clarity about what is right and wrong in this area, they are highly likely to go the way of least resistance. Consider this: when a behavior is obviously harmful to oneself and also causes intense pain, a person rarely has reason or motivation to engage in that behavior, and in such cases there is therefore rarely a need to try to dissuade people from it. For example, hardly anyone needs to be told that it would be morally wrong to hold one's hand over a flame and let the flesh burn off. The intense pain and serious damage caused by the flame obviate the need to warn people against such behavior. It is quite a different situation when a behavior is not just not painful but is intensely pleasurable, and when the damage it does is not immediately evident.

This is what theologians and pastoral ministers are up against in proclaiming the truth about sexual morality. How, then, should they handle the situation? The problem obviously cannot be solved by somehow removing the pleasure from illicit sexual activity. Sexual union is a great good created by God himself, and its concomitant pleasure, which is itself good, bears witness to the goodness of such union. But, of course, sex can be and often is abused and distorted, and people find themselves tempted to seek the pleasure of sex while setting their hearts against the good of life—as they do when they practice contraception, since the very object of their act is to prevent a life from coming into existence. They also find themselves tempted to engage in sexual activity in ways that conflict with its meaning as a communion of bodily persons.

People inclined to any kind of nonmarital sexual activity need support in their efforts to live chaste lives. One way theologians and pastoral ministers can offer that support is to help them see what it is about marriage and sexual activity within marriage that is so good, and what it is about nonmarital and otherwise illicit sexual activity that makes it so harmful. Such an explanation is necessary for people to understand the Church's teaching on sexual morality, as Grisez puts it, "not as arbitrary and outdated rules meant to spoil their enjoyment and make them feel guilty, but as ever-relevant truths that direct them toward real happiness and away from the burden of real guilt, which is the harm people do to their innermost selves when they follow the lure of their feelings and violate the truth."[54] One such harm is that those who engage in nonmarital sexual acts find it more difficult to recognize fruitful marriage as both an icon of the Trinity and a prefiguring of the everlasting wedding feast of Christ the bridegroom with the Church his bride. Of course, since chaste living requires sacrifice, it is necessary to help people see that remaining true to Christ, who desires our own happiness even more than we do, is worth any sacrifice, no matter how great. We must help people appropriate the truth that St. Paul so beautifully articulated: "I consider that the sufferings of this present time are not worth comparing with the glory that is to be revealed to us" (Rom 8:18).

Besides helping people understand how nonmarital sexual activity harms people, theologians and pastoral ministers should confidently communicate the Church's teaching about the grave immorality of nonmarital sex. The Church's proposal of that teaching infallibly by the ordinary universal Magisterium is a gift that enables us to have the necessary confidence. Only if people are convinced that sin leads to everlasting death and fidelity to Christ leads to everlasting life are they likely to imitate St. Augustine, who finally and wholeheartedly followed Paul's exhortation to "put on the Lord Jesus Christ, and make no provision for the flesh, to gratify its desires" (Rom 13:14).

Infallible Teaching and Discernment

I wish to conclude by drawing attention to a crucial point about discernment that confirms the importance of the Church's infallible teaching that the choice to engage in nonmarital sexual activity is intrinsically and gravely wrong.

54. Germain Grisez, *The Way of the Lord Jesus*, vol. 3, *Difficult Moral Questions* (Quincy, IL: Franciscan Press, 1997), q. 22, http://twotlj.org/G-3-22.html.

Discernment bears only on morally good or indifferent options,[55] and the question arises: How can I know which of *those* options I might choose is the one God wants? This is the point at which discernment begins. People who try to discern before that point are in effect asking whether God wants them to do something they should have excluded before beginning to discern. If they treat nonmarital sexual activity as a discernable option, they court disaster by opening themselves up to deception. Theologians and pastoral ministers who recognize and accept the Church's infallible teaching on sexual morality are in a position to help them avoid that disaster.

This point will become clear if we recall St. Ignatius Loyola's Rules for the Discernment of Spirits. He calls them "Rules for becoming aware of and understanding ... the different movements which are caused in the soul, the good, to receive them, and the bad to reject them."[56] His first two rules explain how the actions of the good and evil spirits are very much opposed to each other. The first reveals their action in lives of people moving from bad to worse.

The first rule: in persons who are going from mortal sin to mortal sin, the enemy is ordinarily accustomed to propose apparent pleasures to them, leading them to imagine sensual delights and pleasures in order to hold them more and make them grow in their vices and sins. In these persons the good spirit uses a contrary method, stinging and biting their consciences through their rational power of moral judgment.[57]

The second rule shows how the good and evil spirits act in the lives of people going from good to better.

The second: in persons who are going on intensely purifying their sins and rising from good to better in the service of God our Lord, the method is contrary to that in the first rule. For then it is proper to the evil spirit to bite, sadden, and place

---

55. St. Ignatius initiates his consideration of "what matters an election ought to be made about" with this observation: "It is necessary that everything about which we want to make an election should be indifferent, or good, in itself, and should be allowed within our Holy Mother the hierarchical Church, and not bad nor opposed to her." *The Spiritual Exercises of St. Ignatius Loyola*, no. 170, translated by Father Elder Mullan, SJ (New York: P. J. Kenedy & Sons, 1914), https://www.sacred-texts.com/chr/seil/seil28.htm.

56. St. Ignatius Loyola, translated by Timothy M. Gallagher, OMV, in *The Discernment of Spirits: An Ignatian Guide for Everyday Living*, New York: Crossroad, 2005), 7.

57. Gallagher, *Discernment of Spirits*, 7.

obstacles, disquieting with false reasons, so that the person may not go forward. And it is proper to the good spirit to give courage and strength, consolations, tears, inspirations, and quiet, easing and taking away all obstacles, so that the person may go forward in doing good.[58]

As Fr. Timothy Gallagher explains in his masterful commentary, St. Augustine's discussion of his interior state before and during his conversion beautifully illustrates what St. Ignatius is telling us through these rules. As for the first rule, Augustine says that in his youth, when he was turned away from the Lord, "I burned to fill myself with evil things."[59] That is, he experienced a powerful interior motion toward self-indulgence. That is the dominant movement he experienced at that time, and it is plainly a temptation brought on by the evil spirit. But Augustine also experiences what he calls "fruitless seedlings of grief" and "restless weariness."[60] Those are caused by the good spirit, who is "stinging and biting" Augustine's conscience in order to bring him to his senses.

Augustine illustrates the second rule by recounting that when he experienced his spiritual awakening and sought to be purified of his sins, he felt himself "held back by mere trifles, the most paltry inanities, all my old attachments."[61] That is clearly the movement of the evil spirit, but the dominant motion is toward the Lord, who provides Augustine with great consolation in the vision of "the chaste beauty of Continence in all her serene, unsullied joy, as she modestly beckoned me to cross over and to hesitate no more."[62]

In short, when a person is moving from bad to worse, the evil spirit supplies temptations to strengthen the pull away from God, and the good spirit stings the conscience to weaken that pull. When a person is moving from good to better, the evil spirit places obstacles in order to weaken the movement toward God, while the good spirit offers consolation and encouragement in order to strengthen it. Ignatius exhorts us to be aware

---

58. Gallagher, *Discernment of Spirits*, 7.
59. St. Augustine, *Confessions*, Book II.1, translated by Gallagher in *Discernment of Spirits*, 28.
60. St. Augustine, *Confessions*, Book II.2, translated by Gallagher in *Discernment of Spirits*, 28.
61. R. S. Pine-Coffin, trans., *Saint Augustine: Confessions* (Harmondsworth: Penguin, 1961), 175, quoted in Gallagher, *Discernment of Spirits*, 29.
62. Pine-Coffin, *Saint Augustine: Confessions*, 176, quoted in Gallagher, *Discernment of Spirits*, 30.

of these interior motions, and he supplies the Rules for the Discernment of Spirits to help us understand what they mean and respond properly.

These rules come into play only after one has exercised one's reason to exclude all of the morally bad options. One obviously cannot discern whether one should commit adultery or pay an unjust wage, for discernment bears only on what is morally good or indifferent. Nevertheless, sometimes discernment is mentioned in discussions of options for choice that are excluded by Catholic moral teaching. For example, an unmarried couple may claim they need to discern whether to move in together and live as a married couple before their wedding. A priest may claim that he needs to discern whether to leave the priesthood and attempt marriage. A married couple may say they need to discern whether to use contraception or natural family planning. And a divorced person might say he or she must discern whether to receive Holy Communion despite living as though married to someone else. But I reiterate: discernment applies only to options that God *might* want a person to choose. If we try to discern whether God wants us to choose something we ought to know he cannot possibly want, we invite deception.

How does deception come about? Those who treat as a legitimate option a course of action they should have recognized as illicit and eliminated on that basis set themselves up to misread the interior movements they experience. They are in grave danger of assuming that their very willingness to "discern" God's will indicates that they fit into the category of those who are going from good to better. With that assumption in place, they are liable to read the sting of conscience caused by the good spirit as an obstacle set up by the evil spirit, and to read the apparent pleasures proposed by the evil spirit as consolations from the good spirit to encourage them to move in the direction they want. Consider the couple trying to "discern" whether to cohabitate without benefit of marriage. Not having excluded that option from the outset as wrong and therefore unavailable for discernment, the couple all too easily assume that the appealing emotions associated with the course of action they should not be considering—the prospect of enjoying regular sexual intercourse, which stirs up powerful emotions indeed, and the desire for other aspects of the intimacy and oneness that are proper to the good of marriage—are stirred by the Holy Spirit to encourage the choice of cohabitation. Conversely, they easily assume that the unpleasant emotions associated with the prospect of remaining abstinent are the work of the evil spirit, who saddens and places obstacles in the path of those going from good to better.

The failure to understand this dynamic is a serious problem in the contemporary Church, and the only way to overcome it is to begin with clarity about whether an option should be regarded as available for discernment. That clarity comes through sound reasoning about moral norms and humble acceptance of God's revelation about those norms as interpreted by the Church's Magisterium. St. Ignatius makes this clear in his "Rules for Thinking, Judging, and Feeling with the Church"[63]—but that is matter for another essay. Here it suffices to recognize that the infallibility of the Church's teaching about the grave wrongness of nonmarital sex is a gift that theologians and pastors should cherish because it protects from deception those who wholeheartedly accept it and preserves them in the grace that leads to the intimate life of God's kingdom.

63. See Ignatius of Loyola, *Spiritual Exercises and Selected Works*, edited by George E. Ganss (Mahwah, NJ: Paulist, 1991), 211–14 (*Sp. Ex.* nos. 352–70) and 429n152.

CHAPTER 9

Catholic Sexual Morality and the Problem of Dissent

ROBERT FASTIGGI

Introduction: The Meaning of Dissent

The word "dissent" derives from the Latin verb *dissentire*, which means "to differ or disagree in thought, opinion or sentiment."[1] As used by Catholics today, dissent refers to "opposition or disagreement (often public) with certain Church teachings on faith or morals."[2]

Dissent from teachings on faith and morals must be distinguished from ignorance. Some people simply don't know what the Church teaches on various points. Their opposition to certain teachings, therefore, is not due to willful rejection but to ignorance, that is, lack of knowledge. Because Catholics have the responsibility to seek the truth, such ignorance can be either culpable or non-culpable.[3]

Dissent must also be distinguished from failure or sin. Many Catholics know the moral teachings of the Church and accept them, but they fail at times to live up to them. Such failures do not constitute dissent but sins. Unfortunately, human beings have a tendency to rationalize or justify their actions. When certain sins are engaged in repeatedly, these

---

1. Robert L. Fastiggi, ed., "Dissent," in *New Catholic Encyclopedia Supplement 2009*, (Detroit: Gale Cengage Learning, 2010), 225.
2. Fastiggi, "Dissent," 225–26.
3. See the *Catechism of the Catholic Church*, 2nd ed. (Vatican City State: Libreria Editrice Vaticana, 1997), nos. 1790–93.

sins might no longer feel sinful. If people are told by a priest or a teacher that these repeated actions are not sinful, they might begin to accept them as not sinful. Dissent by Catholic priests and teachers, therefore, might lead to dissent on the part of the people they influence. Justifying sinful actions can be more spiritually harmful than the sinful actions themselves. It is "far better to be a sinner who recognizes sin than someone who has learned to rationalize immoral behavior."[4]

Dissent can involve disagreement with a wide variety of teachings on faith and morals. This essay, though, will focus on dissent from Catholic sexual morality in which dissent is expressed in practice as well as in words and ideas. In fact, the justification of dissent by Catholic theologians only became widespread in the aftermath of St. Paul VI's 1968 encyclical *Humanae Vitae*.[5] According to Msgr. William B. Smith, the word "dissent" was not found in any standard encyclopedia or dictionary of Catholic theology prior to 1972. As he writes:

> A careful review of the standard theological encyclopedias and dictionaries finds no entries under the title of "Dissent" prior to 1972. Standard manuals of theology did raise possible questions about the rare individual who could not offer personal *assent* to formal Church teaching, and such questions were discussed under treatments of the Magisterium or the Teachings of the Church, examining the status of such teaching and its binding force and/or extent.[6]

As William E. May notes, three bishops at Vatican II—in reference to *Lumen Gentium* (LG) 25—raised the theoretical case of a learned person who, "in the face of a doctrine not infallibly proposed, cannot for well-founded reasons, give his internal assent (*interne assentire non potest*).[7] With regard to this theoretical case, the Theological Commission at Vatican II replied that "approved theological treatises should be consulted."[8] Msgr. William B. Smith notes that "the question posed to

---

4. Robert Fastiggi, *Catholic Sexual Morality* (Eugene: OR: Wipf & Stock, 2017), 93.

5. See Fastiggi, "Dissent," 226.

6. William B. Smith, "The Question of Dissent in Moral Theology," in *Persona, Verità, e Morale: Atti del Congresso Internazionale di Teologia Morale*, edited by A. Ansaldo (Rome: 1987), 235.

7. William E. May, *An Introduction to Moral Theology*, 2nd ed. (Huntington, IN: Our Sunday Visitor, 2003), 258.

8. *Acta Synodalia Concilii Oecumenici Vaticani Secundi*, III/8 (Rome: Typis Polyglottis Vaticanis, 1976), no. 159, p. 88.

the Commission concerned the *negative* inability to give positive assent ... which is not at all the same as a *positive right* to dissent."[9]

The Church's Historical Resistance to Dissent

Opposition to teachings on faith and morals is not new. As noted above, this opposition sometimes arises from ignorance or the failure to recognize the sinfulness of various actions. Church leaders since apostolic times have had to remind the faithful of the disordered nature of certain forms of sexual behavior. St. Paul warned the Christians of Corinth and Rome about the sins of fornication and homosexual actions (cf. 1 Cor 6:9–20; Rom 1:26–27). In 1054, Pope Leo IX wrote to St. Peter Damian expressing his dismay over sexual sins of clerics such as masturbation and sodomy.[10]

How, though, did the Church deal with those who opposed Catholic teachings? In the early Christian centuries, there were various forms of exile, penance, or deprivation of full ecclesiastical communion.[11] During the Middle Ages, there were minor excommunications (deprivation of the sacraments) and major excommunications (solemn expulsion from the Church). Dissenters from Church doctrine and discipline were also subject to the various inquisitions, whether papal or national (e.g., the Spanish Inquisition).[12] Recourse to excommunications and other punishments were sometimes excessive. By way of response, the Councils of Lateran III (1179), Lateran IV (1215), and Trent (1563) asked for circumspection and sobriety in the use of such penalties.[13]

After the Council of Trent, more refined distinctions began to emerge.

---

9. Smith, "Question of Dissent in Moral Theology," 239.

10. Heinrich Denzinger and Peter Hünermann, *Compendium of Creeds, Definitions, and Declarations on Matters of Faith and Morals*, 43rd ed. (San Francisco: Ignatius Press, 2012), nos. 687–88. [Henceforth D-H.]

11. Fastiggi, "Dissent," 226.

12. Fastiggi, "Dissent," 226.

13. Norman P. Tanner, SJ, ed., *Decrees of the Ecumenical Councils*, 2 vols. (London and Washington, DC: Sheed & Ward and Georgetown University Press, 1990), Lateran III (canon 6, p. 214); Lateran IV (canons 47–49, pp. 255–57); Council of Trent (Session 25, chap. 3, pp. 785–86).

Some forms of dissent were qualified as heretical, while others were designated as close to heresy (*haeresi proxima*), rash (*temeraria*), scandalous (*scandalosa*), offensive to pious ears (*piarum aurium offensiva*), and evil sounding (*male sonans*).[14]

Prior to the 1960s, there were only occasional efforts to justify dissent from authoritative magisterial teachings. In the seventeenth and eighteenth centuries, some Jansenists claimed that only exterior assent needed to be given to certain magisterial decisions. Pope Clement XI, however, in his 1705 constitution, *Vineam Domini Sabaoth*, ruled that the Jansenist errors must be rejected as heretical "not only in the mouth but also in the heart" (*non ore solum, sed et corde*).[15]

In the nineteenth century, some German-speaking theology professors, led by Ignaz von Döllinger, "sought a maximum of academic freedom for themselves and minimized the binding force of the official Magisterium."[16] These theologians tried to limit the obligation of assent only to doctrines set forth infallibly by the Magisterium. Pius IX rejected this position in his 1863 letter *Tuas libenter*, to the Archbishop of Munich-Freising.[17] In the same letter, he also affirmed the obligation to submit to decisions of the Pontifical Congregations as well as matters upheld as "theologically certain" by the constant and common consensus of Catholics.[18] In his 1864 *Syllabus of Errors*, Pius IX condemned the error, which holds that "the obligation by which Catholic teachers and writers are absolutely bound is restricted to those matters only that are proposed by the infallible judgment of the Church to be believed by all as dogmas of faith."[19]

Pius IX clearly rejected the position that Catholics may dissent from magisterial teachings that have not been proposed as infallible dogmas.

---

14. Cf. D-H, Systematic Index H 3bc, p. 1292.
15. D-H, 2390.
16. Avery Cardinal Dulles, SJ, *Magisterium: Teacher and Guardian of the Faith* (Naples, FL: Sapientia Press of Ave Maria University, 2007), 31.
17. D-H, 2879–80.
18. D-H, 2880.
19. D-H, 2923.

The Magisterium and Sexual Morality

With regard to sexual morality, dissent was never justified by the Magisterium. When some laxist moralists in the seventeenth century began to develop clever ways to justify sexual sins, the Magisterium reacted. On March 18, 1666, the Holy Office under Pope Alexander VII condemned the laxist proposition that "a keeper of a concubine is not bound to dismiss the concubine if she is very useful for the pleasure of the keeper provided that if she were missing, he would carry on life with very great difficulty and other feasts would affect the keeper with great disgust, and another maidservant would be found with great difficulty."[20] On March 2, 1679, the Holy Office under Pope Innocent XI condemned sixty-five propositions of the laxists. Among these condemned propositions was one that stated "pederasty (*mollities*) is not prohibited by natural law. Therefore, if God had not forbidden it, it would often be good and sometimes obligatory under pain of mortal sin."[21]

Over the centuries, the Magisterium has consistently condemned various sexual acts as sinful. The condemned acts include masturbation,[22] fornication or premarital sex,[23] and homosexual acts.[24] These condemnations are rooted in the witness of Scripture the natural law and the constant tradition of the Church. In 1975, the Congregation for the Doctrine of the Faith issued *Persona Humana*, which was a declaration on certain questions concerning sexual ethics. This document notes that the Magisterium of the Church "in the course of a constant tradition" as well as the sense of the faithful "have declared without hesitation that masturbation is an intrinsically and seriously disordered act."[25] Fornication is explicitly condemned in Scripture (1 Cor 6:9), as is prostitution (1 Cor 6:15–20). The Church's condemnation of such actions is considered to be definitive

---

20. D-H, 2061.
21. D-H, 2149.
22. See D-H, 687–88, 3684, and 4584.
23. D-H, 835, 2148, 3715, and 4582.
24. D-H, 687–88, 4583, 5100; see also the Congregation for the Doctrine of the Faith's 1986 *Letter to the Bishops on the Pastoral Care of Homosexual Persons*, website of the Holy See, accessed January 2, 2023, https://www.vatican.va/roman_curia/congregations/cfaith/documents/rc_con_cfaith_doc_19861001_homosexual-persons_en.html.
25. D-H, 4584.

and infallible by virtue of the universal and ordinary Magisterium of the Church.[26] Homosexual acts are condemned in Scripture (Gen 19:1–29, Lv 20:13, Rom 1:24–27, 1 Cor 6:10, 1 Tim 1:10), and the Magisterium has described such acts as "intrinsically disordered."[27] Because the Church's teachings on masturbation, fornication, prostitution, and homosexual acts represent the constant tradition of the Magisterium as well as the witness of Scripture and the natural law, dissent from these teachings can in no way be justified.

The Magisterium and Contraception

The Church has consistently taught that that contraception is gravely wrong. The deliberate wasting of the seed by Onan, son of Judah, when he was having relations with his wife, Tamar, was offensive to the Lord (cf. Gn 38:9–10). The Church therefore condemned *coitus interruptus* and referred to it as "the practice of Onanism within marriage" (*de usu onanistico matrimonii*).[28] In 1822, the Sacred Penitentiary stated that a pious woman would be able to offer herself passively to a husband "when previous experience shows that he conducts himself in the abominable manner of Onan."[29] This is because "the woman, for her part, does nothing against nature and endeavors to do what is licit, while the entire disorder of the act comes from the malice of the husband who withdraws before ejaculation in the vagina."[30] In 1851, the Holy Office condemned the practice of onanism within marriage and described as "scandalous, erroneous and contrary to the natural law of marriage."[31]

In addition to *coitus interruptus*, the Magisterium has also condemned other forms of contraception such as the condom. According to the phi-

---

26. See Congregation for the Doctrine of the Faith, *Profession of Faith,* website of the Holy See, accessed January 2, 2023, https://www.vatican.va/roman_curia/congregations/cfaith/documents/rc_con_cfaith_doc_1998_professio-fidei_en.html, no. 11; see also Dulles, "Commentary of Cardinal Joseph Ratzinger and Archbishop Tarcisio Bertone on the Concluding Paragraphs of the 1989 *Professio Fidei,*" in *Magisterium,* 172.
27. D-H, 4583; see also the *Catechism of the Catholic Church* (CCC), §2357.
28. D-H, 2715.
29. D-H, 2715.
30. D-H, 2715.
31. D-H, 2793.

losopher and legal scholar John T. Noonan Jr., various forms of preventing conception have been used over the centuries. Augustine in the fifth century refers to contraceptive poisons.[32] The *Roman Catechism* of 1566 refers to medicines or drugs used to prevent conception.[33] The condom appears around the middle of the seventeenth century.[34] The diaphragm for use as a pessary is developed in 1880.[35] By 1935, a wide variety of chemical solutions such as spermicides or occlusive agents are available.[36]

The Fathers, Doctors, and the Magisterium of the Church have consistently condemned all forms of contraception. In his monumental study on the history of contraception, John T. Noonan offered this summary:

> Since the first clear mention of contraception, when a harsh third-century accused a pope of encouraging it, the articulated judgment has been the same. In the world of the late Empire known to St. Jerome and St. Augustine, in the Ostrogothic Arles of Bishop Caesarius and the Suevian Braga of Bishop Martin, in the Paris of St. Albert and St. Thomas, in the Renaissance Rome of Sixtus V and the Renaissance Milan of St. Charles Borromeo, in the Naples of St. Alphonsus Liguori and the Liège of Charles Billuart, in the Philadelphia of Bishop Kenrick, and in the Bombay of Bishop Gracias, the teachers of the Church have taught without hesitation or variation that certain acts preventing procreation are gravely sinful. No Catholic theologian has ever taught, "Contraception is a good act." The teaching on contraception is clear and apparently fixed forever.[37]

When forms of contraception began to be promoted in the nineteenth century, the Magisterium reaffirmed the Church's traditional stand against contraception. The Holy Office rejected both onanism and the condom in an April 1853 response:

QUESTION 1: Is the imperfect use of marriage licit, whether it happens by onanism or "condomistically" (or, as the abominable instrument is commonly called, "the condom")?

---

32. John T. Noonan Jr., *Contraception: A History of Its Treatment by the Catholic Theologians and Canonists* (Cambridge, MA: Belknap Press of Harvard University Press, 1965), 138.
33. Noonan, *Contraception*, 349.
34. Noonan, *Contraception*, 347.
35. Noonan, *Contraception*, 408.
36. Noonan, *Contraception*, 408.
37. Noonan, *Contraception*, 6. In spite of this clear assessment of the consistent Catholic condemnation of contraception, Noonan believed the Church's teaching against contraception was subject to change. According to him, the environment in which Christians live has changed; therefore the reasons for condemning contraception no longer apply.

QUESTION 2: Is the wife, aware of the "condomisite" union, able to yield herself passively?

RESPONSE TO 1 (Decree 6, published April 19, 1853): No, indeed, it is intrinsically evil.

RESPONSE TO 2: No, she would indeed give assistance to an act which is intrinsically illicit.[38]

The Magisterium did, however, allow couples for serious reasons to limit marital union only to days when conception is more difficult. This is clear from a June 16, 1880, response of the Sacred Penitentiary:

QUESTION: Is it permitted to have marital union only on those days when conception is more difficult?

RESPONSE: Spouses who use this above-mentioned method need not be troubled, and they can follow the opinion of confessors about this practice who, with caution, deal with those spouses for whom other reasoning has tried in vain to have them abandon the detestable crime of Onanism.[39]

While limiting marital union to times more likely to be infertile could be acceptable (for serious reasons), recourse to *coitus interruptus* and condoms was forbidden. The Catholic Church's prohibition of contraception was the general position of most other Christian communities. This consensus, though, began to erode when gynecologists in the 1920s and 30s began to accept the use of contraceptives.[40] 1930, as Janet E. Smith, observes, "Anglicans broke ranks with nearly the whole of the traditional Christian opposition to contraception with a declaration at the Lambeth Conference that permitted use of contraception by married couples, for grave reasons."[41]

Pius XI responded to the Lambeth Conference's approval of contraception in his December 31, 1930, encyclical *Casti Connubii*. Pius XI covers a wide range of topics on marriage and the family in this encyclical, but he clearly has the Lambeth Conference in mind when he speaks

---

38. D-H, 2795.
39. D-H, 3148.
40. See Noonan, *Contraception*, 408–9.
41. Janet E. Smith, *Humanae Vitae: A Generation Later* (Washington, DC: Catholic University of America Press, 1991), 5. See also Noonan, *Contraception*, 409.

of some recently judging it possible to depart "from the uninterrupted Christian tradition"[42] on the question of contraception. Pius XI teaches that the deliberate frustration of the natural power and purpose of the marital act is "shameful and intrinsically vicious."[43] He goes on to say that "any use whatsoever of matrimony exercised in such a way that the act is deliberately frustrated in its natural power to generate life is an offense against the law of God and of nature, and those who indulge in it are branded with the guilt of grave sin."[44]

Pius XII reaffirmed Pius XI's condemnation of contraception in his October 29, 1951, Discourse to the Participants in the Congress of the Italian Catholic Union of Midwives, which is commonly referred to as his "Allocution to the Midwives." In this address he states:

> Our predecessor, Pius XI of happy memory, in his encyclical, *Casti Connubii* of December 31, 1930 once again solemnly proclaimed the fundamental law of the conjugal act and of conjugal relations: that every attempt of the spouses in carrying out the conjugal act or in the development of its natural consequences that is directed at depriving it of its inherent force and impeding the procreation of a new life is immoral; and no "indication" or necessity can change an intrinsically immoral act into a moral and licit act.[45]

Pius XII made it clear that this norm is permanent and unchanging by saying, "This prescription is in full vigor today as yesterday, and so also will it be tomorrow and always because it is not a simple precept of human law but an expression of a natural and divine law."[46]

In the 1950s—during the pontificate of Pius XII—various forms of pessaries such as the diaphragm were being promoted. The Holy Office

---

42. D-H, 3717.
43. D-H, 3716.
44. D-H, 3717.
45. Pius XII, Allocution to the Midwives, *Acta Apostolicae Sedis* (AAS) 43 (1951): 843. My translation of the Italian, which reads: "Il Nostro Predecessore Pio XI di felice memoria nella sua Enciclica *Casti Connbii* del 31 dicembre 1930 proclamò di nuovo solennemente la legge fondamentale dell'atto e dei rapporti coniugali: che ogni attentato dei coniugi nel compimento dell'atto coniugale o nello sviluppo delle sue conseguenze naturali, attentato avente per scopo di privarlo della forza ad esso inerente e di impedire la procreazione di una nuova vita, è immorale; e che nessuna 'indicazione' o necessità può mutare un'azione intrinsecamente immorale in un atto morale e lecito."
46. AAS 43 (1951): 843. The Italian reads: "Questa prescrizione è in pieno vigore oggi come ieri, e tale sarà anche domani e sempre, perchè non è un semplice precetto di diritto umano, ma l'espressione di una legge naturale e divina."

in 1955 issued a decree—directed to some North American bishops—that condemned the use of the use of pessaries (sterilet, diaphragm) by married couples in the exercise of their marital rights. These methods of contraception were rejected as "intrinsically evil."[47]

The magisterial condemnations of contraception consistently refer to the natural and the divine law. Contraception itself is described variously as intrinsically vicious, intrinsically illicit, and intrinsically immoral. This is why Pius XII holds that the prescription against contraception is in "full vigor today as yesterday and so also will it be tomorrow and always."[48] In light of the constant and consistent condemnations of contraception as intrinsically immoral, it is no wonder that Fr. John C. Ford, SJ, and Germain Grisez would argue that this teaching fulfills the conditions for an infallible judgment of the ordinary and universal Magisterium as articulated at Vatican II in LG 25.[49] Later, Fr. Ermenegildo Lio, OFM, would argue that Pope Paul VI's condemnation of contraception in *Humanae Vitae* fulfilled the requirements of an *ex cathedra* infallible papal teaching.[50]

The Birth Control Pill, the Papal Commission, and the Rise of Dissent

As we have seen, the Catholic Church has consistently condemned all deliberate attempts to impede the marital act of its procreative purpose. These contraceptive methods included *coitus interruptus* or onanism and barrier methods such as the condom or the diaphragm. In 1953, biologists John Rock and Gregory Pincas developed the first birth control pill.[51]

---

47. D-H, 3917a.

48. AAS 43 (1951): 843.

49. John C. Ford, SJ, and Germain Grisez, "Contraception and the Infallibility of the Ordinary Magisterium," *Theological Studies* 39, no. 2 (1978): 258–312.

50. Ermenegildo Lio, OFM, *Humanae Vitae e Infallibilità: Il Concilio, Paolo VI e Giovanni Paolo II* (Vatican City: Libreria Editrice Vaticana, 1986). See also "Humanae Vitae and Infallibility," a book review of *Humanae Vitae e Infallibilità* by Fr. Brian W. Harrison published in the *Roman Theological Forum* 12 (July 1987): http://www.rtforum.org/lt/lt12.html; and "The Ex Cathedra Status of the Encyclical *Humanae Vitae*," first published in the *Roman Theological Forum* 43 (September–November 1992) and then later published in *Faith and Reason: The Journal of Christendom College* 19 (1993): https://media.christendom.edu/wp-content/uploads/2016/10/Brian-W.-Harrison-The-Ex-Cathedra-Status-of-Humanae-Vitiae.pdf.

51. See "A Brief History of Birth Control in the US," Our Bodies, Ourselves Today at Suffolk

In 1960, the anovulant pill known as Enovid was approved for use in the United States by the Food and Drug Administration. It consisted of a mix of the hormones progesterone and estrogen.[52] The Pill—as it became known—soon began to be marketed in other countries. Pius XII, in a September 12, 1958, address to a congress of hematologists, taught that the anovulant pills could be used for therapeutic purposes but not with the specific intention of impeding conception. As he explained:

> If the wife takes this medicine, not in view of preventing conception, but only on the advice of a physician as a necessary remedy on account of a malady of the uterus or the organism, she provokes an indirect sterilization, which is permitted according to the general principle of actions with a double effect.[53]

Pius XII clearly ruled out the use of anovulant pills for the sole purpose of preventing conception.

In spite of Pius XII's rejection of anovulant pills used solely for contraceptive purposes, some Catholics began to promote the use of such pills as means of birth control. Dr. John Rock, the Catholic physician who helped develop the birth control pill, published a book in 1963 titled *The Time Has Come: A Catholic Doctor's Proposal to End the Battle over Birth Control*.[54] Even before the publication of Dr. Rock's book, a number of Catholic theologians had already begun to argue that that the use of anovulant pills could be used to suppress the possibility of conception.[55] One of these theologians was Louis Janssens, who in 1958 published an article arguing for the lawful use of anovulants to inhibit ovulation.[56] Some believe that Pius XII's reference to the anovulant pills in his September 12, 1958, address was in direct response to Janssens' position.[57]

University, accessed January 12, 2023, https://www.ourbodiesourselves.org/health-info/a-brief-history-of-birth-control/.

52. "A Brief History of Birth Control in the US."

53. AAS 50 (1958): 735; my translation of the original French, which reads: "Si la femme prend ce médicament, non pas en vue d'empêcher la conception, mais uniquement sur avis du médecin, comme un remède nécessaire à cause d'une maladie de l'utérus ou de l'organisme, elle provoque une stérilisation indirecte, qui reste permise selon le principe général des actions à double effet."

54. John Rock, *The Time Has Come: A Catholic Doctor's Proposal to End the Battle over Birth Control* (New York: Alfred A. Knopf, 1963).

55. Noonan, *Contraception*, 465–66.

56. Louis Janssens, "L'Inhibition de l'ovulation est-elle moralement licite?," *Ephemerides theologicae lovanienses* 34 (1958): 357–60.

57. Noonan, *Contraception*, 466.

The majority of Catholic theologians between 1958 and 1963 agreed with Pius XII "that the direct use of anovulants to prevent procreation was an immoral interference with the generative process."[58] Beginning in 1963, several other theologians—including Bishop William Bekkers of the Netherlands and Bishop J. M. Reuss of Germany—began to publish articles taking the side of Janssens.[59]

In 1963, Pope John XXIII established a Papal Commission on Population, the Family, and Birth Control to discuss the anovulant pill and other related issues. He appointed six members to the commission, but he died shortly afterward on June 3, 1963.[60] Pope Paul VI continued the commission and greatly expanded its membership to seventy-two.[61] Among the members were cardinals, bishops, experts on population matters, physicians, and married couples. The Second Vatican Council was in session from 1962 to 1965. Pope Paul VI, in a June 23, 1964, address to a group of cardinals, made it clear that certain questions related to the regulation of birth were in need of further and more careful investigation, and they were being discussed by the papal commission.[62] He therefore did not wish the Council to propose immediately concrete solutions. Instead, he would give his judgment after the commission had completed its work.[63] Even though the Council did not resolve all the questions being discussed by the papal commission, *Gaudium et Spes* 51 offered an important instruction:

Hence when there is question of harmonizing conjugal love with the responsible transmission of life, the moral aspects of any procedure does not depend solely on sincere intentions or on an evaluation of motives, but must be determined by objective standards. These, based on the nature of the human person and his acts, preserve the full sense of mutual self-giving and human procreation in the context of true love. Such a goal cannot be achieved unless the virtue of conjugal chastity is sincerely practiced. Relying on these principles, sons of the Church may not un-

---

58. Noonan, *Contraception*, 468.

59. See Noonan, *Contraception*, 469 (on Bekkkers) and Smith, *Humanae Vitae,* 8 and 373 (on Reuss).

60. See Charles W. Norris, "The Papal Commission of Birth Control—Revisited," *Linacre Quarterly* 80, no. 1 (2013): 8–16, https://www.ncbi.nlm.nih.gov/pmc/articles/PMC6081774/.

61. Norris, "Papal Commission of Birth Control—Revisited," 8–9.

62. AAS 56 (1964): 581–89.

63. See footnote to Vatican II's *Gaudium et Spes* 51 (n. 119 in the Latin text).

dertake methods of birth control which are found blameworthy by the teaching authority of the Church in its unfolding of the divine law."[64]

The Council Fathers therefore affirmed the need for married couples to have recourse to "objective standards" when harmonizing marital love with the responsible transmission of life. Furthermore, couples "may not undertake methods of birth control which are found blameworthy by the teaching authority of the Church in its unfolding of the divine law." The footnote cited after this statement includes references to Pius XI's 1930 encyclical *Casti Connubii* and to Pius XII's 1951 "Allocution to the Midwives."[65]

The Birth Control Commission met from 1963 to 1966.[66] During these years, more and more Catholic theologians and bishops began to argue that contraception might be permissible in some circumstances.[67] On August 10, 1963, seven bishops from the Netherlands issued a statement that "in special situations" the use of oral, chemical means to prevent conception might be accepted.[68] Various factors were at play in these departures from traditional Catholic teaching. After the Lambeth Conference and the Anglican acceptance of contraception in hardship cases, other Christian groups began to allow for contraception in some cases, including various Lutheran, Calvinist, and Methodist communions.[69] There were also social influences such as "the fear of overpopulation, the new role of women in society, and the increased financial strains in raising a family well."[70] Many Catholic theologians and bishops, however, continued to uphold the traditional Catholic rejection of contraception. On May 7, 1964, Archbishop John Heenan of Westminster, in the name of the Catholic bishops of England and Wales, issued an opposing statement,

---

64. *Gaudium et Spes* 51; translation taken the website of the Holy See, accessed January 11, 2023, https://www.vatican.va/archive/hist_councils/ii_vatican_council/documents/vat-ii_const_19651207_gaudium-et-spes_en.html.

65. These references can be found in the footnote to *Gaudium et Spes* 51 in AAS 58 (1966): 1072.

66. See Norris, "Papal Commission of Birth Control—Revisited," 10–16, and Smith, *Humanae Vitae*, 12–14.

67. Noonan, *Contraception*, 469–74.

68. Noonan, *Contraception*, 470.

69. Noonan, *Contraception*, 490.

70. Smith, *Humanae Vitae*, 9.

which made it clear that "Contraception ... is not an open question, for it is against the law of God."[71]

The Papal Birth Control Commission—as it came to be known—was divided. Although the proceedings were to be strictly confidential, portions of a 1966 draft intended for Paul VI were leaked and published in the spring of 1967 by *The Tablet* and the *National Catholic Reporter*.[72] This draft came to be known as the "Majority Report," and it argued that a change in Catholic teaching on contraception was possible.[73] Among those endorsing this report were a number of prominent cardinals, including Cardinal Doepfner of Munich, Cardinal Suenens of Malines-Brussels, and Cardinal Shehan of Baltimore.[74] Two appendices were attached to the draft. Although they were only working documents, they came to be understood as primary documents.[75] One of these appendices was a rebuttal to those on the commission who argued that a change in Church teaching on contraception was not possible. This can be referred to as the "Majority Rebuttal."[76] The appendix, which argued that the Church is not able to change her position on contraception, was signed by four theologians—John C. Ford, SJ; Jan Visser, CSSR; Marcelino Zalba, SJ; and Stanislas de Lestapis, SJ—came to be known as the "Minority Report."[77]

We don't need to go into detail about all the arguments offered by those on the commission who believed the Church could change her position. Nor do we need to go into the details of the arguments of those of the "Minority Report" who argued that the Church cannot change her teaching on contraception.[78] Our concern is with dissent from the authoritative teaching of Paul VI in *Humanae Vitae* and dissent from other Catholic teachings on sexuality. There is no doubt, though, that the publi-

---

71. Noonan, *Contraception*, 472–73.
72. Smith, *Humanae Vitae*, 12.
73. See Norris, "Papal Commission of Birth Control—Revisited," 10–16, and Smith, *Humanae Vitae*, 12–16.
74. Smith, *Humanae Vitae*, 12.
75. Smith, *Humanae Vitae*, 12–13.
76. Smith, *Humanae Vitae*, 13.
77. Smith, *Humanae Vitae*, 13.
78. Smith provides a good account of these arguments in *Humanae Vitae* (15–35). Germain Grisez has also provided some interesting documents related to the commission; see http://www.twotlj.org/Ford.html.

cation of the leaked drafts from the birth control commission contributed to the development of a theology of dissent. In his encyclical *Humanae Vitae*, St. Paul VI made it clear that he was appealing to "the precepts of the natural law" and the "constant doctrine" of the Church.[79] In light of the natural law and the constant Church teaching, Paul VI taught that "*each and every marital ac*t must of necessity retain its intrinsic relationship to the procreation of human life" (*id docet necessarium esse, ut quilibet matrimonii usus* ad vitam humanam procreandam per se destinatus permaneat).[80] The English translation in the *Catechism of the Catholic Church* of this sentence reads: "So the Church ... teaches that 'it is necessary that each and every marriage act remain ordered *per se* to the procreation of life'" (§2366). It is significant that the footnote to *Humanae Vitae* 11 refers to Pius XI's 1930 encyclical *Casti Connubii* and Pius XII's 1951 "Allocution to the Midwives," which clearly teach that contraception is against the law of God and nature and that this is a teaching that cannot change.

As mentioned above, Fr. John C. Ford, SJ, and Germain Grisez have argued that the teaching of *Humanae Vitae* is infallible by virtue of the ordinary and universal Magisterium.[81] Fr. Brian Harrison, OS, supports the position of Fr. Ermenegildo Lio that Paul VI exercised his *ex cathedra* papal authority in *Humanae Vitae* and pronounced a definitive, infallible teaching. Fr. Harrison points out that Bishop Gasser, in his official *Relatio* on Vatican I's *Pastor Aeternus*, offered the following understanding of a papal definition:

the word "defines" signifies that the Pope directly and conclusively pronounces his sentence about a doctrine which concerns matters of faith or morals and does so in such a way that each one of the faithful can be certain of the mind of the Apostolic See, of the mind of the Roman Pontiff; in such a way, indeed, that he or she knows for certain that such and such a doctrine [i.e., the condemned teaching] is held to be heretical, *proximate to heresy, certain or erroneous, etc., by the Roman Pontiff.* Such, therefore, is the meaning of the word defines.[82]

---

79. *Humanae Vitae*, no. 11; D-H, 4475.
80. *Humanae Vitae*, no. 11; emphasis in original.
81. Ford and Grisez, "Contraception and the Infallibility of the Ordinary Magisterium."
82. Cited by Harrison, "Humanae Vitae and Infallibility," 10; emphasis added. Bishop Gasser's statement can be found in Fr. James T. O'Connor, *The Gift of Infallibility: The Official Relation of Bishop Vincent Gasser at Vatican I* (Boston: Daughters of St. Paul, 1986), 74. The same statement can

I believe that Ford and Grisez offer a convincing argument that the teaching of *Humanae Vitae* fulfills the requirements of an infallible teaching of the ordinary and universal Magisterium. I also believe that Fathers Lio and Harrison offer a compelling case that Paul VI exercised *ex cathedra* authority in *Humanae Vitae*. Because St. Paul VI was appealing to the natural law and the constant teaching of the Church, it seems clear that his teaching in *Humanae Vitae* is definitive, irreformable, and infallible. Why, then, do some Catholic theologians believe it is acceptable to dissent from this teaching? This will be the subject of the next section.

Fr. Charles Curran and His Dissent from Catholic Sexual Morality

After *Humanae Vitae*, a number of Catholic moral theologians began to argue that Catholics in good conscience could dissent from the teaching of the encyclical. Among the more prominent were Hans Küng, Karl Rahner, SJ, and Bernard Häring, CSsR.[83] Perhaps, though, the case of Fr. Charles E. Curran is the most instructive. This is because the Congregation for the Doctrine of the Faith in 1986, after years of attempted dialogue with Curran, rejected his arguments in favor of public dissent from the ordinary Magisterium of the Church.[84]

Fr. Curran was born on March 30, 1934, and he was ordained a priest for the Diocese of Rochester, New York, in 1958. In 1961, he obtained his STD from the Accademia Alfonsiana in Rome as well as another STD from the Pontifical Gregorian University.[85] In 1965, after teaching at the diocesan seminary in Rochester, Curran joined the faculty at the Catholic University of America (CUA) in Washington, DC. Though only 31 at the

---

be found on p. 92 of the subsequent edition of Fr. O'Connor's book, published by Ignatius Press in 2008.

83. Smith, *Humanae Vitae*, 162.

84. See the Congregation for the Doctrine of the Faith's *Letter to Father Charles Curran* of July 25, 1986, published in Italian in AAS 79 (1987): 116–18. The letter is also available in English at the website of the Holy See, accessed January 12, 2023, https://www.vatican.va/roman_curia/congregations/ cfaith/documents/rc_con_cfaith_doc_19860725_carlo-curran_en.html.

85. See Fr. Curran's faculty profile from Perkins School of Theology at Southern Methodist University, accessed January 15, 2023, https://www.smu.edu/Perkins/FacultyAcademics/ FacultyListingA-Z/Curran.

time, he had already become known as a progressive in moral theology because he advocated for a change in Catholic teaching on contraception.[86] During his first month at CUA, Msgr. Joseph McAllister, the vice rector, advised Fr. Curran "to be careful in espousing his views on birth control."[87] Fr. Curran, though, continued to espouse controversial views. He soon began arguing for a change in Church teaching on masturbation.[88] In 1967, Fr. Curran applied for tenure at CUA, and his application was approved "by the school of theology committee and the academic senate."[89] Some members of the university Board of Trustees—such as Archbishop Hannan of New Orleans and Archbishop Krol of Philadelphia—were concerned about Curran's views, and they persuaded the board not to renew his CUA contract.[90]

The mid to late 1960s were times of turmoil and protest in the United States (and elsewhere). There were race riots and student protests over the Vietnam War. The firing of Fr. Curran led to student and faculty protests at CUA. The faculty voted 400 to 18 to strike until Fr. Curran was reinstated, and some 6,600 students became involved.[91] The campus strike received national attention, and some members of the US Catholic hierarchy—such as Archbishop Shehan of Baltimore and Cardinal Cushing of Boston—expressed support for Curran. Finally, Archbishop Patrick O'Boyle of Washington, DC, the chancellor of CUA, intervened. He decided to rescind the Board of Trustees decision and give a two-year contract to Fr. Curran. He made it clear, though, that this decision should not be interpreted as detracting from the Church's moral teachings, especially on birth control.[92]

On July 29, 1968, Paul VI's encyclical *Humanae Vitae* was made public (though the encyclical is dated July 25, 1968). The encyclical was presented to the press by Msgr. Ferdinando Lambruschini, who stated that the

---

86. Larry Witham, *Curran vs. Catholic University: A Study of Authority and Freedom in Conflict* (Riverdale, MD: Edington-Rand, 1991), 18.
    87. Witham, *Curran vs. Catholic University*, 19.
    88. Witham, *Curran vs. Catholic University*, 19–20.
    89. Witham, *Curran vs. Catholic University*, 22.
    90. Witham, *Curran vs. Catholic University*, 22.
    91. Witham, *Curran vs. Catholic University*, 23.
    92. Witham, *Curran vs. Catholic University*, 24.

encyclical was not pronounced infallibly but did merit "loyal and full assent, interior and not only exterior" because it represents the authority of the Supreme Pontiff.[93] Msgr. Lambruschini's presentation of the encyclical has led some to conclude that the teaching of *Humanae Vitae* is not definitive and infallible. His assessment of the encyclical's authority, however, does not rule out the possibility that the *teaching* of *Humanae Vitae* is infallible by virtue of the ordinary and universal Magisterium. It is also possible to take Msgr. Lambruschini's words as the expression of his own opinion, which is not beyond challenge. According to Fr. Emenegildo Lio, "there was considerable dismay behind the scenes about Msgr. Lambruschini's remarks, which were purely his own opinion, with no official backing whatever.... [I]n the report of Lambruschini's press conference given in the official Vatican newspaper, *L'Osservatore Romano* (daily Italian edition, 29/30 July 1968, p. 4), his statements to the journalists about the 'non-infallible' nature of *Humanae Vitae* are conspicuous by their absence."[94] As Fr. Brian W. Harrison has noted, the serious question of the infallibility of a papal document should not be decided by the words of a Vatican spokesman.[95]

Even before *Humanae Vitae* was issued, there were reports that Paul VI would reaffirm the Church's traditional teaching against contraception.[96] Because of these rumors, "a network of theologians around the country was quickly prepared to launch a public dissent from the encyclical."[97] Fr. Curran was in Upstate New York when he was alerted by the US press that the encyclical was to be released on July 29. He flew back to Washington, DC, and he prepared, with ten other theologians, a statement of dissent from the encyclical.[98] Soon after, eighty-seven other theologians signed the statement, and eventually a total of six hundred would endorse it.[99]

The reaction of Catholic bishops was more supportive. The statements

---

93. Smith, *Humanae Vitae*, 161–62.
94. As reported by Harrison in his book review of *Humanae Vitae e Infallibilità* by Ermenegildo Lio, accessed January 10, 2023, http://www.rtforum.org/lt/lt12.html.
95. See Harrison, "Ex Cathedra Status," 15.
96. Witham, *Curran vs. Catholic University*, 25.
97. Witham, *Curran vs. Catholic University*, 25.
98. Witham, *Curran vs. Catholic University*, 26.
99. Witham, *Curran vs. Catholic University*, 26.

of most conferences of bishops upheld the teaching of *Humanae Vitae*, though about a third of them were qualified in such a way as to suggest that Catholics, in good conscience, could use contraception.[100] The US Bishops issued a pastoral letter on November 15, 1968, titled *Human Life in our Day*. It was subsequently published in the weekly English edition of *L'Osservatore Romano*.[101] The letter has many excellent insights on the sanctity of human life, the dignity of the family, and conscience. With regard to the authority of Paul VI's encyclical *Humanae Vitae*, the letter states:

> [*Humanae Vitae*] is an authoritative statement solemnly interpreting imperatives which are divine rather than ecclesiastical in origin. It presents without ambiguity, doubt or hesitation the authentic teaching of the Church concerning the objective evil of that contraception which closes the marital act to the transmission of life, deliberately making it unfruitful. United in collegial solidarity with the Successor of Peter, we proclaim this doctrine.[102]

The letter recognizes that there may be circumstances that reduce moral guilt, but it nevertheless states that "no one following the teaching of the Church can deny the objective evil of artificial contraception itself."[103]

The most controversial section of the 1968 letter is that on "the norms of licit theological dissent." With regard to "non-infallible authentic doctrine," the letter states that "there is always a presumption in favor of the magisterium." Moreover, "non-infallible authentic doctrine ... remains binding and carries with it a moral certitude, especially when it is addressed to the universal Church." The letter, however, does not rule out the possibility of licit theological dissent, and it states:

> The expression of theological dissent from the magisterium is in order only if the reasons are serious and well-founded, if the manner of the dissent does not ques-

---

100. Smith, *Humanae Vitae*, 163. Among the bishops' statements that seemed to make room for the use of contraception in good conscience were those of Austria, Belgium, Canada, France, Indonesia, Italy, the Netherlands, Scandinavia, Switzerland, and West Germany.

101. The letter was published in the weekly English edition of December 12, 1968 (6) and the weekly English edition of December 19, 1968 (5). US Bishops, *Human Life in Our Day*, EWTN, accessed January 2, 2023, https://www.ewtn.com/catholicism/library/human-life-in-our-day-3895.

102. US Bishops, *Human Life in Our Day*.

103. US Bishops, *Human Life in Our Day*.

tion or impugn the teaching authority of the Church and is such as not to give scandal.[104]

The letter goes on to express hope for "fruitful dialogue between bishops and theologians," and it notes that "even responsible dissent does not excuse one from faithful presentation of the authentic doctrine of the Church when one is performing a pastoral ministry in Her name."

There is no doubt that *Human Life in Our Day* was well intended. Nevertheless, theologians such as Fr. Charles Curran used the letter's "norms of licit theological dissent" to justify their own dissent from *Humanae Vitae* and other Catholic moral teachings. Curran, for example, in his August 10, 1983, response to the doctrinal observations of the Congregation for the Doctrine of the Faith, asks: "Is the congregation willing to accept the norms proposed by the American bishops, who recognize the possibility of public dissent and propose three norms to govern the expression of such dissent—if the reasons are serious and well-founded, if the manner of the dissent does not question or impugn the teaching authority of the Church and is such as not to give scandal?"[105]

Curran's appeal to *Human Life in Our Day* shows the problem with recognizing dissent as "licit." In a 1999 article, Dr. Kenneth D. Whitehead applauded the US bishops' strong defense of the *Humanae Vitae*. He believed, though, that the letter helped to institutionalize dissent among Catholic theologians in the United States. As he writes: "Merely to characterize dissent as ever possibly 'licit' was perhaps already to give the game away; once this point was conceded, it inevitably became merely a question of what specific cases of dissent were therefore 'licit.'"[106] For Fr. Curran, the question of dissent was at the heart of his conflict with the Congregation for the Doctrine of the Faith. On March 8, 1986, Curran met with Cardinal Ratzinger in Rome, and he offered a compromise solution to the conflict. The compromise would be his willingness not to teach sexual ethics at Catholic University. The compromise also included his

---

104. US Bishops, *Human Life in Our Day*.

105. Fr. Charles Curran, "Response to Doctrinal Congregation's Observations," *Origins: NC Documentary Service* 15, no. 41 (March 27, 1986): 673.

106. See Kenneth D. Whitehead, "How Dissent Became 'Institutionalized' in the Church in America," *Homiletic and Pastoral Review* (July 1999): 27, https://www.catholicculture.org/culture/library/view.cfm?recnum=1209.

willingness to have the congregation issue a document pointing out the errors and ambiguities in his theological writings "while still recognizing that I am a Catholic theologian in good standing."[107] In essence, Curran was willing to allow the congregation to point out his errors and ambiguities as long as it recognized his right to dissent from "non-infallible" Catholic teachings and remain a Catholic theologian in good standing. As Curran writes:

The core of the difference between the congregation and myself concerns the legitimacy of dissent from authoritative non-infallible church teaching. Note clearly that I do not disagree with any dogmas or defined truths of the Catholic faith.[108]

He further states: "I continue to hold my basic position that dissent from authoritative, non-infallible church teaching is possible and in certain cases justified. It is a position in keeping with longstanding tradition. I cannot and do not retract this position."[109]

The Congregation for the Doctrine of the Faith rejected Fr. Curran's compromise solution. It recognized the danger in allowing Catholic theologians to dissent from authoritative magisterial teachings—even if some of these teachings have not been set forth in an infallible, definitive, and irreformable manner. Moreover, Fr. Curran's dissent was extensive. In a September 17, 1985, letter, Cardinal Joseph Ratzinger noted Curran's dissent from Catholic teachings on contraception, direct sterilization, abortion, euthanasia, masturbation, premarital intercourse, homosexual acts, and the indissolubility of sacramental and consummated marriage.[110] How is it possible for a priest and professor—teaching in a pontifical Catholic university—to dissent from Catholic teaching on these matters and still remain a Catholic theologian in good standing?

Fr. Curran tried to argue that his positions on these issues are in agreement with other members of the Catholic theological community, and he said that he remains "open to further nuance or change in the light

---

107. Fr. Charles Curran, Press statement of March 11, 1986, as published in *Origins: NC Documentary Service* 15, no. 14 (March 27, 1986): 667.
108. Curran, Press statement, 666.
109. Curran, Press statement, 667.
110. Cardinal Joseph Ratzinger, Letter to Fr. Curran (September 17, 1985), *Origins: NC Documentary Service* 15, no. 14 (March 27, 1986): 668–69.

of persuasive and convincing reasons."[111] Here it would seem that magisterial teachings are binding only if one is persuaded by the arguments that support these teachings. Fr. Curran also claimed that his position on the legitimacy of dissent from non-infallible church teaching has the support of many prominent Catholic theologians. As he writes:

> This position has been proposed by many world-acclaimed Roman Catholic theologians such as Karl Rahner, Yves Congar, Bernard Häring. In addition, many U.S. Catholic theologians such as Avery Dulles, Richard McBrien, Richard McCormick, David Tracy and many others have accepted the possibility in theory and practice for a Catholic and a Catholic theologian to dissent from non-infallible church-teaching. On particular issues, there is no doubt that many Catholic theologians and faithful do disagree sharply with official teachings, such as those on contraception, sterilization, and the indissolubility of marriage. From this it should be evident that the positions taken by me are neither radical nor rebellious, but are in the mainstream of contemporary Roman Catholic theology. In 1968, for example, more than 600 U.S. Catholics with expertise in the sacred sciences publicly expressed the right of Catholics in theory and in practice to dissent from the official church teaching on contraception.[112]

Because Fr. Curran continued to maintain the right of Catholics and Catholic theologians to dissent from Catholic teachings on contraception, direct sterilization, abortion, euthanasia, masturbation, premarital intercourse, homosexual acts, and the indissolubility of sacramental and consummated marriage, the Congregation for the Doctrine decided to resolve the matter in a decisive way. In a July 25, 1986, letter, the congregation informed Fr. Curran that, with the agreement of the Congregation for Catholic Education as well as the approval of Pope John Paul II, he "will no longer be considered suitable nor eligible to exercise the function of a professor of Catholic theology."[113]

Contrary to some popular reports, Fr. Curran was not fired from

---

111. Fr. Charles Curran, in a memorandum outlining his positions issued during his March 11, 1986, press conferences in Washington, DC; published in *Origins: NC Documentary Service* 15, no. 14 (March 27, 1986): 670.

112. Curran, Press statement, 666.

113. Congregation for the Doctrine of the Faith, *Letter to Father Charles Curran*, July 25, 1986 [in Italian], AAS 79 (1987): 116–18. The letter is also available in English at the website of the Holy See, January 12, 2023, https://www.vatican.va/roman_curia/congregations/cfaith/documents/rc_con_cfaith_doc_19860725_carlo-curran_en.html.

CUA after the 1986 decision of the Congregation for the Doctrine of the Faith. His tenure was honored, but he would no longer be able to teach theology. Instead, he would be able to teach social ethics in the Department of Sociology.[114] Fr. Curran, however, refused to accept these conditions. Instead, he filed a lawsuit against the university, which he eventually lost.[115] Curran decided to leave CUA. After several temporary positions, he accepted a position in 1991 at Southern Methodist University in Dallas, Texas, where he remains today (though he retired from full-time teaching in 2014). Curran has never changed his position on the right of Catholic theologians to dissent from what they considered non-infallible magisterial teachings. He expressed his reasons in several books, including *Faithful Dissent* (Kansas City, MO: Sheed and Ward, 1986) and *Loyal Dissent: Memoir of a Catholic Theologian* (Washington, DC: Georgetown University Press, 2006).

Is Dissent from Catholic Teachings on Sexual Morality Justified?

The case of Fr. Curran raises the question of the legitimacy of dissent from Catholic moral teachings on sexuality. Dissent, of course, is present in other areas of Catholic doctrine, but this essay is focused on dissent from Catholic sexual morality. The Magisterium has found it necessary to intervene in cases other than that of Fr. Curran with regard to sexual morality. For example, on July 13, 1979, it issued observations about the book *Human Sexuality: A Study Commissioned by the Catholic Theological Society of America*, edited by Rev. Anthony Kosnik.[116] The US Bishops' Committee on Doctrine had already issued some warnings about this book in 1977, and the Congregation for the Doctrine of the Faith (CDF) further criticized the volume for reducing the moral evaluation of sexual acts to subjective rather than objective criteria. On January 31, 1992, the CDF published a "Note on the Book by Fr. André Guindon, OMI, *The*

---

114. Witham, *Curran vs. Catholic University*, 145.
115. Witham, *Curran vs. Catholic University*, 263–78.
116. Website of the Holy See, accessed January 15, 2023, https://www.vatican.va/roman_curia/congregations/cfaith/documents/rc_con_cfaith_doc_19790713_mons-quinn_en.html.

Sexual Creators: An Ethical Proposal for Concerned Christians (University Press of America, 1986)." This book was censured for legitimating contraception, homosexual acts, and premarital sex.[117]

In what follows, I examine the arguments used by Fr. Curran and others to support dissent from Catholic sexual morality. Each of these arguments will be examined in light of Catholic magisterial documents and interventions, especially Cardinal Ratzinger's July 25, 1986, letter to Fr. Curran, the CDF's 1990 *Instruction on the Ecclesial Vocation of the Theologian, Donum Veritatis,* and the CDF's 1998 Doctrinal *Commentary on the Concluding Formula of the Professio Fidei.*

Is Dissent from "Non-Infallible" Magisterial Teachings a Long-Standing Catholic Tradition?

As we have seen, Fr. Curran claims that dissent from "non-infallible" teachings of the Magisterium has been a "longstanding tradition."[118] This claim is not accurate. Pope Pius IX, in his December 21, 1863, letter *Tuas libenter* to the Archbishop of Munich, made it clear that Catholic theologians are not only bound to accept the dogmas of the Church. It is also necessary "to subject themselves to the decisions pertaining to doctrine that are issued by the Pontifical Congregations."[119] In his *Syllabus of Errors* published on December 8, 1864, Pius IX censured the view that "the obligation by which Catholic teachers and writers are absolutely bound is restricted to those matters only that are proposed by the infallible judgment of the Church to be believed by all as dogmas of the faith."[120] Pius XII, in his 1950 encyclical *Humani Generis,* recognized that popes do not always exercise their supreme teaching authority in encyclical letters, but he rejected the idea that what is expounded in such letters "does not of itself demand consent."[121] He further states,

---

117. Website of the Holy See, accessed January 15, 2023, https://www.vatican.va/roman_curia/congregations/cfaith/documents/rc_con_cfaith_doc_19920131_book-guindon_en.html.

118. Curran, Press statement, 667.

119. D-H, 2880. If the teachings of Roman congregations are to be accepted, then certainly teachings of the ordinary papal Magisterium are to be accepted.

120. D-H, 2922.

121. D-H, 3885.

But if the supreme pontiffs in their official documents purposely pass judgment on a matter up to that time under dispute, it is obvious that that matter, according to the mind and will of the pontiffs, cannot be any longer considered a question open to discussion among theologians.[122]

Vatican II reaffirmed this position in LG 25 by noting the need for Catholics to adhere to teachings on faith and morals of the bishops with "religious assent."[123] *Lumen Gentium* 25 goes on to say:

This religious submission of mind and will must be shown in a special way to the authentic Magisterium of the Roman pontiff, even when he is not speaking *ex cathedra*; that is, it must be shown in such a way that his supreme magisterium is acknowledged with reverence, the judgments made by him are sincerely adhered to, according to his manifest mind and will. His mind and will in the matter may be principally known either from the character of the documents, from his frequent repetition of the same doctrine, or from his manner of speaking.[124]

Are Catholic Teachings on Sexual Morality Subject to Revision?

With regard to sexual morality, Fr. Curran and others assume that they are dealing with teachings that are "non-infallible," and therefore subject to revision. Fr. Maurizio Chiodi, a member of the Pontifical Academy for Life, likewise maintains that "it is a common opinion among theologians that the ecclesiastical magisterium has not spoken on moral issues in an infallible way so far, although of course this does not exclude that it may do so in the future."[125] The Italian reads: "Ora, è opinione comune tra i

---

122. D-H, 3885.
123. D-H, 4149.
124. D-H, 4149. This requirement for adherence with religious submission of intellect and will is also incorporated into Can. 752 of the 1983 *Code of Canon Law*, which reads: "Although not an assent of faith, a religious submission of the intellect and will must be given to a doctrine which the Supreme Pontiff or the college of bishops declares concerning faith or morals when they exercise the authentic magisterium, even if they do not intend to proclaim it by definitive act; therefore, the Christian faithful are to take care to avoid those things which do not agree with it."
125. Fr. Maurizio Chiodi, "Infallibility on Moral Issues?," an interview with Fabrizio Mastrofini translated from the original Italian by Leonardo Stefanucci, *Settimana News*, August 19, 2022, [in Italian] http://www.settimananews.it/teologia/infallibilita-sulle-questioni-morali/; [in English] https://www.academyforlife.va/content/dam/pav/documenti%20pdf/2022/Etica%20Teologica/interviste_interventi/CHIODI_DEF_ENG.pdf.

teologi che su nessuna questione morale il magistero ecclesiastico sia finora intervenuto in modo infallibile, anche se ovviamente ciò non esclude che possa farlo."

Fr. Chiodi's claim that the Magisterium has not yet spoken on any moral question (*su nessuna questione morale*) in an infallible manner seems to limit infallible interventions to formal definitions. The Magisterium, however, has intervened to confirm that certain moral judgments are infallible by virtue of the ordinary and universal Magisterium. In his March 25, 1995, encyclical *Evangelium Vitae*, John Paul II confirms that the direct and voluntary killing of an innocent human being is always gravely immoral. His language makes it absolutely clear that he is confirming a definitive and infallible teaching:

> Therefore, by the authority which Christ conferred upon Peter and his Successors, and in communion with the Bishops of the Catholic Church, *We confirm that the direct and voluntary killing of an innocent human being is always gravely immoral.* This doctrine, based upon that unwritten law which man, in the light of reason, finds in his own heart (cf. Rom 2:14–15), is reaffirmed by Sacred Scripture, transmitted by the Tradition of the Church and taught by the ordinary and universal Magisterium.[126]

As can be seen, St. John Paul II draws upon the authority Christ conferred upon Peter and his successors, and he speaks "in communion with the Bishops of the Catholic Church." Moreover, the teaching is based on the natural moral law, and it is a doctrine "reaffirmed by Sacred Scripture, transmitted by the Tradition of the Church and taught by the ordinary and universal Magisterium." The wording chosen by John Paul II conforms exactly to the requirements for an infallible judgment of the ordinary and universal Magisterium as expressed by both Vatican I and Vatican II.[127] With regard to direct abortion, John Paul II draws upon the same authority conferred by Christ upon Peter and his successors, and he declares that "direct abortion, that is, abortion willed as an end or as a

---

126. D-H, 4990; emphasis original. The entire encyclical can be found at the website of the Holy See, accessed January 16, 2023, https://www.vatican.va/content/john-paul-ii/en/encyclicals/documents/hf_jp-ii_enc_25031995_evangelium-vitae.html. In the 2012 English Denzinger–Hünermann edition, *confirmamus* is translated as "We confirm" rather than "I confirm," to correspond more exactly to the Latin.

127. See Vatican I, *Dei Filius*, chap. 3, D-H, 3011 and Vatican II, LG 25, in D-H, 4149.

means, always constitutes a grave moral disorder, since it is the deliberate killing of an innocent human being"; he further notes that "this doctrine is based upon the natural law and upon the written Word of God, is transmitted by the Church's Tradition and taught by the ordinary and universal Magisterium."[128] In *Evangelium Vitae* 62, John Paul likewise confirms that "euthanasia is a grave violation of the law of God," and he makes it clear that this doctrine "is based upon the natural law and upon the written word of God, is transmitted by the Church's Tradition and taught by the ordinary and universal Magisterium."[129]

Have there been any infallible teachings on sexual morality? The answer is yes. As we have seen, the Magisterium has consistently taught that contraception is intrinsically vicious, intrinsically illicit, and intrinsically immoral. In his 1993 encyclical *Veritatis Splendor*, John Paul II—citing *Humanae Vitae* 14—included contraception among those acts that are intrinsically evil.[130] Fr. Ermenegildo Lio has argued that the teaching of *Humanae Vitae* pertains to a secondary object of infallibility, namely, a teaching that must be definitively held (*tenendum*).[131] In his 1968 encyclical, Paul VI, according to Fr. Lio, made it abundantly clear that he intended to hand down "a decisive certain judgment."[132]

The teaching of *Humanae Vitae* can also be understood as infallibly taught by virtue of the ordinary and universal Magisterium. As we have seen, Fr. John C. Ford, SJ, and Germain Grisez have argued convincingly that the Church's teaching against contraception is infallible by virtue of the ordinary and universal Magisterium. More recently, E. Christian Brugger and John M. Finnis have argued along the same lines.[133]

Fr. Chiodi tries to counter this argument by noting that that many theologians—indeed the greater part (*la gran parte*)—do not believe the

---

128. John Paul II, *Evangelium Vitae* 62; D-H, 4992.
129. John Paul II, *Evangelium Vitae* 65; D-H, 4993.
130. John Paul II, *Veritatis Splendor*, August 6, 1993, no. 80, https://www.vatican.va/content/john-paul-ii/en/encyclicals/documents/hf_jp-ii_enc_06081993_veritatis-splendor.html.
131. See Harrison, "*Humanae Vitae* and Infallibility."
132. See Harrison, "*Humanae Vitae* and Infallibility."
133. See E. Christian Brugger and John M. Finnis, "Contraception and Infallibility, Parts 1 and 2," *National Catholic Register*, August 21, 2022, https://www.ncregister.com/commentaries/contraception-and-infallibility-part-1; https://www.ncregister.com/commentaries/contraception-and-infallibility-part-2 .

teaching of *Humanae Vitae* is infallible. Although the teaching is authoritative, it nevertheless pertains to "reformable doctrine," and therefore the possibility of dissent "is not excluded."[134] The infallible status of the Church's teaching against contraception, however, is not decided by what the majority of theologians believe. If the teaching is already infallible, Catholic theologians are required to give full assent. Moreover, the Magisterium does not justify dissent even with respect to teachings that are not per se irreformable.[135]

In addition to the Church's teaching against contraception, there are other teachings on sexual morality that have been set forth infallibly by the Magisterium. The Congregation for the Doctrine of the Faith, in its December 29, 1975, declaration on sexual ethics, *Persona Humana*, draws upon divine revelation, the natural law, and traditional Catholic doctrine to condemn certain sexual acts. In light of these sources, the CDF teaches that "the use of the sexual function has its true meaning and moral rectitude only in true marriage."[136] Therefore fornication or "the carnal union between an unmarried man and an unmarried woman"[137] is always wrong. Indeed, "this is what the Church has always understood and taught."[138] The Church therefore cannot someday declare fornication to be morally permissible. The CDF, in its 1998 *Doctrinal Commentary on the Concluding Formula of the Professio Fidei*, listed the immorality of fornication as an example of a definitive and infallible teaching that must be held as of the faith (*de fide tenenda*).[139]

The condemnation of homosexual acts is also definitive. As noted above, such acts are condemned in Scripture (Gn 19:1–29, Lv 20:13,

---

134. Fr. Maurizio Chiodi, "Infallibility on Moral Issues?"

135. See Congregation for the Doctrine of the Faith, *Instruction on the Ecclesial Vocation of the Theologian, Donum Veritatis*, esp. nos. 24–32, website of the Holy See, accessed January 18, 2023, https://www.vatican.va/roman_curia/congregations/cfaith/documents/rc_con_cfaith_doc_19900524_theologian-vocation_en.html.

136. Congregation for the Doctrine of the Faith, *Declaration on Certain Questions concerning Sexual Ethics, Persona Humana*, no. V (December 29, 1975), website of the Holy See, accessed January 18, 2023, website of the Holy See, https://www.vatican.va/roman_curia/congregations/cfaith/documents/rc_con_cfaith_doc_19751229_persona-humana_en.html.

137. This is how CCC §2353 defines fornication.

138. CDF, *Persona Humana*, no. VII.

139. CDF, *Doctrinal Commentary on the Concluding Formula of the Professio Fidei*, no. 11, website of the Holy See, June 29, 1998, https://www.vatican.va/roman_curia/congregations/cfaith/documents/rc_con_cfaith_doc_1998_professio-fidei_en.html.

Rom 1:24–27, 1 Cor 6:10, 1 Tm 1:10), and the Magisterium has described such acts as "intrinsically disordered."[140] In a similar way, "both the Magisterium of the Church—in the course of a constant tradition—and the moral sense of the faithful have declared without hesitation that masturbation is an intrinsically and seriously disordered act."[141] Catholic teachings on the immorality of contraception, fornication, homosexual acts, and masturbation have been set forth by the Church in a definitive, irreformable manner. These are not teachings that can change in the future. The only thing that can change or develop is the Church's pastoral approach to those who commit such acts. Because the Church's teachings on fornication, homosexual acts, and masturbation represent the constant tradition of the Magisterium as well as the witness of Scripture and the natural law, dissent from these teachings can in no way be justified.

Can Dissent Contribute to Doctrinal Development and the Good of the Church?

Father Curran has argued that dissent can sometimes be justified for the good of the Church.[142] According to him, erroneous teachings of the non-infallible Magisterium in the past have been corrected "because of the dissent of theologians."[143] Fr. Chiodi has also noted that theological discussions on doctrines subject to reform have led to doctrinal developments on issues such as lending at interest, the death penalty, and the "just war" theory.[144] The question, of course, is which doctrines are subject to reform and which are not. In the case of the death penalty, Pope Francis has noted that from the earliest centuries of the Church, there have always been some—including Pope St. Nicholas I (ca. 800–867)—who were clearly opposed to the death penalty.[145] From the earliest centuries

---

140. CDF, *Doctrinal Commentary*, no. 8.
141. CDF, *Doctrinal Commentary*, no. IX.
142. This is a major theme in the book Curran coauthored with Robert E. Hunt, *Dissent in and for the Church: Theologians and Humanae Vitae* (New York: Sheed & Ward, 1970).
143. Curran, "Response," 673.
144. Chiodi, "Infallibility on Moral Issues?"
145. Pope Francis, Encyclical *Fratelli Tutti*, no. 265, website of the Holy See, October 3, 2020, https://www.vatican.va/content/francesco/en/encyclicals/documents/ papa-francesco_20201003_enciclica-fratelli-tutti.html.

of the Church, however, there have not been reputable Catholic authors and popes who have approved of contraception, fornication, homosexual acts, or masturbation.

We also need to ask whether public dissent is ever good for the Church. The CDF, in *Donum Veritatis*, speaks of dissent as a "problem" and not something good.[146] There is a difference between dissent and communicating difficulties with a certain teaching to magisterial authorities. The CDF offers this guidance:

> If, despite a loyal effort on the theologian's part, the difficulties persist, the theologian has the duty to make known to the Magisterial authorities the problems raised by the teaching in itself, in the arguments proposed to justify it, or even in the manner in which it is presented. He should do this in an evangelical spirit and with a profound desire to resolve the difficulties. His objections could then contribute to real progress and provide a stimulus to the Magisterium to propose the teaching of the Church in greater depth and with a clearer presentation of the arguments.[147]

The CDF recognizes that respectful communications of difficulties with certain magisterial documents can lead to a deeper and clearer presentation of the teachings involved. This is not the same as justifying dissent for the good of the Church. Fr. Curran communicated his difficulties with certain Catholic teachings to the Magisterium, but he did not accept the response he received. Instead, he justified his dissent, and he claimed a right to dissent because he was not challenging any infallible teachings. Cardinal Ratzinger was not persuaded by Fr. Curran's arguments. After reminding Curran that the Church can teach infallibly by the ordinary and universal Magisterium, Ratzinger writes:

> In light of these considerations, it is clear that you have not taken into adequate account, for example, that the church's position on the indissolubility of sacramental and consummated marriage, which you claim ought to be changed, was in fact defined at the Council of Trent and so belongs to the patrimony of the faith. You likewise do not give sufficient weight to the teaching of the Second Vatican Council when in full continuity with the tradition of the church it condemned abortion, calling it an "unspeakable crime." In any case, the faithful must accept not only the infallible Magisterium. They are to give the religious submission of intellect and will to the teaching which the supreme pontiff or the college of bishops enunciate

---

146. CDF, *Donum Veritatis*, no. 32.
147. CDF, *Donum Veritatis*, no. 30.

on faith or morals when they exercise the authentic Magisterium, even if they do not intend to proclaim it with a definitive act. This you have continued to refuse to do.[148]

Ratzinger's response rejects Curran's claim that he was not challenging any infallible teaching. He likewise rejects Curran's claim that Catholic theologians have the right to dissent from teachings that are not per se infallible. The argument that dissent on Catholic sexual morality can be for the good of the Church fails to understand that Catholic teachings on sexual morality are needed to promote the authentic good of the faithful. These teachings are also rooted in the natural law, Scripture, and the constant and traditional pronouncements of the Magisterium. The good of the Church demands adherence to magisterial teachings because the bishops, teaching in communion with the Roman Pontiff, are to be respected by all as witnesses to divine and Catholic truth.[149]

Are Magisterial Teachings Only Binding if They Are Received or Accepted by the Faithful?

Some theologians argue that non-infallible teachings of the Magisterium only become binding if they are received and accepted by the faithful.[150] Recourse is made to the sense of faith (*sensus fidei*) of the People of God, recognized by Vatican II in LG 12. According to this position, widespread resistance to a particular magisterial teaching is an indication that it is not from the Holy Spirit. This position, though, fails to note that LG 12 teaches that the *sensus fidei* must be guided by sacred teaching authority of the Church and manifest obedience to this authority. LG 25 also affirms the need for religious assent to teachings of the Magisterium, even when they are not set forth in an infallible manner.

If magisterial teachings only become binding when the faithful (or the majority of theologians) accept the teaching, then magisterial authority ceases to be authoritative. There is the added question of how we can determine whether the faithful have given adequate consent to a teaching.

---

148. CDF, *Letter to Fr. Charles Curran*.
149. Vatican II, LG 25.
150. Richard Gaillardetz, *Witnesses to the Faith: Community, Infallibility and the Ordinary Magisterium of Bishops* (New York: Paulist Press, 1992), 143.

If the authority of a teaching depends on popular acceptance, then the faithful become vulnerable to various pressures to withhold their consent. The Church, then, can be subject to pressures from various interest groups that seek to manipulate the opinion of the faithful.

Should Dissent Be Permitted Out of Respect for the Freedom of Conscience?

The Church recognizes the dignity and importance of conscience because it "bears witness to the authority of truth in reference to the supreme Good to which the human person is drawn."[151] Conscience, though, must be properly formed, and it is subject to error.[152] Catholic theologians should help the faithful form their consciences according to "the objective norms of morality"[153] as articulated by the natural law, Scripture, and the constant and traditional teachings of the Church. A well-formed conscience discerns the voice of God and the objective norms of morality. Conscience does not create the moral law. Instead, it perceives the moral law and applies it concretely. The freedom of conscience does not justify dissent from magisterial teachings. The Magisterium is the teaching authority of the Church, not individual conscience. The Congregation for the Doctrine of the Faith has made it clear that "the judgment of the subjective conscience of the theologian" does not justify dissent "because conscience does not constitute an autonomous and exclusive authority for deciding the truth of a doctrine."[154] The Congregation further explains that

> Setting up a supreme magisterium of conscience in opposition to the magisterium of the Church means adopting a principle of free examination incompatible with the economy of Revelation and its transmission in the Church and thus also with a correct understanding of theology and the role of the theologian. The propositions of faith are not the product of mere individual research and free criticism of the Word of God but constitute an ecclesial heritage. If there occur a separation from the Bishops who watch over and keep the apostolic tradition alive, it is the bond with Christ which is irreparably compromised.[155]

---

151. CCC §1777.
152. CCC §1783–94.
153. Vatican II, *Gaudium et Spes*, 16.
154. CDF, *Donum Veritatis*, no. 28.
155. CDF, *Donum Veritatis*, no. 38.

Is Dissent Permitted if the Theologian Is Not Convinced by the Arguments of the Teaching?

In his memorandum issued during his March 11, 1986, press conference, Fr. Curran said he was "convinced of the truthfulness" of his positions, but he remained "open to further nuance or change in these positions in the light of persuasive and convincing reasons."[156] Fr. Curran's position therefore implies that theologians are justified in dissenting from magisterial teachings if they are not convinced by the teachings. The Congregation for the Doctrine of the Faith notes that such a position ultimately means that the documents of the Magisterium "reflect nothing more than a debatable theology."[157] Certainly, theologians can raise questions about how to understand certain magisterial teachings. If their difficulties with certain teachings persist, they can communicate these difficulties to the Magisterium. These communications, though, must be carried with "an evangelical spirit and with a profound desire to resolve the difficulties."[158] The Congregation for the Doctrine of the Faith recognizes that there are cases in which theologians might have serious difficulties "in accepting a non-irreformable magisterial teaching."[159] These difficulties, however, do not justify dissent or public disagreement with the teaching. As the CDF notes, "Such a disagreement could not be justified if it were based solely upon the fact that the validity of the given teaching is not evident or upon the opinion that the opposite position would be the more probable."[160] If dissent is justified simply because the reasons behind a certain magisterial teaching are not persuasive to an individual theologian, then documents of the Magisterium lose their authority. In the end, they come to represent nothing more than "debatable theology."

---

156. Curran, Memorandum of March 11, 1986, 669.
157. CDF, *Donum Veritatis*, no. 34.
158. CDF, *Donum Veritatis*, no. 30.
159. CDF, *Donum Veritatis*, no. 28.
160. CDF, *Donum Veritatis*, no. 28.

Should Dissent Be Permitted Because of Academic Freedom?

In his March 11, 1986, press statement, Fr. Curran claims that "a disciplinary action taken by Rome which directly affects the status of a professor in a Catholic university in the United States is a violation of the academic freedom, autonomy, and integrity of that institution."[161] He further states that "the leaders of Catholic higher education in the United States" have affirmed that Catholic universities "must have a true autonomy in the face of authority of whatever kind, lay or clerical, external to the academy community itself."[162] John Paul II rejected the idea that Catholic universities should regard the Magisterium as something "external" to their mission. In his August 15, 1990, apostolic constitution *Ex Corde Ecclesiae*, he said:

> Bishops have a particular responsibility to promote Catholic Universities, and especially to promote and assist in the preservation and strengthening of their Catholic identity, including the protection of their Catholic identity in relation to civil authorities. This will be achieved more effectively if close personal and pastoral relationships exist between University and Church authorities, characterized by mutual trust, close and consistent cooperation and continuing dialogue. Even when they do not enter directly into the internal governance of the University, Bishops "should be seen not as external agents but as participants in the life of the Catholic University."[163]

Bishops in communion with the Roman Pontiff constitute the Magisterium of the Catholic Church. If a university is Catholic, it cannot regard the Magisterium as external to its mission. This is so especially in the teaching of theology at Catholic universities. Freedom of research means openness to accepting the truth, but Catholic theology has its own methodology. As the CDF explains:

---

161. Curran, Press statement, 666.
162. Curran, Press statement, 666–67. Fr. Curran is here citing the Land O'Lakes Statement, issued by some North American Catholic higher education leaders who met in Land O'Lakes, Wisconsin, in July 1967. See Witham, *Curran vs. Catholic University*, 113.
163. John Paul II, Apostolic Constitution *Ex Corde Ecclesiae*, no. 28, August 15, 1990, https://www.vatican.va/content/john-paul-ii/en/apost_constitutions/documents/hf_jp-ii_apc_15081990_ex-corde-ecclesiae.html.

In theology this freedom of inquiry is the hallmark of a rational discipline whose object is given by Revelation, handed on and interpreted in the Church under the authority of the Magisterium, and received by faith. These givens have the force of principles. To eliminate them would mean to cease doing theology.[164]

Those teaching theology in Catholic colleges and universities enjoy a legitimate freedom of inquiry, but this freedom must be conducted according to the principles of Catholic theology, which by necessity involves the Magisterium of the Church. If professors of Catholic theology openly dissent from magisterial teachings in front of their students, the students will be given the impression that dissent is justified. This can lead to scandal and injury to ecclesial communion. Cardinal Ratzinger was aware of such dangers. In his July 25, 1986, letter to Fr. Curran, he repeated what he had said in a prior letter of September 17, 1985: "It must be recognized that the authorities of the Church cannot allow the present situation to continue in which the inherent contradiction is prolonged that one who is to teach in the name of the Church in fact denies her teaching."[165]

Conclusion

In this essay, I have examined Catholic sexual morality and the problem of dissent. I have tried to argue that magisterial teachings on contraception, fornication, homosexual acts, and masturbation have been set forth by the Magisterium in a definitive infallible manner. I have also examined the Magisterium's resistance to dissent from teachings on sexual morality as well as dissent in general. The arguments of Fr. Charles Curran and others in support of the right to dissent from what they consider to be "non-infallible" magisterial positions have been rejected by authoritative magisterial documents. The dissent that followed St. Paul VI's 1968 encyclical *Humanae Vitae* led to a crisis, which has harmed the Church. God, though, can bring good even out of such crises. The arguments in favor of dissent put forward by Fr. Curran led to interventions that have clarified the need for Catholic theologians to give irrevocable assent to infallible teachings of the Magisterium and to adhere with religious submission of

---

164. CDF, *Donum Veritatis*, no. 12.
165. Cardinal Ratzinger, Letter to Fr. Curran, 668.

will and intellect to authoritative teachings of the Magisterium, even if they are not per se irreformable.

The deeper issues, though, are truth and the salvation of souls. With respect to sexual morality, the teachings of the Catholic Church on the indissolubility of marriage and the dignity of the marital act—as well as the harms of fornication, homosexual acts, and masturbation— are much needed today. This is so especially in cultures in which many men and women are deeply injured by sexual promiscuity and exploitation. Those theologians who promote dissent from Catholic sexual morality are not helping the Church or the world. The truth and meaning of human sexuality come from God. Catholic theologians need to listen to God, who speaks through the natural law, divine revelation, and the constant and traditional teachings of the Catholic Church.

PART III

THE
ANTHROPOLOGICAL
DIMENSION

CHAPTER 10

Humanae Vitae and the Unity of the Human Person

MICHAEL WALDSTEIN

Introduction: The Priority of the Gospel

Pope Francis underlines a fundamental order of human life according to which God's gifts come first, moral imperatives second.

> We cannot insist only on issues related to abortion, gay marriage, and the use of contraceptive methods.... I have not spoken much about these things, and I was reprimanded for that. But when we speak about these issues, we have to talk about them in a context.... This is also what fascinates and attracts more, what makes the heart burn, as it did for the disciples at Emmaus.... Otherwise even the moral edifice of the church is likely to fall like a house of cards, losing the freshness and fragrance of the Gospel. The proposal of the Gospel must be more simple, profound, radiant. It is from this proposition that the moral consequences then flow.... The proclamation of the saving love of God comes before moral and religious imperatives.[1]

John Paul II's extensive commentary on *Humanae Vitae*, his *Theology of the Body* (TOB), displays the same order. It is the fruit of an early seminal experience that shaped Karol Wojtyła's whole ministry.

> As a young priest I learned to love human love. This has been one of the fundamental themes of my priesthood—my ministry in the pulpit, in the confessional and

---

1. Pope Francis, "Interview with Antonio Spadaro," *America Magazine*, September 30, 2013, 15–38, at 69.

also in my writing. If one loves human love, there naturally arises the need to commit oneself completely to the service of fair love, because love is fair, it is beautiful. After all, young people are always searching for beauty in love. They want their love to be beautiful.[2]

"*Tota pulcha es Maria.* You are all-beautiful, Mary." Wojtyła wrote these words as the motto in the top right corner of the first page of the manuscript of his *Theology of the Body*, probably the first words of the *Theology of the Body* to be written. They are based on the cry of joy in the Song of Songs addressed by the man to the woman. "You are all-beautiful, my friend, and there is no stain in you." *Tota pulchra es, amica mea, et macula non est in te* (Song 4:7, Vulgate). In the form quoted by Wojtyła, with *Maria* replacing *amica*, they serve as the antiphon for the Feast of the Immaculate Conception. "You are all-beautiful, Mary and there is no stain, no *macula* in you." Next to this motto, he wrote the date of the first page, December 8, 1974, Feast of the Immaculate Conception.

The words "commit oneself completely to the service of fair love" echo the self-praise of personified Wisdom in Sirach, which is applied to Mary in the liturgy. "I am the Mother of fair love" ἐγὼ μήτηρ τῆς ἀγαπήσεως τῆς καλῆς *Ego mater pulchræ dilectionis* (Sir 24:24). John Paul's acute sensibility for the beauty of love, combined with attention to experience, is clear in a text that expresses the spiritual center of his *Theology of the Body*.

Although keeping one's own body "with holiness and reverence" (1 Thess 4:4) is formed *by abstaining from "lustful passion"*—and this way is indispensable—nevertheless it always bears fruit in the deeper experience of the love that has from the "beginning" been inscribed in the whole essence of man and thus also in his body according to the image and likeness of God himself. For this reason, Paul ends his argument in 1 Corinthians 6:13–20 with a significant exhortation: "Therefore glorify God in your body" (v. 20).

Purity as a virtue or ability of "keeping one's own body with holiness and reverence," allied with the gift of piety as a fruit of the Holy Spirit's dwelling in the "temple" of the body, causes in the body such a fullness of dignity in interpersonal relations that *God himself is thereby glorified*. Purity is the glory of the human body before God. It is the glory of God in the human body, through which masculinity and femininity are shown. From purity springs that singular beauty that permeates every sphere of reciprocal common life between people and allows them to express

---

2. John Paul II, *Crossing the Threshold of Hope*, ed. Vittorio Messori (New York: Knopf, 1994), 123.

in it the simplicity and depth, the cordiality and unrepeatable authenticity of personal trust. (TOB 57:3; emphasis original)

Beauty and experience combine in John Paul's pastoral method. One can stand on one leg, but it is difficult to run on one leg alone. Beauty alone would be a strong leg to stand on. Yet it is the pairing of beauty with experience that gives to the argument of John Paul II's *Theology of the Body* its intellectual and pastoral power. A detached beauty seen from afar as an object of admiration and longing, out of reach of experience, can stir nostalgia, but it cannot change lives. Beauty understood as realizable in the body and as connected with daily experience in all its complexity, humor, obscurity, and suffering—this has great power to change lives.

Pressures against the Gospel Vision in Our Age

It is difficult to sustain this vision of the human body in a culture dominated by the ambition for power over nature. The ambition for power, which lies at the root of the scientific revolution in the sixteenth and seventeenth centuries, led to the adoption of mechanics as the master-science of nature. The mechanist image of nature inevitably implies in turn a split between spirit and body.

The philosopher who formulated the principle of "cogito, ergo sum"—I think, therefore I am—also gave the modern concept of man its distinctive dualistic character. It is typical of rationalism to make a radical contrast in man between spirit and body, between body and spirit. But man is a person in the unity of his body and his spirit. The body can never be reduced to mere matter....

The human family is facing the challenge of a new Manichaeism, in which body and spirit are put in radical opposition; the body does not receive life from the spirit, and the spirit does not give life to the body. Man thus ceases to live as a person and a subject. Regardless of all intentions and declarations to the contrary, he becomes merely an object.

This neo-Manichaean culture has led, for example, to human sexuality being regarded more as an area for manipulation and exploitation than as the basis of that primordial wonder which led Adam on the morning of creation to exclaim before Eve: "This at last is bone of my bones and flesh of my flesh" (Gn 2:23). This same wonder is echoed in the words of the Song of Solomon: "You have ravished my heart, my sister, my bride, you have ravished my heart with a glance of your eyes" (Song 4:9). (John Paul II, *Letter to Families*, 13).

When *Humanae Vitae* was published in 1968, the year of a decisive step in the sexual revolution, a wave of rejection had been prepared beforehand to overwhelm it. Contraception, many argued, is simply part of scientific-medical progress in the modern age. It is self-evident, like antibiotics. The encyclical repeats the Church's mistake in the Galileo affair. It is a throwback to medieval obscurantism, motivated by clerical power interests.

TOB reaffirms *Humanae Vitae* in a manner that has attracted and fascinated many men and women. They find an unexpected beauty and freedom in John Paul II's vision. "What is at stake here is an authentically 'humanistic' meaning of the development and progress of human civilization" (TOB 129:2). Is contraception part of fully human progress? Or is it part of a narrow and violent practice of reason that has colonized progress?

Etica Teologica, Chapter VII, Section 1: The Joy of Life Received

Chapter VII of *Etica Teologica della Vita* begins with a section titled "Being Born and the Joy of Life Received." It sketches a profound understanding of the unity of the human person, which converges with *Humanae Vitae* and John Paul II's vision of the human body. It is worth taking a close look at the heart of the argument, found in paragraphs 151–53 of the Base Text. These paragraphs follow immediately after a discussion of children conceived by heterologous insemination or carried to term by surrogate motherhood. Such children, the Base Text points out, often experience their origin as undermining trust in the source of life, as "ambiguity of belonging."

Base Text 151

The development of artificial reproductive technologies, especially in their more extreme forms such as heterologous [insemination] and surrogate motherhood has its place in the heritage of dualist anthropology. Anthropology always reflects an ontological vision: in this sense, the mechanization of the body is better understood if it is seen within the horizon of a more general neutralizing of reality. As neutral, the "natural" order does not have its own speech, no deeper message to transmit to an observer who is ready to see or listen. The reason is that a great perplexity has now taken the place of the ancient wonder faced with the intrinsic goodness of being. In this perspective, the subject has become the only source of value in the moral sense: the good is not "that which all want" (*bonum est quod omnes appetunt*); rather, what we want we call good.

Base Text 152

In this perspective, the moral subject places itself before the good as a self that is not incarnate, an autonomous self, inasmuch as it is separated not only from what it sees as the heteronomy of nature, including that of its own body, but separated also from the heteronomy of the great claims of social solidarity, as in the various versions of individualist liberalism. The "modern self" stops being "porous." It becomes the "unencumbered self" (Michael Sandel), an atomistic individuality that does not recognize the incarnate form of historically defined communitarian bonds.

Base Text 153

We need to rethink the meaning of the incarnation. To do so, we can draw on the philosophical and theological resources of the Christian tradition. One says the obvious when one says that the incarnation is absolutely central for faith according to the gospel. The *kerygma* [=proclamation], the good news of Christianity, is "the Word became flesh" (Jn 1:14) and the community that witnesses to this event before the world is the community of those who have heard, seen with their eyes, contemplated and touched with their hands, namely, life made visible (cf. 1 Jn 1). The incarnation is no longer the indeterminate condition of life that has lost or still waits for its ontological perfection but the Presence of a real manifestation, an epiphany of the true, the good, and the beautiful *in the full glory of a concrete historical event*. For the believing Christian, *it is in the flesh of Jesus, not beyond or next to it, that the presence of the absolute reveals itself*.... "The glory of God is man alive," says Irenaeus with an emphasis on the incarnate self... The body is in the final analysis sacramental.

Let us take a closer look at the argument.

Comments on Base Text 151

Base Text 151 argues that the roots of problematic practices of reproductive technology lie in the dualist vision of the human person that became dominant in the scientific revolution. On the one side of the dualism stands the body seen through the eyes of mathematical physics, the body as a mere mechanism, or in Descartes's terms, as an *extended thing* (*res extensa*) and therefore as completely neutral. "As neutral, the 'natural' order **does not have its own speech, no deeper message to transmit to an observer who is ready to see or listen.**" *The language or speech of the body* is a central concept in John Paul II's *Theology of the Body*.

On the other side stands the conscious personal self that cannot find a meaningful home in this neutral world of mechanical bodies. Deprived of "the ancient wonder faced with the intrinsic goodness of being," it finds itself in a great perplexity. The one place left for the self to find meaning is in itself alone. When the good is not encountered in the world of matter as the reason for desire, the relation between desire and what we call good reverses itself. As paragraph 151 puts it,

> The subject has become the *only* source of value in the moral sense: the good is not "that which all want" (*bonum est quod omnes appetunt*); rather, what we want we call good.

There is much common ground between this analysis and John Paul II's account of our cultural situation in his *Letter to Families* (1994).

Comments on Base Text 152

Base Text 152 uses Michael Sandel's concept of the "unencumbered self" to draw out the consequences of shifting the ground of meaning to the detached subject. Let's reread the paragraph.

> [Base Text 152] In this perspective, the moral subject places itself before the good as a self that is not incarnate, an autonomous self, inasmuch as it is separated not only from what it sees as the heteronomy of nature, including that of its own body, but separated also from the heteronomy of the great claims of social solidarity, as in the various versions of individualist liberalism. The "modern self" stops being "porous." It becomes the "unencumbered self" (Michael Sandel), an atomistic individuality that does not recognize the incarnate form of historically defined communitarian bonds.

Comments on Base Text 153

Base Text 153 turns to the Incarnation as guidance in this situation. The Incarnation, it argues, is "the presence of a real manifestation, an epiphany of the true, the good, and the beautiful in the full glory of a concrete historical event." It concludes, "It is in the flesh of Jesus, not beyond or next to it, that the presence of the absolute reveals itself."

Again, there is a remarkable convergence with John Paul II. In the main thesis statement of his *Theology of the Body*, John Paul writes,

> The sacrament, as a visible sign, is constituted with man, inasmuch as he is a "body," through his "visible" masculinity and femininity. The body, in fact, and only the body, is capable of making visible what is invisible: the spiritual and the divine. It has been created to transfer into the visible reality of the world the mystery hidden from eternity in God, and thus to be a sign of it. (TOB 19:4)

To complete the emphasis on bodily concreteness as the bearer of definitive meaning, one should focus most concretely on bodily acts. It is only in such concrete acts that a definitive meaning can be expressed and realized.

As ministers of a sacrament that is constituted through consent and perfected by conjugal union, man and woman are called to express the mysterious "speech" of their bodies in all the truth that properly belongs to it. Through gestures and reactions, through the whole reciprocally conditioned dynamism of tension and enjoyment—whose direct source is the body in its masculinity and femininity, the body in its action and interaction—through all this man, the person, "speaks." (TOB 123:4)

Chapter VII, Section 2: The Joy of Life Given

The second section of chapter VII turns from the joy of life received to the joy of life given. In paragraph 172, it turns to the question of contraception. *Humanae Vitae* 14 formulates the following general norm.

> Excluded is any act which either before, at the moment of, or after sexual intercourse, intends, whether as an end or a means, to prevent procreation.

Paragraph 172 of the Base Text rejects the general validity of this norm. Let us take up this text in four parts without any omissions.

First Part of Base Text 172

One can understand the undeniable demand inscribed in the formulas expressed by *Humanae Vitae* 10–14. The norm always points to a good that precedes and exceeds it. Its truth is not reducible to the literal statement, because, while it designates a moral imperative, it symbolically attests and refers to the experience of a good that calls for being willed. The truth of the norm, also in *Humanae Vitae*, holds more aspects together: it points beyond literal observance of a law that would be purely physical, urging the spouses to bring the mystery of generation together with the response to this gift.

It is true that ethical norms are not primary, as they are in Kant. They depend on the good. The attractive power of the good stands behind and over them. It is also true, therefore, that mere literal or physical observance of the norm of *Humanae Vitae*, that is, the mere refusal to use contraceptives, would be a sorry reduction of meaning. The spouses need "to bring the mystery of generation together with the response to this gift," that is, with a mentality of taking joy in the goodness of giving life.

These truths do not show that the norm formulated by *Humanae Vitae* is not universally valid. The Base Text bypasses an account of particular acts. It shifts attention away from them to focus on a general mentality of taking joy in the goodness of giving life, that is, the opposite of what it mentions later, namely, "the contraceptive or anti-birth mentality." In this shift away from particular bodily acts, it compromises the incarnate perspective proposed so clearly in section 1. It envisions the self as detached from particular acts, hovering above them in a general mentality of joy in the gift of life. *Humanae Vitae* is without any doubt in favor of such a mentality, but the impression that on a deeper level such a mentality satisfies its demands is simply false. It is simply a way of ignoring what the bodily person does in performing a contracepted act.

Second Part of Base Text 172

Responsibility in generation calls for a practical discernment that cannot coincide with the automatic application and material observance of a norm, as is evident in the case of natural methods. (Footnote: Already Pius XII recalled that recourse to non-conceptive (natural) methods cannot and should not mean that the spouses decide to have sexual relations only in the periods of sterility, because this would call forth an "essential defect in their matrimonial consent" that nullifies the sacrament.)

Let us begin with the general statement that "practical discernment cannot coincide with the automatic application and material observance of a norm." Does the Base Text really hold this general statement as true? The answer is clearly no. In the case of abortion, reasonably, the Base Text *does* approve automatic application and material observance. "The wise choice will be made by evaluating for the occasion all techniques possible in reference to their specific situation and obviously excluding abortive ones." In the case of abortion, the automatic application and material observance of the norm is fine, but in the case of contraception it is not. Why?

The immediately following phrase suggests an argument without working it out in detail, "as is evident already in the case of natural methods." The footnote points to Pius XII's teaching that the decision of spouses "to have sexual relations only in the periods of sterility" causes an "essential defect in matrimonial consent." This defect nullifies the sacrament. This is not what Pius XII says. What he says is more specific.

If already in contracting marriage, at least one of the spouses had the intention of limiting to the periods of infertility *the marital right itself and not only its use*, in such a manner that during the other days the other spouse would not even have the right to ask for the act, then this would imply an essential defect in the marriage consent, which would bring with it the invalidity of the marriage itself, because the right that flows from the marriage contract is a lasting right, uninterrupted, and not intermittent, of each of the spouses in front of the other. *If, by contrast, this limitation of the act to the days of natural infertility refers, not to the right itself, but only to the use of the right, the validity of the marriage stays out of discussion.*[3]

---

3. "Se già nella conclusione del matrimonio almeno uno dei coniugi avesse avuto l'intenzione di restringere ai tempi di sterilità *lo stesso diritto matrimoniale, e non soltanto il suo uso*, in modo che negli altri giorni l'altro coniuge non avrebbe neppure il diritto di richiedere l'atto, ciò implicherebbe un difetto essenziale del consenso matrimoniale, che porterebbe con sè la invalidità del matrimonio stesso, perché il diritto derivante dal contratto matrimoniale è un diritto permanente, ininterrotto, e non intermittente, di ciascuno dei coniugi di fronte all'altro. Se invece quella limitazione dell'atto ai giorni di naturale sterilità si riferisce *non al diritto stesso, ma solo all'uso del diritto, la validità del matrimonio resta fuori di discussione.*" Pius XII, "Allocution to Congress of the Italian Union of Midwives, October 29, 1951," AAS 43 (1851): 835–54, at 845; emphasis added.

Pius XII explicitly excludes from invalidity the case of spouses who want to limit *the use of the right* rather than *the right itself* to periods of infertility. The Base Text applies invalidity without any distinction and thus also to cases in which only the *use of the right* is at stake.

Let us set this difference aside and assume contrary to fact that the Base Text correctly reports Pius XII's words. What exactly is this point about natural family planning supposed to show?

It is supposed to show that "Responsibility in generation calls for a practical discernment that cannot coincide with the automatic application and material observance of a norm." The proof is not spelled out. I am not sure what it is. It might be something along the following lines. The norm that limiting sexual relations to times of sterility is morally unobjectionable cannot be applied to each case. If spouses limit themselves to infertile times throughout their lives, they create "an essential defect in the marriage consent." In this pattern of behavior, natural family planning is morally objectionable. What, then, follows for the counterpart of natural family planning, for contraception? I am not sure. Does the Base Text attempt to make an a fortiori argument along the following lines? If the moral legitimacy of natural family planning is not universal without any restriction, then all the more so (a fortiori) the moral illegitimacy of contraception cannot be universal without any restriction. This argument would level the ground, as it were, between the two ways of avoiding conception. Again, the Base Text might have some other argument in mind, but it does not say what it is.

Third Part of Base Text 172

There are in fact practical conditions and circumstances under which the choice to generate would be irresponsible, as the same ecclesial magisterium recognizes precisely by admitting the "natural methods." Hence, as happens in these methods, which already make use of specific techniques and of scientific knowledge, there are situations in which the two spouses, who have or will decide to welcome children, can make a discernment in the concrete case, which, without contradicting their openness to life, does not provide for it [i.e., for welcoming children] in this moment. The wise choice will be made by evaluating for the occasion all techniques possible in reference to their specific situation and obviously excluding those that are abortive. These choices are far from the "contraceptive" or "anti-birth" mentality justly criticized by *Humanae Vitae* and *Familiaris Consortio* 6.

Let us take a closer look at two points. First, the Base Text argues that the adjective "artificial" should be applied not only to contraception, but also to natural family planning, because natural family planning makes use of specific techniques and scientific knowledge.

In response, the problem is not that contraceptives are artificial, but that their artificiality implies an intention that conflicts with the intention of performing an act that is procreative in its nature. A condom is not particularly high-tech or scientifically advanced, but it excludes the intention of performing an act that is procreative in its nature.

Let me illustrate the point with an example from another area of life altogether. It does not depend on the contrast between natural and artificial and makes no use of scientific knowledge, but clearly highlights the intention of the agent. If my friend asks me to look at him and I turn toward him with an eager expression on my face but close my eyes, I am not looking. Closing my eyes voluntarily excludes the intention of performing an act that is by its nature an act of looking. Closing my eyes does not depend on any artificial means, and it can be done without scientific knowledge.

If I keep my eyes open, but the room is too dark to see my friend, I can still be looking, even though I don't see anything. The outcome and the nature of an act are not the same thing. I destroy the nature of the act only if I am myself responsible for excluding the end that establishes the nature of the act.

Let's take a look at a second point in the Base Text. It claims that spouses can use contraceptives "without contradicting their openness to life," without falling into "a contraceptive or anti-birth mentality."

In response, it is certainly true that a contracepting couple has a general mentality of openness to life and has not adopted an overall anti-birth mentality. Yet to focus only on this global mentality, as already argued above, sidesteps what a person does in a particular act.

Fourth and Final Part of Base Text 172

In the perspective we have outlined, the alternative between "natural" and "artificial" methods is overcome: at root, the question plays itself out in the concretely possible forms of a generous and no less demanding responsibility with respect to the gift of generating.

The main question is not the alternative between natural and artificial in a general sense, but the alternative between performing a genital act with the intention of performing it according to its nature as a procreative act or performing it with an opposite intention that changes the very nature of the moral act. Man and woman should mean what they say to each other by a procreative act.

Conclusion

There is a sharp contrast between the first section of Chapter VII and the second section, specifically Base Text 172. The contrast has many levels. On the deepest level, the two passages contradict each other.

The first section is clear and eloquent in presenting a vision of the human person as a bodily being. Christ's incarnation, and within that incarnation the definitive act of giving himself, has "*the full glory of a concrete historical event.*" Concrete human acts can have a similar concrete and definitive meaning. The first section resists the disincarnate vision that dominates our culture.

Base Text 172, which deals directly with *Humanae Vitae*, is vague. Instead of arguing, it gestures. Its effect (or intention?) is to veil or obscure differences. Its main purpose is to contradict *Humanae Vitae* and at the same time to use various diplomatic means to soften the tension between the Christian incarnate vision and the dominant disincarnate vision of the person in contemporary culture. It thereby loses many of the great gains made in the first section.

Most important, Base Text 172 fails to focus on the concrete conjugal act itself, on what man and woman do in it and what they say to each other by it *in the full glory of a concrete historical event,* in full incarnate particularity. It directs attention away from the particular act to a general state of mind that can be present even when no conjugal act is being performed.

If Base Text 172 had been written as a student paper in one of my courses, I could not give it a passing grade. It avoids the question it addresses.

A passage in Maurizio Chiodi's comments on the Base Text explains why this escape into vagueness became inevitable.

> One of the fundamental challenges that underlies working out the Base Text springs from the intention of overcoming the opposition between continuity and discontinuity. If the one as well as the other are placed in a reciprocal and virtuous relation, continuity ceases to be understood as mere repetition and discontinuity is not a break. The hermeneutics of renewal knows how to put together the continuity of universal human experience and the discontinuity of its history, in fidelity to Scripture, which addresses the believing conscience and challenges it to responsibility. (Maurizio Chiodi, p. 326)

There may be forms of continuity and discontinuity that allow ways of bringing them into a new whole that in some ways overcomes the opposition. Black and white can be blended in a gradient beginning with black and going through shades of gray all the way to white. Opposition between the good of individual members of a family and the common good of the family as a whole can often be reconciled.

Yet if continuity means continuing to hold "*Yes*, a *is* b!" and discontinuity means saying "*No*, a is *not* b!" then the attempt to overcome the opposition is doomed to failure. The only alternative is to bring in a veil of studied vagueness that covers the failure.

The purpose of this veil is diplomatic rather than intellectual. It is designed for consumption by others, not by its authors. It does not hinder the clear vision of those who use the veil to soften the blow in the eyes of others. It is difficult to see this use as anything other than a lack of intellectual honesty.

In the case of abortion, reasonably, the drafters of the Base Text do not see a need to overcome the opposition between continuity and discontinuity. In this case, they do not dismiss strict continuity as "mere repetition."

Professor Chiodi occupies the chair of bioethics at the new John Paul II Institute in Rome. His intention of overcoming the opposition between continuity and discontinuity between John Paul II's arguments and his own denial of their conclusion explains why he ignores John Paul's arguments. If keeping the name John Paul II Institute is in any way honest, there is hope that at some point the new John Paul II Institute will face John Paul II's arguments directly and dispassionately, under the guidance of its grand chancellor, Archbishop Vincenzo Paglia. He would surely agree, would he not, that addressing the question of truth is incomparably more important than gaining a temporary administrative and diplomatic victory in ecclesiastical politics and diplomacy.

It would be interesting to hear what the drafters of Base Text 172 think about *Amoris Laetitia* 80. Pope Francis begins with a discussion of the place of children in the enduring mutual love of spouses for each other. He ends by focusing clearly on particular conjugal acts. It is in these acts, in which they renew their sacramental marital covenant, that man and woman express and realize this covenant of procreative love in full incarnate concreteness.

The child who is born "does not come from outside as something added on to the mutual love of the spouses, but springs from the very heart of that mutual giving, as its fruit and fulfilment" (Catechism, no. 2360). He or she does not appear at the end of a process but is present from the beginning of love as an essential feature, one that cannot be denied without disfiguring that love itself. From the outset, love refuses every impulse to close in on itself; it is open to a fruitfulness that draws it beyond itself. *Hence no genital act of husband and wife can refuse this meaning, Humanae vitae 11–12.* (*Amoris Laetitia* 80)

In agreement with the first section of *Etica Teologica*, chapter VII, Pope Francis focuses on *the full glory of a concrete historical event, a sacramental event* that expresses a final and definitive meaning in the covenant of procreative love between spouses.

CHAPTER 11

The Language of the Body and Intrinsically Evil Acts

FR. JOSÉ GRANADOS

The teaching on intrinsically evil acts seems difficult to accept today, for these acts are impossible to order toward the good of the person, regardless of the circumstances and the intention of those who perform them, which is seen as a limitation of freedom imposed on personal conscience. It seems easier for our society to accept the Christian doctrine regarding the salvation of the flesh, for here it is a question of the meaning of the human body, capable of putting us in relationship with one another and with God. I would like to show that both doctrines are intertwined. Christianity defends that there are intrinsically evil acts precisely on the basis of the Christian view of the body. A proper theology of the body would make it possible better to understand the need for moral absolutes.

(1) I begin by analyzing a recent text proposed for theological discussion by the Pontifical Academy for Life (PAL) edited by Msgr. Vincenzo Paglia (*Etica Teologica della Vita*, or ETV).[1] The document, while showing appreciation for the body, relativizes the teaching on the existence of intrinsically evil acts. It would seem, therefore, to contradict the thesis I am proposing in this paper. (2) I will show, however, that ETV presents only an apparent appreciation for the body and that the Christian view of the body, when fully understood, consolidates the doctrine on moral

---

1. Archbishop Vincenzo Paglia (ed.), *Etica Teologica della Vita* (Vatican City: Libreria Editrice Vaticana, 2022).

absolutes. (3) I go on to argue for the foundational role of our bodily condition in showing that there are intrinsically evil acts. I further argue that, given its connection with the Christian view of the body, the doctrine on intrinsically evil acts is also essential to sustain the fulfillment of the Christian view of the body, that is, the Incarnation of the Son of God and his salvific mission to redeem the flesh.

An Ambiguous Vision of the Body in the PAL Text

ETV has acquired a certain notoriety for defending that contraceptive acts and homologous in vitro fertilization (IVF) are morally licit. It thus breaks with the teachings of *Humanae Vitae, Familiaris Consortio* (FC 32), *Donum Vitae,* and *Amoris Laetitia* (AL 222; cf. *Relatio finalis* of the Synod of Bishops, no. 63).

Interestingly enough, however, ETV explicitly rejects any dualism between the person and his body.[2] In this way, its line of argument moves away from other attempts to modify the moral teaching of the Church denounced by *Veritatis Splendor* 48.[3] It does not seem, in fact, that these authors treat the body "as a raw datum, devoid of any meaning and moral values until [a freedom that claims to be absolute] has shaped it in accordance with its design" (VS 48). Nor is the body for them just "*a presupposition or a preamble,* materially necessary for freedom to make its choice, yet *extrinsic* to the person, the subject and the human act" (cf. VS 48).

On the contrary, ETV proposes a phenomenology of the body that discovers in the body a witness of human life's basic receptivity (ETV 155). According to ETV, the body is given to us as the primordial foundation of our presence and action in the world. As a testimony of all that man receives as a previous given (including his biological dimension), the body possesses an original meaning, which ETV calls "filial." The body refers to a language written in it by the Creator.

When the PAL carries out the moral analysis of contraception and in vitro fertilization, however, it forgets about this language of the body. This

---

2. ETV, chap. VII, nn. 147–73.
3. Todd A. Salzman and Michael G. Lawler, "Quaestio Disputata: Catholic Sexual Ethics: Complementarity and the Truly Human," *Theological Studies* 67 (2006): 625–52.

is clear when ETV discusses the use of technology in family planning. The authors point out that there is no difference between contraceptive techniques and methods based on fertility awareness. But would not the acceptance of a language originating from the body make it possible to establish precisely this difference? Something similar occurs with the acceptance of homologous IVF and the condemnation of heterologous IVF, proposed by ETV. The difference between the two is based on criteria extrinsic to the body itself, since both techniques are performed outside the couple's concrete bodily experience.

The text of the PAL does not develop an adequate vision of the body. What has been forgotten about its language?

Meanings of the Sexual Body in Reference to *Humanae Vitae* and *Donum Vitae*

ETV's beginning sounds promising when it emphasizes that the body possesses above all a filial character. The body contains a meaning prior to that which man bestows upon it. The expression "filial language of the body" has been used in the Magisterium of Benedict XVI.[4] The body possesses its own grammar, which avoids an autonomous look on one's own life, as if our identity could be created from scratch. As it happens with a mother tongue, which is given to us through conversation with our mother and which allows us to participate in society, so it happens with the language of the body, which is also a language received from the mother.

Although not from the mother only. In fact, a filial language of the body is possible because every child proceeds from the sexual difference of his parents. The filial body refers necessarily to the spousal language the body itself speaks. In fact, when Benedict XVI uses the expression "filial meaning of the body," he immediately refers to "our parents, who have transmitted life to us," and have thus opened a way to find the Creator. In short, the ability to accept one's own body as good depends on the good-

---

4. See Benedict XVI, *Discourse of May 13, 2011*: "We can affirm that the body, in revealing its origin, has a filial meaning, because it reminds us of our generation, which, through our parents who transmitted life to us, is attentive to God the Creator."

ness of the origin from which our body comes. And in order to recognize this goodness, it is essential to recognize that our body is the fruit of the union of two bodies, male and female.

For if the origin of the body were only in the planning and decision of two persons, the child would be totally dependent on those persons. Here lies the problem of the "child of desire," described by Marcel Gauchet. This way of seeing the child originates when the direct desire or will of the parents is at the root of the child's coming to be. Consequently, the child tends to measure the success of his own life according to whether he is able to correspond to his parents' desire.[5] This radical dependence harms the growth of his freedom. Equality between people, a crucial foundation of all society, is no longer possible, for one generation would depend excessively on the previous one. ETV does well to distance itself from this vision of the "child of desire," but it does not point out the essential element to avoid this reductive mentality. What is this element?

Precisely because the child is born of the sexual difference engraved in the flesh of his father and mother, the bodily reference to the child's origin does not stop at the projects of his parents because the difference that unites his parents goes beyond them, insofar as the masculine surpasses the woman and the feminine surpasses the man, for neither the man nor the woman is the origin of their sexual difference. The child's body possesses a filial character only because his origin is rooted in the common body of the parents, and not only in their common decision, separate from the body.

We must say that man and woman give themselves to each other in a common body that is also filial, since it draws its unity from a higher origin. It is not only that each human body separately contains the language of receptivity, but that the bodily conjugal union, insofar as it associates two bodies marked by the sexual difference, also refers to that origin. One can thus speak of a *filial meaning of the conjugal union*. It is this point that is silenced in ETV. Let us consider some of the consequences of acknowledging this filial meaning:

---

5. See Marcel Gauchet, *Il figlio del desiderio: Una rivoluzione antropologica* (Milan: Vita e Pensiero, 2010).

1. The filial meaning of the conjugal body is crucial for understanding what is proper of the one-flesh union. In the conjugal union, man and woman are united in that precise place where they themselves have been generated. Hence in the Song of Songs, the bride speaks to the bridegroom of their union "beneath the apple tree; there your mother conceived you; there she who bore you conceived" (Song 8:5). John Paul II insisted on this reference of the conjugal union to the Creator in his Catechesis on human love when dealing with the biblical phrase: "Adam knew his wife, Eve" (Gn 4:1). According to the Holy Pontiff, man and woman in the conjugal union know themselves as created by God, since they are united in that place where God creates each new human being.[6]

2. Moreover, the filial meaning of the conjugal body allows us to understand the total gift required in the conjugal union. By being united in the place of their deepest memory, man and woman share their deepest identity and destiny. The radicality of what they share calls for the total gift of their persons: a love that is faithful, exclusive, integral, fruitful (cf. Paul VI, *Humanae Vitae* 7).

3. The filial meaning of the one-flesh union is also crucial to understanding the generative meaning of the body—that is, its capacity to transmit life—for openness to life is part of the original language of the conjugal union.

4. Finally, only when the spouses honor this filial character of the conjugal body, which is to be received as an original gift, can their union in the body allow them to grow beyond themselves. This is reflected both in the wonder experienced by the first woman: "I have received a man with the help of God" (Gn 4:1), and in the capacity of the first man to transmit to his son the "image and likeness" (Gn 5:1–3). The word "procreation" also says that much.

In summary, *we have identified the shortcoming of the text edited by Msgr. Paglia*. Even if the authors refer to a filial meaning of the body, this filial meaning does not embrace the whole language of the body, which includes the generative conjugal union. This has consequences for the ETV's judgment regarding homologous IVF and contraception.

---

6. Cf. John Paul II, *Man and Woman He Created Them*, translated by Michael Waldstein (Boston: Pauline Books & Media, 2006), Cat. 22,2 (March 26, 1980), 214–15.

i) On the one hand, homologous and heterologous IVF are contrary to the filial meaning of the child's body since conception takes place outside the parents' bodies. Absent the filial meaning of the conjugal body, neither can a filial meaning be mediated to the body of the child that is born. The child won't be able to recognize his body's origin in the body of the parents, but in the disembodied decision of both.

ii) The filial meaning of the conjugal body is also necessary to understand the moral evil of contraception. By directly eliminating the openness of the conjugal act to procreation, not only do the spouses cancel the generative meaning of the body, but they cancel as well the filial meaning of the conjugal body. It is as if, in order to cut the fruits of the tree, it were necessary to cut the roots, which can only lead to the death of the tree. Sexual difference is then deprived of the capacity to open beyond the couple, like a river without its wellspring. Contrariwise, spouses who use fertility awareness methods to distance births are not depriving the conjugal body of its filial meaning, but on the contrary, they recognize and honor this filial meaning, so that their love makes them grow beyond themselves, even when they do not conceive a child.

There is a necessary unity, then, between these three meanings of the body: filial, unitive, and generative. They are so intertwined that one cannot be canceled without canceling the two others. If we compare these meanings to a language, eliminating one of the meanings is not like eliminating some terms from the language, for while this elimination impoverishes the language, it does not completely deprive it of its ability to communicate. A more appropriate comparison would be with a language from which affirmation or negation were removed, making it impossible to distinguish true and false. Or with a language deprived of the distinction between past, present, or future, which would make it impossible to tell a narrative in time.

From here we can clarify some problematic elements in ETV's position.

1. If one does not acknowledge the filial sense of the conjugal body, then this filial sense could refer to the body as each individual feels it. There would be no difficulty here with maintaining that homosexual tendencies are not intrinsically disordered. For, in fact, these tendencies are considered innate, so that each one can accept them as if they came from God, as if this were how God fashioned the person. All would work as if there were a filial sense also in so-called sexual orientation, whether toward persons of the same sex or of the other sex.

Now, the filial sense of the body refers not to how each individual feels his own body but to the relational constitution of the body, which includes the relationship to the male-female difference through which every human being is born. If the mediation of filiation through sexual difference is not mentioned, as it happens in ETV, then the "filial" sense of the body refers to a God who does not mediate his action through the created relation of man and woman. This is a Gnostic God to which it corresponds a Gnostic meaning of the body.

2. The unity of the three meanings of the body (filial, spousal, generative) makes it possible to understand what a rightful way is of using technology in matters related to sexuality. ETV says that the natural recognition of fertility also needs to use technology, which is true. But this point is not new, for *Humanae Vitae* does not oppose what is natural to what is artificial, since "natural" refers in this encyclical to what corresponds to the "nature of man" (as in "natural law") and the use of technology is a feature of man's nature.

The question, therefore, is not whether to use technology. The question is rather which technological interventions enhance the meanings of the body, and which nullify these meanings. The moral evil of contraception does not derive from the fact that it is artificial, but from the fact that it goes against the meanings of the body. Contraception artificially eliminates the procreative meaning, and therefore the filial meaning, without which the true unitive meaning cannot subsist. Therefore the problem is not technology but an anti-corporeal technology. To make the difference clearer, perhaps we should speak not so much of natural and artificial methods, but rather of corporeal or anti-corporeal.

3. It is remarkable that the PAL insists on rejecting the traditional teaching on the hierarchy of the ends of marriage (ETV 192). It does so by claiming that the Second Vatican Council rejected such a hierarchy. But the proceedings of the Council's discussions show that this interpretation is false. Indeed, when 190 Council Fathers asked that the language of the hierarchy of ends be introduced in *Gaudium et Spes*, the doctrinal commission replied that this language is not used not because the doctrine is not true, but because it does not seem adequate to the nature of a pastoral text ("in textu, qui stylo directo et pastorali mundum alloquitur, verba nimis technica [hierarchia] vitanda apparent"). Moreover, the doctrinal

commission added that the conciliar document already alludes several times to the primordial importance (*momentum primordiale*) of the generation and education of children.[7] St. John Paul II teaches, indeed, that *Gaudium et Spes* reaffirms the traditional hierarchy of ends.[8]

In fact, this hierarchy is necessary to safeguard the order of the meanings of the body and, in particular, the primacy of the filial meaning, which is the primacy of God's gift over human action. The generative meaning, in turn, has primacy over the unitive meaning, precisely because it bears witness to the filial meaning and depends directly on it, leading the spouses beyond themselves. Certainly, as St. John Paul II taught, reaffirming the hierarchy of ends, it is not a matter of the primacy of the institutional over the interpersonal (this is how ETV 162 presents it), but of different dimensions of personal love, which are hierarchically ordered. Love comes first from God and leads to God, and only so can it unite man and woman.[9]

Once we reject the unity of the three meanings of the body, admitting the moral goodness of a contraceptive act, there is no reason not to admit other types of acts that eliminate the procreative meaning, such as homosexual acts. Of this opinion are authors of such opposite positions on contraception as Elizabeth Anscombe and Charles Curran. The latter affirms that it is necessary to change the teaching of *Humanae Vitae*, not so much because of the Church's teaching on contraception, which, according to him, is already de facto rejected by the majority of the faithful, but because this teaching blocks other necessary reforms, including accepting the moral licitness of homosexual acts.[10]

---

7. The response begins by recognizing different ways of ordering the goods of marriage, in reference to *Casti Connubii*, which had spoken of a certain primacy of love in Christian marriage. See *Acta Synodalia Sacrosancti Concilii Oecumenici Vaticani II*, vol. 4, pars VII (Roma: Typis Polyglottis Vatticanis 1978), 477–78: "Notetur *hierarchiam bonorum* sub diverso aspectu considerari posse: cf: *Casti Connubii: A.A.S.,* 22 (1930), 547. Insuper in textu, qui stylo directo et pastorali mundum alloquitur, verba nimis technica (hierarchia) vitanda apparent. Ceteroquin momentum primordiale procreationis et educationis saltem decies in textu exponitur."

8. See St. John Paul II, *Man and Woman He Created Them*, Catechesis 127,3 (October 10, 1984).

9. See John Paul II, *Man and Woman He Created Them*, Catechesis 127,3.

10. See Charles Curran, "*Humanae Vitae*: Fifty Years Later," *Theological Studies* 79 (2018): 537: "Although most Catholics in the US have settled this issue by deciding to follow their consciences and by not following the church's teaching, the issue is perhaps even more important and significant than it was fifty years ago. Why? Artificial contraception is a linchpin both with regard to issues of

The Language of the Body and Intrinsically Evil Acts

The analysis I have just made leads us to a conclusion. The existence of a language of the body explains the existence of intrinsically evil acts in the sphere of sexuality and the procreation of life. If the body possesses a language that precedes human action, then the acts that contradict this language can never be ordered toward the good of man, independently of the other *circumstances* and the *intention* with which they are carried out. It could also be said that the body itself is the fundamental *circumstance*, prior to the other circumstances and radical with respect to them. And that the body bears an original *intention*, so that further intentions cannot modify it. Thus the acts that deny corporeality and disembody the person become unfruitful acts, just as a tree uprooted from the earth becomes unfruitful.

This relationship between intrinsically evil acts and the language of the body is taught by the encyclical *Veritatis Splendor*, in the section dedicated to avoiding an opposition between freedom and law. Now, freedom

---

sexuality and issues of authoritative magisterial teaching. With regard to sexual issues, the reasoning behind the condemnation of contraception gives strong support to questioning teaching regarding other issues. For example, if every sexual act must be open to the procreation of offspring, and if the model of natural law employed by *Humanae Vitae* is invoked, then there is no possibility of ever accepting the validity of homosexual relationships. If the hierarchical Magisterium cannot allow for development, i.e., change in its teaching on contraception when the vast majority of its people no longer follow such a teaching, how could it ever consider that other teachings might be subject to change? There will most likely never be any development in other teachings while the teaching condemning artificial contraception is considered impervious to development or change. For this very same reason those who oppose any other development in the church teachings being discussed today logically recognize the fundamental importance of not changing the teaching against contraception. If that teaching is changed, the door opens to changing teaching about other issues as well." See also Elizabeth Anscombe, "On Humanae Vitae [1978]," in *Faith in a Hard Ground: Essays on Religion, Philosophy, and Ethics by G.E.M. Anscombe*, edited by Mary Geach and Luke Gormally (Exeter: Imprint Academic, 2008), 192–98, at 197: "Make no mistake: it is the whole Catholic Christian idea of chastity that is under fire in the modern world. It is also under fire from those Catholics who reject *Humanae Vitae*. I used to think you could argue, sufficiently to convince a Catholic, that no sort of sexual acts could be excluded if once you admitted contraceptive intercourse. But the enemies of *Humanae Vitae* seem now to embrace that conclusion. Not indeed without any restriction, but at least as far as concerns sexual activity between two people; I suppose adult people. For though I know Catholics who solemnly defend and commend homosexual activity, I don't know any who make propaganda for bestiality, group-sex or paedophilia. No doubt, however, all that will come as the world at large becomes accepting of these things."

and law are opposed only from the viewpoint of a master-slave dialectic, but not if the optic is the father-son relationship. In fact, the will of the father is not a will extrinsic to the son himself, since in the very life of the son there is a reference to his origin in the father. This is why the ancient idea of freedom was linked to belonging to a house, while the slave was the one who had no house of his own. Recall in this light Jesus' saying, "If the Son sets you free, you will be free indeed" (Jn 8:36). Freedom is not simply autonomy, but the capacity to act on the basis of belonging to a common home, whose origin lies in the Father.

This filial character of the Law is found in the Decalogue, where two precepts are formulated as positive commandments. On the one hand, there is the Sabbath, which honors the Creator from whom life proceeds. On the other hand, there is the respect due to father and mother, who witness to the bodily mediation through which the Creator's goodness has come to us. The "no's" of the divine Law, which set limits to human action, are ways of honoring these two "yeses" that contain the first gift of God. The no's are necessary so that our action can always proceed from a source that makes it fruitful.

Well, this filial precedence of the Law is engraved on our body, for the body bears witness to a meaning that precedes us and constitutes our identity. Honoring the Creator (by keeping the Sabbath) as well as father and mother presupposes our acceptance of the body as a filial body. The first "law" is the law inscribed in the body, which invites us to receive our life as an original gift and to respond to this gift. The body, through its reference to our parents and to the Creator, teaches us to relate freedom and law.

The commandments, with its many no's, would seem to limit freedom. In a similar way, the body, which we have not chosen, would seem as well to limit our freedom. Now, precisely because the body witnesses to a gift that precedes us, the body moves us beyond ourselves to welcome this gift and, in responding to it, to bear a fruit greater than ourselves. Now, this fruitfulness is the core of true freedom. The body thus appears not as a limit to freedom, but as a region or space where freedom can germinate (*provincia libertatis*; *Deus Caritas Est* 5). Again, the no's of moral absolutes are rooted in the yeses of the meanings of the body.

ETV 160 accepts this filial character of freedom, although, as we have seen, it does not adequately relate it to the filial language of the conjugal union. There is a key text where *Veritatis Splendor* takes up this vision of the body, insisting on the aspect that escapes ETV:

> The person, by the light of reason and the support of virtue, discovers in the body the anticipatory signs, the expression and the promise of the gift of self, in conformity with the wise plan of the Creator. It is in the light of the dignity of the human person—a dignity which must be affirmed for its own sake—that reason grasps the specific moral value of certain goods towards which the person is naturally inclined. And since the human person cannot be reduced to a freedom which is self-designing, but entails a particular spiritual and bodily structure, the primordial moral requirement of loving and respecting the person as an end and never as a mere means also implies, by its very nature, respect for certain fundamental goods, without which one would fall into relativism and arbitrariness. (VS 48)

The human being discovers, in light of the love that orients his life ("by the light of reason and the support of virtue"), a bodily language that witnesses to his life being a gift and that orients man in turn toward this gift ("the precursor signs, the expression and the promise of the gift of self"). This means that the gift of self, which is uniquely realized in the conjugal union, also comes from the Creator. There is thus a grammar of the body where the filial, unitive, and procreative meanings of the body intertwine. That is why acts that contradict this grammar can never help the person flourish. These acts refer above all to the fifth, sixth, and eighth commandments, where moral absolutes can more easily be formulated.

The fifth commandment ("thou shalt not kill") recognizes the body as the place where life is received from a source that surpasses us. It is a matter of recognizing the dignity of all life as life received and as life called to relationship. This is why the fifth commandment is not equivalent to respect for the autonomy of the other. On the contrary, it is a commandment that has to do with brotherhood, insofar as the commandment invites us to perceive the same source of life for us and for our neighbors. This is why this commandment is rooted in the body, which is the first and most radical witness to the dependence and the relationality of human life. The areas where our culture does not respect the fifth commandment are precisely those where life unambiguously demonstrates its relational character (abortion) or when life seems to oppose the will of the individual (euthanasia).

Regarding the sixth commandment, we have already highlighted the relationship with the body. When either the filial or the generative meaning of the body is rejected, the sexual act is incapable of acknowledging an origin that precedes the lovers and helps them grow beyond themselves.

Finally, there is the eighth commandment, where we can also point out some acts that can never be performed. To bear false witness can be linked to the body, first, because we bear witness by uttering a word before others to establish or to reject a certain relationship between persons. Speech acts in general are linked to the body because they acknowledge or reject the fundamental bonds attested by the flesh. Thus an act that publicly denies human dependence on the Creator can never be oriented toward our good. And neither can be justified the public denial of the spousal promise that was pronounced for life, in the attempt to replace it with a new spousal promise. We see that these are two cases of an act of language radically opposed to the central relationships of the person (filial and spousal), inscribed in his or her body. This use of language, by radically contradicting the relational language of the body, can in no way be oriented toward the good of the person.

The teaching on intrinsically evil acts is related to the Christian view of the body and of its language. Consequently, this doctrine is also important in defending the center of the Christian faith, for Christ assumed the language of the body in order to save us, and his salvation consisted in purifying and empowering this language. Let us consider this last point.

Faith in Christ and the Moral Absolutes

What is at stake for the Christian faith in the defense of moral absolutes? ETV 153 points out the relationship between the language of the body and faith in the Incarnation. This means that the reduced vision of the body proposed by the PAL also has an impact on the confession of faith in Christ.

We have already seen that the denial of moral absolutes touches faith in the Creator. Indeed, by rejecting the existence of intrinsically evil acts, we reject a grammar of the body that allows us to welcome the body as the original gift of the Creator. This rejection makes it difficult to accept, then, that God has inscribed his word in matter itself, so that a "truth of the body" exists. This latter teaching his crucial to the confession of faith that God created the world *ex nihilo* by means of his Logos.

Besides, given the link between creation and redemption, the doctrine on intrinsically evil acts also affects the confession of faith in the redemptive Incarnation of the Son of God. The Church teaches about moral absolutes because this doctrine is at the heart of her faith and therefore of her evangelization. *Veritatis Splendor* recognizes this fact when it starts with Jesus' encounter with the rich young man and concludes with martyrdom.

In his *Summa Theologiae* (I-IIae, q. 108, a. 1), St. Thomas Aquinas offers us a key to illuminate this link between morality and the center of Christian faith.[11] Aquinas asks the following question: Does the New Law contain precepts that command or prohibit concrete external acts? The answer seems to be "no," since the New Law is the law of the Spirit, and where the Spirit is, there is freedom (I-IIae, q. 108, a. 1, obj. 2). But Aquinas answers that there are indeed such precepts in the New Law. The reason is that the New Law of the Spirit is possible because the Word has become flesh and has himself lived the fullness of the Law. It is necessary, therefore, that we come into contact with Christ by means of external acts that communicate his grace to us. These are the sacraments. Moreover, once filled with Jesus' grace, it is necessary that this grace be manifested in our body by our own external acts, as was the case with Christ. This is the moral life in charity, a life according to the precepts that are necessary to practice the virtues (I-IIae, q. 108, a. 2).

In the background is the idea that the Spirit is not opposed to the flesh. To the contrary, since the Spirit is a force for communion, and since the body is the place where we open to communion, then the body is a place where the Spirit can act. The Spirit, who blows wherever it wishes, has wished to blow only in the order of relationships opened by Jesus in his body, which assumes in itself the order of creation. By accepting the order of relationships of the body of Christ, which is communicated to us in the sacraments, we are able to receive the Spirit of Christ.

The matter affects some key affirmations for the Christological mystery.

---

11. On this topic, see Livio Melina, "Cristocentrismo e assoluti morali nell'enciclica Veritatis Splendor," *Scripta Theologica* 55 (2023) 127–63.

1. First, Christ redeems us with a concrete action in the body: his self-giving unto death on the cross. This means that *in the narrowness of a bodily action, it is at stake the definitive orientation of human life and indeed of all history.* The Gnostics taught that Christ escaped from the cross before dying. This would have been the case if human action did not pass through the body, but only through an internal decision of conscience. But Christ did not evade the cross because he did not evade his crucified flesh.

Moreover, if Christ's human action was able to decide on the orientation of the whole of history, this is because our human actions decide on the orientation of our life. In other words, *the body allows the eternal to be expressed in time.* This capacity of the body to enact our eternal fate forms the horizon of martyrdom. It is not licit for the Christian to say, with the Gnostics, "the tongue has sworn, but the mind has not sworn."[12] On the contrary, the call to martyrdom reminds us that in the here and now of the body, we are called to perform an act on which depends life's eternal salvation or loss.

Paul Claudel has illustrated this bodily conformity to the will of God at the beginning of his work *The Satin Slipper*. There we read about a Jesuit father whom the pirates have left tied to the mast of the ship, and who considers this mast-cross as the concrete place of God's will, where he is nailed inch by inch: "Lord, I thank you for having fastened me so! And, sometimes, I have chanced to find your commandments painful. / And my will, at sight of Your rule, / perplexed, restive / But, to-day, it is not possible to be closer bound to You than I am, and, verify each limb as I will, there is not one that can withdraw from You ever so little."[13]

2. Second, *if the body expresses what is definitive and eternal, this is because it possesses an original language coming from the Creator. This bodily language has been assumed and enriched by Christ, who bestows it upon us in the sacraments.*

According to the Letter to the Hebrews, Christ, on entering this world, exclaimed: "A body you prepared for me" (Heb 10:5). Christ brings

---

12. The phrase is from Euripides and is quoted by St. Justin Martyr in *Apol.* 1,39; on its use by the Gnostics, see A. Orbe, *Los primeros herejes ante la persecución: Valentinian Studies V* (Rome: Gregorian University Press, 1956).

13. Paul Claudel, *The Satin Slipper* (London: Sheed and Ward, 1932), 2.

human action to its fullness because he accepts the concrete coordinates of his life in the body as a gift from the Father. Through his acceptance of the Father's will, he transformed the body he assumed from us, thus making it capable of expressing full love. Being our brother, he can share with us this new language of the body, so that we can participate in it.

It is crucial, in this way of living the body, that Christ does not eliminate, but fully assumes, the original meaning of the created body. For this reason, in his Last Supper, he used the framework of the Old Testament sacrifices, which places God at the center of human relationships. These are especially relationships of fatherhood and filiation (as in the case of Abraham or in the ransom of the first-born from Egypt) or spousal relationships (as in the Mosaic covenant in the blood; Ex 24). The Eucharist, in fact, assumes the very meanings of the created body: the body for which Christ gives thanks to the Father (filial sense), the body given for mankind (spousal sense), the body for the life of the world (generative sense). The rejection of the original meanings of the body would make it impossible for Christ to assume them and, through them, to renew and fulfill love.

Therefore, in the new body of the sacraments, Christ includes the ancient meanings of Adam and Eve's body. This is confirmed if we note that there are two sacraments where the sacramental sign contains concrete human actions. There is, on the one hand, penance, whose matter is the acts of the penitent who converts. And then there is marriage, where the conjugal covenant is assumed in the love between Christ and the Church. Respect for the language of the body, on which the doctrine of intrinsically evil acts is based, thus enters into sacramental language.

Jesus' assumption of the meanings of the body also has to do with martyrdom. If the body is capable of expressing the definitive and eternal, it is because the body is a place of radical receptivity, a place where we have been born and therefore where we also can be reborn. But if one rejects the body as an original gift (i.e., if one rejects the filial, spousal, and generative language of the body), then one cannot grasp the seriousness of bodily acts, and all is decided by an enlightened decision of conscience. This disembodied conscience will always be able to escape from the cross by saying, "the mind has not sworn."

3. Third, *the existence of an original language of the body, which Christ*

assumed and redeemed, is essential to ensure that Christ's action can be communicated to all, so that he redeems our own humanity.

The filial, unitive, and generative meanings of the body ensure that the relationships instituted in the body do not remain outside the person but constitute his identity as child, brother, spouse, father, or mother. By sharing this language of the body, human beings form a unity. And so the father's actions are not foreign to the child, any more than it was the bodily action that generated the son. Nor are the actions of the spouses alien to each other, any more than was the covenant that united them in one flesh.

This is key to understanding, on the one hand, how Christ has been able to assume all that is human in order to redeem it. As St. Augustine said, explaining how Adam's sins could affect his children, even though these sins are alien to them: *Aliena sunt, sed paterna sunt*.[14] They are alien, but they are also paternal, and therefore they are in some way his children's. This reasoning also serves to explain how Christ has redeemed us. His action seems to be alien to us, but it is fraternal and spousal and paternal, and for this reason it is not really alien.

There exists, therefore, a communication in corporeality (Merleau Ponty would say "intracorporeality") that allows all human beings to share the same origin and destiny. This communication explains both the fatherhood of Adam over all men and the new fatherhood of Christ. The rejection of the meanings of the body (as in the practices proposed by ETV) goes against this experience. Thus this rejection makes it impossible to access a central element of Christ's redemption, which is his bodily presence in us and our presence in him. Consequently, we can no longer grasp St. Leo the Great's teaching when he affirms that, in baptism, "the body of the baptized becomes the flesh of the crucified."[15] Nor can we understand St. Hilary's saying that Christ, in the Incarnation, assumed our flesh and that in the Eucharist we assume his.[16] In short, in this way we lose the realism of the Church as the body of Christ, which becomes only a mystical metaphor.

A consequence of this rejection of the language of the body is the rejection of the universal mediation of Jesus Christ as the only savior of

---

14. St. Augustine, *Contra Iul.* I 48: CSEL 85/1, p. 40, l. 108.
15. St. Leo the Great, *Sermo* LXIII (CCL 138A, l. 114).
16. St. Hilary of Poitiers, *De Trinitate* VIII 15.

mankind. And today, in fact, many reject that Christ is the savior of all, after having lost the experience that we are all one by sharing in the same bodily condition.

Conclusion

An attempt is underway to undermine the Church's traditional teaching on sexuality, especially with regard to the existence of intrinsically evil acts. On the basis of this rejection, it is possibly to justify intrinsically evil acts, such as contraception or in vitro fertilization.

In this essay I have shown, on the one hand, that such a justification implies the rejection of the relational language of the body. The body, in this view, ceases to be a place where the person's destiny is at stake.

To avoid this conclusion, it is not enough to refer to a general filial meaning of the body that opens the body to the Creator. It is also necessary to affirm that the "one flesh" of man and woman also is open to the Creator. An acceptance of a filial language of the body that does not include the filial meaning of the conjugal body is an attempt to find the origin of the body apart from its concrete bodily mediation. The result would be a Gnostic flesh.

On the other hand, I have shown that this rejection of the meaning of the body has consequences not only for the creatural language of the body, but also for faith in the redemptive incarnation of the Son of God. To question the grammar of the body, which underlies the existence of moral absolutes, is to question the redemptive power of Christ's death on the Cross, as well as the sacramental language that mediates this salvation to all men.

The conference at which this essay was presented took place during the feast of the Immaculate Conception. I spoke of Christ's offering on the Cross as a bodily act in which the definitive orientation of history is at stake. There is another act that also shows how the body enacts the definitive and the eternal. This is Mary's yes who welcomes the Incarnation of the Word in her womb. This is why Dante calls the Virgin *termine fisso d'eterno consiglio* ("fixed term of the eternal counsel").[17] In the Virgin

---

17. Dante, *Paradiso* XXXIII 3.

"capable of God" (*capax Dei*),[18] we see how the flesh is capable of the power of God (*capax virtutis Dei*),[19] precisely in its feminine and maternal dimension.

The Immaculate Conception flows from Mary's motherhood. By preserving his mother from original sin, Christ redeemed the very innocence of the beginning of creation and therefore the original goodness of the body, prior to sin. Thus Mary Immaculate witnesses at the same time to the original language of the body and to the bodily newness that Christ inaugurated.

She is thus a witness of the incorruptible faith of the Church, traditionally compared to Mary's virginity. To this faith's deposit belongs the truth about human actions, which, redeemed by Christ, can reach, in the limitations of space and time, what is divine and eternal. It belongs to the Lord's promise that the Church will always preserve this virginity, in order to be able to await the final coming of the Bridegroom.

18. St. Cromatius, *In Math.* III (CCL 9a, l. 12).
19. St. Irenaeus, *Adv. Haer.* V 3,2 (SCh 153, l. 48).

CHAPTER 12

The Body Matters
Moral Implications of an Integrated versus Fragmented Anthropology

PAUL GONDREAU

In its famous no. 12, *Humanae Vitae* insists that there exists an "inseparable connection [*nexu indissolubili*], established by God, which man on his own initiative may not break, between the unitive significance and the procreative significance which are both inherent in the marital act." What ultimately stands behind this assertion, I submit, is a certain vision of being human, that of a body-soul composite unity. I can put it no more directly than this: where one stands on the fundamental metaphysical structure of the human person determines where one stands on the meaning and purpose of human sexuality, since one's position on the moral quality of sexual action is necessarily predicated on a deeper anthropology. As a consequence, any so-called radical paradigm change in the Church's moral teaching, such as the Pontifical Academy for Life proposes in its recent base text *Theological Ethics of Life*, whether as it concerns artificial contraception or any other sexual practice, would call this anthropology into question. That is, it would involve a radical change in anthropology.

The upshot is clear: at stake in the dispute over the moral use of our sexuality, including contraceptive use, is nothing less than the truth of the human person. By upholding the proper meaning and direction of human sexuality as articulated by *Humanae Vitae*, we are at bottom safeguarding and proclaiming the truth of the human person as a body-soul composite unity. The teaching of *Humanae Vitae* is irreformable because the truth of the human person as an integrated whole is irreformable. Period. Full stop.

In what follows, I endeavor to spell out how "opening up theological dialogue on *Humanae Vitae*" by proposing a "radical paradigm change" in the Church's moral teaching, to cite *The Tablet*'s interview with the President of the Pontifical Academy for Life, Archbishop Paglia, necessarily implies a radical change in how the Church views the human person.[1] At the crux of the issue—there can be little doubt—is a clash of anthropologies, a clash between an integrated, hylemorphic anthropology and a fragmented, distorted anthropology. Let me trace this out.

Rival Anthropologies

An Integrated, Hylemorphic View of the Human Being

Painting in broad strokes, we can say this clash of anthropologies rests upon two vastly divergent ways of viewing the role of the human body, inclusive of its biological hardwiring, in our human identity. On the one side (the side of *Humanae Vitae* and of the Church's common tradition), we find, as already indicated, an integrated anthropology. This anthropology identifies the human being as a body-soul unity, wherein the individual is as much identified with his body as with his soul. A paradoxical union of body and soul, the human being is yet one.

According to this integrated anthropology, the body shares in the dignity and moral responsibility of one's personal identity. St. Paul unequivocally affirms as much. Holding in mind the fact that "the immoral man sins against his own body," the Apostle charges us to "glorify God in (our) body," as the body "is the Temple of the Holy Spirit" (1 Cor 6:18–20). "Radiance of the flesh" is how Dante's *Divine Comedy* expresses the exalted view that this anthropology accords the human body, where the body, hardly a mere husk or shell, acts as a glorious royal "robe" for the human soul (Dante's language).[2]

In the Church's common tradition, the most ardent proponent of an

---

1. See Christopher Lamb, "Life in Abundance," *The Tablet*, November 12, 2022, 4–5. Paglia issued the call for a radical paradigm change in the Church's moral teaching in his presentation of the base text, *Theological Ethics of Life*.

2. This view of the human body comes in Dante's discussion of the resurrection of the flesh in *Paradiso*, Canto XIV, translated by Anthony Esolen (New York: Modern Library, 2004), 147.

integrated anthropology is St. Thomas Aquinas. Aquinas fuses a robust Aristotelian view that all things (save God and the angels) are composed of matter and form (material "stuff" arranged or specified and actualized, via the form, into particular kinds of things) with the biblical account of creation, especially Genesis 2:7 ("then the Lord God formed man of dust from the ground, and breathed into his nostrils the breath of life; and man became a living being").

On Aquinas's account, the human person is a unified composite of organic matter that he shares with all other animals and a rational form or soul that is unique to the human species. As a result, this anthropology can also be termed hylemorphic (from the Greek *hylē* for matter and *morphē* for form). What constitutes the human person is an animal body ("dust from the ground") and an immaterial or spiritual soul ("the breath of life"). Human beings are not angels, not free-floating disembodied spirits that happen to become accidentally attached to material bodies.

Underscoring the nobility that such an account accords the body, and aware that matter (or body) is for the sake of form (or soul), Aquinas in one standout passage asserts that the human body, because of its dignity of being fitted for a rational soul, stands apart from all other bodies as the most excellent expression "of the divine art" (*ab arte divina*).[3] For Aquinas, the human body marks God's artistic masterpiece!

Citing the Council of Vienne (1311–12), the *Catechism of the Catholic Church* appropriates this same integrated, hylemorphic view of the human being: "The unity of soul and body is so profound that one has to consider the soul to be the 'form' of the body ... Spirit and matter, in man, are not two natures united, but rather their union forms a single nature" (no. 365). John Paul II appeals to this same anthropology as the foundation of the natural law in *Veritatis Splendor*, no. 50, and in *Fides et Ratio*, no. 68, he insists that a "sound philosophical vision of human nature" must underpin any moral theology worthy of its name. Benedict XVI, for his part, places this same integrated view of the human person at the centerpiece of his inaugural encyclical letter *Deus Caritas Est*; he writes: "It is neither the spirit alone nor the body alone that loves: it is man, the person, a unified creature composed of body and soul, who loves" (no. 5).

---

3. *Summa Theologiae* (*ST*) I, q. 91, a. 3.

A Fragmented Anthropology

Opposed to this is an anthropology that we can term Cartesianist, though some call it by other names, like Gnostic-dualistic, Manichaean, or angelistic. Whatever the name, it is an anthropology that defines the human being not as a body-soul unity but as an autonomous thinking-choosing "self" who is only loosely or accidentally bound to a body. Moral agency belongs exclusively to the thinking "self," with the body relegated to the biological sphere of the "subhuman." As Descartes puts it, "this 'I,' that is to say, the Soul by which I am what I am, is entirely distinct from the body."[4] Such an anthropology places us in the foyer of Gnosticism, whereby the body stands inimically opposed to the soul and to all things spiritual.

According to this anthropology, the body with its biological hardwiring weighs upon the soul as a kind of albatross and stands as a threat to the autonomy of the thinking, choosing "self." Considered completely malleable, the body must by exploited and conquered, if only to free the soul from its bonds, or recast to fit unbridled, solipsistic free will. Descartes himself expressly asserts that the goal is to "make ourselves as it were the masters and possessors of nature"—and, by extension, the masters and possessors of our embodied nature.[5]

This Cartesian-styled anthropology has gained considerable traction in modern times. The modern secular approach to sexual choices and lifestyles is largely predicated, even if implicitly, upon it. We know this because of the attitude taken toward our biological structuring. Today the biological ordering to procreation is largely seen as impertinent—if not outright hostile—to sexual love (unless we choose to make it otherwise) and as placing no inherent moral obligation upon us. Sex, for the most part, is an affair of internal desire and love, with the biologically struc-

---

4. René Descartes, *A Discourse on the Method of Correctly Conducting One's Reason and Seeking Truth in the Sciences*, Part 4, translated by Ian Maclean (Oxford: University of Oxford Press, 2006), 29. The fuller passage in which this statement appears reads: "I thereby concluded that I was a *substance* whose whole *essence* or nature resides only in thinking, and which, in order to exist, has no need of place and is not dependent on any material thing. Accordingly this 'I,' that is to say, the Soul by which I am what I am, is entirely distinct from the body and is even easier to know than the body; and would not stop being everything it is, even if the body were not to exist."

5. Descartes, *A Discourse on the Method*, Part 6 (trans. Maclean, 51).

tured body standing on the outside looking in (save for the pleasure enjoyed).

In a little-known address to the Roman Curia in 2012, Benedict XVI observes that a veritable "new philosophy of sexuality" has taken hold of Western culture. Denying the fact that "bodily identity serves as a defining element of the human being," this philosophy, notes Benedict, conceives of the human being instead as "merely spirit and will."[6] Consider, for instance, how Benedict's assessment resonates with what the first director of the Johns Hopkins Gender Identity Clinic said of transgender individuals at the clinic's opening in 1966: "If the mind cannot be changed to fit the body, then perhaps we should consider changing the body to fit the mind."[7] Or consider how taking biology seriously (as when insisting that one's sexual self-identity, or gender, must correspond to one's biological sex) is now seen as tantamount to transphobic bigotry. Possessing no inherent moral worth because it is nonessential to our human identity, the body can be molded like clay to fit purely utilitarian purposes, or treated recreationally, like a toy or like a morally neutral playground. Consent, nebulously defined and provided by the "self" (the soul), meets the only necessary condition for morally acceptable sexual activity.

We should note in passing that many proponents of a Cartesian-styled approach to sexual choices and lifestyles are materialists who deny outright the existence of the soul. This is yet unsurprising, since only a material body that is united to a rational soul enjoys inherent moral worth and agency. Logically speaking, then, a strict materialist must insist (like a Cartesianist) that one's body can be treated in whatever way one wishes, whether as a plaything, as a technological specimen, as a tool, and so on. It is an ironic fact that the new philosophy of sexuality is home to polar opposite anthropologies that yield the same moral consequences.

---

6. See "Address of His Holiness Benedict XVI on the Occasion of Christmas Greetings to the Roman Curia," website of the Holy See, December 21, 2012, https://www.vatican.va/content/benedict-xvi/en/speeches/2012/december/documents/hf_ben-xvi_spe_20121221_auguri-curia.html.

7. This director was the plastic surgeon Dr. John Hoopes, as reported by Laura Wexler, "Identity Crisis," *Baltimore Style* (January–February 2007): www.baltimorestyle.com.

"A Debasement of the Human Body"

A Cartesianist disdain for the body is not difficult to find in Catholic moralists who dissent from the Church's official line on sexual love, marriage, and family—moralists, we should say, who have long advocated for a "radical paradigm change" in the Church's moral teaching. Their disparaging references to the procreative purpose of sex give away their anthropological leanings. One takes issue with the way Catholic moral teaching views "biological givenness as normative," while another proposes a moral theory that goes "beyond physicalism."[8] A third tells us that Church teaching is driven by an "obsession" with the "mechanics of the pro-creative process," a view echoed by another who accuses Catholic moral teaching of "turn[ing] human sexuality into a barnyard-animal affair."[9] If other authors revert to less caustic language, their disregard for the procreative purpose of sex reveals all the same the near identical anthropological approach to sexual practice.[10] Of note, this includes the Pontifical Academy of Life's base text, *Theological Ethics of Life*, which courts the same disparaging attitude toward biology and procreative processes.

We should not be fooled here, nor should we take the Cartesian bait. Charges of "physicalism" or of "normative" value given to biological processes and ends camouflage an underlying Cartesian-styled bias

---

8. The former comes from Richard McCormick, "The Consistent Ethic of Life: Is There a Historical Soft Underbelly?," in *The Critical Calling* (Washington, DC: Georgetown University Press, 1989), 211–32, cited in Romanus Cessario, OP, *Introduction to Moral Theology* (Washington, DC: Catholic University of America Press, 2001), 72n5c; the latter is from Philip S. Keane, *Sexual Morality: A Catholic Perspective* (New York: Paulist Press, 1977), 46.

9. The first is from the Catholic priest and sociologist/novelist Andrew Greeley, *Sex: The Catholic Experience* (Allen, TX: Thomas More, 1994), 75 and 82; the second is from the psychotherapist and moral theologian Daniel A. Helminiak, *Sex and the Sacred: Gay Identity and Spiritual Growth* (New York: Harrington Park Press, 2006), 92–93; here Helminiak also writes: "Psychological studies show that the *distinctive* function of human sex is intimacy and relationship, not procreation" (emphasis his).

10. Thus Jean Porter, "Natural Law and Innovative Forms of Marriage: A Reconsideration," *Journal of the Society of Christian Ethics* 30 (2010): 79–97, at 93: "if the sexual function can credibly be seen as serving other natural purposes [than the procreative one], then arguably, *these can legitimately be pursued independently of one another*, even through sexual acts that are structurally or deliberately nonprocreative" (emphasis mine). Tellingly, Porter provides no argument for why these natural purposes can be pursued independently of each other (her principal aim in this article is to legitimize same-sex unions). Though appealing to thirteenth-century natural law doctrine, Porter uses as her main authority not Thomas Aquinas but Philip the Chancellor and his *Summa de Bono*.

against the physical or biological order. How else to interpret such language—"obsession with the mechanics of procreation," "barnyard-animal affair"—than as a disdainful relegating of the body with its biological structuring to the subhuman, detached from the rational dimension of human life? Commenting on this approach to human sexuality, the noted moral theologian Servais Pinckaers observes: "The predominant criterion for judging sexual behavior will then be health [rather than moral excellence], which remains chiefly in the biological order."[11] Descartes' dream of our becoming "masters and possessors of nature"—in this case, masters and possessors of our bodily sexuality—has been realized. Not mincing words, Benedict XVI charges this approach to sexual practice as tantamount to a veritable "debasement of the human body" and a "hatred of [human] bodiliness" (*Deus Caritas Est*, no. 5).

Integrated Whole or Fragmented Self?

There stand before us, then, two anthropological alternatives, each defined by its distinct regard for the human body: either the human body as God's artistic masterpiece, as the Temple of the Holy Spirit, or the body as a "barnyard-like," "physicalist" accessory. If the former sees the human being as a paradoxical unity, as an integrated, hylemorphic whole, the latter reduces the human being to a "fragmented self," to use the term that St. Augustine employs when describing his earlier life of sexual dissipation in the *Confessions* (II:1).

The Church, to repeat, has cast her lot with the view of man as a paradoxical unity. And with good reason, since this view coheres both with a realist metaphysics of human nature and with the revealed biblical view of the human being. What emerges from this integrated, hylemorphic anthropology is the entirety of Catholic moral teaching, inclusive of the meaning and purpose of sex, of which *Humanae Vitae* is but one iteration.

That said, let us consider how the Church's account of the moral meaning and purpose of human sexuality is indeed expressive of our body-soul composite nature, and how this bears on our moral responsibility to act in view of genuine human flourishing.

---

11. Servais Pinckaers, OP, *The Sources of Christian Ethics*, translated by Mary Thomas Noble, OP (Washington, DC: Catholic University of America Press, 1995), 441.

The Ordering of Sex to Procreation and Unitive Love

Embodied Complementarity and the Ordering to Procreation

That human sexuality follows primarily upon our embodied nature is plainly obvious. Because they are linked to the animal kingdom, our bodies are by their very design of a sexually complementary, dimorphic (male-female) sort, deriving specifically from the genetic karyotypes of XX for females and XY for males. Without this binary biological complement, which accounts for all respective physical sexual characteristics (genitalia, bone and muscular structure, breast formation, larynx and beard development, sex-specific neurotransmitters that release sex-specific biochemicals and hormones, etc.), it is nonsensical even to begin to speak of sexuality. Sexual difference pertains neither to angels nor God because neither possess bodies. We do. And so we are sexed.

Eyeing the hylemorphic structure of the human being, Thomas Aquinas observes that certain essential human attributes proceed immediately, and thus essentially, upon the definition of man as a rational animal. We find certain essential compositional attributes that follow immediately both upon our animality (expressive of the body or of our matter) and upon our rationality (expressive of the soul or of our form). If risibility provides an example of an attribute following upon human rationality, sexuality, or binary sexual difference (maleness and femaleness), stands out as a compositional attribute that proceeds upon our animality, or upon our animal bodiliness: "the diversity of male and female among animals derives from matter," Aquinas writes.[12] Human sexuality, inclusive of our affective loves and desires, necessarily implies embodied altereity, embodied complementarity. As risibility is to the rational soul, so is binary sexual difference to the animal body.

That human sexuality as an embodied reality is teleologically hardwired for a predetermined end—namely, procreation—is plainly obvious. Unless we wish to abstract biology outright from our sexed nature, it is impossible to deny or dismiss this. Male-female sexual dimorphism,

---

12. Thomas Aquinas, *De ente et essentia*, cap. 5.

looked at on the level of strict biology, targets procreation in the same way that, say, respiration targets the oxygenation of blood, since male-female sexual union possesses the inherent power of generation.

We live in times when today's new philosophy of sexuality holds up pleasure as the primary purpose of sex. Of course, by giving priority to the ordering of our sexuality to procreation, the Church does not by that very fact hold pleasure in some kind of contempt, as modern authors are wont to suggest. Indeed, such an accusation is patently absurd, since without pleasure, few would find interest in the very act from which procreation follows. Further, pleasure is natural, and God is the author of all things natural. Yes, the Church recognizes the goodness of pleasure, but only as a subordinate good. Nature orders our sexuality to a higher good—procreation—to which pleasure is secondary. Just as the pleasures associated with eating and drinking are a means to the higher end of preserving the life of the individual, so sexual pleasure acts as a means to the higher end of procreation, which ensures the continuation of the human species.

The Body Matters

Here it must be stressed that if Catholic moral teaching harbors an "obsession" with the "mechanics" of procreation or with "biological givenness," to quote again those Cartesian-styled authors we cited above, it is because the Church seeks to honor and respect the human body. Committed to a biblical view of creation and to an Aristotelian understanding that matter enters into the essential definition of all things, the human being included, the Church refuses to shortchange our biological structuring. By giving priority to the procreative (biological) ordering of our sexuality, Catholic moral teaching indicates its esteem for the nobility and sacred dignity of the body.

The nobility and sacred dignity of the body derive, of course, from the inherent moral worth it enjoys. Because the body marks a constitutive part of every human person, Catholic moral teaching understands that what we do to our bodies, we do to our very selves as persons; hence the Pauline charge to "glorify God in your body" (1 Cor 6:20). Put negatively, to abuse our bodies, particularly in its sexed design, is to commit a gravely immoral act, since this is to abuse our very selves as persons. Misusing one's sexual organs, as when engaging in a sexual act that is opposed to the procreative and/or unitive ordering, is tantamount, say, to misusing one's head to hammer a nail. No one would deny that this latter act is gravely abusive, since, deep down, most people intuitively know that their bodies are integral to their human identity. The body in all its parts (whether the sexual organs or the head) shares in the moral worth and responsibility of the acting person.

So if the Cartesianist, fragmented anthropology that drives the modern secular vision of human sexuality favors, as Benedict XVI suggests, an underlying hatred of the human body, particularly in its biological structuring, then it is no less true to affirm the converse: the integrated, hylemorphic anthropology, from which the Catholic vision of the meaning and purpose of human sexuality (see *Humanae Vitae*) flows as from a wellspring, champions the body—God's artistic masterpiece.

Face to Face: The Ordering to Unitive Love

By giving priority to sex as an embodied reality, Catholic moral teaching does not thereby intend to signal that sex serves no purpose other than procreation, let alone to undersell this other purpose. As the human person is no mere body, so neither is human sexuality merely expressive of our embodied nature, nor ordered simply to a bodily good. After all, if we say human sexuality is ordered exclusively to procreation, we in no way distinguish human sex from purely animal sex.

That we know there is a difference—a radically profound difference—is betrayed by the distinctive phrase we use to signify sexual union among humans: "making love," a phrase we would never use to signify sex among animals. Indeed, the very physical manner of sexual union among humans, namely, frontal and face-to-face—unique in the animal kingdom—in its own way testifies mightily to this difference. Further, animals always derive the gratification they seek in coitus, but humans often come away from sexual encounters unfulfilled emotionally and with a foreboding sense of moral or spiritual emptiness. Animals do not plod the "walk of shame" after a sexual encounter, nor do they attempt to cover themselves when caught with their nakedness exposed.

What this indicates, of course, is the fact that in human sexual encounters there is, or at least should be, something much more than the mere physical union of bodies. The sexual joining of two human beings encompasses not simply a physical union, but an encounter of persons, or what John Paul II terms a *communio personarum*. How else to look upon the bodily frontal posture of face-to-face than as expressive of a union that serves spiritual, moral, and emotional needs, in addition to physical needs? "In the human person the biological dimension [inclusive of our sexuality] is vitally integrated in a spiritual nature" is how Servais Pinckaers puts it.[13]

Human sexuality thus enjoys a per se teleological ordering not merely to procreation but also to a complementary love-making union. Because this latter ordering is proper to us as rational beings, as persons, moralists term this the *personalist* or *unitive* ordering.[14]

In short, sexuality as characteristic of the animal kingdom becomes so profoundly integrated in the human condition that it undergoes a thorough transformation. Our bodies in their very physical design bespeak the rational souls to which they are substantially joined, and thereby stand apart from all other animal bodies even as they continue to resemble them. Likewise, our sexed nature participates in and reflects that which is unique to us—our rationality—even as it continues to link us to the animal kingdom.

Consider, for instance, the ability of the human body, given the unique design of the innominate bone (hipbone), to stand upright and erect indefinitely, a feat no other animal can accomplish. Or how the human hand with its opposable thumb and fine motor skills serves more than a mere "animal" need to eat: it serves the proper *human* need to prepare and share in a meal (animals do not experience mealtime). And so it is with the frontal, face-to-face posture of human sex. We are not centaur-like creatures—half rational, half bestial, with a clean line of separation between the sub-rational and rational spheres. We are integrated, unified beings comprising both rational and animal dimensions. It bears repeating: the human being is inseparably one.

---

13. Pinckaers, *Sources of Christian Ethics*, 440–41.
14. One finds the near equivalent in Aquinas, who terms marriage a "domestic fellowship" (*domesticae conversationis*) in *Summa contra Gentiles* III, chap. 123, and a "union of souls" (*coniunctione animorum*) in *ST* III, q. 29, a. 2. He also calls marriage a "conjugal society" (*associatio matrimonium*) in *IV Sent*, d. 26, q. 1, a. 1.

The Great Paradox

To say human sexuality enjoys a teleological ordering to both procreation and unitive love is to place us at the crux of the Catholic vision of human sexuality. As sex is intended to generate human progeny, so at the same time is it intended to unite in love a man and a woman in the most intimate of unions possible. Human sexual union is (or is meant to be) at once physical or bodily and spiritual or moral. To express this in the terms of the fundamental metaphysical structure of human nature examined above, the procreative ordering of our sexuality follows immediately upon our embodied, animal-like nature, and the unitive ordering follows immediately upon our rational nature. Cardinal Georges Cottier (theologian of the pontifical household under John Paul II) thus dubs human sex the "great paradox," since it reflects the paradoxical union of body and soul in man.[15] With good reason did Paul VI, given the inseparable connection between body and soul in the human person, insist that there is correspondingly an "inseparable connection, established by God, which man on his own initiative may not break, between the unitive significance and the procreative significance" (*Humanae Vitae*, no. 12).

The inseparable union of both the procreative and unitive orderings, reflective of and following upon the inseparable union of body and soul, thus provides the normative good of human sexuality. From this it follows that any sexual act that violates or inhibits either the procreative and/or the unitive orderings of human sexuality violates the fundamental meaning and purpose of our sexuality. The Church's common tradition enumerates well these practices: under "procreative-free" practices we find artificial contraception, homoerotic practices and all forms of same-sex intimacy, autosexual practices (pornography, masturbation, cybersex, etc.); and under "unitive-free" practices we find adultery, remarriage after divorce, rape, fornication and all forms of premarital sex, artificial methods of reproduction, and so on. There is also, of course, transgenderism and the ideology associated with it. These acts—all of them—deny, at least in practice, the fundamental unity of the human being as a body-soul (procreative-unitive) composite. As such, they are deeply dehumanizing.

15. Georges Cottier, OP, *Défis éthiques* (Saint-Maurice, Switzerland: Editions Saint-Augustin, 1996), 25.

Conclusion

I close where I began: that to call for a "radical paradigm change" in the Church's moral teaching is to call into question the truth of the human person as a body-soul composite unity; indeed, it is to deny this truth, espousing as it does a fragmented, distorted view of the human person. Predicated on an integrated, hylemorphic anthropology, *Humanae Vitae* gets the paradigm right. It is a paradigm that is irreformable and unchanging, since the hylemorphic structure of the human being, "established by God" (*Humanae Vitae*, no. 12), is itself irreformable and unchanging.

CHAPTER 13

Disordered Desire and Contraception

ANGELA FRANKS

Many Catholic theologians debating contraception assume that postlapsarian desire is intrinsically altruistic. In this essay, I argue that this assumption is misguided and naive. I will develop the ways in which classical sources, especially St. Thomas Aquinas, and the recent Magisterium enable a deeper understanding of human sexual desire and the disorder caused by sin. The *testo base* in the recent book by the Pontifical Academy of Life on contraception is naive because it neglects to consider these points.

Contemporary Sex: Messy versus #MeToo

Let me summarize two opposing accounts of contemporary sexuality; one of these I label "messy" and the other "#MeToo." The messy view tends toward reading any ambiguous experience of sexuality as part of its inherent "messiness." The #MeToo approach highlights the negative aspects of sex, centering in particular on dynamics of consent and pressure.

As a representative of the messy account, Luke Timothy Johnson in

---

This essay is an abbreviated and slightly edited version of Angela Franks, "End-Less and Self-Referential Desire: Toward an Understanding of Contemporary Sexuality," *National Catholic Bioethics Quarterly* 18, no. 4 (Winter 2018): 629–46.

The author thanks John Grabowski, Michael Hanby, Matthew Levering, Adrian Walker, and the participants in the Catholic Women's Forum in June 2018 and in the International Catholic Jurists Forum's conference in December 2022 who provided comments on earlier drafts of this essay.

his book *The Revelatory Body* asserts the inherently positive and revelatory power of the body and its experiences. In Johnson's reading, Pope St. John Paul II's theology of the body, in contrast, "fantasiz[es] an ethereal and all-encompassing mode of mutual self-donation between man and woman that lacks any of the messy, clumsy, awkward, charming, casual, and yes, silly aspects of love in the flesh."[1] These aspects of love arise out of human experience. Johnson's positive presentation of the body and desire has many strengths, although he appears to be unaware that, on those points, he does not diverge significantly from the theological tradition influenced by Aristotle. But his overall approach is a theological version of what we might call "sex positivity."[2] Sex positivity views sexual expression, as long as it is consensual, as fundamentally positive and good.[3] It has sought to valorize sexual expression, often tying it to personal and societal liberation.[4]

Yet in the secular domain, sex positivity as grounded simply in sexual experience has recently been problematized as hopelessly naive. The outbreak of revelations of widespread sexual harassment and assault that rallied under the banner of the social media hashtag #MeToo has reframed the contemporary debate.

Without presuming that all the accused were guilty, and while acknowledging that #MeToo had little to provide in terms of a positive sexual ethics, we can still safely say that the contemporary status quo of sexuality has been unmasked as being too often marked by aggression and entitlement.[5] Many questions could profitably be pursued regard-

---

1. Luke Timothy Johnson, *The Revelatory Body: Theology as Inductive Art* (Grand Rapids, MI: Eerdmans, 2015), 24.

2. An early proponent, with whom Johnson may or may not agree, is Hans Hoffman, *Sex Incorporated: A Positive View of the Sexual Revolution* (Boston: Beacon Press, 1967). For a summary, see Chantelle Ivanski and Taylor Kohut, "Exploring Definitions of Sex Positivity through Thematic Analysis," *Canadian Journal of Human Sexuality* 26, no. 3 (December 2017): 216–25. For a (Marxist) critique of sex-positive feminism in its queer forms, see Elisa Glick, "Sex Positive: Feminism, Queer Theory, and the Politics of Transgression," *Feminist Review* 64, no. 1 (Spring 2000): 19–45, here 31.

3. For a related approach from within moral theology, see Todd A. Salzman and Michael G. Lawler, *The Sexual Person: Toward a Renewed Catholic Anthropology* (Washington, DC: Georgetown University Press, 2008).

4. The issue of consent is its own vexed question, one that I shall not engage here. See Angela Franks, "Consent Is Not Enough: Harvey Weinstein, Sex, and Human Flourishing," *Public Discourse*, November 26, 2017, http://www.thepublicdiscourse.com/2017/11/20563/.

5. I present an overview of the #MeToo claims in "Consent Is Not Enough" and in Angela

ing #MeToo, including the degree of possible responsibility of the women involved. But my concern here is different. #MeToo reveals another interpretation of contemporary sexuality, one far removed from Johnson's optimistic sex positivity. Is concupiscence simply a matter of a little messiness? Perhaps the Christian tradition was onto something when it emphasized the ambiguity—indeed, the tendency toward domination—within desire, especially of the sexual kind. Aquinas's thought in particular combines these traditional notes of caution with a robust appreciation of the goodness of the passions (including sexual desire). To this treatment I now turn.

Desire's Ends

For Aquinas, we cannot treat desire without turning to the question of the good.[6] In the *prima pars* of the *Summa Theologiae*, drawing on the first sentence of the first book of the *Nicomachean Ethics* of Aristotle, Aquinas affirms that "goodness is what all desire."[7] Aristotle insisted that our desires must be structured toward an ultimate good, that toward which all subsidiary goods are ordered, or else we would be stuck in "an infinite progression, making our desire fruitless and vain."[8] The reorientation of the question of desire to the good enables a properly ethical account, one that provides hope to victims of aggressive sexual desire. In this way, we can turn the conversation away from the merely legalistic toward something more ethically robust.[9]

Franks, "#MeToo Shows the Dangers of 'End-less' Sex: 'Humanae Vitae' Shows the Way Forward," *America Magazine*, April 17, 2018, https://www.americamagazine.org/.

6. Gilles Deleuze and Félix Guattari give a representative, contrary sample of contemporary thought: "The unconscious poses no problem of meaning, solely problems of use. The question posed by desire is not 'What does it mean?' but rather *How does it work?*'... Desire makes its entry with the general collapse of the question 'What does it mean?'" Gilles Deleuze and Félix Guattari, *Anti-Oedipus*, vol. 1, *Capitalism and Schizophrenia*, translated by Robert Hurley, Mark Seem, and Helen R. Lane (New York: Penguin, 1977), 109, original emphasis.

7. Thomas Aquinas, *Summa Theologiae* (*ST*) I, q. 5, a. 1. I have used the online edition of the English translation by the English Dominican Fathers (New York: Benziger Brothers, 1920), available at http://www.newadvent.org/summa.

8. Aristotle, *Nicomachean Ethics*, rev. ed., edited and translated by Roger Crisp (Cambridge: Cambridge University Press, 2014), 1.2.

9. In addition to the sources cited below, I am here indebted to the lucid summary of Aquinas's

Aquinas further argues that "goodness has the aspect of the end."[10] But this implies that there is something that moves toward the end. In living things, the appetite is what drives them toward the good. The appetite is the desiring power of the human soul.[11] Key for our purposes is the sensitive appetite, which tends toward the good as it is apprehended by the senses.[12] The acts of this appetite are the passions, which are the motions of the appetite toward a good (or away from an evil), united to a bodily change.[13]

At this point, a terminological clarification is in order. The term *concupiscence* will be necessary to our discussion, but it can refer to one of three distinct realities. Concupiscence can mean disordered desire, which is the inclination to sin after the Fall. But it has also a second, neutral sense, as designating one of the two kinds of powers of the sensitive appetite: the concupiscible and the irascible. The concupiscible passions are the motions to a sensible good that is easy to obtain or the motions away from an evil easy to avoid.[14] Third, it can refer to one of the concupiscible

---

anthropology in Thomas Petri, *Aquinas and the Theology of the Body: The Thomistic Foundations of John Paul II's Anthropology* (Washington, DC: Catholic University of America Press, 2016).

10. *ST* I, q. 5, a. 2, ad 2.

11. *ST* I, q. 5, a. 6. The appetite is further divided into the rational appetite (the will) and the sensitive appetite (*ST* I, q. 80, a. 2). This essay confines itself to discussing the sensitive appetite only. I am also bracketing the natural appetite, which is not dependent on apprehending an object. Rather, the natural appetite is the orientation of the living thing for the goods of nature, such as generation, nutrition, and the other goods that sustain it in being (see *ST* I, q. 80, a. 1 as well as I-II, q. 30, a. 1 and 3). The sensitive appetite is above the natural appetite because the former is a "superior inclination [that] belongs to the appetitive power of the soul, through which the animal is able to desire what it apprehends, and not only that to which it is inclined by its natural form" (*ST* I, q. 80, a. 1). See also Diana Fritz Cates, "Love: A Thomistic Analysis," *Journal of Moral Theology* 1, no. 2 (2012): 9, and Robert Miner, *Thomas Aquinas on the Passions: A Study of* Summa Theologiae *1a2ae 22–48* (Cambridge: Cambridge University Press, 2009), 154–59.

12. See the summary and the issues discussed by Miner, *Aquinas on the Passions*, 13–28. See also Mark P. Drost, "In the Realm of the Senses: Saint Thomas Aquinas on Sensory Love, Desire, and Delight," *The Thomist* 59, no. 1 (January 1995): 47–58. The sensitive appetite requires the prior sensible apprehension of the good; as Kevin White puts it, "Wanting... presupposes awareness." "Wanting Something for Someone: Aquinas on the Complex Motions of Appetite," *Review of Metaphysics* 61 (September 2007): 4.

13. *ST* I-II, q. 22, but also I, q. 20, a. 1, ad 1. See the controversies summarized in Miner, *Aquinas on the Passions*, 29–46. Miner points out that I-II, q. 28, a. 5 and I-II, q. 44, a. 1 both explain the relation of appetite to bodily change in terms of the relation of form to matter.

14. *ST* I, q. 81, a. 2. As restated in *ST* I-II, q. 23, a. 1, "the object of the concupiscible power is sensible good or evil, simply apprehended as such, which causes pleasure or pain." The irascible

passions, namely, desire for a sensible good. The complete list of the concupiscible passions are, according to Aquinas, love and hatred, desire (or concupiscence) and avoidance, and joy and sorrow.[15]

The last meaning—concupiscence as the desire for the apprehended good that is pleasant—is important for our purposes.[16] The trio of passions pertaining to the sensibly desirable good work together: love is the inclination for the good, while concupiscence is the movement toward it, and pleasure is the delight arising from resting in it.[17] For example, I love drinking cappuccino in the Piazza Navona, and I have this inclination even when I am in Boston. But when in Rome (or when my memory calls up an image of Roman cappuccino), the internal motions of desire urge me toward that good. Once I am actually sipping cappuccino by Bernini's fountain, I experience pleasure in my happy state.

From this overview, we can conclude that desire by its nature is oriented to an end, and that end is a good (even if it is a misconstrued or partial good). As a movement of the sensitive appetite, desire is always intrinsically connected to the body. For Aquinas, the passions are natural and good, part of the perfectibility of the human person.[18]

So how can things go wrong, as they so obviously do in the most egregious examples of contemporary sexual aggression? Obviously, desire can direct itself toward a merely apparent and not true good. But Aquinas's account is richer than that; the question is not only an intellectual problem—what is the true good?—but also one rooted in the nature of desire itself. In particular, he provides three key insights lacking in contemporary

---

passions concern goods difficult to obtain or evils difficult to avoid. These passions are hope and despair, fear and daring, and anger.

15. *ST* I-II, q. 23, aa. 2–3.

16. *ST* I-II, q. 30.

17. See, inter alia, Miner, *Aquinas on the Passions*, 109–211, for an overview of the concupiscible passions, with many helpful diagrams. See also Nicholas E. Lombardo, *The Logic of Desire: Aquinas on Emotion* (Washington, DC: Catholic University of America Press, 2011), 54–62. Christopher J. Malloy unpacks the development of Aquinas's thought on this issue in "Thomas on the Order of Love and Desire: A Development of Doctrine," *The Thomist* 71, no. 1 (January 2007): 65–87.

18. We can also listen directly to Aquinas on this point: "Accordingly just as it is better that man should both will good and do it in his external act: so also does it belong to the perfection of moral good, that man should be moved unto good, not only in respect of his will, but also in respect of his sensitive appetite; according to Psalm 83:3: 'My heart and my flesh have rejoiced in the living God': where by 'heart' we are to understand the intellectual appetite, and by 'flesh' the sensitive appetite" (*ST* I-II, q. 24, a. 3).

accounts, such as Johnson's, of the "messiness" of sexuality. These insights are the natural inclination of love toward the self, the infinitude of our desires, and the power of desire to hijack reason.

First, Aquinas notes that love contains within itself two naturally opposing movements, *amor concupiscentiae* and *amor amicitiae*.[19] The distinction is captured by the phrase "wanting something (*amor concupiscentiae*) for somebody (*amor amicitiae*)."[20] I could love ice cream for myself. I could even love kale, qua healthy, for myself. The originary *amor amicitiae* is to oneself, to preserve oneself in being, because it is unnatural and wrong to hate oneself.[21] As Josef Pieper puts it, "Friendship is the image and self-love is the original; we love our friends as we love ourselves."[22] But self-love is not supposed to be the only *amor amicitiae*; I can also love a promotion for my friend, or a good meal for a hungry person.

The distinction between the two loves, however, is still subtler.[23] Thomas explains:

Because in love of concupiscence, the lover is carried out of himself, in a certain sense; in so far, namely, as not being satisfied with enjoying the good that he has, he seeks to enjoy something outside himself. But since he seeks to have this extrinsic good for himself, he does not go out from himself simply, and this movement remains finally within him. On the other hand, in the love of friendship, a man's affection goes out from itself simply; because he wishes and does good to his friend, by caring and providing for him, for his sake.[24]

---

19. See related discussions in White, "Wanting Something for Someone"; Miner, *Aquinas on the Passions*, 122–26; Kucharski, "Thomas Aquinas, Josef Seifert"; Guy Mansini, "Duplex Amor and the Structure of Love in Aquinas," in *Thomistica*, edited by Eugène Manning (Leuven: Peeters, 1995), 137–96; and Peter A. Kwasniewski, "St. Thomas, *Extasis*, and Union with the Beloved," *The Thomist* 61, no. 4 (October 1997): 587–603, in particular 592–94. William C. Mattison III provides a lucid summary of the question, relying on Mansini, in "Movements of Love: A Thomistic Perspective on *Agape* and *Eros*," *Journal of Moral Theology* 1, no. 2 (2012): 31–60, esp. 34–42.

20. White, "Wanting Something for Someone."

21. See *ST* I-II, q. 29, a. 4. See also Tobias Hoffmann, "The Pleasure of Life and the Desire for Non-Existence: Some Medieval Theories," *Res Philosophica* 90, no. 3 (July 2013): 323–46.

22. Josef Pieper, *Faith, Hope, Love* (San Francisco: Ignatius Press, 1997), 236, quoted in Miner, *Aquinas on the Passions*, 133.

23. The following discussion of the *amor concupiscentiae* is indebted to the contributions in Mansini's "Duplex Amor and the Structure of Love" and Graham McAleer's *Ecstatic Morality and Sexual Politics: A Catholic and Antitotalitarian Theory of the Body* (New York: Fordham University Press, 2005).

24. *ST* I-II, q. 28, a. 3.

In other words, *amor concupiscentiae* returns to the self because "the telos of any concupiscent motion toward a thing outside the self is always to possess the thing for oneself."[25]

This tendency of the love of concupiscence to return to itself explains why the passion of *concupiscentia* is named by Aquinas to be the matter (the material cause) of original sin.[26] The vector of such love already tends toward the self. The loss of original justice (the formal cause) distorts and exaggerates the vector of self-love. Thus "it is evident that inordinate love of self is the cause of every sin."[27]

The self-referential vector of *amor concupiscentiae* is the first reason why desire itself, even before the Fall, is marked by instability and the potential for selfishness. For a second reason, let us turn to a quality of desire that has particular contemporary relevance, namely, its tendency toward infinity.

Recall Aristotle's emphasis on the importance of a final good. Without this final end, the process of desire would go on to a futile infinity. In question 30, article 4 of the *prima secundae*, Aquinas returns to this idea, agreeing with Aristotle that concupiscence ordered to the end is naturally infinite. A concupiscence of means is finite; I want this thing for that end—a certain sum of money to fix my broken fence—and once I obtain that means, I should cease wanting it. But if money itself is the end, then my desire for it is infinite. "Consequently those who place their end in riches have an infinite concupiscence of riches; whereas those who desire

---

25. Miner, *Aquinas on the Passions*, 136. When one wishes the good for a friend, it is concupiscent in that the friend is "another self" (see *ST* I-II, q. 28, a. 1, inter alia, drawing on Augustine). McAleer compares the treatment in the *Summa* with that of the *De Malo* (4.2), in which Aquinas discusses the *pronitas ad inordinate appetendum* that is intrinsic to concupiscence even before the Fall. In the state of original justice, this *pronitas* is ordered by reason, but with the loss of that original harmony, the *pronitas* becomes an *inclinatio* (see McAleer, *Ecstatic Morality*, 45–48). McAleer might overstate the sinister nature of *amor concupiscentiae* qua natural. He interprets the union desired by such love (*amatum perfecte habere, quasi ad intima illius perveniens*, *ST* I-II, q. 28, a. 2) as "reduc[ing] [the other] to the lover" (46), which is a valence not obviously found in Aquinas's more neutral wording. Nevertheless, McAleer's larger point in this passage is a significant contribution.

26. "Now the inordinateness of the other powers of the soul consists chiefly in their turning inordinately to mutable good; which inordinateness may be called by the general name of concupiscence. Hence original sin is concupiscence, materially, but privation of original justice, formally." *ST* I-II, q. 82, a. 3, inter alia.

27. *ST* I-II, q. 77, a. 4.

riches, on account of the necessities of life, desire a finite measure of riches, sufficient for the necessities of life, as the Philosopher says."[28]

Further, as Aquinas argues in the same article, the concupiscence proper to man is by nature "altogether infinite" because reason itself is ordered to the infinite. But infinity properly speaking belongs only to God, who does not have a form contracted by matter, who is fully in act, and who is completely simple.[29]

This leaves the desiring creature in a quandary because our desires have an infinite quality with no infinite created object. Yet the infinity of our desire is not meant to be a trap but a call. Such infinity need not breed disorder, if our desire is ordered by our reason to the true good. But when desire is unmoored from good ends (and, ultimately, the *bonum honestum*), its infinite orientation manifests itself in a kind of insatiability. In contemporary terms, the infinity of our desires can breed addiction, in which no amount of the desired good is ever enough.

Thus Aquinas, following Aristotle, compares the insatiable man to an epileptic who cannot stop the spasms in his limbs.[30] His desire is literally endless. That is, it is not bent toward an end that naturally orders it, and the only natural limit to endless desire is fatigue. The spasm peters out. John Paul II in his theology of the body highlights this insatiability of fallen concupiscence by quoting the book of Sirach: "Hot passion that blazes like a fire will not be quenched until it burns itself out" (23:16).[31] Without a good that naturally orders desire to it as the end, desire becomes endless.

To summarize our progress thus far: we have seen that concupiscence naturally has two qualities that become disordered by sin, namely, a movement toward the self and a tendency to infinity. Further, the naturally infinite nature of concupiscence requires reason to order it to the good. Now I will explicate the third aspect of concupiscence: without the grace that orders desire to reason, desire will order itself toward arbitrary and

---

28. *ST* I-II, q. 30, a. 4.
29. *ST* I, q. 7, a. 2; see also I, q. 3.
30. *ST* I-II, q. 77, a. 3 (citing *Nicomachean Ethics* 7.8).
31. Pope John Paul II, *Man and Woman He Created Them: A Theology of the Body*, edited and translated by Michael Waldstein (Boston: Pauline Books and Media, 2006), 39:2, 282–84.

self-referential ends, justifying itself after the fact through rationalization, that simulacrum of reason.

Rationalization is a word that was unknown to Aquinas, but he describes the phenomenon with acuity. Because desire is meant to work in harmony with reason, it will always bring reason along with it, even when desire is going rogue. Thus when desire runs the show, "the movement of passion, as passion, begins in the appetite, and ends in the reason, since the appetite tends to conformity with reason. On the other hand, the movement of virtue is the reverse, for it begins in the reason and ends in the appetite, inasmuch as the latter is moved by reason."[32]

For example, if I am governed by virtue, my reason will tell me that having a cappuccino at 7:00 p.m. is a poor choice, because the caffeine will keep me up and because Romans look down on tourists having cappuccino after 10:00 a.m. My reason will then moderate my desire (even though the stable love for cappuccino remains strong). My will would then choose other, more appropriate goods, such as a walk through the piazza. Conversely, if my passion directs my reason, I begin to rationalize that I don't need the sleep or even that this time it will be different. My desire continues unabated or even strengthens, and my will then bends my feet into a café.

Rationalization would be impossible if the world were not full of finite goods that have a role to play in man's happiness. Virtue enables man to order all these good things to the one true good, God himself—not by stamping out the passions (as Aquinas understood Stoicism to require), but by bending their affective power to the cause of the pursuit of the good.[33] This is a kind of political rule rather than a totalitarian and Gnostic control: "The reason governs the irascible and concupiscible not by a 'despotic supremacy,' which is that of a master over his slave; but by a 'politic and royal supremacy,' whereby the free are governed, who are not wholly subject to command."[34]

32. *ST* I-II, q. 59, a. 1.
33. *ST* I-II, q. 59, a. 5: "Whereas it is not the function of virtue to deprive the powers subordinate to reason of their proper activities, but to make them execute the commands of reason, by exercising their proper acts. Wherefore just as virtue directs the bodily limbs to their due external acts, so does it direct the sensitive appetite to its proper regulated movements."
34. *ST* I-II, q. 17, a. 7. See McAleer, *Ecstatic Morality*, and also his "The Politics of the Flesh: Rahner and Aquinas on *Concupiscentia*," *Modern Theology* 15, no. 3 (July 1999): 355–65:

Sex: End-Less or Ordered

With the loss of original justice, the passions are no longer governed by reason, a situation that unleashes their latent tendencies toward self-referential and infinite desire. This affects human sexuality in particularly acute ways.

Citing Aristotle, St. Augustine, and St. Gregory of Nyssa, Aquinas observes that the sexual organs manifest a particular "insubmission" to reason.[35] In other words, the sexual organs do not docilely respond to reason's directives. Aquinas grants, following Augustine, that this insubmission is partly a result of the punishment due to the Fall.[36] He does not leave the matter there, however, but goes on to emphasize the intrinsic reason for such insubmission: the natural state of the organs of generation (in particular, it would seem, the male organ) is to be the principle of life. Outside of grace, as we have seen, the natural principles of man are not completely docile to reason.[37]

In other words, of all the bodily functions and pleasures, sexuality is particularly strong.[38] All this is naturally good and necessary; as Benedick declares with newfound resolution in *Much Ado about Nothing*, "The world must be peopled!" Yet this natural imperative also means that, outside of grace, sexual desires are also potentially destructive, precisely because of their intrinsic power.

On account of this power, sexual desire has a particular ability to upset the balance of virtue in which reason, rather than the passions, directs the will. As Aquinas puts it forthrightly, "venereal pleasures ... more than anything else work the greatest havoc in a man's mind."[39]

"Concupiscence is thus to be understood as a problem of political persuasion and obedience (and oftentimes disobedience) and not as a metaphysical problem" (358).

35. *ST* I-II, q. 17, a. 9, ad 2 and 3.

36. *ST* I-II, q. 17, a. 9, ad 3: "The soul is punished for its rebellion against God, by the insubmission of that member whereby original sin is transmitted to posterity."

37. *ST* I-II, q. 17, a. 9, ad 3. In this passage, he speaks also (following Aristotle) of the heart as principle of life.

38. As Edward Feser drily notes, "Sexual arousal occurs very frequently and can often be very hard to resist even for a short while" (*The Last Superstition: A Refutation of the New Atheism* [South Bend, IN: St. Augustine Press, 2008], 142). See also Feser's "In Defense of the Perverted Faculty Argument," in *Neo-Scholastic Essays* (South Bend, IN: St. Augustine Press, 2015), 378–413.

39. *ST* II-II, q. 153, a. 1, ad 1.

What does this look like, concretely? Sex, when uprooted from its natural ends, tends toward unrestrained *amor concupiscentiae*. C. S. Lewis, speaking of his awakening into sexual desire, writes, "What I felt for the dancing mistress was sheer appetite, the prose and not the poetry of the Flesh. I did not feel at all like a knight devoting himself to a lady; I was much more like a Turk looking at a Circassian whom he could not afford to buy. I knew quite well what I wanted."[40]

The only significant difference between Lewis's description of his experience and the contemporary scene is cultural. While Lewis "could not afford to buy" his Circassian, the now-fallen leaders in Hollywood apparently felt no such limitation. In a culture marked by what I have elsewhere called "the default of the 'yes,'" in which sex is cheap and everyone assumes everyone else's compliance with the sexual revolution, anyone can feel entitled to sex with anyone else.[41]

What, then, happened between Lewis's experience of sexual costliness and our contemporary situation (only a century or so later) of sexual bargains?[42] The key change, I will now argue, has been the easy availability of contraception, which validates endless sex by structuring sex's aims as purely internal to the user.[43]

In particular, contraception requires that the end of sexual intercourse be detachable from the end of procreation.[44] The desire for children might still be operative in the partners, in the sense of the principle of totality, but contraception makes even that desire a purely subjective and

---

40. C. S. Lewis, *Surprised by Joy* (London: Geoffrey Bles, 1955), 70, quoted in McAleer, *Ecstatic Morality*, 124.

41. See Franks, "Consent Is Not Enough."

42. For the theoretical and empirical development of this metaphor, see the work of Mark Regnerus, in particular *Cheap Sex: The Transformation of Men, Marriage, and Monogamy* (Oxford: Oxford University Press, 2017). Obviously, sexual abuse and exploitation were not invented in the past fifty years. What has occurred, however, is the elimination of cultural barriers that protected at least some classes of women from the default of the yes. Before contraception, the default was assumed to be no. Contraception has reversed the default position, providing cultural support for an increased sense of sexual entitlement on the part of men, which then has caused increased cultural pressure on women.

43. For an elegant statement of this conviction, see Feser, "In Defense of the Perverted Faculty Argument."

44. In this essay, I do not take a position on whether the sexual act has a single end (procreation) or a dual one (procreation and marital union). While I am skeptical that union is a final cause, rather than the formal cause, of sex, my argument here is separate from that conviction.

not objective reality. Contraceptive sex is not structurally oriented to any objective end. The end of sex must be imposed, not received, by the subject. Sex and its end(s) thereby become purely subjective.

This displacing of the end of sex from the nature of the act to the desires of the subject is tantamount to making sex endless. Sex-positive theologians assume that love is reliably the motive for sex, but #MeToo testifies to a reality somewhat different. Sex can just as easily be the expression of aggression, misogyny, entitlement, insecurity, pleasure-seeking—the list is as long as all the varieties of postlapsarian selfishness. When we make up an end for ourselves, it is reliably a self-referential and infinite one.

The reason this situation is worse than "messy" has to do with the intrinsic vulnerability of sex. The nakedness of the partners is a physical symbol of their vulnerability to each other, analyzed by John Paul II in his phenomenology of sexual "shame."[45] This shame is deeply self-protective, in that it safeguards us from the disordered "look of desire" against which Jesus warns in the Sermon on the Mount (Mt 5:28).[46] The possibility of children helps to explain why sex makes the partners so vulnerable: because of the sexual act, a couple might be yoked to each other forever as the parents of a child. This makes the possible costs of a one-night stand very high indeed, especially for the woman, who cannot simply walk away from her own womb.

A further reason explains the vulnerability of sex. As John Paul II argues, the body expresses the person.[47] The naked body expresses the person without filters. In this way, the very interiority of the person is at stake in the sexual act. This reality explains why unemotional hookups are so difficult to achieve, especially for women.[48]

---

45. See Pope John Paul II in his *Man and Woman He Created Them*, 26:4–30:4 (236–51). This later treatment depends on his earlier work in *Love and Responsibility*, 158–77.

46. Explored by Pope John Paul II in *Man and Woman He Created Them* at 34:1–43:7 (264–301).

47. See *Man and Woman He Created Them*, 9:4 (164) and 55:2 (345–46), inter alia.

48. Mark Regnerus and Jeremy Uecker, *Premarital Sex in America: How Young Americans Meet, Mate, and Think about Marrying* (Oxford: Oxford University Press, 2010), 139–43: "The more lifetime [sexual] partners women have had, the higher their depression-scale score and likelihood of diagnosis, the more crying they report, the lower their life satisfaction, and the more likely it is that they are currently taking antidepressants" (143). On hook-ups in particular, see Donna Freitas, *The End of Sex: How Hookup Culture Is Leaving a Generation Unhappy, Sexually Unfulfilled,*

Because of the indelible vulnerability of the sexual act, women find sexual aggression to be deeply traumatic. In sex that is coerced or forced, what should be a deeply personal gift is taken without consideration for the would-be giver. I am not arguing that users and apologists for contraception have no consideration for victims of sexual violence; that would be an absurd and unjust contention. Rather, my point is that *contraception itself* (and not the intentions of the partners) turns the sexual act into a self-referential act. Perhaps the end in mind is good, à la Johnson. But perhaps it is not; structurally, contracepted sex need not be about love at all.[49] Contraception thereby surrenders one to the uncertain dynamics of endless, self-referential, and infinite desire, and we have seen from Aquinas why, in the case of sexuality, that is so dangerous. By validating endless sex, birth control has removed the cultural barriers that previously might have protected one from someone else's sense of sexual entitlement. It should not be controversial to say that, in such a setting, women are more frequently the losers.

The only alternative to structuring sex according to self-chosen ends is structuring sex according to the ends objectively required by the act. This is what *Humanae Vitae*, as interpreted by the recent Magisterium, enables us to do. By refusing to uncouple union and procreation from each other, and by refusing to uncouple both from sex itself, *Humanae Vitae* defends persons from becoming the victims of others' selfishness. In his famous predictions concerning a contracepting world in no. 17, Paul VI notably calls attention to the possibility that men would treat women not as companions but as instruments for the service of sexual desire.

By now one can read a robust literature on *Humanae Vitae*.[50] Less notice has been given to how Pope Francis's development of "technocracy," most famously in *Laudato Si'*, no. 106, harmonizes deeply with Paul VI's

---

and Confused about Intimacy (New York: Basic Books, 2013); and Laura Sessions Stepp, *Unhooked: How Young Women Pursue Sex, Delay Love and Lose at Both* (New York: Riverhead Books, 2007).

49. Of course, contraception is not the only way to make sex self-referential. One could also make sex solely about procreation, a temptation especially acute for infertile couples. This too places a self-chosen end—a baby *must* come from this act—over the self-gift and surrender demanded by the sexual act in the context of spousal love. This question is worthy of a more detailed treatment that will not be attempted here.

50. See, e.g., the essays compiled in Janet E. Smith, *Self-Gift:* Humanae Vitae *and the Thought of John Paul II* (Steubenville, OH: Emmaus Academic, 2018).

presentation of the utilitarian, technological mentality of contraception, especially in *Humanae Vitae*, no. 2. In *Laudato Si'*, Pope Francis presents the technocratic paradigm: "This paradigm exalts the concept of a subject who, using logical and rational procedures, progressively approaches and gains control over an external object."[51] John Paul II also criticized this worldview in his Letter to Families, calling it a "new Manichaenism," in which "body and spirit are put in radical opposition; the body does not receive life from the spirit, and the spirit does not give life to the body."[52] Likewise, the Congregation for the Doctrine of the Faith under Pope Francis has criticized a "new form of Gnosticism," which "presumes to liberate the human person from the body and from the material universe."[53]

All of these tendencies lead to technocracy, "a technique of possession, mastery and transformation. It is as if the subject were to find itself in the presence of something formless, completely open to manipulation."[54] *Laudato Si'* restates the Magisterium's opposition to this view of the natural world, but it should not be forgotten that the material world includes the body.[55] Thus Francis's emphasis follows the anti-Gnostic trajectory of the recent Magisterium in opposing the hegemony of the detached reason over and above the body. It is not the job of the mind to impose ends on the blank slate of either nature or sexuality. Rather, for both, it is the mind's job to discern the ends that are already present within them.

Hence Francis proposes the alternative of receptivity, of being "in tune with and respecting the possibilities offered by the things themselves." The

---

51. Pope Francis, *Laudato Si'*, May 24, 2015, no. 106. The technocratic paradigm appears also in the 1966 majority report of the Papal Birth Control Commission, which demonstrates a Cartesian anthropology in which the body is pictured as passive matter, detachable from the rational person who freely acts upon it. Papal Commission, "Majority Report," in *The Catholic Case for Contraception*, edited by Daniel Callahan (New York: Macmillan, 1969). See Michael Waldstein's introduction in John Paul II, *Man and Woman He Created Them*, 36–44 and 94–105.

52. John Paul II, *Gratissimam Sane*, Letter to Families, February 2, 1994, no. 19.

53. Congregation for the Doctrine of the Faith, *Placuit Deo*, February 22, 2018, no. 3.

54. Pope Francis, *Laudato Si'*, no. 106. For an analysis, see Michael Hanby, "The Gospel of Creation and the Technocratic Paradigm: Reflections on a Central Teaching of *Laudato Si'*," *Communio* 42, no. 4 (Winter 2015): 724–47.

55. See Pope Benedict XVI, Address to the Bundestag, September 22, 2011, concerning an "ecology of man": "Man too has a nature that he must respect and that he cannot manipulate at will. Man is not merely self-creating freedom. Man does not create himself. He is intellect and will, but he is also nature, and his will is rightly ordered if he respects his nature, listens to it and accepts himself for who he is, as one who did not create himself."

ends are within the natural order, and the human person's relation to this order is "a matter of receiving what nature itself allowed, as if from its own hand."[56] Just as the earth has a purpose prior to man's manipulation of it for his own ends, so too does sex. The imposition of purely subjective ends leads to the exploitation of both the earth and the body. It leads to self-love smothering self-gift.

The Necessity of Virtue

What, then, is a more realistic and hence livable anthropology? Aquinas, as well as the recent Magisterium, emphasizes the role of virtue in bringing order to the passions. Reason must choose a truly good end, certainly, yet the role of reason is necessary but not sufficient. The human person must also be purified through virtue in order to understand the good, choose well, and moderate her passions. The virtues order the powers of the soul, which then are properly ordered to the ultimate good.[57] Three virtues in particular are relevant for our purposes: temperance, charity, and hope. For our purposes here, let us not forget that periodic continence stands out for the Magisterium *not* because it is one method among others and better merely because it does not involve chemicals. It is not the case that an ethical sexual act involves simply purifying motives and then choosing among many possible "methods," which are in themselves morally neutral.[58]

Rather, only periodic continence is a truly moral method because

---

56. Pope Francis, *Laudato Si'*, no. 106.

57. See Miner, *Aquinas on the Passions*, 287–89, for an exegesis of the moral virtues' "matter about which" (i.e., the matter about which the virtues are concerned) and the "matter in which" (the subject of the virtues). Miner denies that the subject of the moral virtues is in the *activity* of the powers; it is, he argues, in the powers themselves.

58. As implied in the *testo base* of the Pontifical Academy for Life's recent book, *Etica Teologica della Vita: Scrittura, tradizione, sfide pratiche* (Vatican City: Libreria Editrice Vaticana, 2021), 304, no. 172: "Ci sono infatti condizioni e circostanze pratiche che renderebbero irresponsabile la scelta di generare, come lo stesso magistero ecclesiastico riconosce, appunto ammettendo i 'metodi naturali.' Perciò, come accade in questi metodi, che già si servono di tecniche specifiche e di conoscenze scientifiche, ci sono situazioni in cui due sposi, che hanno deciso o decideranno di accogliere figli, possono operare un saggio discernimento nel caso concreto, che senza contraddire la loro apertura alla vita, in quel momento, non la prevede. La scelta saggia verrà attuata valutando opportunamente *tutte le tecniche possibili* in riferimento alla loro specifica situazione ed escludendo ovviamente quelle abortive" (emphasis added).

it demands of its users two things: respect for the generative (and not self-chosen) end of the marital embrace (and thus true responsibility in acting accordingly), and self-denial in order to abstain during the fertile time. In other words, the acts themselves either of contraception or of periodic continence form desire, respectively, according to a selfish/self-chosen or a selfless end.

In contrast, the merely "messy" view of sex positivity that is also reflected in the Pontifical Academy's *testo base* at no. 172 ignores the distorting effect of sin. As Wojtyła argues, "when encountering a person of the other sex, man does not know how to 'love' simply and spontaneously, but his whole approach to this person becomes interiorly disturbed by the desire to 'use' ... man cannot quite safely trust the reactions of sensuality."[59] By means of virtue, however, the person can have a genuine experience of robust human functioning and flourishing, even in his loving and desiring.

Rather than being self-referential, endless, and prone to misleading the reason, desire can instead be integrated within the whole psychosomatic reality of the rational person. Contemporary sexual culture provides no such hope in its oscillation between sex positivity and sexual anxiety. The resources of the Christian tradition, as delineated in this essay, provide a robust response to the hopelessness found in the contemporary sexual mission field.

---

59. Wojtyła, *Love and Responsibility*, 143–44.

CHAPTER 14

St. John Paul II on Conscience

ADRIAN J. REIMERS

This essay on the notion of conscience according to Pope St. John II has three parts. The first examines Karol Wojtyła's treatment of conscience in his philosophical works. The second considers his development of this concept in *Veritatis Splendor* and its relationship to the concepts of *heart* and *ethos*. The third and final part looks at the work of the Holy Spirit in the formation of the conscience.

Ethics is central to the study of man. As a person man lives from his interiority, which is constituted by intellect and will. By his acts the person exteriorizes himself. In his essay "Person: Subject and Community," Karol Wojtyła writes,

> To be free means not only to *want*, but also to *choose* and to *decide*, and this already suggests a transcendent subordination of the good to the true in action. Conscience, however, is the proper place for this subordination. The person's authentic transcendence in action is realized in conscience, and the *actus humanus* takes shape as the willing and choosing of a "true good" thanks to conscience.[1]

"To be free means not only to *want*, but also to *choose* and to *decide*." In this rich text, the point is simply that the human person is not compelled by his *wants* or *desires*. In *Person and Act*, Wojtyła argues at length that the human act transcends what "happens in a man," which is beyond the control of the will. A person acts when he engages his efficacy by his

---

1. Karol Wojtyła, "Person: Subject and Community," in *Person and Community: Selected Essays* (New York: Peter Lang, 1993), 234.

will. Efficacy refers to the person's engagement with the world by exercising his own efficient causality. It is the experience of being the agent.[2] As such, he is responsible for the act and is therefore morally responsible. The act is therefore different from anything that merely *happens* in the man.

The human being is free, that is, capable of self-determination. The experience "I can, but I do not have to" is the moment of freedom, the characteristic discovery of freedom.[3] Wants and desires occur as events that may happen in a person, and one may respond to them by acting. Because decision is for one cognized good among several alternatives, Karol Wojtyła argues that it is the dependence on truth that makes the will independent from its objects.

With Thomas Aquinas, Karol Wojtyła accepts the Boethian definition of the person as an individual substance of a rational nature, a definition that the authors of *Etica Teologica della Vita* find to be inadequate: "A hermeneutic of the person in terms of freedom-in-relation represents a definitive surpassing of the traditional notion of the person as *rationalis naturae individua substantia*."[4] That the person is a substance of a rational nature means that the person lives from the interior, from reason.[5] By his power of reason, the person can know truth and form himself in truth.

Although the object of a desire is a good of some sort, desire is incapable of itself of determining the truth about the good. Reason—and only reason—can recognize truth. Wojtyła writes, "Truth is in man a function and a task of reason."[6] Therefore, to know the truth about the good, it is necessary to transcend the realm of sense experience and emotion to that governed by reason and understanding. The normative power of truth is rooted in the intellect, which is subordinate to truth as its end or purpose, standing, as it were, beyond subjectivity. If, as St. Thomas Aquinas argues, truth is the adequation of intellect to thing (*adequaetio res et intellectus*),[7] then truth cannot be created by the mind.

---

2. Karol Wojtyła, *Person and Act* (Washington, DC: Catholic University of America Press, 2021), 168.

3. Wojtyła, *Person and Act*, 203.

4. Vincenzo Paglia, ed., *Etica teologica dell aviate: Scrittura, tradizione, sfide pratiche* (Vatican City: Librería Editrice Vaticana, 2022), 183.

5. Karol Wojtyla, *Love and Responsibility* (Boston: Pauline Books & Media, 2013), 4.

6. *Love and Responsibility*, 61.

7. Thomas Aquinas, *Disputed Questions on Truth* (Chicago: Regnery, 1951), q. 1, a. 1.

Conscience, Truth, and Duty

The ethical question concerns the truth about *good*. Ever since David Hume raised the sharp challenge that from a fact one cannot infer a value—"is" cannot imply "ought"—philosophers and undergraduates alike have been stymied by his apparently inexorable logic. Indeed, many contemporary moral theologians continue to insist on a sharp distinction between fact-concepts (*Tatsachenbegriffe*) and value-concepts (*Wertbegriffe*).[8] Karol Wojtyła addresses this issue.

> It is in conscience that the particular *linking of truthfulness with duty takes place, linking that is manifested as the normative power of truth*. The human person in his every act is an eyewitness of the transition from "is" to "should": from "*x* is truly good" to "I should perform x."[9]

His point here is the simple but inevitable consequence of the nature of human acting. Underlying Hume's argument is a conception of the person as a mere observer of facts and not an efficacious agent. Whenever a person acts, however, he acts for some good that he recognizes.[10] One cannot act without intending some end, which he takes to be a good according to some standard that preexists his choice. This standard (or good) is called a *norm*. A norm is a *truth about the good*, which conscience can recognize.

> The point here is not only the objective truthfulness of the norms *in abstracto* but also *the lived experience of this truthfulness, which is expressed by the conviction, that is, by a subjective certitude*, that this or that norm indicates a true good.[11]

We must note Wojtyła's understanding of the concept of norm. In both his philosophical writings and in his pastoral works as pope, he understands *norm* as some *truth about the good* and not as a rule or law. From a moral norm, a truth, one can infer an imperative or law. For instance, from the personalistic norm that a person is not an object for use but rather a good to be loved, we can infer the Gospel commandment to

---

8. Richard A. McCormick, SJ, *The Critical Calling: Reflections on Moral Dilemmas Since Vatican II* (Washington, DC: Georgetown University Press 1989), 58.
9. *Person and Act*, 264.
10. Thomas Aquinas, *Summa Theologiae* Ia, IIae, q. 1, a.1.
11. *Person and Act*, 266.

love.[12] Wojtyła writes, "norm, in the most general sense of the term, is the name we give to a principle of moral good and evil."[13] The norm is a truth about some good.[14] Therefore, although an imperative may admit of exceptions—killing is prohibited but may be allowable in self-defense—the norm, which is a truth—a person is possessed of inherent dignity as a child of God—is always and everywhere true. The fundamental moral obligation or duty is therefore to live in and act according to truth. This distinction is notably important when we consider the question of divorce and remarriage.

Experience of Guilty Conscience

In his essay "The Problem of the Theory of Morality," Karol Wojtyła addresses the problem of the guilty conscience, which is particularly relevant to our concerns here. Wojtyła writes:

The experience of guilt is in its essential core an experience of moral evil. This evil is contained in a human act, in a conscious and free action whose author is a human being—or, one could say, a concrete human self.[15]

In his apostolic letter on suffering, John Paul II remarks: "It can be said that man suffers whenever *he experiences any kind of evil.*"[16] Arising precisely as an effect of the efficacy of the person, guilt is the experience of the evil of one's own acts. Efficacy is far more than the ability effectively to change things in the world beyond one's subjectivity. Acting in truth, the human being creates and integrates himself.[17] Therefore the pangs of guilt reflect the harm one has done to his own self, disintegrating it by violating a norm of morality, by directing his will not by the truth as known by reason but by some disvalue incompatible with the truth about the good.

---

12. *Love and Responsibility*, 25.
13. Karol Wojtyła, "The Problem of the Theory of Morality," in *Person and Community*, 139.
14. Adrian J. Reimers, *The Truth about the Good* (Washington, DC: Catholic University of America Press, 2011), 148; also Karol Wojtyła "L'uomo nel campo della responsabilità," in *Metafisica della persona* (Roma: Bompiani, 2003), 1272.
15. Wojtyła, "Problem of the Theory of Morality," 137.
16. John Paul II, Apostolic Letter *Salvifici Doloris* (Vatican City: Libreria Editrice Vaticana, 1984), §7.
17. *Person and Act*, 173.

Unlike other evils that may afflict a person—pain resulting from injury to the body, bitterness from failure to accomplish a goal, or even despair of finding some meaning in one's life[18]—moral evil affects the entire person *as person,* because moral evil entails the disintegration of the person in his self-determination.[19] This disintegration arises precisely because the agent has refused to form his acts according to truth. To be sure, the victim of severe burns or the recently widowed who finds herself alone feels an immediate pain that cannot be easily alleviated, whereas grave sinners (think of Macbeth or Michael Corleone[20] after committing their respective murders) may not immediately be consciously aware of the harm they have done to themselves. Both Shakespeare's play and Coppola's films illustrate artistically the spiritual disintegration of the respective killers, however.

Conscience and the Moral Law

[C]onscience is the application of the law to a particular case; this application of the law thus becomes an inner dictate for the individual, a summons to do what is good in this particular situation.[21]

The Second Vatican Council teaches, "Always summoning him to love good and avoid evil, the voice of his conscience when necessary speaks to his heart: do this, shun that."[22] The judgment of conscience thereby acquires an imperative character.[23] Responding to (or ignoring) the voice of conscience, the person chooses and acts, and in this choice of act the encounter between conscience and freedom comes to the fore, as William F. Murphy Jr. argues in *Etica Teologica della Vita*.[24]

---

18. Adrian J. Reimers, "Human Suffering and the Theology of the Body," *Nova et Vetera* 2, no. 2 (Fall 2004): 447–48.
19. *Person and Act*, 298–302.
20. In Francis Ford Coppola's *Godfather* film trilogy.
21. *Veritatis Splendor*, §59.
22. Second Vatican Council, Pastoral Constitution on the Church in the Modern World *Gaudium et Spes*, §16.
23. *Veritatis Splendor*, §60.
24. William F. Murphy Jr., "Reflections on Fundamental Morality, Conscience, Norms, and Discernment," in *Etica Teologica della Vita*, edited by Vincenzo Paglia (Vatican City: Libreria Editrice Vaticana, 2022), 217–43.

The human act is free, for freedom is a fundamental prerogative of the person.[25] Freely to perform an act is itself a kind of good, a personalistic good. Nevertheless, that an act is one's own, freely chosen, does not make that act good of itself. Here we are reminded of Charles Curran, who carries this further. "For moral maturity one must be one's own person. It is not enough to follow what one has been told. The morally mature person must be able to perceive, choose, and identify oneself with what one does."[26] As we parse it, however, this statement becomes confusing. Curran speaks of moral maturity as being one's own person, that is, of being morally adult, no longer living according to the directions of others. This is reminiscent of Kant's insistence that the person is to be autonomous, indeed a law unto himself.[27] The autonomous agent may follow another's instructions, but only insofar as he personally validates them as his own choice.

From this Kantian principle, Curran goes on to characterize the morally mature person as the one who can "perceive, choose, and identify oneself with what one does." In this we see much more than Kant's autonomous self-legislating subject. Curran's conception of conscience implies a strong assertion of self. What is decisive, then, is not that I have *decided for the good*, but that *I* have decided, and by that personal decision it is good. Implicit in this is the claim that the speaker is so identified "in conscience" with his judgment that to speak or act otherwise would be a betrayal of his own self. St. John Henry Newman characterizes this conception:

When men advocate the rights of conscience, they in no sense mean the rights of the Creator, nor the duty to Him, in thought and deed, of the creature; but the right of thinking, speaking, writing, and acting, according to their judgment or their humour, without any thought of God at all. They do not even pretend to go by any moral rule, but they demand, what they think is an Englishman's prerogative, for each to be his own master in all things, and to profess what he pleases, asking no one's leave, and accounting priest or preacher, speaker or writer, unutterably impertinent, who dares to say a word against his going to perdition, if he like it, in his own way. [...] Conscience is a stern monitor, but in this century it has been

---

25. *Person and Act*, 222.
26. Charles Curran, *Conscience: Readings in Moral Theology No. 14* (New York: Paulist Press, 2004), 58.
27. Immanuel Kant, *Grounding for the Metaphysics of Morals* (Indianapolis: Hackett, 1993), 434–36.

superseded by a counterfeit, which the eighteen centuries prior to it never heard of, and could not have mistaken for it, if they had. It is the right of self-will.[28]

The last sentence of this text captures the point. Conscience is to be identified with self-will, to which the person has a fundamental right. As such, the conscience becomes essential to the person's own identity. To violate it is to betray one's deepest self and most fundamental values. It is this sense of conscience that appears to dominate many contemporary discussions of freedom of conscience. According to this conception, conscience can claim its rights and insist on its inviolability vis-à-vis heteronomous authority. But as Newman also insists, this is not the proper understanding of conscience.

If conscience is the application of knowledge to the act, then the proper concern of conscience is *truth*, not the *will's decision*. John Paul II writes:

In their desire to emphasize the "creative" character of conscience, certain authors no longer call its actions "judgments" but "decisions": only by making these decisions "autonomously" would man be able to attain moral maturity.[29]

The knowledge at stake is the person's knowledge of the moral law, and herein lies the rub. Every human act occurs within a rich nexus of circumstances and may potentially issue in a wide variety of results, some desirable and some not. Any choice can and ordinarily will issue in a variety of conflicting values and disvalues. The *creative conscience* sees its task as balancing these values in such a way that the core values embraced by the subject are realized. The question of truth, however, need not be addressed.

The Heart

With these considerations we turn to John Paul II's concept of the *heart*. Pope John Paul II frequently cites St. Augustine's dichotomy between love of God to the contempt of self and, by contrast, love of self to the con-

---

28. John Henry Newman, "A Letter Addressed to the Duke of Norfolk on Occasion of Mr. Gladstone's Recent Expostulation," in *The Newman Reader*, 250, accessed January 3, 2023, https://www.newmanreader.org/works/anglicans/volume2/gladstone/index.html.

29. *Veritatis Splendor*, §55.

tempt of God.[30] The person who is formed by the love of God has necessarily adopted a different system of values from one who is formed for love of self. We may call this system of interiorized values an *ethos*,[31] and one's ethos is what forms his heart. Thus in his Theology of the Body he lays out at length the nexus of values that constitute the *ethos* of the redemption and of Christian marriage.[32]

The importance of these concepts of *ethos* and heart lies in the fact that one's acts arise from a subsisting person as from a common source. Every person's values fall into some kind of order or nexus, which constitute an *ethos*. A man may be a hero and martyr for justice but unfaithful to his wife. Nevertheless, he has a fairly consistent *ethos* by which he habitually lives. If his *ethos* is internally inconsistent in some respect, he will come to sense a need to bring his values into harmony with each other. The moral life cannot be reduced to a serious of discrete moral decisions but is in fact *a life* flowing from its living source. We call this source the *heart*.

This heart is, in fact, identical with the conscience.[33] In his encyclical on the Holy Spirit, John Paul II writes,

> By becoming "the light of hearts," that is to say the light of consciences, the Holy Spirit "convinces concerning sin," which is to say, *he makes man realize his own evil and at the same time directs him toward what is good.*[34]

Elsewhere he writes, "The sacredness of life gives rise to its inviolability, written from the beginning in man's heart, in his conscience."[35] And in *Ver-*

---

30. Augustine of Hippo, *City of God*, Book XIV, chap. 28; Karol Wojtyła, *Teachings for an Unbelieving World* (Notre Dame, IN: Ave Maria Press, 2020), 53.

31. Karol Wojtyła, "Valutazione sulla possibilità di costruire l'etica cristiana sulle base del sistema di Max Scheler," in *Metafisica della persona*, 284–86, 305.

32. John Paul II, *Man and Woman He Created Them*, 228, 278, 264ff., 294ff., 312–400, etc.

33. With respect to the heart, it's important to note the description of conscience given by Vatican II *in Gaudium et Spes*, 16: "In the depths of his conscience, man detects a law which he does not impose upon himself, but which holds him to obedience. Always summoning him to love good and avoid evil, the voice of conscience when necessary speaks to his heart: do this, shun that. For man has in his heart a law written by God; to obey it is the very dignity of man; according to it he will be judged. Conscience is the most secret core and sanctuary of a man. There he is alone with God, Whose voice echoes in his depths. In a wonderful manner conscience reveals that law which is fulfilled by love of God and neighbor."

34. John Paul II, Encyclical *Dominum et Vivificantem* (Vatican City: Libreria Editrice Vaticana, 1986), §42.

35. John Paul II, Encyclical *Evangelium Vitae* (Vatican City: Libreria Editrice Vaticana, 1995), §40.

itatis Splendor, he identifies the heart with the conscience (§54). As the site of the person's beliefs about the truth concerning the good, the heart can then rightly be called the person's *inner core*. If conscience is application of knowledge to the act, and *if knowledge cannot be reduced simply to one's belief concerning a particular fact*, then conscience addresses the fact not only in its existential singularity but also in its relationship with other truths. A direct implication of this is that the formation of conscience is more than the memorization of a set of moral rules. To form one's conscience is to adopt and internalize a nexus of values, which is to form one's heart.

"Well-Formed" Conscience

As the final subjective judge of what is the good to be done, conscience is infallible. That is, one is always obliged to follow his conscience.[36] When Catholic pastors defend this prerogative of conscience, they always add the qualification that the conscience is to be "well formed." To follow one's conscience is always right—provided that the conscience is "well formed." The question must inevitably arise concerning the characteristics of a well-formed conscience. How does the individual know whether his conscience is well formed? Let us consider an instance of conscience formation.

Conscience and the "Winnipeg Statement"

When we examine a *crisis of conscience*, we find at the core of the crisis lies a choice of the will concerning the good for which one lives. In *Humanae Vitae*, Pope Paul VI had solemnly presented the moral requirement that in their marital union couples must refrain from using contraceptives. The Bishops of Canada in their "Winnipeg Statement" acknowledged that "[m]any Catholics face a grave problem of conscience" in receiving the encyclical. This grave problem does not exempt them from "the responsibility of forming [their] conscience according to truly Christian values and principles."[37] But the Canadian bishops allowed that the married

---

36. *Catechism of the Catholic Church*, §§1778–82.
37. Bishops of Canada, "Canadian Bishops' Statement on the Encyclical Humanae Vitae," Winnipeg, 1968.

couple who find this requirement to be unduly burdensome can disobey the teaching "in good conscience." The bishops write,

> In accord with the accepted principles of moral theology, if these persons have tried sincerely but without success to pursue a line of conduct in keeping with the given directives, [pastoral counsellors] may be safely assured that, whoever honestly chooses that course which seems right to him does so in good conscience.[38]

Let us consider this closely. If the conscience is a judgment of reason, then the unduly burdened couple is called to examine the truth concerning contraception. In the first instance, this entails consideration of the moral instruction received from Pope Paul VI. *Humanae Vitae* makes clear that to have contracepted marital relations is without exception a moral evil. To reject this judgment is effectively to reject Paul VI's authority to teach this as a truth concerning morality. It is to claim that in this instance, at least, there is some higher authority than the pope or that they are themselves capable of arriving at a contrary moral evaluation. Most revisionist moral theologians (and possibly the Canadian bishops[39]) will allow that it is this second alternative which applies in such cases, that is, that ordinary Catholics are in a position to judge whether contraceptives may be used without sin in their conjugal relations.[40] It follows, therefore, that the Catholic who will not accept the teaching of *Humanae Vitae* effectively denies the authority of the pope to teach definitively about conjugal relations.

We generally assume that most human beings are qualified to recognize moral goods and evils, but this may not be true. Aristotle seemed to recognize that some individuals may be morally blind. He attributes some moral blindness to poor upbringing.[41] Indeed, if we examine human behavior attentively, we find that many people do not actually have a well-developed sense for right and wrong, that many continue to live by childhood rules. Therefore professional associations and government legislatures must define legal standards or professional ethical codes. It is

---

38. "Canadian Bishops' Statement."
39. We may also mention those of Austria and Germany. Cardinal Schönborn expressly apologized for a similar statement by the Austrian bishops.
40. Charles Curran et al., "Text of the Statement by Theologians," *New York Times*, July 31, 1968, 16.
41. Aristotle, *Nicomachean Ethics*, II, 1 1103b23.

common for young men at universities not to recognize that the sexual exploitation of young women is wrong. Despite clear evidence that the entity within a pregnant woman's belly is a baby, many people in Western societies refuse to acknowledge that abortion is a grave evil. The point of these examples is simply that we have little reason to believe that most human beings have well-developed powers of moral reasoning.

In the case of contraception, readily available and reliable contraceptives obviate many difficulties and make life easier. The sentiment that once opposed contraceptives as obscene has largely disappeared. Save for the Catholic Church, no prominent moral authority opposes contraception. If our hypothetical Canadian couple is to choose in good conscience while rejecting papal authority, then they must find other resources for their moral evaluation. As good, moral persons, the hypothetical Canadian couple recognize that they are obliged to behave with love toward each other and their neighbors. They want to cause no harm. This is not only a moral fact; it is also written into their kindly Canadian bones, as it were. They live according to what Karol Wojtyła calls an *ethos*,[42] a nexus of values, which they have to a great extent received and often uncritically. The concept of *ethos* sheds light on the minds of our hypothetical Canadian couple who have chosen *in conscience* to reject the teaching of *Humanae Vitae*. They adhere to the values by which decent Canadians and (to a great extent, at least) their southern neighbors live. According to these values, by the shape of this *ethos*, sexual pleasure is prima facie a good; as Thomas Nagel writes, "bad sex is generally better than none at all."[43] We may characterize this *ethos* as bourgeois, middle-class morality. Those who behave according to it are generally seen to be good, and their consciences accord with that morality.

Here we encounter the critical issue. Can our hypothetical couple rely on this *ethos* to guide them in their decision about contraception? Joseph Ratzinger is especially helpful here:

---

42. Karol Wojtyła, "Separation of Experience from the Act in Ethics," in *Person and Community*, 35.

43. Thomas Nagel, "Sexual Perversion," in *Moral Problems: A Collection of Philosophical Essays*, edited by James Rachels (New York: Harper and Row, 1975), 15.

Liberalism's idea of conscience ... is the faculty which dispenses with truth. It thereby becomes the justification for subjectivity, which would not like to have itself called into question. Similarly, it becomes the justification for social conformity.[44]

In other words, one cannot safely rely on the socially received *ethos* to form one's own grasp of moral values. It does not suffice simply for this couple to consider their own situation, whether they can afford another child, whether they can forgo sexual intimacy for a time, and so on. Having called into question the moral teaching authority of the pope, they must examine the roots and structure of the *ethos* by which they form their choices. What this means is that the human person is to critique the morality received from the culture in which he lives according to criteria from a higher authority.

From this the error underlying the Winnipeg Statement, an error that also appears in the *Etica Teologica della Vita*[45] becomes clear. What is proposed is that the Catholic can appeal to a higher principle of authority than the Catholic Church. But the Christian *ethos* is formed by the recognition that the highest good is union with God through the encounter with Christ. Furthermore, "In order to make this 'encounter' with Christ possible, God willed his Church."[46] Therefore a conscience based on an *ethos* other than that proposed by the Church is inevitably ill formed. To follow Jesus is to embrace a new way of life, a different *ethos*, which will form the person's moral values and decisions. In this way he will rightly form his conscience. Therefore our hypothetical Canadian couple is not challenged to find a source of argumentation or valuation besides that of the Church in order to weigh different traditions or perspectives. Rather, because the Church has so consistently insisted that the use of contraceptives is morally illicit, the couple is called to the *obedience of faith* (Rom 1:5).

Fundamental to all this is that conscience is not a decision, that is, an

---

44. Joseph Ratzinger (Benedict XVI), *Faith and Politics: Selected Writings* (San Francisco: Ignatius Press, 2018), 110.

45. Sigrid Müller, "Moral Responsibility as an Answer to God's Call," in *Etica Teologica della Vita: Scrittura, tradizione, sfide pratiche*, edited by V. Paglia (Vatican City: Libreria Editrice Vaticana, 2022), 208.

46. *Veritatis Splendor*, §7.

act of the will. Good and evil are not determined by the acting person's decision to act. That the Church teaches on specific kinds of behavior does not violate consciences. One who acts according to his conscience, according to the truth about the moral good, is most free. John Paul II writes, "The relationship between man's freedom and God's law is most deeply lived out in the 'heart' of the person, in his moral conscience."[47]

And Hence...

Conscience is the final court of decision, but the conscience must be well formed, which means that conscience is formed according to truth. To be formed by truth means that conscience must be guided by reason, which is the person's power to know truth. Conscience is not, therefore, a kind of inner sense or feeling, however deep or intense, that some act is right, permissible, or wrong. The discernment of conscience is not an examination of one's inner self, of his most persistent feelings or even convictions. Moral good and evil can be given to reason and known by human intelligence.

In his encyclical on the Holy Spirit, Pope John Paul II reflects on the Lord's words at John 16:7–11:

And when [the Holy Spirit] has come, he will convict the world of sin, and of righteousness, and of judgment: of sin, because they do not believe in me; of righteousness, because I go to the Father and you see me no more; of judgment, because the ruler of this world is judged.[48]

Dependent as it is on human reasoning and on the social ethos in which one lives, the conscience is indeed susceptible to error. Furthermore, it is easy to minimize the seriousness of one's personal missteps. Because conversion requires the "convicting concerning sin," the Holy Spirit confers a *"double gift*: the gift of the truth of conscience and the gift of the certainty of redemption."[49] In practical terms, what this means is that the Christian needs an active engagement with the Lord in prayer, Scripture reading, and reception of the sacraments, which if practiced dai-

---

47. *Veritatis Splendor*, §54.
48. *Dominum et Vivificantem*, §27.
49. *Dominum et Vivificantem*, §31.

ly will open one to the Holy Spirit's illumination of the conscience. This illumination is a matter not so much of resolving conflicts of conscience by seeking specific answers to particular issues, but of opening one's mind and heart generally to the Lord and his will. As one practices his faith, with especial attention to Christ's sacrifice on the cross, the Holy Spirit can gradually shed light on the truth, one's personal responsibility, and the requirements of the moral law.

PART V

THE BEAUTY AND WISDOM OF CATHOLIC SEXUAL MORALITY

CHAPTER 15

The Beauty of Chastity

OANA GOTIA

Introduction

Speaking about the virtue of chastity today goes against all the pre- or post-pandemic trends invading our culture, as we have recently seen with the aggressive promotion of the sexualization of children through different movies and ads (the Netflix movie *Cuties* and Balenciaga advertisements, for example), with the aggressive push to insert pornographic material into schoolbooks in the United States and in Europe, as well as the promotion of pornography consumption in recent years.[1] Pornographic websites today are free, leading to an increase of 42 billion views on Pornhub—a kind of *pacifier* to numb the consciences of people at the time of the lockdowns.

Why is chastity one of the most attacked virtues today? And why would the Church not just cease to promote it for us all, especially the youth and couples today? (I refer specifically to the virtue of *conjugal* chastity and not to the vow of virginity and celibacy.) Why does the Church, as a Mother and a Teacher, not stop proclaiming the cultivation of this virtue?

It is, in a nutshell, because she cares deeply and truly for our freedom and for human love. Contrary to the many misunderstandings, chastity has to do with *freedom and love*.

---

1. F. Zattoni et al., "The Impact of COVID-19 Pandemic on Pornography Habits: A Global Analysis of Google Trends," *International Journal of Impotence Research* 33 (2021): 824–31.

The Saving Gaze of Love

I presented the talk on which this essay is based in the early hours of Saturday morning in my time zone, a time that liturgically points to the coming of Sunday, the day of the Resurrection. This time reminds us, especially during Holy Week, of Christ's descent into hell to bring light and life to the first couple, Adam and Eve. This context also stimulated me to start my presentation with imagery taken from Franz Schubert's opera *The Devil's Pleasure Palace* (*Der Teufels Lust-schloss*).

It tells the love story of Oswald and Luitgarde. Oswald is penniless, but he still marries Luitgarde in secret, even though her father—a nobleman—is furious about this financial mismatch. They are banished to the Black Forest, which is known for hiding a Magic Castle (the devil's pleasure palace) to which, it is said, only "the brave" have access. Oswald goes there to test his bravery. All of a sudden, all the fleshly delights (beautiful women, food, music, etc.) present themselves and surround him with their alluring charms, attempting to seduce him. He resists them to a certain point, but then, since these enticements keep multiplying, he almost starts to give in. Just when he is on the verge of collapsing into the arms of these temptations, his wife Luitgarde comes to his rescue. With his eyes focused on her loving gaze, he regains his inner strength and firmly rejects the allurements of the devil's palace. In that same moment, the palace disappears, since it was nothing but an illusion created by his father-in-law, who puts him through all manner of trials in an effort to test his character and his worthiness for his daughter.

We see that Oswald is awakened by Luitgarde's gaze of love: so clearly different than what surrounds him in that moment, so resplendent in its pure beauty, profundity and quality, that it brings him to his senses. Luitgarde's gaze frees his heart and thus allows him to regain access to the depth of his heart, where he can then recognize what he really desires from life.

Children, young people, and couples experience that same deep thirst for this kind of love and for its gaze, which can first be received through the foundational experiences of the family. Teenagers today state that the deciding factor for shaping their decision-making regarding their sexuality is, in fact, the family.[2] But, even more evidently so, there is a propitious disenchantment with all the counterfeits of love in our culture (which cause significant depression in girls and boys[3]), prophesied in *Humanae Vitae* (HV 17) and dramatically fulfilled today. These are *surrogate* loves that can, yes, momentarily blur one's inner moral perceptions, but can never offer what is truly sought. Jason Evert, who speaks on chastity in hundreds of schools around the United States, often states how attentive the kids are when listening, and how much they long for someone to show them *what* true love is and *where* to find it.[4]

Some of these young people are so addicted to porn[5] that they are actually disgusted with it, since it is deeply alienating, yet despite their own disgust, they don't know the way out of this habit, nor do they know the way toward someone with whom they can have a meaningful relationship. They don't actually know the way back to what they intuit and interiorly recognize as already written in their hearts: a love that embraces not just "bits and pieces," but the whole person (HV 7).

The Counterfeit Love or the *Shipwrecked* Promise

The endless visual stimulation and explicit sexual images that imbue apps and all the media today[6] may make the youth think that perhaps there is no mystery, nothing left to know about sexuality that is not already understood. But is this true?

---

2. Bill Albert, *With One Voice 2010: America's Adults and Teens Sound Off about Teen Pregnancy: A Periodic National Survey* (Memphis, TN: National Campaign to Prevent Teen and Unplanned Pregnancy, December 2010), https://idecideforme.com/wp-content/uploads/2021/09/19756-With_One_Voice_2010.pdf.

3. Kirk Johnson, Lauren Noyes, and Robert Rector, "Sexually Active Teenagers Are More Likely to Be Depressed and to Attempt Suicide," Heritage Foundation, June 2, 2003, https://www.heritage.org/education/report/sexually-active-teenagers-are-more-likely-be-depressed-and-attempt-suicide.

4. Jason Evert, "On Catholic Chastity," *The Augustine Institute Show* with Dr. Tim Gray, June 1, 2021, https://www.youtube.com/watch?v=ffaF6xPKyeU&ab_channel=AugustineInstitute-CatholicChurchExplained.

5. J. Wolak et al., "Unwanted and Wanted Exposure to Online Pornography in a National Sample of Youth Internet Users," *Pediatrics* 119 (2007): 247, 248–49.

6. S. Villani, "Impact of Media on Children and Adolescents: A 10-Year Review of the Research," *Journal of the American Academy of Child and Adolescent Psychiatry* 40 (2001): 392, 399.

This fascination is not without some ambiguity. If the beauty of bodies does not open a horizon, if it is not inscribed in the search for *meaning* proper to the human heart, it deeply disappoints, like a shipwrecked promise or a "dull" beauty, incapable of moving, as Plotinus would say.[7] Man's gaze seeks in the bodily beauty of the other the possibility of a deep relationship, an access way to the *person* for whom he/she was made.

Roger Scruton states in his book *Beauty* that the capacity to see the beauty of the human body is strongly rooted in the way our eyes see the other person's body:

There is a distinction, familiar to all of us, between an interest in a person's body and an interest in a person as embodied. A body is an assemblage of body parts; an embodied person is a free being revealed in the flesh. When we speak of a beautiful human body we are referring to the beautiful embodiment of a person, and not to a body considered merely as such.[8]

Our eyes, however, can also attempt to destroy the mystery of the other, eclipsing the person through the approach of his or her body. Think of the fragmentary vision offered by porn, which does not allow that individuality of the body to shine forth, but instead transforms it into a merchandise of pleasure through a depersonalizing experience:

When the eclipse of the person by his body is deliberately produced, we talk of obscenity. The obscene gesture is one that puts the body on display as pure body, so destroying the experience of embodiment [...] Those thoughts suggest something important about physical beauty. The distinctive beauty of the human body derives from its nature as embodiment. Its beauty is not the beauty of a doll, and is something more than a matter of shape and proportion.[9]

If the beauty of the human body is not that of a toy and is more than merely a question of form and proportion, what then is its true source?

Scruton asserts that in the transfiguring moment of admiration—for example, admiring the beauty of an *Apollo* Belvedere or Bernini's *Daphne*—we are led out of ourselves, out of an attitude of immediate consumption of pleasure that bends/closes us upon ourselves.[10] We perceive, in

---

7. Plotinus, *Enneads* VI, 7, 22:3–7, 22–27.
8. Roger Scruton, *Beauty* (Oxford: Oxford University Press, 2009), 47.
9. Scruton, *Beauty*, 48–49.
10. Scruton, *Beauty*, 49: "When we find human beauty represented in a statue, such as the

fact, a human beauty that is defined in *personal* terms because it is the fruit of the contemplation of an irreducible mystery of the other. If we indeed seek a pleasure that lasts, which does not vanish in the instant, in reality we seek nothing other than the joy of being with the person, since only the pleasure that arises as the fruit of this personal bond of love can fill our hearts. That is where the difference lies between the two gazes.

What makes this love different and unique, so much so that John Paul II calls it fair and beautiful?[11]

Beauty and Conjugal Chastity

St. John Paul II is deeply influenced by St. Thomas's description of the virtue of chastity and its unique relationship with love and beauty. In fact, St. Thomas Aquinas ascribes the characteristic of beauty (*pulchritudo* and *honestas*) only to the virtue of chastity, a component of the cardinal virtue of temperance,[12] thus fitting into the great ancient Greek tradition that temperance (*sophrosyne*) and beauty (*kalos*)[13] are closely related (*kalokagathia*).[14]

The Beauty of Love: A Transforming Instant

In the treatise on love in the *Summa,* Aquinas points to *goodness* and *beauty* as the *causes* of love.[15] On the one hand, he associates them, since both are attractive, and on the other hand, he distinguishes them, since beauty adds to goodness a connection with knowledge.[16]

We saw that Oswald *knows* what he desires most when he *sees* Luit-

---

Apollo Belvedere or the Daphne of Bernini, what is represented is the beauty of a person-flesh animated by the individual soul, and expressing individuality in all its parts.... Whether it attracts contemplation or prompts desire, human beauty is seen in personal terms."

11. See John Paul II's *The Jeweller's Shop* and *Crossing the Threshold of Hope.*

12. St. Thomas Aquinas, *Summa Theologiae* II-II, qq. 141–70. On the connection between beauty and conjugal chastity, see Oana Gotia, *L'amore e il suo fascino: Bellezza e castita' nella prospettiva di San Tommaso d'Aquino* (Siena: Cantagalli, 2011).

13. Plato, *Republic,* 589 c-d.

14. F. Bourriot, *Kalos kagathos—kalokagathia: D'un terme de propagande de sophistes à une notion sociale et philosophique. Étude d'histoire athénienne* (Zurich: Georg Olms Verlag, 1995), 285.

15. *ST* I-II, q. 27, a. 2, co.

16. *ST* I-II, q. 27, a. 1, ad. 3. See also Georgette Dorval-Guay, "Sur le sens du terme 'placet' dans la définition thomiste du beau," *Laval théologique et philosophique* 41 (1985): 443-47.

garde's clear and loving gaze. What kind of beauty triggers this saving knowledge in spousal love?

In Aquinas, understanding the profound truth of human love starts with the analysis of the novelty of the event constituted by the love encounter between a man and a woman (*amor est passio*[17]): the beloved irrupts into and touches the depths of the subject's heart (*amor dicitur intimus*[18]), thus becoming a precious *presence* (*amor facit amatum esse in amante et converso*[19]) that then illuminates his/her existence. Each one of us can relate to this original experience: of being enriched in a fundamental and irrevocable way by the impact the presence of the beloved has upon us. The *experience* of love, in its richness, awakens different dynamisms in man and woman: their affectivity and intellect, together with their sensitivity and corporality, and each of these dimensions is important and connected (*proportio*), since each one brings a specific richness to human life (*integritas*). When we fall in love deeply, we don't just experience a sensation, but our minds and hearts as well are also touched and involved by this presence of the person we love.

Human love therefore has an interpersonal sense not only in the elective moment (*dilectio*), but already in the receptive moment—that of the affective union between man and woman, as we can see in Aquinas (and then later on in Wojtyla's analysis of love[20]). In Aquinas, the affective union generates an affective harmony (*immutatio, complacentia, coaptatio*[21]) between the two lovers and allows for their *presence* in each other's hearts not just to endure, but also to blossom. From this receptive movement of love, without which reciprocity cannot spring, man and woman experience a new desire. A desire to share a life together, a desire that takes them out of themselves, which Aquinas calls *ecstatic*[22] and which aims to reach their real union[23] (*unio realis*) with the beloved.

As we can see, true love is never static. It requires a *response*; it requires

17. *ST* I-II, q. 26, a. 2, co.
18. *ST* I-II, q. 28, a. 2, co.
19. *ST* I-II, q. 28, a. 2, sc.
20. See K. Wojtyla's multidimensional analysis of love in *Love and Responsibility*, translated by Grzegorz Ignatik (Boston: Pauline Books & Media, 2013).
21. *ST* I-II, q. 26, a. 2, co.
22. *ST* I-II, q. 28, a. 3, co.
23. *ST* I-II, q. 28, a. 1, ad 2.

a mutual interest and intentional choice to make the other flourish in all that makes him unique in his identity. This is why, for Aquinas, this response to the presence of the beloved, the *dilectio,* means nothing other than to reciprocally choose the other as an end[24] (*amatum simpliciter et per se amatur*[25]), as worthy of guiding one's emotions, thoughts, desires toward a deep relationship with him and toward all the goods that nourish and strengthen this personal communion (*bonum alicui velle*[26]).

Aquinas uses the threefold traits of beauty (based on Aristotle and Pseudo-Dionysius)—proportion (*proportio/consonantia*), *integrity* (*integritas/perfectio*), and *splendor* (*claritas*)—to describe the interpersonal structure of love in which the lover's interiority, inhabited by the beloved, shines forth. For St. Thomas, and for the Tradition of the Church, true interpersonal love never loses these intrinsic elements of richness and excellence that constitute its beauty.

When Love Becomes Mature

This is where the virtue of chastity comes in. We all desire to know and possess not just the *instant* of love, but rather the *art* of loving. Oswald and Luitgarde need to get to know each other over time, overcoming specific temptations, but most especially also being able to nourish their spousal love in a creative way during the various *seasons* of their love.

This quality of interpersonal love can only strengthen over time. Only through chastity, aided by the other virtues, as principles of unity of man's action,[27] is it possible to face, with intelligence and sensitivity, the challenges of contingency and fragility of human action, those misunderstandings inherent to bringing together two different ways of thinking and feeling in daily life, those difficulties such as sickness or job precarity, the constant temptations to give up on purifying one's love from selfishness and to take the easy but shallow way out, the challenge of educating children and welcoming new ones, and so on.

Thus through the virtue of chastity guided by prudence (with which

---

24. *ST* I-II, q. 26, a. 2, co.
25. *ST* I-II, q. 26, a. 4, co.; I-II, q. 26, a. 1, co.
26. *ST* I-II, q.26, a.4, co.
27. See Giuseppe Abba, *Lex et virtus, Studi sull'evoluzione della dottrina morale di san Tommaso d'Aquino* (Rome: LAS, 1983), 195.

it is synergistically bound[28]), reason does not impose an extrinsic order. To the contrary, the *ordo* that chaste reason generates refers to the very structure of interpersonal love.[29] It requires creativity and imagination, an attentive dialogue, a selfless listening to one another, a constant practice of channeling the emotions and the sexual desires toward the communion of persons (and not toward a self-absorbed attitude), as *Humanae Vitae* states when referring to the benefits of periodic continence (HV 16, 21, 22).

Nothing that is truly good and human is lost in the process of acquiring this art of relating to one another according to his/her personal dignity.[30] Thus desires do not die, but instead are purified and strengthened. Intelligence becomes the art of *intus-leggere* the reality of the beloved and not a projection of one's imagination. Because of the virtue of the *beautiful-chaste love*, the gaze becomes clearer and deeper in each spouse, for it has witnessed the gift of being forgiven and of forgiving, of learning the hard way to remain open to rising up again after each fall, rather than embracing a self-pitying attitude, which is in fact another form of narcissism.

The chaste person is thus enabled to reach the specific *bonum* of chastity: the integration of the sexual desires toward conjugal union of love with the other, while open (*conveniens*) to life,[31] as Aquinas would put it. True love brings forth life. It is only in this way that the conjugal act can be an expression of interpersonal love and not an act of emotivistic need, since it transcends the communion of the spouses and opens it up to a new relationship with the fruit of this communion: the child.

Therefore it is only through the collaboration of prudence, fortitude, and justice that chastity allows for the gradual disappearance of disordered passions that, without guidance, would condemn the person to dissolution and would leave him abandoned to the destructive assault of the vices of intemperance and lust, since vice is a loss of freedom, according to Aquinas.[32]

---

28. *ST* I-II, q. 58, a. 4, co.
29. J. Noriega, "*Ordo* amoris e *ordo rationis*," in *Limiti alla responsabilità: Amore e giustizia*, edited by L. Melina and D. Granada (Rome: LUP, 2005), 187–205.
30. *ST* II-II, q. 141, a. 3, co.
31. *ST* II-II, q. 153, a. 2, co.
32. *ST* I-II, q. 76–77.

Thus chastity has to do with a gain in freedom and love. It frees us to love the other in his full dignity. If chastity makes us see and promote the personal value of the beloved, the vice opposed to chastity does the opposite. This vice, lust (*luxuria*), causes a certain blindness of the heart and mind (*caecitas mentis*[33]) since the beloved is no longer perceived in his/her personal dignity. To this vice St. Thomas attributes moral turpitude and moral ugliness.[34]

Chastity is beautiful, therefore, because it introduces and allows the subject to remain permanently within a person-to-person relationship, which is the only one that is capable of offering that profound *joy*[35] to both.

The Family: The School of the "Fair" Love

Can man attain this art of loving by himself? Of course, the answer is negative. We can only learn from someone/Someone how to acquire the pure gaze of love, by *seeing* it lived out, by *experiencing* the reality that love is possible in our relationships. This is why the school of love is the family, where we receive precious tools to build a mature spousal love in the future.

Witnessing Spousal Love

The first way for parents to educate their child in this art is to love each other as spouses.[36] This is a fundamental aspect in the child's life: seeing, experiencing that he is the fruit of his parents' spousal love, a love that is not limited to feeling but endures in time, because it intentionally places the good of conjugal communion at the center. The parents exemplify and witness a love that is capable of uniting, even though the differences between the parents are maintained. This shining truth of love, along with the child's healthy relationship with his siblings, inspires in him the confidence to approach serenely the otherness implied in all relationships,

---

33. *ST* II-II, q. 153, a. 5, co.
34. *ST* II-II, q. 162, a. 6, ad. 3.
35. *ST* I-II, q. 31, a. 3, co.
36. Jason Evert and C. Stefanick, *Raising Pure Teens* (San Diego, CA: Catholic Answers 2010), 217.

especially in those with the opposite sex. Thus loving one's spouse and cultivating his or her best qualities are not distractions from caring for one's children, but are in reality a secure investment in education and in its solid foundation. The credibility of the values one wants to pass on to one's children is generated by the very life of the parents who deeply care about growing and renewing their bond as a couple.

The Education of the Heart

Manifesting an unconditional love to the child is a goal to be achieved; it is not automatic. Alasdair MacIntyre proposes an enlightening model to parents for offering this unconditional love. He says it is useful to consider the model of parents of disabled children.[37] For this Scottish philosopher, it is in the disabled child's utmost fragility and dependence on parents that true parental love manifests itself. This love is not focused on or animated by the mere expectation of advantage or retributive reward on the child's part. This love does not focus solely on the qualities or performance of the child, nor does it cease to be given because of the mistakes the child makes[38]—although excellence should always be encouraged in education.

The heart of the child's affective maturation therefore implies, on the part of the parents, their presence of care, sensitivity, and closeness with respect to the child's needs. Otherwise, there is a danger that the child will take refuge in an unreal world, detached from the reality that frightens him, because he perceives it to be hostile and insensitive to his needs. In fact, we can see that the brokenness of the postmodern family goes hand in hand with the rise in the addictions related to the escapist trends promoted by our digital culture, especially among the youth who experience such brokenness,[39] who have difficulty facing reality—especially that of relationships—and its challenges. As we well know, facing reality and one's responsibility to take one's place in it is normally learned for a child with the support of a nurturing and present family.

---

37. See Alasdair MacIntyre, *Dependent Rational Animals* (Chicago: Open Court, 1999).

38. See Oana Gotia, "Educazione delle emozioni e sessualità in Martha Craven Nussbaum," in *La soggettività morale del corpo (VS 48)*, edited by Levio Melina and J. J. Pérez-Soba (Siena: Cantagalli, 2012), 245–60.

39. Susan Villani, "Impact of Media on Children and Adolescents: A 10-Year Review of the Research," *Journal of the American Academy of Child and Adolescent Psychiatry* 40 (2001): 392–401.

For this reason, in order to help the child cope with the reality external to him, the education of imagination, sensitivity, and memory through narrativity is decisive for the child's growth. The great books, the great narratives are a precious instrument for the affective and sexual education of children. For MacIntyre,[40] the mediation of the narrative centered on true heroes who are faced with challenges and yet who choose brave deeds instead of easy escapes (and thus distinguish themselves from false and cowardly "heroes"), helping children develop a sense of the meaning of life. True relationships, true friendships take time to be built, but it is worth spending one's life to achieve them. The little boy and girl make true moral choices, by both intellectually and affectively embracing and adhering to these true heroes—be it a just prince or a brave orphan, a hardworking and honest father, or a selfless and sweet mother. This is why reading stories is so important in the family. Good stories take us out of our own universe, and they open up the interior world of others, showing how our good is intrinsically connected to the good of others.

The healthy narrativity of the child's human emotions also depends on the knowledge of the models and figures of his or her own family stories that are told and commemorated by grandparents. Grasping his genealogical roots and thus his historic origin, understanding the intergenerational layers of his identity, helps the child see his relational nature as a good to embrace and cherish always. Thus stories mediate reality, prepare for reality, and make the child want to embrace reality with courage and in all its richness.

This is why the emotivistic culture also attacks these great classical stories through the many twists that turn heroes into ambiguous characters and transform evil into a diluted harmless character, blurring for the child the salutary differences between good and evil, which help him develop a moral sense. This is why it is paramount to choose those great (unmodified) stories (movies, games, toys, etc.) with great care and detail, so that these deliberate distortions do not creep into the educational growth of the child.

Education of the child's great desires means also being introduced intentionally to good practices: learning to do good for others, starting with

---

40. See MacIntyre, *Dependent Rational Animals*.

parents and siblings, but then also for the poor and the sick, the less able, those with different traditions and cultures. The child needs not only to be *instructed* about good, but to actually see it practiced and shared with others. And one of the first essential and valuable exercises in the education of the child consists in learning *to give thanks* for a love received, that is, to discover the gift of one's own existence as a gift from the Other and from one's parents.

The practice of introducing the child to the world of art and craftsmanship is also precious in the affective-sexual education of children. Seeing the meticulous care, inventiveness, and effort invested in one's craft helps the child see that real art—including that of building up relationships—takes time and practice, and requires models to live up to. Learning from mistakes is also a salutary experience that is an integral part of that facing the reality of love and its intricate pathways leading to its growing in quality.

Learning to say *yes* to the love of the person and to say *no* to selfishness is why parents know that to love their child means to also to be able to say *no*. Emotivistic role models in fact alienate the child because they transform the family into an emotivistic refuge, instead of a school for socialization, for learning to take responsibility within the larger community.

Learning the Gift of Self

Through this education of desire, the little boy and girl also come to understand naturally the meaning of their sexuality as being intrinsically connected to gift of self. By learning to wait for small things, they learn to wait to build great friendships and to conquer great loves.

For both St. Thomas[41] and Wojtyla,[42] the education of desire implies also the education to modesty/shame (Italian: *pudore*, Latin *verecundia*), which is not a reaction rooted in a self-deprecating complex. Modesty/shame is an affective reaction that shows that only the gaze of true love can correspond to the dignity of our sexuated body. It is the sign of an acquired self-respect that has only been obtained because the boy or little girl has been loved *for his/her own sake* within the family. Cultivating

---

41. *ST* II-II, q. 144.
42. See the explanation of shame in Wojtyla's *Love and Responsibility*.

modesty in the family shows that love is the only proper gesture toward one's body, and anything short of that, anything that reduces the dignity of the body, is actually an attack on the person itself. The commodification of the human body through the pornographic pandemic can only be fought with the intentional cultivation of one's dignity through the beauty of love, proper to a person created for true love in marriage.

How important today is for fathers to teach—and witness! —to their little girls that they are made for a true great love[43] and also how to recognize counterfeit loves: to help them see that being asked by a boyfriend to send nude selfies is actually a sign of cowardice, since it avoids the courage and maturity to build true friendships that lead to a great marriage and friendship. How important for parents to teach the art of loving, instead of giving in to the temptation of taking the easy way out and providing the children with contraception, expecting them to fail[44] (as you know, so many girls today do not even know that they have a fertility cycle). How important it is today to have strong fathers who witness to their sons that to be a good man is not just to be *a male*! True manhood is attained when boys learn to care for another and to take on responsibilities for the destiny of the other.[45] Great men are capable of great loves because they have learned to employ their strength for something constructive, something that endures in time.

I am talking especially of the fatherly model, because it is under attack today by the "toxic masculinity" trend pushed by the radical feminism: as if a woman can manifest her value and uniqueness only by ridiculing men. What a deception, what a distortion of the heart of the woman! A woman's heart longs for a complementarity that does not efface otherness, but nourishes the individuality of the other out of love. How much good the family can do to prepare the kids for the adventure of love and thus to attain its mission in the Church!

---

43. Meg Meeker, *Strong Fathers, Strong Daughters: 10 Secrets Every Father Should Know* (Washington, DC: Regnery, 2015).

44. Evert and Stefanick, *Raising Pure Teens*, 101.

45. Meg Meeker, *Boys Should Be Boys: 7 Secrets to Raising Healthy Sons* (Washington, DC: Regnery, 2008); F. Nembrini, *Di padre in figlio: Conversazioni sul rischio di educare* (Milan: Ares, 2011).

The Fullness of the Beauty of Chaste Love Is Rooted in Eternity

The family can become what it is called to be—a school of a communion of love—only when it knows, is nourished, and remains rooted in a *filial* love with its own Origin, the communion of persons in God himself.

The spouses learn to love with an *integral* and therefore "fair" love because they have first *received* such a love from the Divine Source. They learn not to despair and not to give in to the pleasures of the devil's palace because they know it is an empty promise, an illusion. They have experienced through the grace of their marriage that only the gaze of true love, rooted in Divine love, can awaken them from the deadly prison of the counterfeit loves that surround them. The hearts of spouses are gradually configured, attuned, and harmonized with the heart of God, from which the gift of conjugal charity arises.

The beauty of this renewed conjugal love doesn't forget that Christ's beauty, in which it is rooted, is paradoxical. The spouses come to know that it is the Cross of Christ, the place of manifestation of the beauty of divine Love Incarnate: to put it with St. Augustine, "He had neither beauty nor decorum, to give you beauty and decorum. What beauty? What decorum? The love of charity; that you may run loving and may love running" (*In Joh. Epist. ad Parth.* IX, 9, 31). Joseph Ratzinger states that a pure concept of harmony, such as the Platonic one, is not sufficient and cannot exhaust the concept of beauty, but demands to be surpassed as it is confronted with the drama of life and the atrocities of history: "but precisely in this Face so disfigured appears the authentic, extreme beauty: the beauty of love that spends itself, and that, precisely in this, reveals itself stronger than lies and violence."[46]

Spouses and parents are thus called to contemplate Christ's face, shining that Love spent to the end. Thus they receive the strength to purify their love in a constant manner, in order to learn from him how to truly love and how to root their love in the sure foundation of eternal love. This strength of the redeemed spousal love, which passes through the daily Cross, becomes a strength from which the children will benefit immense-

---

46. Joseph Ratzinger, *La bellezza: La Chiesa* (Castel Bolognese: Itaca, 2006), 23

ly too, because it teaches them to embrace the greatness and radicality of Love in all its integral Beauty. Spouses thus come know the greatness of their vocation, which becomes, because it is anchored in God through the sacrament of marriage, the means for the spouses of communicating to their children God's presence in their lives.

When the gift of friendship with God—charity—becomes a vital source for their conjugal love chastity, spouses become true missionaries, true evangelizers of the fair love.

CHAPTER 16

Natural Family Planning versus Contraception

THERESA NOTARE

Introduction

In the life of the Church, there has always been tension between God's invitation to embrace his truth as expressed in Church teaching and how the faithful receive that invitation. It therefore should not be surprising that some, even many, in the Church would on occasion clamor for a change in Church teaching, especially with regard to the moral prohibition of contraception. They say that modern times have placed unique stresses on married couples, and that the burden of human fertility should be lifted from the shoulders of husband and wife. Afterall, contraception would allow a couple to turn fertility on and off as they desire—where is the harm in that?

On the surface, these thoughts seem practical, even acceptable pastoral advice if spoken by a Catholic leader. This is, however, an illusion and a dangerous one at that. My remarks will explain why through comparing contraception and the methods of Natural Family Planning. I will set this comparison within the context of a true story that reveals what a misguided pastoral decision can foster.

On a hot August afternoon in 1930, a vote to approve a pastoral decision among a worldwide group of Anglican bishops at Lambeth Palace, the home of the Archbishop of Canterbury, initiated a revolution in

Christian sexual morals.[1] The cautiously worded Resolution 15 permitted the use of contraception in marriage for serious reasons.[2] The decision intended to address the "hard cases"—to support those married couples who needed to limit births for serious reasons, such as the physical or mental health of the wife, economic hardships, and so forth. It was not made lightly.

In their debate, the bishops grappled with various concerns, including whether medicine can help or hinder the natural process of human fertility and when that intervention was moral. They discussed the truth about marriage and the Christian moral tradition regarding the evil of contraceptive practices. They were aware that if they allowed contraceptive use in marriage, they would break the Christian moral tradition. And they admitted that they did not have the theological language to defend that tradition, as did the Roman Catholic Church.[3] They discussed other influential issues such as eugenics, or who should reproduce and who should not reproduce; the "woman's question"; and the implications of the acceptance of contraception in marriage and its effect upon youth and living a virtuous life. In the end, the majority voted to accept Resolution 15.

Although the intention was to help married couples, the bishops' decision had a terrible fallout. Unbeknownst to them, their qualified acceptance of contraception lent a respectable hand and gave a blessing to the key destructive messages of the then young, modern sexual revolution, namely that:

- It is good to decouple procreation from sex

and

- Contraception is acceptable to facilitate the decoupling.

---

1. Theresa Notare, "A Revolution in Christian Morals: Lambeth 1930–Resolution #15, History and Reception," PhD diss. (Catholic University of America, 2008). The thesis asserts that the Anglican bishops who voted to accept contraceptive use in marriage did so owing to pastoral concerns for married couples in difficult circumstances and were influenced not by the truth of the Christian moral tradition but by cultural forces that mixed human goods with falsehoods.

2. See Appendix A below.

3. Some bishops suggested that they postpone the decision and appoint a group of theologians to work on developing an Anglican moral theology. See Notare, "Revolution in Christian Morals," 399–400.

The story of Resolution 15 represents a misguided pastoral strategy whose negative consequences were unforeseen by the well-meaning Anglican bishops of 1930. Today, Catholic clergy and lay leaders find themselves caught in a similar crossroad—how best to minister to married couples who are confronted with modern stresses and human fertility. I submit that the response is twofold:

- First, teach the truth about God's gifts of human sexuality, the virtue of chastity, the nature of marriage, the unitive and procreative nature of conjugal relations, and the sacred responsibility that husband and wife have to cooperate with the Lord God in conceiving and caring for children.
- Second, provide pastoral support in the way of Natural Family Planning education so that couples can live these truths.

The question of spacing or limiting births in marriage is a reasonable one, as the Church teaches.[4] It is, however, critical to remind married couples that they are not "masters of the powers of life and love," to quote Paul VI in *Humanae Vitae*, "but rather, the ministers" of these gifts."[5] Most Catholic couples do not understand this noble mandate. They are not aware either of the dark side of contraception, or of the benefits of Natural Family Planning (NFP). They do not know, as the US bishops wrote, that "the Church's support for NFP" is based on NFP's ability to respect "the God-given power to love a human life into being even when we are not actively seeking to exercise that power."[6] Contraception does not respect these powers and in fact harms God's design.

Let's now compare the differences between contraception and NFP. We will review their effects on the health of the body and the mind and human behavior. By way of conclusion, I will address the spiritual well-being of the married couple.

---

4. See *Humanae Vitae* (HV) 10, website of the Holy See, accessed July 12, 2023, vatican.va/content/paul-vi/en/encyclicals/documents/hf_p-vi_enc_25071968_humanae-vitae.html.
5. HV 10.
6. United States Conference of Catholic Bishops (USCCB), *Married Love and the Gift of Life* (Washington, DC: USCCB, 2006), usccb.org/issues-and-action/marriage-and-family/natural-family-planning/catholic-teaching/upload/Married-Love-and-the-Gift-of-Life-English-version.pdf.

Contraception and Natural Family Planning: Comparison

The differences between contraception and NFP begin with their definitions.

- Contraception is the title for those pharmaceutical drugs or devices that are designed to suppress or block human fertility. Some contraceptives are designed to prevent a woman's body from ovulating (as in hormonal birth control pill). Others are chemical solutions that kill sperm or devices that block the meeting of sperm and ovum (as in the male condom or female diaphragm).[7]
- NFP is the title for the natural methods of family planning that assist couples to either postpone or achieve conception through education about "the naturally occurring signs and symptoms of the fertile and infertile phases" of the wife's menstrual cycle.[8] In this way, couples can identify their window of fertility and either plan to "to avoid pregnancy" by abstaining "from intercourse and genital contact during the fertile phase of the woman's cycle"[9] or target the most fertile time to attempt conception.

Regarding who can use contraception, each method carries its individual recommendations. For example, a person who is allergic to latex could not use a latex condom. With regard to chemical contraceptives, much will depend upon a woman's individual health to make her a candidate for specific prescriptions. NFP methods carry no restrictions—any woman can apply the individual method information to her own menstrual cycle—and she does not need to have "regular" cycles to use the informa-

---

7. Note that all hormonal contraceptives carry a secondary action of interrupting fetal development after conception. This action is called "anti-nidation" or, in popular language, "abortifacient." The evidence is not clear as to how often this occurs, but it can and does happen. In addition, some prescriptions of hormonal contraception are designed to be used in strong doses to prevent ovulation in emergency situations or cause spontaneous abortion if conception has occurred. These "emergency contraceptives" are to be taken after non-contraceptive sexual intercourse.

8. See Administrative Committee of Bishops, *Standards for Diocesan NFP Ministry* (Washington, DC: USCCB, 2022), usccb.org/resources/2022%20Standards%20approved.pdf. Hereafter *Standards for Diocesan NFP Ministry*.

9. *Standards for Diocesan NFP Ministry*.

tion. If some women experience hard-to-interpret fertility signs or are in special circumstances, such as postpartum, breastfeeding, or perimenopause, additional instruction will be needed.

In terms of access, in developed nations, contraceptives are readily available. They can be purchased in a store, with some requiring a physician's prescription. Other contraceptives may have to be prescribed to patients in a medical setting. Some nations, through their public health departments, provide free or subsidized contraception. In the United States, Title X, a federal government program, provides contraception at little or no cost to low-income women.[10] And many American insurance plans will cover physician-prescribed contraception.[11] This ease of availability might not exist in low- or middle-income nations. But, interestingly, the US federal government has had a commitment since 1965 to provide contraception to low-income nations through the US Agency for International Development (USAID).[12] In addition, nongovernmental organizations such as Planned Parenthood, International Planned Parenthood Federation, and the Gates Foundation subsidize contraception for low-income people both in the United States as well as overseas.

Access to NFP education, on the other hand, is not as easily obtained as contraception. And there continues to exist some confusion regarding what NFP is. For example, some think it is still the calendar rhythm method, withdrawal, or even a fertility app that claims women can identify their fertile time (most of these apps are not based on NFP science and are not accurate[13]). In any case, NFP methods are available via the Internet through an NFP provider. On-site instruction is also available and

---

10. See Helen Alvaré, "No Compelling Interest: The 'Birth Control' Mandate and Religious Freedom," *Villanova Law Review* 58 (2012): 379–436.

11. Despite the US federal government's attempt in recent years to require coverage of contraception through the Affordable Care Act, employers can refuse to include contraception in their health insurance plans if they have religious or moral objections.

12. USAID reports that in 1965, "fewer than 10 percent of women in the developing world (excluding China) were using a modern contraceptive method, and the average family size was over six. Today, in the 31 countries where USAID focuses its support, modern contraceptive prevalence has increased to 32 percent, and the average family size has dropped to 4.3." See "Fact Sheet: Family Planning Program Overview," USAID, June 1, 2023, https://www.usaid.gov/global-health/health-areas/family-planning/resources/family-planning-overview.

13. For a review of current fertility apps, see "Facts about Fertility," accessed July 12, 2023, factsaboutfertility.org/category/fertility-apps.

dependent upon local teachers. In the United States, for example, there are teachers in every diocese—but the number of teachers varies and can be low compared to the local Catholic population. Finally, NFP methods meet the US federal requirements for insurance coverage (ICD-10 codes), allowing medical providers to receive reimbursement.[14]

With regard to effectiveness rates for pregnancy avoidance, most contraceptives are highly effective. Each contraceptive will have its rates for both perfect use—when the method is used correctly and consistently, and typical use—when it is not used correctly and consistently. These effectiveness rates can range from 80% to 99%.[15] Some contraceptives have extremely high effectiveness rates because they do not rely on the user's behavior (e.g., shots, intrauterine devices, etc.).

NFP methods are completely reliant on user behavior. Users will have high rates of effectiveness (up to 99%) if certain conditions are met: (1) that the couple has learned the method guidelines for pregnancy avoidance correctly from a reliable source (e.g., a certified teacher or online provider program); and (2) understands the guidelines and applies them according to their family planning intention.[16] When these conditions are not met, NFP methods will have lower effectiveness rates that are similar to failure rates of barrier methods. Unlike contraception, NFP methods can be highly effective in achieving pregnancy within 1–6 months.[17] Without knowing the time of the fertile window, it takes about twelve months for 85% of couples to become pregnant.

---

14. ICD is medical shorthand for International Classification of Diseases. Insurance companies use the codes to verify consistency between a condition and treatment rendered.

15. For contraceptive effectiveness rates, see Robert Hatcher et al., *Contraceptive Technology*, 21st ed. (Atlanta: Managing Contraception, 2018).

16. See, e.g., a review of NFP effectiveness studies by Michael D. Manhart, Marguerite Duane, April Lind, Irit Sinai, and Jean Golden-Tevald, "Fertility Awareness-Based Methods of Family Planning: A Review of Effectiveness for Avoiding Pregnancy Using SORTS," *Osteopathic Family Physician* 5 (2013): 2–8.

17. See, e.g., T. W. Hilgers, K. D. Daly, A. M. Prebil, and S. K. Hilgers, "Cumulative Pregnancy Rates in Patients with Apparently Normal Fertility and Fertility-Focused Intercourse," *Journal of Reproductive Medicine* 37 (1992): 864–66; "Billings Ovulation Method," FACTS: Fertility Appreciation Collaborative to Teach the Science, accessed August 26, 2023, https://www.factsaboutfertility.org/wp-content/uploads/2014/09/BillingsPEH.pdf. This study of the Billings method found that 78% of couples were able achieve pregnancy after an average of just 4.7 months. The Hilgers et al. study found that 76% of the couples studied were able to conceive in the first month that they used the Creighton model. Ninety percent had conceived after the third month, and 100% after seven months.

"The Body and Its Health"

From the above, it may appear that contraception has an edge over NFP; after all, they are not only effective but also accessible and mostly easy to use. NFP methods, in contrast, require education, commitment, consistency, couple communication, and cooperation. Since periodic sexual abstinence is the NFP means to avoid pregnancy, the couple has to accept this as part of the practice. It can be a challenge. That said, NFP actually has the upper hand when it comes to the health of the body.

NFP methods have no harmful side effects. Anyone can use these methods—there are no restrictions. The information that is typically part of an NFP method's education helps the couple to achieve fertility literacy. In fact, the information gained in NFP use can assist a woman and her physician to pinpoint problems in her reproductive health should they arise.[18]

Contraception, however, does not teach its users about the human body. Instructions are typically given about how to use the device or medication. In the case of long-acting and reversible contraception (LARC), little information is provided to the patient except when to return to a physician because of a negative side effect, receive another injection, or have the LARC, such as an IUD, removed.

Each contraceptive method carries its own contraindications—those reasons why certain people cannot use them safely. Each also carries negative side effects, with hormonal contraceptives for women being among the most dangerous. This last statement requires further discussion.

Research about chemical contraceptives reveals abundant evidence demonstrating many harmful side effects, including reduction of a woman's libido; rise in depression;[19] physiological changes in a woman's brain;[20] blood clots; heart attack; stroke; cancer (e.g., breast, cervical);

---

18. See, e.g., information about NFP methods as an aid to women's health at factsaboutfertility.org. In the United States, Dr. Thomas Hilgers (Omaha, Nebraska) has conducted pioneering work to develop ethical women's health care at the St. Pope Paul VI Institute; see popepaulvi.com.

19. See Charlotte Wessel Skovlund, Lina Steinrud Mørch, Lars Vedel Kessing, and Øjvind Lidegaard, "Association of Hormonal Contraception with Depression," *JAMA Psychiatry* 73 (2016): 1154–1162.

20. See C. H. Kinsley and E. A. Meyer, "Women's Brains on Steroids: Birth Control Pills Appear to Remodel Brain Structure," *Scientific American*, September 28, 1010, scientificamerican.com/article/womens-brains-on-steroids.

ulcerative colitis; liver tumors; lupus; multiple sclerosis; bladder pain syndrome; and osteoporotic bone fractures. So harmful are chemical contraceptivs that a group of health care professionals and scientists in the United States submitted a Citizen's Petition documenting the evidence to the US Food and Drug Administration (FDA).[21] They asked for a warning label to be included on the boxes of all such contraceptive drugs. In addition, they asked that the injectable product Depo Provera[22] be removed from the American market because of conclusive evidence that it facilitates the transmission of HIV from men to women.

When considering the above health risks, NFP methods stand out as the healthy option for men and women, while most contraceptives not only include some restrictions for use but also have adverse side effects.[23]

"The Mind and Human Behavior"

Turning from the body to the mind and human behavior, it should not be surprising that the choice of a family planning method has both personal and societal consequences. Once more, there are distinct differences between contraception and NFP use.

Beginning with the modern notion of consciously regulating births, research demonstrates that about 53% of couples worldwide use contraception, with use at 48% in developing nations and 71% in developed countries.[24] This suggests that a significant majority of people agree that the regulation of births is needed—and that they are using contraception to achieve that end. Unfortunately, few people worldwide would identify the methods of NFP as helpful because NFP methods are not well

---

21. Contraceptive Study Group, *Petition on Hormonal Contraceptives* (2019), usccb.org/resources/Citizens%20petition%20-%20Hormonal%20Contraceptives%202019May9%20submitted_0.pdf.

22. Depot medroxyprogesterone acetate, or DMPA.

23. Helpful charts showing a summary of the differences between contraception and NFP can be found in Richard Fehring, "Contraception and Natural Family Planning: The Impact on the Sexual Lives of Couples," *Anthropotes* 34 (2018): 125.

24. See United Nations, *Contraceptive Use by Method 2019* (New York: United Nations, 2019), un.org/development/desa/pd/sites/www.un.org.development.desa.pd/files/files/documents/2020/Jan/un_2019_contraceptiveusebymethod_databooklet.pdf. About 80% of contraceptive use in developing countries is accounted for by sterilization, IUDs, and oral contraceptives.

known, well funded, or commonly promoted by health care professionals.[25] NFP leaders continuously address these difficulties.

A person's motivation to regulate fertility is also a strong factor in the use of a family planning method. A person's motivation can be good or bad. When good—a couple may have to carefully space births for the sake of caring for others, such as children already born or elderly relatives. Other circumstances such as poor health of the mother or father, harsh economic factors, and so forth play their role in a couple's decision. The Catholic Church agrees with these reasonable motivations.[26] In fact, it is part of the Church's theology of responsible parenthood.[27] To this practical concern, Catholic teaching adds that the spacing of births must be done by respecting God's laws—so couples ought not take just any means to avoid pregnancy.[28] This is where the methods of NFP emerge as a real aid to married couples. They respect the powers of love and life in marriage. Contraceptives are different. Their actions are precisely designed to suppress or block human fertility as well as cause one or both partners to withhold him/herself from the other—they fail to support God's design.

With the practice of NFP, husband and wife will have to consider why they want to postpone or achieve a pregnancy. This can have a positive effect upon the individual and the couple. For the individual, the NFP discipline can prompt self-reflection about one's motivation and love for the other—it can foster self-mastery. As a couple, spouses have to think about each other and work together. They will have to discuss their combined fertility, which can lead to other meaningful conversations—this can strengthen couple's communication. And NFP research shows that this bears good fruit. NFP users have higher levels of self-esteem, levels of intimacy, and spiritual well-being (both religious and existential) compared to contraceptive users.[29] Women currently using an NFP method

---

25. So unknown is NFP science and methodology among health care professionals that several organizations and institutes in the United States are committed to their outreach education, notably the St. Pope Paul VI Institute for the Study of Human Reproduction (popepaulvi.com), the Institute of Natural Family Planning, Marquette University College of Nursing (marquette.edu/nursing/natural-family-planning.php), and Fertility Appreciation Collaborative to Teach the Science (FACTS; factsaboutfertility.org).

26. See HV 10.

27. See HV 10, 13.

28. See HV 10, 13.

29. See R. Fehring, D. Lawrence, and C. Sauvage, "Self-Esteem, Spiritual Well-Being, and

"had fewer health concerns, were less irritable, less depressed, had high levels of sexual pleasure, and a higher sex drive than with ... methods of contraception." [30] In fact, in studies that reveal the challenge of the NFP lifestyle, couples often remark that it is "worth the effort."[31] And NFP couples often admit their journey from a more self-centered motivation to a deeper "we-centered" perspective that appreciates God's gift of love and life in the conjugal embrace.[32]

Turning to contraception, its nature as a block to human fertility can lull a person into a false mentality where fertility is viewed as a burden—something alien to their persons. It can also prompt a person to place walls around their hearts as they "protect" themselves from each other. The cumulative fallout is that a person can slide into the mentality that procreation is not part of sex, and that self-gift and mutuality are not essential ingredients. This shift or slide—because most people are not consciously aware of it—from "we" to "me" can foster selfishness and isolation. It is a mentality that opposes the strengthening of the couple relationship. An example is demonstrated in one study of contraceptive use. It found that a person's fertility is commonly viewed as an obstacle to the "good life."[33] In this case the good life means the pursuit of sexual pleasure for its own sake and/or being free from responsibilities. With this mindset, sexual intercourse can become the goal to fill a personal need rather than a sacred exchange of persons where mutual support and love are given and received and the gift of life can bloom.

The contraceptive mentality has social effects. It has fueled the hook-up culture where couples meet only for sex, with no interest in a

---

Intimacy: A Comparison among Couples Using NFP and Oral Contraceptives," *International Review of Natural Family Planning* 13 (1989): 227–36; see also R. Fehring and D. Lawrence, "Spiritual Well-Being, Self-Esteem, and Intimacy among Couples Using Natural Family Planning," *Linacre Quarterly* 61 (1994): 18–29.

30. R. J. Fehring and M. D. Manhart, "Natural Family Planning and Marital Chastity: The Effects of Periodic Abstinence on Marital Relationships," *Linacre Quarterly* 88 (2021): 45.

31. Natural Womanhood, *Love, Marriage, Sex and the Gift of Natural Family Planning: A Study of the Experience and Insights of Catholic Couples Who Strive to Be Faithful to the Church Teachings* (Texas: Natural Womanhood, 2022), https://naturalwomanhood.org/nfpreport2022/.

32. Natural Womanhood, *Love, Marriage, Sex and the Gift of Natural Family Planning*.

33. See J. E. Anderson, D. J. Jamieson, L. Warner, D. M. Kissin, A. J. Nangia, and M. Macaluso, "Contraceptive Sterilization among Married Adults: National Data on Who Chooses Vasectomy and Tubal Sterilization," *Contraception* 85 (2021): 552–557.

relationship or having and caring for children. As sociologist Mark Regnerus suggests in his landmark study on the sexual behavior of contemporary Americans,[34] this mentality has created "cheap sex." Cheap sex eliminates the meaning of the nature of sex with its power to bind a man and a woman as well as bring new life into the world. Cheap sex places a woman at a disadvantage, since she is the one who will bear new life if the contraceptive fails and the man wants nothing to do with the child. Cheap sex fosters emotional immaturity and places an inordinate emphasis on "the genital life." This, notes Regnerus, is dangerous for both the individual and society. Cheap sex fosters more isolation rather than community. It will not make people happier and society stable. Regnerus says that the "the exchange relationship," best seen in the marriage between one man with one woman, is where true happiness can be found. When men and women only focus on genital sex for the sake of pleasure, they contribute to a cultural mentality that

is misanthropic, anti-woman, and not sustainable. The exchange relationship, on the other hand, is old. It is deeply human. It fosters love when navigated judiciously. And it remains the historic heartbeat, and the very grammar, of human community and social reproduction.[35]

The above indicates that besides motivation to use a family planning method, the actual method will have a bearing on the couple's relationship. Looking at this more carefully, NFP appears to have surprising benefits. As one of the scientists who conducted foundational research on a woman's time of ovulation said in 1934, there is a value to periodic sexual abstinence as a means to manage human fertility. Dr. Kyusaku Ogino, a non-Catholic, noted that this would "help a person be more open to the needs of one's spouse."[36] And this has been validated over the years by NFP couples.

Studies confirm that although an NFP method may take some effort to learn and can be challenging at times—especially with regard to the use of periodic sexual abstinence as the NFP means to avoid pregnancy—

---

34. See Mark Regnerus, *Cheap Sex: The Transformation of Men, Marriage, and Monogamy* (New York: Oxford University Press, 2017).

35. Regnerus, *Cheap Sex*, 215.

36. Paraphrased by Fehring and Manhart, "Natural Family Planning and Marital Chastity," 43.

most NFP couples are satisfied with their method and agree that it has helped their relationships.[37] NFP couples admit to having "a greater understanding of their combined fertility, a sense of increased communication, an increase in ways of expressing intimacy, and a sense of shared responsibility for family planning."[38] Since periodic sexual abstinence is the NFP means to avoid conception, couples also say that it gives them an "appreciation of sexuality ... and ... enhances their spiritual wellbeing as well as their sexual desire."[39] Overall, NFP couples admit how the NFP lifestyle helps them to improve their sex lives and relationships.[40] In fact, NFP users are known to have lower divorce rates compared to the wider population (most of whom, it can safely be said, use contraception). To quote an NFP study,

Studies using population-based samples indicate in those who ever-used NFP, [that] divorce was at significantly lower rates compared to those who never-used NFP. These studies also demonstrated that regular church attendance and importance of religion are at least as strongly associated with decreased divorce rates. Conversely, use of contraceptives, sterilization, and abortion are all associated with an increased risk of divorce.[41]

The strength of living married love in an integrated way as in the practice of an NFP method, where the whole person is accepted—including

---

37. Fehring and Manhart, "Natural Family Planning and Marital Chastity," at 44. Fehring and Manhart write that across "all studies, large majorities (60 percent to 85 percent of respondents) of both men and women users consistently perceive that practice of periodic abstinence and NFP has helped their marriage despite the common acknowledgment that it can be difficult at times" (51).

38. Fehring, "Contraception and Natural Family Planning," 110.

39. Fehring and Manhart, "Natural Family Planning and Marital Chastity," 44. See also M. Unseld, E. Rötzer, R. Weigl, E. K. Masel, and M. D. Manhart, "Use of Natural Family Planning (NFP) and Its Effect on Couple Relationships and Sexual Satisfaction: A Multi-Country Survey of NFP Users from US and Europe," *Frontiers in Public Health* 13 (2017): 42; L. Vande Vusse, L. Hanson, and R. J. Fehring, "Couples' Views of the Effects of Natural Family Planning on Marital Dynamics," *Journal of Nursing Scholarship* 35 (2003): 171–176.

40. Fehring and Manhart, "Natural Family Planning and Marital Chastity," 44.

41. Fehring and Manhart, "Natural Family Planning and Marital Chastity," 51. Note that a common quoted divorce rate of 3% or 4% among NFP users has been repeated in the past. This percentage is taken from two studies, that of M. A. Wilson, "The Practice of Natural Family Planning versus the Use of Artificial Birth Control: Family, Moral and Sexual Issues," *Catholic Social Science Review* 7 (2005): 185–211; and W. Rhomberg and H. Weissenbach, "Natural Family Planning as a Family Binding Tool: A Survey Report," *Catholic Social Science Review* 18 (2013): 63–70. Fehring notes that both studies were poorly constructed because they were not population based and lacked external validity. See Fehring, "Contraception and Natural Family Planning," 113–14.

his or her fertility—affirms the whole person and shines a bright light on the importance of mutuality as strengthening the marital bond. As one NFP husband noted, "Being in tune with your wife's cycle builds empathy and understanding. It's a unitive process not just during the act but in-between."[42]

As already discussed, contraception does little to enhance a couple's relationship—except to remove the fear of unwanted pregnancy or protect against some sexually transmitted infections. Its users can falsely think that fertility can easily be turned on and off. This can lead couples to delay pregnancy until it becomes too late for the woman to conceive. It can also lead a person to trust more in the methods rather than their bodies and partners. And when the contraceptive unexpectedly fails, it can trigger shock in its users who are then more apt to tragically turn to abortion as backup for the failure. The bottom line with contraceptive use is that it does little to foster mutuality between a man and a woman, and it certainly opposes new life. Contraceptive sex facilitates cheap sex, where the meaning and nature of sex is greatly diminished and even twisted with its exaggerated preoccupation with genital value and devaluing of procreation or the family that can be created from the conjugal embrace.

One more word about the negative impact of contraception from the public or societal perspective. Recall that contraception has played the supporting role in the two central messages of the modern sexual revolution that the 1930 Anglican bishops unknowingly supported: the decoupling of procreation from sex and sex from marriage. There is a relationship, therefore, between contraceptive use and a host of negative social outcomes. We do not have time to consider all of these now, but it is enough to end with two poignant examples. With more women agreeing to have nonmarital sex, more children are born without the benefit of married parents when the contraceptive fails. More single women and their children live in poverty because of this cycle.[43] In addition, with the introduction of contraception (with sterilization being the number one

---

42. Anonymous NFP husband quoted in Natural Womanhood, *Love, Marriage, Sex and the Gift of Natural Family Planning*, 18–19.

43. See George A. Akerlof, Janet L. Yellen, and Michael L. Katz, "An Analysis of Out-of-Wedlock Childbearing in the United States," *Quarterly Journal of Economics* 111 (1996): 277–317.

method of contraception in developed nations),[44] a nation's population rate will drop, even dangerously, to below replacement level. Currently, most developed nations are below population replacement or just hovering at it. Contraception is the instrument that has effectively facilitated these trends.

Conclusion: The "Spiritual Well-Being" of Men and Women

In conclusion, the evidence is clear: contraception is associated with a host of unforeseen adverse effects for men, women, and the wider society, while the methods of NFP are associated with many wholesome benefits. In the United States, NFP scientist Richard Fehring[45] has labored to understand the benefits of NFP—especially with regard to the couple's spiritual well-being. He has found that NFP couples have higher levels of spiritual and existential well-being than contracepting couples.[46] That said, living a life of acceptance of one's fertility, self-gift, wonder over the nuptial meaning of the body, and striving to become "one flesh" as God intended is good for husband and wife. And as a dear friend once wrote,

good theology and good science both lead to truth.... Catholic teaching about contraception does not depend on scientific discoveries, medical findings, or sociology statistics. It rests on an understanding of the meaning and purpose of marriage and human sexuality, through which God continues to speak His "yes" to human life.[47]

Church teaching on the ethical regulation of births in marriage is true and good for married couples. When spouses embrace these truths, they will see a strengthening of their relationship and deepening of their spiritual wellbeing. One NFP husband captured this growth well when he said, "The bond between the husband and the wife ... is something that

---

44. See United Nations, *Contraceptive Use by Method 2019.*

45. Richard J. Fehring, PhD, RN, is the founder of the Marquette Method, a Sympto-Hormonal method of NFP. He is also the founding director of the Natural Family Planning Institute at Marquette University, College of Nursing.

46. See, e.g., Fehring et al., "Self-Esteem, Spiritual Well-Being, and Intimacy: A Comparison among Couples Using NFP and Oral Contraceptives"; see also Fehring and Lawrence, "Spiritual Well-Being, Self-Esteem, and Intimacy among Couples Using Natural Family Planning."

47. Susan Wills, "Truth Pressed to Earth Will Rise Again," *Women for Faith and Family* 15 (Fall 2000): http://archive.wf-f.org/fall2k-wills.html.

deserves to be cherished ... protected and sacrificed for. NFP really facilitates that by facilitating communication between the spouses [and] ... honoring each other's physical presence."[48]

Striving to help the faithful reject contraception and all "cheap sex" and embrace the truth of Church teaching is critical. Church leaders can do this by teaching the faithful about human sexuality as God designed it with its gifts of conjugal love and life. Where this happens, good fruit can be seen in the example of those Catholic dioceses where NFP ministry is well established. When NFP educators lead with Church teaching and explain the "why" behind the effort to learn an NFP method, married couples will listen and typically express frustration that they had not heard these truths at an earlier age.[49]

Some dioceses in the United States are addressing this gap. In the Diocese of Phoenix, for example, engaged couples are required to take a complete course in a method of NFP as part of their marriage preparation. After learning Church teaching and the required NFP method, they have found that more "couples express their desire to accept and respect God's gifts." In their post-program surveys, they have found that couples "want to grow in their faith.... [and] long to know and love God more deeply—especially as a couple."[50]

There is so much more to say, but it is sufficient to close with the words of a twenty-first-century Anglican pastor who posted a review of Regnerus's book *Cheap Sex* on a website. Although I do not know if this pastor rejects contraception, he certainly understands the nature of married love, which should be supported by family planning methods that respect its nature. He said,

Conjugal love is ... based not on mutual ... [agreement], but on total union in which husband and wife give their bodies (and minds and spirits) to each other completely for their mutual joy and help and the procreation of children. Married

---

48. NFP husband, quoted in Natural Womanhood, *Love, Marriage, Sex and the Gift of Natural Family Planning*, 19–20.

49. In the Diocese of Phoenix, they "annually review over 1000+ class-surveys from the engaged couples they teach" and identify NFP education as "an important catalyst for a change of heart and behavior." Quoted in Theresa Notare, Alice Heinzen, and Cindy Leonard, "Diocesan NFP Ministry: Failures and Successes—Lessons Learned," *Anthropotes* 34 (2018): 375–88, at 384.

50. Notare et al., "Diocesan NFP Ministry," 384.

love is not about what I get, but what I give. Sex is not cheap. "With my body I thee worship," the husband vows to his wife, in Bishop Cranmer's time-honored rite.

In preaching, catechesis, and the care of souls, pastors have the joyful privilege to teach what it means to be man and woman in Christ—to live chastely and faithfully within the calling to be male or female. Abstinence apart from marriage and faithfulness within it is not the impossible dream nor is it some weird Christian hang-up. It is a blessed reality for all who are baptized into Christ's death and resurrection. Rather than the "Genital Life," [as what our culture currently promotes] the baptismal life is daily dying to sin and rising to righteousness in order to love and serve the neighbor, offering their bodies as living sacrifices to God, holy and acceptable through faith in Christ Jesus.[51]

With so beautiful a gift as conjugal love and the sacred transmission of new life, only the ethical methods of Natural Family Planning can do honor to this design. Contraceptive sex falls woefully short. To support contraceptive use as a compassionate pastoral strategy to help married couples is simply wrong.

Appendix A. Lambeth Conference, Resolution No. 15

Where there is a clearly felt moral obligation to limit or avoid parenthood, the method must be decided on Christian principles. The primary and obvious method is complete abstinence from intercourse (as far as may be necessary) in a life of discipline and self-control lived in the power of the Holy Spirit. Nevertheless, in those cases where there is such a clearly felt moral obligation to limit or avoid parenthood, and where there is a morally sound reason for avoiding abstinence, the conference agrees that other methods may be used, provided that this is done in the light of the same Christian principles. The conference records its strong condemnation of the use of any methods of conception from motives of selfishness, luxury, or mere convenience.[52]

---

51. Harold Senkbeil, review of *Cheap Sex* by Mark Regnerus, Amazon.com, accessed July 14, 2023, amazon.com/Cheap-Sex-Transformation-Marriage-Monogamy/dp/0190673613/ ref=sr_1_1?crid =Q3M7TNFBO5XT&keywords= Cheap+Sex+Mark+regnerus&qid=1669085521&sprefix= cheap+sex+mark+regnerus%2Caps%2C599&sr=8-1/.

52. *The Lambeth Conference 1930, Encyclical Letter from the Bishops with Resolutions and Reports*

Upon the final verdict the Bishop of Bloemfontein, Dr. Walter Carey "wept bitterly." So overwhelmed and displeased was Carey that "he withdrew in protest and was impervious to Lang's persuasions, not only refusing to attend the final Service in Westminster Abbey, but even sending a petition on the subject to the King."[53]

(London: Society for Promoting Christian Knowledge, 1930), Resolution no. 15, p. 43. The vote was taken on August 7, 1930, with 193 supporting the resolution, 67 opposing it, and 46 abstaining.

53. J. G. Lockhart, *Cosmo Gordon Lang* (London: Hodder and Stoughton Limited, 1949), 350. The Right Rev. Paul Matthews, Bishop of New Jersey, described Bishop Carey as being "overwhelmed" in his account of the passing of Resolution no. 15. Bishop Matthews also indicates in this article that he boycotted the final service due to Resolution no. 15. See *The Church Times* (October 24, 1930): 511.

CHAPTER 17

Magisterial Teaching on Gender Ideology, the Person and Identity Project, and Catholic Schools

THERESA FARNAN

The pontificate of Pope Francis has emphasized building a culture of encounter and accompaniment for the marginalized, including those who identify as transgender. On several occasions, Pope Francis met with transgender-identified individuals and afterward reminded all of us that we must accompany and never abandon the marginalized.[1] But what is the best way to accompany an individual who expressly rejects his or her God-given sexual identity as male or female? How do we show empathy, compassion, and love to vulnerable individuals while remaining faithful to the Church's teaching on the person and human sexuality? This essay examines the claims of gender ideology, the reality of "gender transition," the conflict between Christian anthropology and gender ideology, and the Catholic Church's specific teachings on the person and gender

---

1. Notably, in 2014, Pope Francis met with "Diego," a woman who identifies as a man, after reading her letter expressing her fear that there was no place for her in the Church. Thomas C. Fox, "Report: Pope Francis Meets with, Hugs Transgender Man [sic]," *National Catholic Reporter*, January 30, 2015. Pope Francis has since met with groups of individuals who identify as transgender, most recently with guests of a Church that opened its doors during the COVID-19 pandemic. See Associated Press, "Pope Francis Meets with Transgender Guests of Rome Church," *New York Post*, August 11, 2022, https://nypost.com/2022/08/11/pope-francis-meets-with-transgender-guests-of-rome-church/.

ideology. It concludes with a brief discussion of how to effectively respond to gender ideology in parishes, schools, and dioceses.

First, however, let us begin by recognizing the lived experience of a particular group of marginalized persons. They have experienced identity-related turmoil, pain, and confusion. Many continue to struggle with physical and mental health. And they know well the sting of rejection, particularly from those they counted as friends, or even family. Who are these marginalized persons? They are "detransitioners," individuals who once identified as transgender but no longer do. After a painful journey, they stopped the futile efforts that they once believed would enable them to escape the reality of being born male or female. They finally acknowledged, accepted, and made peace with their natal sex. But they continue to endure suffering. Many of these detransitioners describe their bodies—and their lives—as shattered by the lasting effects of "gender transition" medication and surgeries, interventions often prescribed to them, they point out, when they were mentally unwell. Detransitioner Keira Bell sued the Tavistock clinic in the United Kingdom in 2020, accusing the clinic of conducting a devastating and harmful experiment. In an interview, Bell remarked, "I look back with a lot of sadness. There was nothing wrong with my body, I was just lost and without proper support."[2] Another detransitioner, a young woman named Prisha Mosley, has gone public with her pain, starting a GoFundMe page seeking donations to cover the costs of "breast reconstruction." Prisha wrote, "When I was 15, I began transitioning from female to male. This was the biggest mistake of my life. I medically destroyed my body and I am in extreme grief. I have borderline personality disorder and was suffering with anorexia at the time doctors were allowing me to transition. No one looked into my past, my trauma, my suffering. They just changed my body. Now that I have worked through my childhood sexual trauma, I am devastated by my broken and ruined body. I destroyed it in an attempt to stop it from being touched—and it worked."[3]

2. "Keira Bell: There Was Nothing Wrong with My Body," interview by Raquel Rosario Sanchez reprinted in *Woman's Place UK*, November 30, 2020, https://womansplaceuk.org/2020/11/30/keira-bell-there-was-nothing-wrong-with-my-body/.

3. "Prisha's Breast Reconstruction," GoFundMe, accessed July 14, 2023, https://www.gofundme.com/f/Prishas-breast-reconstruction.

The experiences of other detransitioners are captured in a growing body of documentaries and recent research.[4] While Pope Francis has yet to meet with detransitioners, he has spoken compassionately about his interactions with persons who identify as transgender, while forcefully insisting that gender ideology has a harmful influence on young persons. In 2016, for example, Pope Francis was asked about his pastoral meeting with a transgender-identified woman who had undergone surgery to create a masculine appearance. In a response that appeared to perplex journalists, he approvingly cited the pastoral approach of an elderly priest, who would urge individuals to go to Confession so they could receive Communion. Pope Francis has pushed back on attempts by Western media to characterize his pastoral care of individuals who assert a transgender identity as approval of the phenomenon of transgender identification itself. In one instance, Pope Francis cautioned reporters, saying, "'Please don't say: 'the Pope sanctifies transgenders.' He added 'I want to be clear! It's moral problem [sic]. It's a human problem and it must be resolved always can be [sic] with the mercy of God, with the truth...'"[5]

Nevertheless, controversy continues, as pressure builds on the Catholic Church and other Christian churches to conform their teaching about the human person to the spirit of the world. Is a change in teaching possible? I argue that it is neither possible nor desirable for the Church to alter its teaching on the nature of the human person or to approve of an individual's attempts to reject his or her God-given sexual identity (male or female) and assert a transgender, or self-determined, identity. Although

---

4. Recent documentaries featuring the experiences of detransitioners include "Transgressive: The Cult of Confusion," *Tucker Carlson Originals*, Fox Nation (2022); "The Detransition Diaries: Saving Our Sisters," Jennifer Lahl, Center for Bioethics and Culture Network (2022); "Detransitioning: Reversing a Gender Transition," BBC Newsnight (2019); Don Johnson, *Dysconnected: The Real Story behind the Transgender Explosion* (San Francisco: Ignatius Press, 2022). Recent research exploring the experiences of detransitioners includes Lisa Littman, "Individuals Treated for Gender Dysphoria with Medical and/or Surgical Transition Who Subsequently Detransitioned: A Survey of 100 Detransitioners," *Archives of Sexual Behavior* 50 (November 2021): 3353–69; Elie Vandenbussche, "Detransition-Related Needs and Support: A Cross-Sectional Online Survey," *Journal of Homosexuality* 69 (July 2022): 1602–20; and Alison Clayton, "Gender-Affirming Treatment of Gender Dysphoria in Youth: A Perfect Storm Environment for the Placebo Effect—The Implications for Research and Clinical Practice," *Archives of Sex Behavior* 52 (February 2023): 483–94.

5. "Full Text: Pope Francis' In-Flight Press Conference from Azerbaijan," *Catholic News Agency*, October 2, 2016, https://www.catholicnewsagency.com/news/34671/full-text-pope-francis-in-flight-press-conference-from-azerbaijan.

it is not possible within the time and length constraints of a single essay to provide an in-depth analysis, my argument briefly explains the irreconcilable conflicts between gender ideology and Christian anthropology, unpacks the reality of "gender transition," explains why transitioning, or any rejection of one's sexed identity, even social transition, is objectively harmful, presents Catholic teaching on gender ideology, and addresses several arguments proposed by Catholic theologians who advocate for changes to relevant Catholic teachings. In closing, I briefly describe the work of the Person and Identity Project, which equips Catholics and Catholic institutions to promote the truth about the human person and to counter gender ideology.

What Does It Mean to Be Human? Christian Anthropology's Account

The Christian vision of man is, in fact, a great "yes" to the dignity of persons called to an intimate filial communion of humility and faithfulness. The human being is not a self-sufficient individual nor an anonymous element in the group. Rather he is a unique and unrepeatable person, intrinsically ordered to relationships and sociability. Thus the Church reaffirms her great "yes" to the dignity and beauty of marriage as an expression of the faithful and generous bond between man and woman, and her no to "gender" philosophies, because the reciprocity between male and female is an expression of the beauty of nature willed by the Creator.

—Pope Benedict XVI[6]

For centuries, the Catholic Church has relied on both reason and revelation to come to a deeper understanding of the human person, as well as the person's relation to God and other human beings. For our purposes, a brief summary of some essential elements of Christian anthropology will suffice.[7]

The human person comes into existence through a direct act of cre-

---

6. Pope Benedict XVI, "Address of His Holiness Pope Benedict XVI to Participants in the Plenary Meeting of the Pontifical Council 'Cor Unum,'" website of the Holy See, January 19, 2013, https://www.vatican.va/content/benedict-xvi/en/speeches/2013/january/documents/hf_ben-xvi_spe_20130119_pc-corunum.html.

7. For this account, see *Catechism of the Catholic Church* (CCC), §§355–84; see also all of *Mulieris Dignitatem*, particularly 6–8; and all of *Familiaris Consortio*, particularly 11–18.

ation by God. Each of us is a unity of body and soul, where each soul is the first principle of life and is the form of one particular body. Each person is loved into existence by the same God who sustains him or her in being. And it is this loving act of creation that gives a human his or her "authentic" identity—son or daughter of God.

Each person is created as and exists as either a male or female human being, with one's sex as male or female understood as the person's unchangeable mode of existing as a human. Being male or female is permanent and is "whole body," as every cell of that person's body is male or female in accord with that person's God-given sex.[8] This is the root of sexual difference, with genetic and physiological differences that influence the whole development of a person. In almost all cases, the sex of a baby or even an unborn child is observable and obvious.[9]

Sexual identity is meaningful. At the moment of conception, the person's soul and body are united in such an intimate union that the person's soul will be marked by his or her experiences as either a male or female person.[10] The genetic and physiological differences determined by sex influence the development of the whole person. Moreover, as St. John Paul

---

[8]. "As biologists, we know that sex is a fundamental variable in biomedical research. As such, it must really be considered from the very start. Every cell has a sex. Every part of the body is made of cells, and each of those has a sex, depending on whether the body is a man's or a woman's. Brain cells, lung cells, skin cells: Each is uniquely male or female." See "Filling the Gaps: NIH to Enact New Policies to Address Sex Differences," National Institutes of Health, May 14, 2014, https://orwh.od.nih.gov/about/director/messages/nih-policies-sex-differences.

[9]. In rare cases, persons are born with disorders of sexual development, but even then, in most instances, the sex of the person is still discernible. A disorder of sexual development does not indicate a third sex, as is the claim of lesbian, gay, bisexual, and transgender (LGBT) advocates, but indicates a situation that may call for patience and discernment on the part of patients and doctors. In any case, almost all transgender-identifying individuals have healthy bodies and easily discernible sex. See Cara Buskmiller and Paul Hruz, "A Biological Understanding of Man and Woman," in *Sexual Identity: The Harmony of Philosophy, Science, and Revelation*, edited by John DeSilva Finley (Steubenville, OH: Emmaus Road, 2022), 66, 78–85.

[10]. This simple explanation of how we understand the person as male or female, the one that rings true to the lived experience of men and women and avoids implying the possibility of a masculine or female soul in the "wrong" body, is sketched out by W. Norris Clarke's simple explanation in *The One and The Many* (Notre Dame, IN: University of Notre Dame Press, 2001), 103–4. For other accounts, see John Finley, "The Metaphysics of Gender," *The Thomist* 79 (2015): 585–614; Paul Gondreau, "Thomas Aquinas on Sexual Difference: The Metaphysical Biology and Moral Significance of Human Sexuality," *Pro Ecclesia* 30 (2021): 177–215; Timothy Fortin, "Finding Form: Defining Human Sexual Difference," *Nova et Vetera* 15 (2017): 397–431.

II revealed in his teachings on the theology of the body, the body and its bodily instincts have intrinsic meaning, reflecting metaphysical and ethical truths about the person. Finally, men and women are complementary, which is to say that sexual difference mutually enriches men and women and their relationships and mutual endeavors in a wonderfully creative way.[11] Thus sexual difference is the foundation of the family.[12]

This account of the unity of the person not only matters for intellectually understanding who we are as humans and integrating this account with morality. As St. John Paul II observed in both *Veritatis Splendor* and *Fides et Ratio*, anthropology is the foundation of ethics, and both are anchored by a foundation of realist metaphysics.[13] It is also crucial as the foundation of the teachings of the faith about morality, by asserting the unity of the acting person, body and soul. Moreover, Christian anthropology provides the foundation for understanding crucial theological teachings, such as the Incarnation of our Lord as a man ("You will conceive in your womb and bear a son"; Lk 1:26), as well as the Church's beautiful teachings on marriage and family.

The foundational truths of Christian anthropology are knowable by all, Christians and nonbelievers alike—they are borne out by how we experience the world, reflect an intuitive awareness of human nature, and are compatible with a realist metaphysics. Christian anthropology is a universally applicable teaching. It is not true because the Church teaches it—rather, the Church teaches it because it is true.

Postmodern Anthropology of Gender Ideology: Queering the Culture

For decades, the Holy See has been pushing back, not only through Church documents but also through efforts at the United Nations, against gender theory's denial of sexual difference.[14] The Church clearly under-

---

11. For a summary of complementarity in Catholic teaching, see Prudence Allen, RSM, "Man-Woman Complementarity: The Catholic Inspiration," *Logos* 9, no. 3 (2006): 87–108.

12. See *Amoris Laetitia* 56 and *Laudato Si'* 155 for Pope Francis's remarks about the importance of sexual difference for marriage, the family, and our culture.

13. See, e.g., *Veritatis Splendor* 48 and *Fides et Ratio* 80–83.

14. See, e.g., Jane F. Adolphe, "'Gender Wars' at the United Nations," *Ave Maria Law Review* 11, no. 1 (2012): 18–19; Jane F. Adolphe, "Gender Wars I and II: An Overview," *Iustitia: Rivista*

stands that debates about gender are about more than just feminist philosophy.[15] Much has already been written about the incompatibility of gender theory with the Catholic faith, including stellar treatments by Margaret H. McCarthy, Angela Franks, Abigail Favale, John Grabowski, and Sr. Prudence Allen.[16] My analysis here focuses on the specific point that, as disseminated into culture, gender ideology is inseparable from the "philosophy" of queer theory and the project that issues from it, namely "queering culture" in service to a false anthropology.[17]

Queer theory is an amalgamation of postmodern theory, feminism, Marxism, and other influences. For our purposes here, which is to understand its effect on the family, it is a belief system that rejects the binary of sexed identity, challenges the stability and knowability of sexual identity, and deconstructs the heteronormative family (as queer theorists would describe it). Yale scholar Robin Dembroff, for example, openly eschews gender theory for "genderqueer" theory, where genderqueer includes trans, nonbinary, and queer identities as members of a group who "have a felt or desired gender categorization that conflicts with the binary axis and on this basis collectively destabilize this axis."[18] Dembroff notes that genderqueer has both an internal (feelings) component and an external (performative) component.[19]

---

di Cultura Giuridica dell'Unione Giuristi Cattolici Italiani (2019): https://works.bepress.com/ProfessorJaneAdolphe/33/; Jane F. Adolphe, "The United Nations, the Holy See and the Global Reset," *Christianity-World-Politics: Journal of Catholic Social Thought* (2022): 49–85.

15. Congregation for the Doctrine of the Faith (CDF), *On the Collaboration of Men and Women in the Church and in the World* (Rome: CDF, 2004).

16. Abigail Favale, *The Genesis of Gender: A Christian Theory* (San Francisco: Ignatius, 2022); John Grabowski, *Unraveling Gender: The Battle over Sexual Difference* (Charlotte, NC: Tan Books, 2022); Prudence Allen, RSM, "Gender Reality vs. Gender Ideology," *Solidarity: The Journal of Catholic Social Thought and Secular Ethics* 4 (2014): 1–36; Margaret H. McCarthy, "Gender Ideology and the Humanum," *Communio* 43 (2016): 274–98; Angela Franks, "Andrea Long Chu Says You Are a Female, and He's Only Partly Wrong," *Public Discourse*, December 10, 2019, https://www.thepublicdiscourse.com/2019/12/58719/. These scholars all have written extensively on this question—this is just a representative sample of their work.

17. Gender ideology is termed an ideology, not simply a theory or philosophy, because it compels action. The use of the term "philosophy" to describe queer theory is set in quotes, because queer theory functions more like an anti-philosophy, denying the possibility of truth and seeking to deconstruct and subvert norms and natures.

18. Robin Dembroff, "Beyond Binary: Genderqueer as Critical Gender Kind," *Philosopher's Imprint* 20, no. 9 (April 2020): 16.

19. Dembroff, "Beyond Binary," 17.

To queer the culture is to reject God as Creator and deny the truth about the human person, consequently rejecting sexual difference, the family, and human nature itself.[20] It requires smashing social norms and boundaries, rejecting moral rules as expressions of the power and privilege of the dominant group, and deconstructing and subverting language.[21] Once a fringe set of beliefs, queer theory has metastasized through the culture, so that children are immersed in it at school, at libraries, online, while shopping, and even while watching children's programming.[22]

As filtered through social media, culture, and education, gender/queer ideology involves crude assertions that rely on stereotypes. Graphic illustrations are used to catechize and evangelize, including the Genderbread Person and the Gender Unicorn.[23] These graphic illustrations, in digital form or downloadable as coloring pages, are used by teachers and clinicians to help children visualize themselves according to tenets of gender ideology—and to internalize this false anthropology. These "gender" images present the human person as fractured, a collection of disconnected parts, each existing on a spectrum.[24] To really figure out his or her

---

20. See, e.g., this glowing article in *LGBTQ Nation*, describing for a nonscholarly audience the origin and role of queer theory and queering: "What Is Queer Theory and Why Is It Important?," *LGBTQ Nation*, October 4, 2021, https://www.lgbtqnation.com/2021/10/queer-theory-101-matters/.

21. "By challenging what is 'given,' deconstruction [of language and normative assumptions] affirms the infinite possibilities of human existence." See J. M. Balkin, "Deconstructive Practice and Legal Theory," *Yale Law Journal* 96 (1987): 743–86, at 764.

22. Children encounter queer theory through their public schools. See Sexuality Information and Education Council of the United States (SIECUS), *Guidelines for Comprehensive Sexuality Education*, 3rd ed. (Washington, DC: SIECUS, 2004); *Future of Sex Education Initiative: National Sex Education Standards, Core Content and Skills, K-12*, 2nd ed. (New York: Advocates for Youth, 2020); Pride Month, where corporations vie to display LGBT-affirming messaging and products; Drag Queen Story Hour at public libraries; and even the exponential rise of LGBT characters in children's programming. See "The Queering of Kids TV: 259 LGBTQ Characters in Children's Animation as Producers Actively Push Agenda," *CBN News*, July 6, 2021.

23. The Genderbread Person was originally published by Sam Killerman and is found at https://www.genderbread.org. It has been part of the resources offered by the US Agency for International Development (USAID) to countries receiving assistance. See, e.g., page 42 in this gender and sexual diversity training published jointly by USAID, PEPFAR (President's Emergency Plan for AIDS Relief), and the Health Policy Project: http://www.healthpolicyproject.com/pubs/398_GSDGuide.pdf. The Gender Unicorn was created by Trans Student Educational Resources after dissatisfaction with the Genderbread Person for being seemingly too closely aligned with the Western gender binary. It is found at https://transstudent.org/gender/.

24. In these videos, Dr. Angela Goepferd, a pediatrician who identifies as "nonbinary,"

authentic self, the child needs to consider: gender identity (the child's self-perception as boy, girl, neither, or something else); gender expression (how the child dresses and acts, and the child's choice of name and pronouns); anatomical parts (male or female genitals); sex "assigned" at birth (the male or female label assigned to babies by parents and physicians); romantic attraction (physical desires); and emotional attraction (feelings for another person).

Not all dimensions of the person are equally weighted. "Sex assigned at birth" is essentially meaningless, included to explain why the child/young adult previously has thought of him or herself as male or female. "Sex assigned at birth" devalues sex as an arbitrary label imposed by someone else (parents or doctors) that can be rejected by the child. Gender identity, on the other hand, is the most significant category. Gender identity is self-defined, fluid, variable, and premised on the rejection of the significance of sex. Gender identities range from transgenderism (an umbrella term that expresses an identity at odds with biological sex) to cis-genderism (a term invented to be a foil to transgenderism, which expresses that, for now, the person's gender identity is not at odds with biological sex), nonbinary (neither male nor female), queer, or gender fluid (an unstable or fluctuating gender identity), with an infinite number of individualized gender identities as well. Thus gender ideology fragments the person, as the child absorbs the lesson that there is no necessary connection between the body and one's identity. For many young persons, gender identity becomes the primary means of self-actualization and self-validation as they absorb the message, *You possess complete autonomy, and only you can know and decide who you really are. You do you!*

The consequences of absorbing gender/queer theory's anthropology cannot be overstated. As a result, children are taught a dualist view of the person, where personhood is inherent in the mind or the will. *You are the sum of your desires and your feelings about yourself. Your body exists as raw*

---

explains the "queer" understanding of the person and defends the use of medical and surgical interventions to alter the bodies of adolescents to match a desired identity. See "Pediatricians Are under Attack," Human Rights Campaign, December 13, 2022, https://www.youtube.com/watch?v=ptsWH68E4ZI&t=101s, which shows an image of the Genderbread Person. See also "The Revolutionary Truth about Kids and Gender Identity," Dr. Angela Goepferd, TedX Talk, October 26, 2020, https://www.youtube.com/watch?v=knNjvX6eoBI&t=1s.

material with no intrinsic meaning, acting as a canvas on which to project your gender identity to others. Those who question these assertions are doing violence to your very existence. Increasingly, in classroom-"inclusive" puberty education and in public discourse, the body is reduced to parts and functions (person with vagina, person with uterus, pregnant people), often expressed in demeaning misogynistic language (persons with front holes, bleeders).[25] The body is so irrelevant to who you are that propaganda aimed at children asserts literally that you can be a boy trapped in a girl body or vice versa.[26]

As a result of this intensive catechesis, the child *unlearns* the natural knowledge of the unity of body and soul, of the permanence and knowability of the sexed body, and of the complementarity of men and women, whose bodies are ordered toward having children. In its place, the child is taught that the body and soul are not necessarily united; only by accident of birth does the body align with the person's authentic identity.[27] More significant, the child is taught that God the Creator is irrelevant. *Who decides your identity? You decide. What is it based on? Feelings, desires, preferences, aversions, your feelings about social interactions*—everything except the unity of body and soul, or God's plan for your life, as discerned by the gift of your creation as embodied male or female.

True to its postmodern roots, gender/queer theory insists that everything exists on a spectrum, including the sexed body. The child learns that

---

25. Gender Spectrum, a transgender advocacy and education organization, published a "landmark" guide for schools titled "Principles for Gender-Inclusive Puberty and Health Education," accessed July 14, 2023, https://www.genderspectrum.org/articles/puberty-and-health-ed. Healthline published a safe-sex guide that used the term "front hole" instead of "vagina." They defended their decision by stating that it is "terminology accepted by the National Institutes of Health, the LGBT advocacy group Human Rights Campaign, *BMC Pregnancy and Childbirth* journal and Fenway Health in collaboration with Harvard Medical School." See Samuel Smith, "Safe Sex Guide Uses 'Front Hole' as Alternative to Vagina to Not Offend Transgenders," *Christian Post*, August 22, 2018, https://www.christianpost.com/news/safe-sex-guide-uses-front-hole-alternative-vagina-not-offend-transgenders.html.

26. A recent documentary titled *Mama Has a Mustache* asks children: "Is it possible to be a girl and have a boy body or be a boy and have a girl body?" With great certainty, the child interviewed declares, "yes it's called transgender." "Can this person be a parent?" "Yes, MaDad," the child responds. See https://www.mamahasamustache.com.

27. As Crawford, Hanby, and McCarthy observed, we are all trans now. See David Crawford, Michael Hanby, and Margaret McCarthy, "The Abolition of Man and Woman," *Wall Street Journal*, June 24, 2020.

nothing about the person is permanent or stable.[28] Claims that gender identity is innate and fixed serve only to break down parents' opposition to transitioning and vanish as soon as the child's emotions swing in a new direction, signaling the need to try on a new identity.[29] But gender clinicians insist that the persistence or reemergence of negative emotions (anxiety, despair) is never a sign that the newly embraced "transgender" identity is at odds with reality, but instead is a sign that further measures are needed to align the body with the true self. Detransitioner Chloe Cole, for example, describes her experience with gender clinicians. "My doctors knew about my worsening psychological conditions when I went under the knife for a double mastectomy. They didn't care. They just chopped off the breasts of a struggling 15 year old girl and pocketed the money."[30] Gender clinicians promote "gender-affirming" medical and surgical interventions as the path to fulfillment and happiness. They promise their young patients that feelings of discontent or dislike for the body, clinically described as "gender dysphoria," will resolve at the end of a scalpel or through a lifetime of dependency on hormones. Instead of learning to be at peace with their bodies, these vulnerable young people are encouraged to imagine for themselves a quasi- mythical "gender euphoria" at the end of the rainbow.[31]

---

28. As gender ideology/queer theory permeates the culture, the claim that human beings exist not as males or females but on an "infinite gender spectrum" has gone mainstream, appearing even in children's educational resources and entertainment. For example, public schools in Portland, Oregon, teach students that there is an "infinite gender spectrum," and because "gender identity is about how you feel about yourself inside," each student self-determines his or her "gender identity." See Reagan Reese, "Portland Schools Teaching Young Children about 'Infinite Gender Spectrum,'" *Daily Signal*, July 29, 2022, https://www.dailysignal.com/2022/07/29/portland-schools-teaching-young-children-about-infinite-gender-spectrum/. The TV show *Blue's Clues* featured a drag queen leading a pride parade that included characters with an array of various "gender identities." See David Artavia, "'Blue's Clues' Rings in Pride Month in New Sing-Along, Starring Drag Queen Nina West, Celebrating LGBTQ Families," *Yahoo News*, June 1, 2021, https://www.yahoo.com/entertainment/blues-clues-rings-pride-month-drag-queen-nina-west-lgbtq-families-174301686.html.

29. See, e.g., Healthline's description of gender fluid. Sian Ferguson, "What Does It Mean to Be Gender Fluid?," Healthline, June 11, 2020, https://www.healthline.com/health/gender-fluid.

30. Chloe Cole, Twitter, November 29, 2022, https://twitter.com/ChoooCole/status/1597653407459815425.

31. Pediatric endocrinologist Elyse Pine, MD, defined gender euphoria as "the positive feeling that occurs when a person feels recognized and seen in their authentic gender, or feels an alignment between gender identity and body." See Mel Van de Graaff, "What Is Gender Euphoria and

Finally, although trans activists insist that sexual orientation and gender identity are two different issues, including sexual attraction and emotional attraction in the Genderbread Person or Gender Unicorn paradigm muddies the waters for young people, sending the message that the young person who is emotionally unready for sexual intimacy and instead seeks close friendships with members of the same sex might just be trans. Other young persons struggling with mental health issues feel no sexual desire and assume that they are asexual/nonbinary.[32] Anecdotally, it seems that for some young persons, the category of nonbinary functions as an entry point—the point at which he or she rejects the constraints of biological sex—before proceeding to a trans identification. Thus, for some young persons, the gender identity journey is inseparable from the categories of romantic attraction and emotional attraction.

Gender Ideology's Destructive Effects

If gender identity ideology "merely" distorted the anthropology underlying our laws, language, and relationships, the result would be extremely harmful. But it does far worse damage. Gender identity ideology is distorting the self-understanding of an entire generation of young people. In addition, it acts as a corrosive solvent on family relationships, disrupting and redefining natural bonds and relationships. Activists online groom children to "go no contact" with families that are deemed insufficiently supportive.[33] The threat of death by suicide is held over the heads of

---

How Can It Affect Your Health?," Livestrong, June 12, 2022, https://www.livestrong.com/article/13772239-gender-euphoria/.

32. Is it possible that the growing number of young persons who identify as asexual or nonbinary is related to the high numbers of young persons on widely prescribed antidepressants known as SSRI medications (such as Zoloft), for which loss of libido is a side effect? See the side effects listed in "Selective Serotonin Reuptake Inhibitors (SSRIs)," Mayo Clinic, September 17, 2019, https://www.mayoclinic.org/diseases-conditions/depression/in-depth/ssris/art-20044825. An Australian nonprofit, PSSD Network (PSSD stands for post-SSRI sexual dysfunction), has been raising awareness about the link between selective serotonin reuptake inhibitors and sexual dysfunction. See their website at https://www.pssdnetwork.org.

33. Abigail Shrier writes of this phenomenon in her book *Irreversible Damage: The Transgender Craze Seducing Our Daughters* (Washington, DC: Regnery, 2020). A whole host of influencers work in online spaces to separate "trans kids" from their parents. For a sample of this, see the Instagram page of influencer Jeffrey Marsh, and scroll through the comments to see how vulnerable teens react: https://www.instagram.com/thejeffreymarsh/.

parents, dismantling their natural opposition to the dangers posed by gender identity ideology. Parents are given a Hobson's choice: "Would you rather have a dead daughter or a live son?" Gender transitions are hidden from parents by schools, counselors, and doctors unless parents are judged—by the experts, with no evidence—sufficiently supportive, as the child absorbs the unmistakable message that "unsupportive" parents are the enemy.[34] Finally, the threat of the state removing children from the custody of parents who refuse to support their child's gender transition looms over vulnerable families. One Virginia lawmaker recently proposed a bill to make failure to support a child's gender transition a felony. A mother in California lost custody for not affirming her daughter's transition and was forbidden to mention God to her daughter, who tragically committed suicide while in custody of the state. Meanwhile, a father in Canada was imprisoned for "misgendering" his daughter, and a father in Texas watched helplessly as his ex-wife took their son to California, where the father will have no power to prevent the mother from transitioning the boy to a "transgender girl."[35]

Even for those children who are not trans-identifying, the message from books, social media, and public education is that girls can become boys, moms can become dads, brothers can become sisters. All children are affected by gender ideology, as family relationships are emptied of intrinsic meaning. As scholar Mary Hasson observes, writing about the confluence of powerful interests driving the advance of gender ideology globally, "Ideologues working alone lack the power to embed their beliefs in

---

34. See Mary Hasson and Theresa Farnan, *Get Out Now: Why You Should Pull Your Child from Public School Before It's Too Late* (Washington, DC: Regnery, 2018), chaps. 1–3; and Shrier, *Irreversible Damage*, chap. 4.

35. Paul Best, "Virginia State Lawmaker to Introduce Bill Making It a Crime for Parents Not to Affirm Their LGBT Child," FoxNews, October 13, 2022, https://www.foxnews.com/politics/virginia-state-lawmaker-introduce-bill-making-it-crime-parents-not-affirm-their-lgbt-child; Hank Berrien, "'I'm Broken': CA Mom Whose Daughter Committed Suicide after 'Transitioning' Blames School," Daily Wire, March 18, 2022, https://www.dailywire.com/news/im-broken-ca-mom-whose-daughter-committed-suicide-after-transitioning-blames-school; Jesse O'Neil, "Father Arrested for Discussing Child's Gender Transition in Defiance of Court Order," *New York Post*, March 18, 2021, https://nypost.com/2021/03/18/man-arrested-for-discussing-childs-gender-in-court-order-violation/; Snejana Farberov, "Texas Dad Fears Ex-Wife Plans to 'Chemically Castrate' 9-Year-Old Son," *New York Post*, January 6, 2023, https://nypost.com/2023/01/06/texas-dad-fears-ex-wife-plans-to-chemically-castrate-9-year-old-son/.

the culture. But when ideologues join forces with cultural and economic power players ... the results are transformative. And disastrous. The harm extends beyond the confused and suffering individuals ensnared by the 'gender web' to the cultural and social institutions collapsing amidst anthropological deceit and moral chaos."[36]

The Troubling Reality of "Gender Transition"

The damage done by gender identity ideology extends far beyond the child's understanding of himself or herself and his or her relationship with God and family. An entire industry has sprung up around medicalizing children who erroneously believe they are "born in the wrong body" and are told that hormones and surgery will help them become their "authentic selves," if only they reject their natal sex. This gender industry is composed of Big Pharma (the pharmaceutical companies), gender clinics (almost all US children's hospitals now have gender clinics), unscrupulous doctors, Planned Parenthood, and online providers of hormones to young people.[37] In addition, cottage industries have sprung up providing

---

36. Mary Rice Hasson, "Reality Check: Gender Diversity Is Driven by a Top-Down Ideological Movement," Mercatornet, June 9, 2016, https://mercatornet.com/transgender-triumph-time-for-a-reality-check/20818/; Mary Rice Hasson, "The Trans-Industrial Complex," *Humanum* 1, no. 2 (2018): https://humanumreview.com/articles/the-trans-industrial-complex.

37. For an idea of the scope of the pharmacological/surgical industry driving the medicalization of children, the US sex reassignment surgical market was valued at $1.9 billion in 2021 and was expected to continue to expand at a growth rate of 11% for the remainder of the decade. "US Sex Reassignment Surgery Market Size, Share and Trends," Grand View Research, accessed July 15, 2023, https://www.grandviewresearch.com/industry-analysis/us-sex-reassignment-surgery-market. Globally, the sex reassignment market was expected to rise by more than $321 million between 2023 and 2027, at a growth rate of over 10%. See R. Linker, "The Global Gender Reassignment Surgery Market Is Expected to Grow by $321.48 mn [sic] during 2023–2027, Accelerating at a CAGR of 10.73% during the Forecast Period," Yahoo!Finance UK, December 5, 2022. https://uk.finance.yahoo.com/news/global-gender-reassignment-surgery-market-185600203.html?guccounter=1&guce_referrer=aHR0cHM6Ly9kdWNrZHVja2dvLmNvbS8&guce_referrer_sig=AQAAAL qs2tFYJjni6y8eko9dEj6Syw66DUG8fB-GcGBDMDxbGcLc21Er7nvdS9vzkvdcJ34xXrlarnc2 foJz2PYoraVqoNBekX_7SbWXr8wzNLSAADSMWBhq77v-AovitNHvro8csEUQ-s9LQi4l7 lgtOYXm2R2SU9UnEiO3_xhEz7ew. This doesn't even take into account the profits from medical transition using puberty blockers or cross-sex hormones. As Vanderbilt University Medical Center Clinic for Transgender Health's Dr. Shayne Sebold Taylor pointed out, when describing how VUMC made the calculation to become involved in gender transitions, transgender medicine is a lucrative business at every stage of transition but especially bottom surgery, which is a "huge money maker." See Amanda Prestigiacomo, "'Huge Money Maker': Video Reveals Vanderbilt's Shocking

children with tools to use for self-harm: "binders" that flatten the breasts (and impair respiratory function) of girls; tape and special gear for adolescent boys to literally tuck their genitals into their pelvic cavities and tape them in place in order to create a flat appearance. Other vendors sell special swimsuits, clothing, child-size prosthetic penises, and other items that facilitate a psychosocial transition, perpetuating the illusion that a child can "change sex" by changing appearance.

The harm is immense. Psychosocial transition, which is typically seen as the most benign form of transitioning a child, reinforces the child's discomfort with his or her sex so that he or she comes to regard himself or herself as transgender or nonbinary.[38] Not surprisingly, nearly all children whose parents "affirm" the child's psychosocial transition will persist in transgender identification after five years.[39] In the meantime, as a child socially transitions, he or she socially falls further and further behind his or her classmates of the same sex, cementing his or her disassociation from the body and alienation from peers. There is physical harm associated with social transition from the practices of binding and tucking, including fractured ribs and the risk of testicular torsion.[40]

The next stage, medical transition, begins with using puberty-blocking drugs such as Lupron that are intended to suppress and delay natural puberty. Puberty blockers are associated with risks of significant bone density loss, delayed brain maturation, and even swelling in the brain. Cross-sex hormones such as estrogen or testosterone cause the body to be either

---

Gender 'Care,' Threats against Dissenting Doctors," Daily Wire, September 20, 2022, https://www.dailywire.com/news/huge-money-maker-video-reveals-vanderbilts-shocking-gender-care-threats-against-dissenting-doctors.

38. As one parent described the process of socially transitioning her son and eliminating any contact with anyone who might question it: "Looking back, I now see this in a shockingly different light: this was an intentional process of concretizing transgender identity in children as young as 3 years old—the age of the youngest child in this group. When identity is concretized at this young of age, children will grow up *actually believing they are the opposite sex*. How could medicalization not follow?" "I Thought My 4-Year-Old Was Transgender. I Was Wrong," Mercatornet, August 29, 2022, https://www.mercatornet.com/i-thought-my-4-year-old-was-transgender-i-was-wrong.

39. K. Olson et al., "Gender Identity 5 Years after Social Transition," *Pediatrics* 150 (2022): doi.org/10.1542/peds.2021-056082.

40. Incredibly, prominent gender clinics in the United States offer resources on "safer" binding and tucking to children. See, e.g., Sarah Weaver, "'Safer Tucking': Boston Children's Hospital Says Teens Can Use Tape to Hide Genitals," Daily Caller, August 19, 2022, https://dailycaller.com/2022/08/19/safer-tucking-boston-childrens-hospital-trans-teens-duct-tape/.

feminized or masculinized by developing the secondary sex characteristics of the opposite sex, and they have long-term serious consequences for the teenager or young adult's body. Irreversible changes to voice and hair growth, genital atrophy, metabolic syndromes, and high risks of blood clots all are common side effects. One prominent gender surgeon admitted that children who medically transition—using puberty blockers at Tanner stage 2—lose adult sexual function and the ability to experience sexual pleasure.[41] Most alarming, the combination of puberty blockers and cross-sex hormones effectively sterilizes the child.

Finally, surgical transition inflicts irreversible, lifelong injury on a previously healthy young person. It involves carving up the body to create the appearance of the desired identity by amputating breasts, performing hysterectomies, mutilating genitalia, creating neo-vaginas or facsimiles of a penis using skin grafts or the patient's own tissues (such as the flesh from the forearm or from the colon), and performing facial and vocal surgeries to eradicate any trace of the individual's natal sex. A neo-vagina, for example, must be dilated daily to keep it open as the body tries to heal what is essentially a wound. This brief description cannot do justice to the radical nature of these surgeries, the high rates of serious complications, the horrifying results, and the problems healing wounds. (One surgeon who performs phalloplasties admitted the complication rate can be 100%.)[42]

The children and young adults being drawn into this ideology are incredibly vulnerable and universally struggling. Risk factors include autism, previous trauma, unresolved grief, body issues including eating

---

41. "An observation that I had, every single child who was, or adolescent, who was truly blocked at Tanner stage 2, has never experienced orgasm. I mean, it's really about zero." See Libby Emmons, "'Gender Affirming' Surgeon Admits Children Who Undergo Transition before Puberty NEVER Attain Sexual Satisfaction," *Post Millennial*, May 1, 2022, https://thepostmillennial.com/gender-affirming-surgeon-admits-children-who-undergo-transition-before-puberty-never-attain-sexual-satisfaction.

42. For an impartial summary of procedures and risks, see "Benefits, Harms and Uncertainties of the Gender-Affirmative Treatment," Society for Evidence Based Gender Medicine (SEGM), accessed July 16, 2023, https://segm.org. See also "The Facts about 'Gender Affirming Care' (GAC) for Children and Adolescents," Rethink Identity Medicine Ethics, accessed July 16, 2023, https://personandidentity.com/wp-content/uploads/2022/09/ReIME-FACTS-abt-GAC.pdf. See the comments of a surgeon who performs phalloplasty, Dr. Gabriel del Corral, "Phalloplasty Risks and Complications," Phallo, accessed January 11, 2023, https://www.phallo.net/risks-complications/; and "Use It or Lose It: The Importance of Dilation Following Vaginoplasty," MTFsurgery.net, accessed January 11, 2023, https://www.mtfsurgery.net/dilation.htm.

disorders, attachment disorders, poor peer relationships, and other serious problems. The majority of children who identify as trans, nonbinary, or queer also have been diagnosed with comorbid mental health issues.[43] Many detransitioners complain that as soon as they mentioned gender, their other mental health issues were no longer being treated.[44] As a result, when these young women and men eventually address their underlying mental health issues, they find themselves like Prisha Mosley, shattered by trying to resume life with mutilated and disfigured bodies.

Proponents of the gender affirmative care model, with its insistence that children must be affirmed and transitioned, claim that these drastic, experimental treatments are justified in the name of eradicating the risk of suicide. But ample evidence exists that these treatments do not resolve the suicide risk at all. This makes sense, given that the suicide risk is from underlying mental health issues, which the gender affirmative care does not treat and are overshadowed by the trans diagnosis.[45] In fact, research has suggested a powerful placebo effect that is responsible for a short-term sense of feeling better.[46] Long term, though, the child or young adult is

---

43. K. Kozlowska, C. Chudleigh, G. McClure, A. M. Maguire, and G. R. Ambler, "Attachment Patterns in Children and Adolescents with Gender Dysphoria," *Frontiers in Psychology* 11 (January 2021): doi.org/10.3389/fpsyg.2020.582688; V. Warrier, D. M. Greenberg, E. Weir, C. Buckingham, P. Smith, M. C. Lai, C. Allison, and S. Baron-Cohen, "Elevated Rates of Autism, Other Neurodevelopmental and Psychiatric Diagnoses, and Autistic Traits in Transgender and Gender-Diverse Individuals," *Nature Communications* 11 (August 2020): doi:10.1038/s41467-020-17794-1.

44. The interim report of the Cass Review, the United Kingdom's review of the GIDS/Tavistock Clinic, referred to this phenomenon as diagnostic overshadowing: "Another significant issue raised with us is one of diagnostic overshadowing—many of the children and young people presenting have complex needs, but once they are identified as having gender-related distress, other important healthcare issues that would normally be managed by local services can sometimes be subsumed by the label of gender dysphoria." See Hilary Cass, *The Cass Review: Interim Review of Gender Identity Services for Children and Young People: Interim Report* (United Kingdom: Independent Review into Gender Identity Services for Children and Young People, February 2022), 46. Numerous lawsuits against gender clinics and surgeons allege failure to treat the underlying mental health disorder.

45. See discussion of suicidality in "The Facts about Gender Affirming Care (GAC) for Children and Adolescents," Rethink Identity Medicine Ethics, https://personandidentity.com/wp-content/uploads/2022/09/ReIME-FACTS-abt-GAC.pdf, 5. See also Michael Biggs, "Suicide by Clinic-Referred Transgender Adolescents in the United Kingdom," *Archives of Sexual Behavior* 51 (2022): 685–90.

46. Alison Clayton, "Gender-Affirming Treatment of Gender Dysphoria in Youth: A Perfect Storm Environment for the Placebo Effect—The Implications for Research and Clinical Practice," *Archives of Sexual Behavior* 52 (2023): 483–94.

left struggling with the same issue that led him or her to be vulnerable, but now with a mutilated body and a claimed identity that will never align with the reality of his or her body.

No wonder, then, that some countries are beginning to distance themselves from the gender-affirming care model and now prioritize psychotherapy for distressed minors. In 2020, Finland announced its intention to limit transitions in children based on concerns that such care could worsen the condition of vulnerable children. England and Sweden, two countries that had enthusiastically embraced the gender affirming care model, announced their intention to stop or drastically curb routinely "transitioning" children. England in fact closed its main gender clinic, deeming it unsafe for children. Australia, France, and New Zealand have all expressed concern as well. Unfortunately, other Western countries including Canada and United States, have been slow to follow suit.[47]

The Church Has Clear Teaching on Gender Ideology

Christian anthropology and gender ideology are radically incompatible ways of looking at the person, with real-life implications for person and family.[48] Christian anthropology supports a holistic, integrated view of person and sexuality. Shaped by the principles of subsidiarity and solidarity, Christian anthropology respects intermediary institutions like the family and seeks to promote human flourishing in light of the nature of the human person and family, as known by reason and revealed by God. In contrast, gender ideology is a destructive ideology that targets extremely vulnerable children and young adults, subverts social norms, encourages young persons to engage in medicalized self-harm, and deconstructs and shatters families, leaving the most vulnerable children and young men and women defenseless against those who seek to profit from their misery. With the financial backing of medicine, pharmacology, media, and

---

47. See "2022 Year-End-Summary: A Remarkable Year for Safeguarding of Vulnerable Youth," SEGM, January 1, 2023, https://segm.org/gender-medicine-developments-2022-summary.

48. For a comprehensive treatment of gender ideology in light of Christian anthropology, see *Sexual Identity: The Harmony of Philosophy, Science, and Revelation*, edited by John DeSilva Finley (Steubenville, OH: Emmaus Road, 2022). Finley's collaborators include Paul Hruz, MD, PhD; Deacon Patrick Lappert, MD; Cara Buskmiller, MD; Andrew Sodergren, PsyD; and Lawrence Welch, PhD.

corporations, who benefit from the commodification of the body and the ideological colonization of families and cultures, gender activists are modern-day pied pipers, seducing children to leave family, faith, and even themselves behind in search of the myth of gender euphoria.

With prescience and courage, the popes in the modern age have been unsparing in their rejection of gender ideology. The *Catechism of the Catholic Church* teaches, "Everyone, man and woman, should acknowledge and accept his sexual identity," choosing the term sexual identity to convey that one's identity is inseparable from one's sex as male or female. The *Catechism* also stresses the unity of body and soul, the equal dignity of men and women, the importance of complementarity and sexual difference for the family, and reiterates prohibitions against unnecessary amputations, mutilation of the body, or sterilizations.[49]

Pope John Paul II's catechesis on the theology of the body and his apostolic exhortation *Mulieris Dignitatem* provide substantial reflections on the unity of the person (body and soul); the importance of sexual difference; and the dignity, meaning, and importance of the body. In *Mulieris Dignitatem*, John Paul II's reflections on the feminine genius as derived from the somatic reality of the female body provide a genuine response to gender ideology's inherent misogyny as gender ideology encourages trans-identifying men to invade women's sports, women's colleges, women's bathrooms, and even women's prisons.[50] Finally, John Paul II's magnificent trilogy of encyclicals—*Fides et Ratio, Veritatis Splendor*, and *Evangelium Vitae*—provide the framework for understanding the relationship between metaphysics, anthropology, and ethics that is necessary for responding to the problems of postmodern culture. In particular, *Fides et Ratio* warns against scientism—the belief that anything that is technically possible is therefore morally permissible. *Veritatis Splendor* warns against freedom that considers the human body as raw material "to be fashioned in accord with man's desires, devoid of any meaning or values until shaped by human freedom."[51] *Veritatis Splendor* reaffirms that the

---

49. *CCC* §§2333, 2393, 2297.

50. John Paul II, *Man and Woman He Created Them: A Theology of the Body*, translated by Michael Waldstein (Boston: Pauline Books, 2006); John Paul II, *Mulieris Dignitatem* (1988). See also John Paul II, *Letter to Families* (1994).

51. For a critique of scientism, see *Fides et Ratio* 88. It is worth quoting in full the passage in

somatic reality of the sexed body has meaning and conveys metaphysical truths about the person and about humanity.[52]

As Holy Father, Pope Benedict XVI began to sharpen the Church's focus on gender ideology as a specific threat to the family. In his address to the German Bundestag in 2011, Pope Benedict XVI saw clearly the effect of gender ideology on law and culture as well, linking it to the disastrous movement of legal positivism and the scholarship of the German philosopher Hans Kelsen. In that same address, he highlighted the idea of human ecology—that man has a nature that he must accept and respect— and urged the Church to see care for human ecology as inseparable from care for the environment. He proposed that human ecology would thus be a point of engagement with young Catholics.[53] In his 2008 Christmas

---

Veritatis Splendor in which Pope St. John Paul II writes, "A freedom which claims to be absolute ends up treating the human body as a raw datum, devoid of any meaning and moral values until freedom has shaped it in accordance with its design. Consequently, human nature and the body appear as *presuppositions or preambles,* materially *necessary* for freedom to make its choice, yet extrinsic to the person, the subject and the human act. Their functions would not be able to constitute reference points for moral decisions, because the finalities of these inclinations would be merely '*physical*' goods, called by some 'pre-moral.' To refer to them, in order to find in them rational indications with regard to the order of morality, would be to expose oneself to the accusation of physicalism or biologism. In this way of thinking, the tension between freedom and a nature conceived of in a reductive way is resolved by a division within man himself. This moral theory does not correspond to the truth about man and his freedom. It contradicts the *Church's teachings on the unity of the human person,* whose rational soul is *per se et essentialiter* the form of his body. The spiritual and immortal soul is the principle of unity of the human being, whereby it exists as a whole—*corpore et anima unus*—as a person. These definitions not only point out that the body, which has been promised the resurrection, will also share in glory. They also remind us that reason and free will are linked with all the bodily and sense faculties. *The person, including the body, is completely entrusted to himself, and it is in the unity of body and soul that the person is the subject of his own moral acts.* The person, by the light of reason and the support of virtue, discovers in the body the anticipatory signs, the expression and the promise of the gift of self, in conformity with the wise plan of the Creator. It is in the light of the dignity of the human person—a dignity which must be affirmed for its own sake—that reason grasps the specific moral value of certain goods towards which the person is naturally inclined. And since the human person cannot be reduced to a freedom which is self-designing, but entails a particular spiritual and bodily structure, the primordial moral requirement of loving and respecting the person as an end and never as a mere means also implies, by its very nature, respect for certain fundamental goods, without which one would fall into relativism and arbitrariness" (*Veritatis Splendor* 48).

52. *Veritatis Splendor* 50.

53. "Yet I would like to underline a point that seems to me to be neglected, today as in the past: there is also an ecology of man. Man too has a nature that he must respect and that he cannot manipulate at will. Man is not merely self-creating freedom. Man does not create himself. He is intellect and will, but he is also nature, and his will is rightly ordered if he respects his nature, listens to

address to the Curia, Pope Benedict urged that we not disregard the language of creation regarding the nature of the human being as man and woman. "What is often expressed and understood by the term "gender" ultimately ends up being man's attempt at self-emancipation from creation and the Creator."[54] He returned to this theme in his Christmas address to the Curia of 2012, outlining how the attempt to free oneself from one's God-given, sexed bodily identity leads to rejecting God as Creator while attempting to be one's own creator. Prophetically, Pope Benedict XVI warns that rejecting God as Creator leads to a loss of dignity for individual humans and to an attack on the family.[55] It is hard to imagine a

---

it and accepts himself for who he is, as one who did not create himself. In this way, and in no other, is true human freedom fulfilled." See Pope Benedict XVI, "The Listening Heart: Reflections on the Foundations of Law," Visit to the Bundestag, Address of His Holiness Benedict XVI, 2011, website of the Holy See, https://www.vatican.va/content/benedict-xvi/en/speeches/2011/september/documents/hf_ben-xvi_spe_20110922_reichstag-berlin.html.

54. Pope Benedict XVI, "Address of His Holiness Benedict XVI to the Members of the Roman Curia for the Traditional Exchange of Christmas Greetings," 2008, website of the Holy See, https://www.vatican.va/content/benedict-xvi/en/speeches/2008/december/documents/hf_ben-xvi_spe_20081222_curia-romana.html.

55. "The profound falsehood of this theory and of the anthropological revolution contained within it is obvious. People dispute the idea that they have a nature, given by their bodily identity, that serves as a defining element of the human being. They deny their nature and decide that it is not something previously given to them, but that they make it for themselves. According to the biblical creation account, being created by God as male and female pertains to the essence of the human creature. This duality is an essential aspect of what being human is all about, as ordained by God. This very duality as something previously given is what is now disputed. The words of the creation account: 'male and female he created them' (Gn 1:27) no longer apply. No, what applies now is this: it was not God who created them male and female – hitherto society did this, now we decide for ourselves. Man and woman as created realities, as the nature of the human being, no longer exist. Man calls his nature into question. From now on he is merely spirit and will. The manipulation of nature, which we deplore today where our environment is concerned, now becomes man's fundamental choice where he himself is concerned. From now on there is only the abstract human being, who chooses for himself what his nature is to be. Man and woman in their created state as complementary versions of what it means to be human are disputed. But if there is no pre-ordained duality of man and woman in creation, then neither is the family any longer a reality established by creation. Likewise, the child has lost the place he had occupied hitherto and the dignity pertaining to him. Bernheim shows that now, perforce, from being a subject of rights, the child has become an object to which people have a right and which they have a right to obtain. When the freedom to be creative becomes the freedom to create oneself, then necessarily the Maker himself is denied and ultimately man too is stripped of his dignity as a creature of God, as the image of God at the core of his being. The defence of the family is about man himself. And it becomes clear that when God is denied, human dignity also disappears. Whoever defends God is defending man." See Benedict XVI, "Address of His Holiness Benedict XVI on the Occasion of Christmas Greetings to the

more shocking attack on the dignity of the person than to seduce a young woman to amputate her breasts, or to persuade a young man to be castrated in pursuit of the falsehood that one can change sex; it is hard to imagine a more egregious attack on the family than removing a son from his parents because they object to his castration, or a daughter from her parents because they try to stop the amputation of her breasts.

But no pope has been more forceful in denouncing gender ideology than Pope Francis, who has referred to it as "a great enemy to marriage," even as he continually reminds the Church to respond to any individual in need with charity and pastoral care.[56] Pope Francis reminds us that accompaniment must always "lead others ever closer to God in whom we attain true freedom," and that accompaniment is not "a therapy supporting their self-absorption."[57] Pope Francis explicitly denounced gender ideology in his encyclical *Laudato Si'*, highlighting the body as gift from God, the importance of receiving our created nature as a gift from God our Creator, and of cherishing it just as we should also cherish the earth, our home. In fact, Francis notes that sexual difference is essential for basic human relations, for encountering and learning to love another person.[58] In *Amoris Laetitia*, Pope Francis described gender ideology as "envisaging a society without sexual difference and thereby eliminating the anthropological basis of the family." When gender ideology promotes the idea that

---

Roman Curia," 2012, website of the Holy See, https://www.vatican.va/content/benedict-xvi/en/speeches/2012/december/documents/hf_ben-xvi_spe_20121221_auguri-curia.html.

56. Pope Francis, "Address to Priests, Religious, Seminarians and Pastoral Workers during the Apostolic Journey to Georgia and Azerbaijan," October 1, 2016. Pope Francis also criticized gender theory in the following addresses: "Address to the Polish Bishops during the Apostolic Journey to Poland," July 27, 2016; "Address to *Équipes de Notre Dame*," September 10, 2015; "Address to the Bishops of Puerto Rico," June 8, 2015; "Address in Naples," March 23, 2015; "Meeting with Families in Manila," January 16, 2015.

57. *Evangelii Gaudium* 170.

58. "The acceptance of our bodies as God's gift is vital for welcoming and accepting the entire world as a gift from the Father and our common home, whereas thinking that we enjoy absolute power over our own bodies turns, often subtly, into thinking that we enjoy absolute power over creation. Learning to accept our body, to care for it and to respect its fullest meaning, is an essential element of any genuine human ecology. Also, valuing one's own body in its femininity or masculinity is necessary if I am going to be able to recognize myself in an encounter with someone who is different. In this way we can joyfully accept the specific gifts of another man or woman, the work of God the Creator, and find mutual enrichment. It is not a healthy attitude which would seek to cancel out sexual difference because it no longer knows how to confront it." Pope Francis, *Laudato Si'* 155.

one can "choose" an identity by rejecting one's own sexual identity, Francis warns it leads to the sin of "trying to replace the Creator."[59] Finally, on numerous occasions, Francis laments the ideological promotion of gender ideology in schools and culture as a form of ideological colonization, a unique insight into this destructive and invasive attack on families.[60]

In addition, both the Congregation for the Doctrine of the Faith (CDF) and the Congregation for Catholic Education (CCE) have addressed this issue in their own competencies. The CDF issued the letter *On the Collaboration of Men and Women in the Church and in the World* (2004), in which it decried as erroneous the desire to be freed from one's personal constitution as male or female.[61] The CDF also issued a response to a Spanish bishop on the question of a transgender-identifying person serving as godparent, noting that transsexual behavior revealed "an attitude opposed to the moral demand of resolving the problem of one's

---

59. *Amoris Laetitia* (AL) 56, 285, 286. Specifically, Pope Francis writes in AL 56: "Yet another challenge is posed by the various forms of an ideology of gender that 'denies the difference and reciprocity in nature of a man and a woman and envisages a society without sexual differences, thereby eliminating the anthropological basis of the family. This ideology leads to educational programs and legislative enactments that promote a personal identity and emotional intimacy radically separated from the biological difference between male and female. Consequently, human identity becomes the choice of the individual, one which can also change over time.' ... Let us not fall into the sin of trying to replace the Creator. We are creatures, and not omnipotent. Creation is prior to us and must be received as a gift. At the same time, we are called to protect our humanity, and this means, in the first place, accepting it and respecting it as it was created." And again in AL 285: "Beyond the understandable difficulties which individuals may experience, the young need to be helped to accept their own body as it was created, for 'thinking that we enjoy absolute power over our own bodies turns, often subtly, into thinking that we enjoy absolute power over creation ... An appreciation of our body as male or female is also necessary for our own self-awareness in an encounter with others different from ourselves. In this way we can joyfully accept the specific gifts of another man or woman, the work of God the Creator, and find mutual enrichment.' Only by losing the fear of being different, can we be freed of self-centeredness and self-absorption. Sex education should help young people to accept their own bodies and to avoid the pretension 'to cancel out sexual difference because one no longer knows how to deal with it.'"

60. See his "Address to Priests, Religious, Seminarians and Pastoral Workers during the Apostolic Journey to Georgia and Azerbaijan"; "Address to the Polish Bishops during the Apostolic Journey to Poland"; "Address in Naples"; and "Meeting with Families in Manila."

61. "While the immediate roots of this second tendency are found in the context of reflection on women's roles, its deeper motivation must be sought in the human attempt to be freed from one's biological conditioning. According to this perspective, human nature in itself does not possess characteristics in an absolute manner: all persons can and ought to constitute themselves as they like, since they are free from every predetermination linked to their essential constitution." CDF, *On the Collaboration of Men and Women*, 3.

own sexual identity according to the truth of one's own sex," and therefore the individual who identifies as transgender would not be a suitable godparent (a teaching/witness role).[62] The CDF reiterated Pope Francis's clear opposition to gender ideology in a 2021 letter to an Italian political party.[63]

Before examining the teaching of the Congregation for Catholic Education, it is necessary to address, albeit briefly, attempts by Catholic theologians to undermine the Church's teaching on this issue. Some attempts propose that the Church needs to adopt a more compassionate approach by avoiding discussion of Church teaching; others propose an innovative theological anthropology capable of supporting gender ideology, either by accommodating transgenderism or by expanding sexual morality to allow for same-sex sexual activity and relationships. In the first instance, these theologians justify their refusal to even mention the Church's teaching on same-sex issues or gender ideology by arguing that the teaching has not been received by the LGBT community, insinuating that a teaching that is not received by a group does not apply to that group. Would they similarly claim that because the teaching on the Real Presence was not received by those who walked away from Jesus that it does not apply to them? Cardinal Joseph Ratzinger, in a 1991 address to the United States Bishops, criticized similar ideas that, he wrote, "have discernibly crippled the disposition to evangelize. The one who sees the faith as a heavy burden or as a moral imposition is unable to invite others to believe." Invoking the concept of anamnesis, Ratzinger warned that withholding the fullness

---

62. The CDF communication to Bishop Zornoza was private. But New Ways Ministry reported the text of the communication to include the following language. "The same transexual behavior reveals, in a public manner, an attitude opposed to the moral demand of resolving the problem of one's own sexual identity according to the truth of one's own sex. Therefore, the result is evident that this person does not possess the requisite of leading a life conformed to the faith and to the position of godfather (CIC, can 874 §1,3), therefore is not able to be admitted to the position of godmother nor godfather. One should not see this as discrimination, but only the recognition of an objective absence of the requisites that by their nature are necessary to assume the ecclesial responsibility of being a godparent." See Robert Shine, "Vatican Intervention Causes Bishop to (Again) Reject Trans* Man as Godparent," *New Ways Ministry*, September 3, 2015.

63. Andrea Gagliarducci, "Vatican Cites Pope Francis' Condemnations of Gender Ideology in Letter to Pro-Life Association," *Catholic News Agency*, October 28, 2021, https://www.catholicnewsagency.com/news/249425/vatican-recalls-pope-francis-condemnations-of-gender-ideology-in-letter-to-pro-life-association.

of the Gospel is based in the denial of "the original memory of the good and true ... implanted in us ... an inner ontological tendency within man, who is created in the likeness of God, toward the divine," which he calls the "ground of our existence."[64] To withhold the fullness of truth is thus the opposite of mercy; it supposes that some people shouldn't even try to live up to the teachings of Christ, which it sees as an unattainable ideal that brings misery rather than happiness.

The theological innovators similarly use language that blames the Church for being harsh, or unforgiving, but go even farther in suggesting that the Church's understanding of Christian anthropology needed to be updated. One critic of the Church's teaching, Fr. Daniel Horan, wrote, "The time is long overdue to reject specious arguments like those that undergird the right-wing political and ecclesial agendas promoting the boogeyman of 'gender ideology.'"[65] He then advised the Church to study Judith Butler, despite the fact that her understanding of sex and gender as performance is utterly incompatible with both reason and revelation on the person as unity of body and soul. Despite clear teaching on the role of philosophy in the encyclicals *Fides et Ratio* and *Aeterni Patris*, including the insistence that the Church has no official philosophy and that any philosophy employed must have genuine metaphysical range, Horan argues that Thomistic philosophy is outdated (by citing passages in Aquinas that rely on medieval biology, rather than citing foundational principles of Thomistic anthropology), then conflates Thomistic philosophy with Christian anthropology in order to create the impression that the Church's teachings on Christian anthropology are outdated. In its place, he argues that the Church needs a contemporary anthropology that will accommodate gender and identity issues. In doing so, he ignores, disparages, and denies magisterial teaching on Christian anthropology, including teaching by Pope Francis, as well as Pope Benedict and Pope John Paul II.[66] In his book, Horan approvingly cites Cardinal Newman on the

---

64. Joseph Cardinal Ratzinger, "Conscience and Truth," Presented at the 10th Workshop for Bishops, February 1991, Dallas, Texas, https://peped.org/philosophicalinvestigations/article-conscience-and-truth-pope-benedict-on-conscience/.

65. Daniel Horan, OFM, "The Truth about So-Called 'Gender Ideology,'" *National Catholic Reporter*, June 24, 2020, https://www.ncronline.org/news/opinion/faith-seeking-understanding/truth-about-so-called-gender-ideology.

66. In his book *Catholicity and Emerging Personhood: A Contemporary Theological*

development of doctrine but conveniently leaves out Newman's tests to distinguish a corruption from a development of doctrine, a test his writing failed when he lamented the explicit sexism of the account of "gender complementarity" notably found in the writings of Pope John Paul II and in the *Catechism of the Catholic Church*.[67]

In both instances, those who seek to minimize or to change the teaching of the Church studiously avoid acknowledging the harm that is occurring to mentally unwell young persons and children and autistic children through transgender medicine. There is no mention in their writings for example, of the presence of social contagion, the emotional seduction of vulnerable kids, nor of the tangible and lasting harm that is occurring to these very children when they are castrated, undergo double mastectomies, or are bathing their developing bodies in wrong-sex hormones. They ignore the damage to families when the rights of parents to direct the upbringing and education of their children is overridden by aggressively secular bureaucrats who believe that Christian teachings are inherently discriminatory. Moreover, they intentionally avoid acknowledging the inevitable conflict when a young person is told that the Church is becoming more open to LGBT identities and relationships, only to find that the Church's perennial teaching on human sexuality has not changed and cannot change. They push the Church to change in the name of compassion, but their desired change would sideline one of the few voices speaking out against the exploitation of vulnerable children and young persons and would undermine the teachings of the Church, affecting the catechesis of an entire generation.

Anthropology (Maryknoll, NY: Orbis Books, 2019), Fr. Horan expresses a desire to replace Aquinas with a "contemporary retrieval" of Duns Scotus, implying that Scotus would support an understanding of the person compatible with gender ideology, a reading that reflects wishful thinking rather than anything specific to Scotus. A longer treatment of Fr. Horan's work is beyond the scope of this paper. See Horan, *Catholicity and Emerging Personhood*, 153.

67. Horan, *Catholicity and Emerging Personhood*, 10; see also 147–49 for his discussion of the explicit sexism of "gender complementarity," his term for the discussion of sexual difference and the complementarity of men and women found in Pope John Paul II's Theology of the Body as well as in the *Catechism of the Catholic Church*.

The Congregation for Catholic Education Guidance: Male and Female He Created Them

In 2019, the CCE issued a guidance document titled *Male and Female He Created Them*, which specifically addresses how Catholic schools should respond to the challenge of gender ideology. In this document the CCE traces the origin of gender theory from various beliefs: that sexual difference is socially constructed, that sexual difference is inconsequential for sexual relationships and human sexuality and therefore is unnecessary for the family, and that sex has nothing to do with modern uses of the term gender.[68] All of this, the CCE warns, culminates in the queering of sexuality and ushers in a cultural, ideological, and juridical revolution that changes the meaning and nature of marriage.[69] The CCE document was not just diagnostic, however. It mapped out a response in the schools: Catholic schools must re-propose Christian anthropology to cultures and communities that have forgotten or rejected it. Moreover, Catholic schools must form the formators, so that any teacher can answer a question of concern about gender ideology as it arises.[70] In proposing this strategy, the CCE mapped out a blueprint that is useful for parishes and dioceses, as well as schools.

The Person and Identity Project: Equipping Catholics with the Truth

In response, the Person and Identity Project has developed resources for parents, family members, parishes, schools, and dioceses to equip them to respond to gender ideology.[71] We offer resources to assist in forming the formators—teachers, directors of religious education, youth ministers—so that they are able to respond as needed to questions about gender ideology. In light of the corrosive effect of gender ideology on the preambles for catechesis—the child's natural understanding of the person, the family, and even the stability of the created order—we advise teachers

---

68. CCE 10.
69. CCE 19, 21.
70. CCE 30, 47*ff*.
71. See the Person and Identity Project at https://personandidentity.com.

that they need to expect gaps in the child's understanding of foundational concepts and anticipate that the child's understanding of human sexuality has already been shaped by gender ideology. We offer in-person trainings and workshops for clergy, teachers, administrators, parents, and teens, and our website has free online resources (thanks to a grant from Our Sunday Visitor). We work on a consultative basis, partnering with dioceses in order to help them with this issue as much or as little as needed.

When we founded Person and Identity, this issue was strictly theoretical to most of our audiences. Now, at every talk, we encounter distraught parents, grandparents, and even teens who have been harmed by this. Gender ideology is a destructive and devastating force breaking families apart. Just as the Catholic Church led the way in proclaiming the dignity and right to life of the unborn child, so too the Church is leading now, opposing an ideology that harms some of the most vulnerable among us. No other Church has the intellectual resources and the systematic theological tradition to draw on. Proponents of gender ideology know this—it is why they level astonishing vitriol against the Catholic Church and seek to undermine its teachings by amplifying voices that spread confusion about Catholic teaching on the person. Now, as some European countries are beginning to back away from harmful gender transitions for minors, as lawsuits are being filed in the United States and United Kingdom, the Church must not lose courage. For if we lose courage, we strip hope away from desperate families, families of all faiths that respond with gratitude to the Church's defense of these vulnerable young persons, of the family, and of the nature and meaning of the human person.

APPENDIX B. TABLES

The following tables compare contraception to NFP. From R. J. Fehring, "Contraception and Natural Family Planning: The Impact on the Sexual Lives of Couples," *Anthropotes* 34 (2018): 125.

The Health of the Body

Contraception	*Natural Family Planning*
Fertility is a medical problem	Fertility is a natural process
Fertility needs to be controlled	Fertility needs to be lived with
Fertility is suppressed, blocked, or destroyed (harmed)	Fertility is [understood and] monitored
Can be used to avoid pregnancy	Can be used to avoid or achieve pregnancy
Unitive and procreative [nature of intercourse] separated	Unitive and procreative maintained
Sexuality and fertility separated	Sexuality and fertility remain integrated
Can cause [negative] medical side effects	No [negative] medical side effects
Can mask medical problems	Helps identify medical problems
Easy to use	At times a challenge to use

Couple Behavior

Contraception	*Natural Family Planning*
Little/no understanding of fertility	Knowledge/understanding of fertility
Little or no need for self-control	Builds self-control
[Couple] Communicating on whether fertile or not	[Couple] Communicating on whether to use or not
Trust [in] the [contraceptive	Trust partner + woman's signs of fertility
Woman [or man] is the object of sex	Woman [or man] is respected
Not willing to live with … fertility	Accepts and lives with … fertility
Used by one person in relationship	Can be a shared method
Decreased fear of pregnancy	Increased creative tension [challenge to be "open to"]
Increased sexual pleasure	Increased sex drive (libido) [and more satisfaction]
Role mode is sterility	Role model [is] fertility
Increases risk for divorce	Lowers risk for divorce

CONTRIBUTORS

FULVIO DI BLASI is an attorney, legal mediator, and Thomistic philosopher. He is the director of the Thomas International Center for Philosophical Studies (United States), and he has taught at the University of Notre Dame (United States), the LUMSA Law School (Italy), the Pontifical University of the Holy Cross (Rome), and the John Paul II Catholic University of Lublin (Poland).

THERESA FARNAN is a fellow at the Ethics and Public Policy Center and cofounder of the Person and Identity Project. She is the coauthor of two books, *Get Out Now: Why You Should Pull Your Child from Public School Before It's Too Late* and *Where Did I Come From? Where Am I Going? How Do I Get There?* She has taught at St. Paul Seminary in Pittsburgh, Franciscan University of Steubenville, Ohio, and Mount St. Mary's Seminary in Maryland. She received her doctorate in medieval studies from the University of Notre Dame (United States).

ROBERT FASTIGGI is professor of dogmatic theology at Sacred Heart Major Seminary in Detroit, Michigan, where he has taught since 1999. He previously taught at St. Edward's University in Austin, Texas (1985–99). He is the coeditor of the English translation of the 43rd edition of Denzinger-Hünermann (2012) and a member of the Pontifical Marian Academy International.

JOHN FINNIS taught at the University of Oxford for more than forty years. He is an emeritus professor there and at the University of Notre Dame (United States), a fellow of the British Academy, and a former member of the International Theological Commission (1986–91), the Pontifical Council of Justice and Peace (1990–95), and the Pontifical Academy Pro Vita (2001–16).

ANGELA FRANKS is a professor at the Theological Institute at St. John's Seminary in Brighton, Massachusetts. In addition to numerous scholarly articles on systematic theological topics, she is the author of *Margaret Sanger's Eugenic Legacy* (2005) and *Contraception and Catholicism* (2013). She writes and speaks on Trinitarian theology, the theology of the body, and feminism.

PAUL GONDREAU is professor of theology at Providence College in Rhode Island, where he teaches in the areas of moral theology, Christology, and the sacraments. He is the author of *The Passions of Christ's Soul in the Theology of St. Thomas Aquinas* (2002 and 2009), numerous scholarly articles on sexual morality, Christology, and disability, and he serves as an associate editor of the journal *Nova et Vetera*.

OANA GOTIA is associate professor of moral theology at the Sacred Heart Major Seminary in Detroit. She previously taught applied moral theology for ten years at the Pontifical John Paul II Institute for Marriage and Family in Rome. Like Msgr. Melina and Fr. Granados, she is on the scientific council of the *Veritas Amoris* Project; see https://veritasamoris.org/EN/.

FR. JOSÉ GRANADOS is the Superior General of the Disciples of the Hearts of Jesus and Mary, based in Madrid. His doctoral thesis on St. Justin Martyr—directed by Fr. Luis Ladaria, SJ—received the Bellarmine Prize as the best theology thesis at the Gregorian University. Fr. Granados has served as a professor and vice president of the John Paul II Institute in Rome, and he has taught in Washington, DC. Since 2018 he is a consultant to the Dicastery for Laity, Family and Life.

MATTHEW LEVERING holds the James N. Jr. and Mary D. Perry Chair of Theology at the University of St. Mary of the Lake/Mundelein Seminary in Illinois. The author or coauthor of more than thirty-five books, he is the past president (2021–22) of the Academy of Catholic Theology. He serves as the coeditor of two quarterly journals, *Nova et Vetera* and *International Journal of Systematic Theology*.

MONSIGNOR PIOTR MAZURKIEWICZ is a Catholic priest and professor of social science at the Cardinal Stefan Wyszyński University in Warsaw, Poland. He served as the secretary general of the Commission of the Bishops' Conferences of the European Union (COMECE) from 2008 to 2012. Since 1997, he has been associated with the Emmanuel Community.

CONTRIBUTORS

MONSIGNOR LIVIO MELINA taught moral theology at the Pontifical John Paul II Institute for Studies on Marriage and Family in Rome from 1986 to 2019, and he served as the Institute's President from 2006 to 2016. He is an ordinary member of the Pontifical Academy of Theology and a former consultant to the Pontifical Council for the Family. Msgr Melina is a founding member of the *Veritas Amoris* Project.

THERESA NOTARE, assistant director of the Natural Family Planning Program of the United States Conference of Catholic Bishops (USCCB), has been staff to the bishops since 1984. She holds a PhD in Church history from the Catholic University of America. In her role at the USCCB, she has developed numerous pastoral strategies and resources, including several academic books, notably *Humanae Vitae, 50 Years Later, Embracing God's Vision for Marriage, Love, and Life; A Compendium* (2019).

GRÉGOR PUPPINCK is director of the European Centre for Law and Justice. He also serves as an expert representing the Holy See in committees of the Council of Europe since 1999. From 2003 to 2012, he lectured on human rights, international law, and constitutional law at the Universities of Mulhouse and Strasbourg.

ADRIAN J. REIMERS teaches philosophy at Holy Cross College in Indiana. He has also taught and lectured at the University of Notre Dame (United States), the Pontifical University of John Paul II in Krakow, and the John Paul II Catholic University of Lublin, Poland. He has published several books and numerous articles on the thought of Karol Wojtyla/Pope John Paul II.

PETER RYAN, SJ, is the Blessed Michael J. McGivney Chair in Life Ethics at Sacred Heart Major Seminary in Detroit, Michigan. He has served as executive director of the Secretariat of Doctrine and Canonical Affairs at the United States Conference of Catholic Bishops, and he has taught at Kenrick-Glennon Seminary in St. Louis; Mount St. Mary's Seminary in Emmitsburg, Maryland; and Loyola College in Maryland.

FR. LUIS SÁNCHEZ-NAVARRO is a priest of the Disciples of the Hearts of Jesus and Mary, and he has doctorates in both Greek philology and Sacred Scripture. He holds the New Testament chair at the Universidad San

Damaso in Madrid, and he also taught Sacred Scripture at the John Paul II Institute in Spain.

MICHAEL WALDSTEIN is professor of New Testament at Franciscan University, Steubenville, Ohio. He previously was the Max Seckler Professor of Theology at Ave Maria University in Florida. He has published on Gnosticism, St. Thomas Aquinas, and Hans Urs von Balthasar. He is the translator of John Paul II's *Man and Woman He Created Them: A Theology of the Body*.

INDEX

abortion, 39, 46, 66, 68n44, 74, 86n14, 89, 91–92, 94, 96–97, 133, 135, 141, 144, 164–65, 199–200, 204, 208, 217, 225, 229, 241, 288, 313n7, 321, 322
absolutes, moral, 15, 80, 106n10, 143, 231, 240–43, 247
abstinence: complete or total, 50, 149n9, 325; periodic, 84, 316, 319n30, 320–21; prolonged, 137
acts: human, 13, 15, 38–39, 48, 57, 107, 119, 120–21, 123, 228; intrinsically evil, 2, 8, 14, 38–39, 48, 51, 101–4, 106–11, 113–14, 119, 122, 128–30
Adam and Eve, 145, 196
adequation of the intellect, 279
Adolphe, Jane F., 322n14, 333n14
aesthetics, 104
Aeterni Patris (encyclical of Leo XIII, 1879), 351
agathòs (the good), 104–5, 299n114
Alexander VII (pope), 183
Allen, Sr. Prudence, 332n11, 333
Allocution [Address] to the Midwives (of Pius XII), 84, 138, 187, 191, 193, 225n3
Amoris Laetitia (exhortation of Pope Francis, 2016), 9, 16, 45n55, 143, 230, 232, 332n12, 148, 349n59
Anglican/Anglicans, 83, 134, 149, 186, 191, 310, 311n1, 311n3, 312, 322, 324
animals, 44n53, 146, 251, 256, 258–59
animal sex, 258
anthropology, 11, 13, 23, 30, 160, 220, 251, 276, 332, 338, 345; biblical, 35n32; Christian/Catholic, 2, 263n3, 327, 330, 332, 344, 351, 353; contemporary, 351; dualist/Cartesian, 220, 252, 275n51; false, 333–34; fragmented, 249–50, 252; hylemorphic, 250–51, 255; integrated 250–51; John Paul II's, 265n9; postmodern, 332; queer theory's, 335; theological, 73, 76, 350, 352n66; Thomistic, 264n9, 351
Apollo Belvedere, 298
appetites: concupiscible, 265; irascible, 265, 270; sensitive, 265–66, 270n30
Aquinas, St. Thomas, 11, 19, 38, 52n70, 110, 111, 113n19, 116n26, 121n41, 125, 127–28, 143, 145–47, 243, 251, 254n10, 262, 264–71, 274, 276, 279, 280n10, 299–302, 331n10, 351, 352n66, 358, 360

Aristotle, 38–39, 102–6, 110–12, 113n19, 117, 128, 263–64, 268–69, 271, 287, 301
Athanasius, St., 53
atomic bomb, 111
Augustine, St., 41, 83, 114, 156, 174, 176, 185, 246, 255, 268n25, 271, 284, 285n30, 308
Australia, 344
authors, approved, 140
autosexual, 160
Ave Maria University, 1, 360

Barth, Karl, 55
Base Text, 220–30, 249, 250n1, 254. *See also* foundational text
Beauchamp, Paul, 31, 33
Bekkers, Bishop William, 190
Benedictus Deus (constitution of Benedict XII, 1336), 168
Benedict XII, 168
Benedict XVI, 28n12, 31, 41n44, 233, 251, 253, 255, 258, 275n55, 289, 330, 346, 347nn53–55
Bernini, 266, 298, 299n10
Big Pharma, 340
body: and soul, 250–51, 260, 331–31, 336, 345, 346n51, 351; language of, 19, 231–35, 239, 242, 244–48
Bonhoeffer, Dietrich, 55
bonum fides, 146, 148
bonum prolis, 90, 146, 148
Bori, Pier Cesare, 29
Boyle, Joseph, 146
Brugger, E. Christian, 136, 151–52, 153n6, 205

Cabásilas, Nicholas, 43
caecitas mentis (blindness of the mind), 303
Calvinist, 191
Canada, 86, 197n100, 286, 339, 344
Canadian Bishops Conference, 97–98, 286–87
Canterbury, Archbishop of, 310
Casti Connubii (encyclical of Pius XI, 1930), 83–84, 89, 134, 138, 144, 148, 150, 186–87, 191, 193, 238
casuistry, 61, 63, 66, 71, 75
Catechism of the Catholic Church, 22n3, 108, 119n37, 168n50, 179n3, 184n27, 193, 251
Catechism of the Council of Trent, 139. *See also* Roman Catechism

INDEX

cause, material, 123–24, 268
chastity, beauty of, 2, 295, 303; conjugal, 94, 134, 137, 190, 295, 299
child, unborn, 331, 354
Chiodi, Fr. Maurizio, 14n17, 203–5, 206n134, 207, 228–29
Chloe Code, 337
Christological mystery, 243
Church and State, 58, 148
Claudel, Paul, 144
Clement XI (pope), 182
coitus interruptus, 184, 186, 188
collaboration (of men and women), 33n15, 349
Colombo, Bishop Carlo, 94
commandments: of God, 24n7, 34; of Jesus, 36
communion, ecclesiology of, 24
Communion, Holy, 50, 177
communio personarum, 259
concupiscence, 26, 57, 264–69, 271n24
condom, 184–86, 188, 227, 313
conformity, 79; automaton, 63; ideological, 82; social, 289; with the divine law or plan, 138, 241, 244, 346; with the good of the person, 119–22; with the law, 116; with reason, 270
Congar, Yves, OP, 200
connection, inseparable, 249, 260
consequentialist reasoning, 137
conscience, creative, 78–79, 284; formation of, 278, 286; well-formed, 110, 286
contraception, 2, 8, 18, 66, 83n1, 84n4, 85n7, 86, 88–94, 95n31, 96–98, 124, 128–29, 132–33, 135–37, 139–46, 148–52, 156n15, 158n20, 173, 177, 184–88, 189nn55, 57, 190nn58–59, 190–93, 195–97, 199–200, 202, 205–8, 213, 220, 223, 225–27, 232, 235–38, 239n10, 247, 249, 260, 262, 272, 274–75, 277, 287–88, 307, 310–17, 319, 321–24, 354–55, 358
Coppola, Francis Ford, 282
Cottier, Georges, OP, 260
Council of Trent, 84, 144, 155–57, 181, 208
Council of Vienne, 25
courage, 9, 38, 78, 104, 106, 137, 176, 305, 307, 345, 354; absence of, 7
Courage (Catholic apostolate), 172–73
creation *ex nihilo*, 243
Creator, the, 48, 118, 232–33, 235, 240–42, 244, 247, 283, 330, 334, 336, 347n51, 347–49; image of, 41
Cupich, Cardinal Blaise, 45
Curran, Fr. Charles, 56, 97, 194–96, 199–99, 201–3, 207–9, 211–13, 238, 283, 287n40

Damian, St. Peter, 181
Dante, 147
Decalogue, the, 24, 32–33, 40, 57, 82, 240
de la Potterie, Ignace :, SJ, 25, 30 31n21

Dembroff, Robin, 333
Demmer, Klaus, 12n12
Depo Provera, 317
Descartes, René, 22, 252, 255
desire's ends, 264
detransitioners, 328–29, 337, 343
Deus Caritas Est (encyclical of Benedict XVI, 2005), 31, 240, 251, 255
Devil's pleasure palace, 396, 398
dignity, of the human person, 2, 119, 241, 346n51
dilectio, 300–301
discernment, 2, 8, 11, 15, 17, 24n6, 39, 52, 93, 108, 163n36, 174–75, 177–78, 224–26, 331; of conscience, 8, 17–18, 175, 176nn58-62, 177, 290; practical, 225–26; of spirits, 78
dissent, 108, 153, 161n31, 167n48, 179–84, 188, 192–94, 196–202, 206–14, 254
Doepfner (Döpfner), Cardinal Julius, 192
Döllinger, Ignaz von, 182
Donum Vitae (instruction of the Congregation for the Doctrine of the Faith, 1987), 8, 18, 232–33
Dostoevsky, Fyodor, 66
doubt, 59, 73, 75, 127–28, 161, 197
Dulles, Avery, SJ, 182n16, 184n26, 200
duty, 1, 51, 57, 65–66, 93, 98, 116, 208, 280; of conjugal responsibility, 91; legal, 105n7; to God, 283; to hand on teaching, 140, 158; moral, 281; to procreate, 90; of respect for human life, 118, of responsibility, 96

Ecclesial Vocation of the Theologian, Donum Veritatis (instruction of the Congregation for the Doctrine of the Faith, 1990), 101, 142, 202, 206n35
education: of children, 238, 305–6; inclusive puberty, 336; moral, 77; of desire, 306; of the heart, 304; of Natural Family Planning, 314, 316, 318n25, 324n49; public, 339
Emmanuel, 115
Emmanuel Community, 358
end, ultimate, 118, 120–22, 124, 129
England, 191
Epictetus, 38
epikeia, 18
equiprobablism, 59, 75
ethics, authoritarian, 73, 79–80; existential, 55, 69, 70nn47–50, 71; hylemorphic, 81
ethos, consistent, 285
Etica Teologica della Vita, 1, 7n2, 12, 13n14, 15n18, 26, 109n15, 220, 231, 276n58, 179, 282, 289
euthanasia, 97, 164–65, 199–200, 205, 241
Evangelii Gaudium (apostolic exhortation of Pope Francis, 2013), 12n11, 348n57

362

INDEX

Evangelium Vitae (encyclical of John Paul II, 1995), 8, 164–65, 204–5, 285n35, 345
Evert, Jason, 303n36
evil, intrinsic, 88, 107, 151
Ex Corde Ecclesiae (apostolic constitution of John Paul II, 1990), 212
Ezekiel, Book of, 29

Fabro, Cornelio, 12, 13n13, 25n9
Fall, the (original sin), 265, 268, 271
fallacy, naturalistic, 13
family, school of, 303, 308
fatherhood, 42 83n1, 245
fathers, 36n34, 42, 163, 307
Favale, Abigail, 333
Fehring, Richard, 317n23, 318n29, 319nn29–30, 320n36, 321nn37–41, 323, 354
feminism, 263n2
Ferrer, Jorge José, 15n18
fertility, human, 1, 86–87, 92, 310–14, 318–23, 355
Fides et Ratio (encyclical of John Paul II, 1998), 251, 332, 345, 351
fides quae, 27
filial meaning: of conjugal union, 234–35, 237–38; of the body, 233, 235–36
Finnis, John M., 151–52, 153n6, 205, 357
Ford, John C., SJ, 139–43, 156n15, 158, 188, 192–95, 205
forgiveness, 26, 69n45, 78, 81, 105–6, 117
fornication, 148, 159, 181, 183–84, 206–8, 213–14, 260
foundational text, 16–18. See also Base Text
France, 86, 197n100, 344
Francis, Pope, 1–2, 7–8, 10, 1n11, 19, 45nn57–59, 48nn60–62, 169, 207, 217, 230, 274–75, 276n56, 327, 329, 332n12, 348–51
Franks, Angela, 262, 263n4, 264n5, 272n41
freedom, 33–34, 40, 57, 62–64, 66–68, 71, 75–76, 79–80, 101n1, 220, 231–32, 234, 239–40, 243, 279, 281, 290, 295, 302, 345, 346n51, 347n53; academic, 182, 212; authentic, 73, 348; autonomous, 74; of conscience, 210, 282, 284; from concupiscence, 16; creative, 76, 347n55; economic, 63; existential, 72; of inquiry, 213; and law, 120, 239–40; and love, 295, 303; political, 62; radical, 72; self-designing, 241, 275n55, 346n51
French bishops' statement on *Humanae Vitae*, 97–98
French Revolution, 44
Fromm, Erich, 61–64, 66, 73, 79
Fuchs, Joseph, SJ, 55–56, 73
fundamental option, 71–73, 76–78, 80, 112–13

Gadamer, Hans-Georg, 12n12
Gaillardetz, Richard, 161, 163n37, 165n43, 209n150
Gallagher, Timothy M., OMV, 175nn56–57, 176
Gaudium et Spes (constitution of Vatican II, 1965), 48, 51, 96, 137, 147, 150, 190, 191nn64–65, 210n153, 237–38, 282n22, 285n33
gay marriage, 117
gender: bread, 334, 335n24; dysphoria, 329n4, 337, 343nn43–44, 346; ideology, vi, 327, 329–30, 332–35, 337n28, 338–39, 344–46, 348–50, 351n65, 352n66, 353–54; transition, 327–28, 329n4, 339–40, 354; unicorn, 334, 338
German Bundestag, 275n55, 346, 347n53
gift of self, 291, 241, 306, 346n51
Gnostic: dualism, 252; flesh, 247
Gnosticism, 252, 275, 360
Gnostics, 244
goods, 14, 26, 119, 122, 127, 129, 141, 241, 265nn11–14, 301, 346n51; moral, 287
Grabowski, John, 262, 333
Grand Inquisitor, 66
grandparents, 305, 354
Greely, Andrew, Fr., 354n9
Gregory II, Pope, 167
Gregory of Nyssa, St., 44n53, 45n53, 271
Gregory the Great, Pope St., 29–30, 167
Grisez, Germain, 139–43, 145–46, 153n5, 156n15, 158, 159n23, 160, 174, 188, 19n78, 193–94, 205
guilt, 71–72, 93, 125, 134, 174, 281; moral, 197; of mortal or grave sin, 168, 187
Guindon, André, OMI, 201, 202n117

Hannan, Archbishop Philip, 195
Häring, Bernard, CSsR, 55–56, 73–79, 80n83, 85n7, 194, 200
Harrison, Brian W., Fr., 188n50, 193–94, 196, 205nn131–32
Hasson, Mary, 339, 340n36
Hawkins, D. J. B.,144
heart, 19, 22–23, 28n12, 32n, 35–37, 113, 148–49, 159, 182, 204, 217, 219, 243, 266n18, 271n37, 282, 284–86, 290–91, 296, 298, 300, 304; blindness of, 303; change of, 324n49; education of, 304; of God, 308; of the law, 113; of spouses, 308; of the woman, 307
Heidegger, Martin, 55, 61
hell, 166n45, 168–69; Christ's descent into, 196; scriptural images of, 169
Heraclitus, 41
hermeneutics: of renewal, 229; of the Magisterium, 10; primacy of, 11–13
heroism, 105–6
Hesburgh, Theodore, CSC, 86
Hilary, St., 22n3, 246
Hilgers, Thomas, 315n17, 316n18

363

INDEX

Hippocrates, 39
Holy Office, 183–85, 187
Holy See, 41n45, 47n58, 52n69, 85n8, 87n18, 140, 183n24, 184n16, 191n64, 194n84, 200nn113-16, 202n117, 204n126, 206nn135–36, 206n139, 207n145, 253n6, 312n4, 330n6, 332, 333n14, 347nn53–54, 348n55, 359
Holy Spirit (or Holy Ghost), 11, 21, 22n3, 26, 49, 51, 61, 68n44, 71, 74, 76, 78, 80,114, 133–34, 149n9, 155, 158, 160, 163, 171, 177, 209, 218, 250, 255, 278, 285, 290–91, 325
Holy Week, 296
homosexuality, 159, 172, 239n4
homosexual: acts, 97, 143–44, 146, 149–50, 159, 172–73, 181, 183–84, 199, 200, 202, 206–8, 213–14, 238, 239n10; person, 183n14; relationships, 11, 104, 239n10; tendencies, 236; unions, 2
homosexual marriage. *See* gay marriage
Horan, Fr. Daniel, OFM, 351, 352nn66–67
hormones, 189, 246, 337, 340–42, 352
Humanae Vitae (encyclical of Paul VI, 1968), 2–3, 8, 81, 83, 85n7, 85n9, 85n12, 86n13, 89n20, 95, 97, 98n38, 140, 144, 150–51, 180, 188, 192–98, 205–6, 207n142, 213, 217, 220, 223–24, 226, 228, 230, 232–33, 235, 237–38, 239n10, 249–50, 255, 258, 260–61, 264n5, 274–75, 286–88, 297, 302, 312, 359
Human Life in Our Day (pastoral letter of the US Bishops, 1968), 197–98
Hume, David, 280
Humean critique, 13
Hütter, Reinhard, 55, 82n86
hylemorphic: anthropology, 250, 255; view of the human being, 250–51, 255–56, 258, 261
hylemorphism, 251
hypertrophy of conscience, 15

illumination, 74, 291; by the Holy Spirit, 291
image of God (*imago Dei*), 23, 347n55
Immaculate Conception, 218, 247–48
infallibility, 89, 132–34, 142–44, 152n3, 154, 158, 160–61, 163, 164n39, 168, 178, 194n82, 196, 203n125, 205nn131–33, 206n134, 207n144; creeping, 158; of the Fathers, 157; of the ordinary Magisterium, 139, 142, 150–51, 156n15, 158n60, 161, 165, 168, 188n49, 193n81, 209n150; of the ordinary and universal Magisterium, 158, 161, 164–66, 168; secondary objects of, 205. *See also* Magisterium
Innocent XI, Pope, 183
insemination: artificial, 84; heterologous, 110, 220
integritas, 300–301
intention, 2–3, 15, 91, 91, 108, 115, 120; abstract, 111–12; contraceptive, 97; God's, 93, 96; good, 2; of the agent, 57, 112, 119; of the couple, 97; procreative, 91; subjective, 8, 67, 88; unitive, 97
intentions, 128, 219, 239; good, 11,141; of the partners, 274; sincere, 190; subjective, 18
International Catholic Jurists Forum, 1n1, 162
International Theological Commission, 7n1, 52nn69–70
intrauterine device (IUD), 91
in vitro fertilization (IVF), 232, 247
Italian: legal system, 105; penal code, 105n7, 124; political party, 350

Jansenists, 182
Janssens, Louis, 189–90
Jaspers, Karl, 55, 61
Jerome, St., 22n3, 185
Jesus Christ, 11, 42–43, 56, 76, 82, 171, 174, 246; teachings of, 3
John, Gospel of, 19, 37n36
John of the Cross, St., 41n46
John Paul II Institute in Rome, 229, 358–59
John Paul II, St., 8, 21, 34–35, 38, 51, 55, 73, 81, 98, 108, 11, 115, 141–42, 160, 164–65, 169, 200, 204–5, 212, 217, 218n2, 219–20, 222–23, 229, 235, 238, 251, 259–60, 263, 265n9, 269, 273, 274n50, 275, 278, 281, 284–85, 290, 299, 332, 345, 346n51, 351–52
Johns Hopkins Gender Identity Clinic, 253
Johnson, Don, 329n4
Johnson, Kirk, 297n3
Johnson, Luke Timothy, 262–64, 267

kakón (the ugly), 104
kalòs (the beautiful), 104
Kampowski, Stephan, 8n3, 17n22
Kant, Immanuel, 224, 283
karyotypes, genetic, 256
Kasper, Cardinal Walter, 9
Keenan, James, SJ, 56, 81
Kerygma, 221
Kosnik, Fr. Anthony, 201
Krol, Cardinal John, 195
Kuhn, Thomas, 9

Lambeth Conference, 83, 134, 149n9, 186, 191, 310, 331n1, 325
Lambruschini, Msgr. Ferdinando, 195–96
Lateran Council III, 181
Lateran Council IV, 181
Laudato Si' (encyclical of Pope Francis, 2015), 274–75, 276n56, 332n12, 348
law: eternal, 13, 57, 74, 80, 120; new, 113–14, 131, 243. *See also* natural law
Lawler, Michael G., 232n3, 263n3

INDEX

laxism, 60
legalism, Old Testament, 68
legalist, 115
Leo I, Pope St., 246
Leo IX, Pope, 181
Lérins, St. Vincent de, 10, 156n16
Lestapis, Stanislas de, 85n8, 192
Lewis, C. S., 272
LGBT, 331, 334, 336n25, 337n28, 339n35, 352; community, 350
Liguori, St. Alphonsus, 59–60, 185
Lio, Ermenegildo, OFM, 144, 188, 193, 196n94, 205
L'Osservatore Romano, 98n38, 167n48, 197
love, 19–20, 31, 33–37, 43, 50, 61, 64, 73, 81, 87, 92–93, 98, 104, 111–12, 114–15, 130, 138, 230, 235, 238, 241, 263, 266, 274, 277, 281–82, 295–96, 299–301, 304, 306–8, 312, 318–20, 325, 327, 348; and desire, 266n17; and freedom, 303; and responsibility, 86; beauty of, 299, 308–9; between Christ and his Church, 245; bond of, 299; chaste, 302, 308; communion of, 308; conjugal, 93, 95, 98, 138, 190, 302, 308–9, 324–25; counterfeits of, 297, 307; eternal, 308; experience of, 300; fair, 218, 303, 308–9; filial, 308; gaze of, 296; gift of, 319; human, 103, 108, 217–18, 235, 295, 300; interpersonal, 301–2; language of, 92; marital, 137–38, 191; married, 172, 312n6, 321, 324; mutual, 87, 230; of charity, 308; of Christ, 20, 113; of concupiscence, 267–68; of enemy, 82; of friendship, 267; of gain, 44n53; of God, 73, 77, 80, 106, 113, 116–19, 217, 283–84; of honor, 44n53; of neighbor, 32–33, 77, 80, 106, 288; of pleasure, 44n53; of self (self-love), 63, 267–68, 276, 284–85; parental, 304; procreative, 230, 254; sexual, 252, 254; spousal, 300–301, 303; true, 93, 118, 137–38, 190, 297, 302, 306–8; unconditional, 304; unitive, 254, 258–59, 260
Loyola, St. Ignatius of, 71, 175, 178n63
Luño, Ángel Rodríguez, 13n14, 16, 18n24
Lupron, 341
Lutheran, 191
luxuria (lust), 303

MacIntyre, Alasdair, 304–5
Magisterium, 2–3, 8, 10, 18, 34, 51, 68, 83–85, 87, 89–91, 94–95, 98, 101–2, 107, 110–11, 131, 138–39, 142, 153n6, 162–63, 167n48, 178, 180, 182–86, 188, 197, 201–3, 205–14, 216, 233, 239n10, 262, 274–76; extraordinary, 131, 133, 135, 154n7, 158, 167n48; ordinary, 97, 131–33, 135–37, 139, 141–43, 150–53, 154n7, 155, 156n15, 158, 160–61, 165, 166nn45–46, 168, 188n49, 193n81, 194, 202n119; ordinary and universal, 151–54, 156n15, 158, 161–62, 164–68, 174, 184, 193–94, 196, 204–5, 208
Mahoney, E. J., 145
Male and Female He Created Them (Congregation for Catholic Education, 2019), 352
manhood, 24n4
Manichaeism, 219, 275
Maoist origins, 10
marital theology, 4
marriage, 2–3, 9, 46–47, 52, 68n44, 76, 80, 83, 85–86, 88–90, 94–97, 133, 135, 138, 145–48, 150, 152, 160, 173–74, 177, 184–86, 193, 200, 206, 208, 214, 225, 245, 254, 259n14, 307–9, 311–12, 320, 321n37, 322, 325, 330, 332, 348; abuse of, 133; act of, 193; 238n7, 285; as conjugal society, 259n14; Christian, 145, 149n9; consent for, 225–26; contraceptive use in, 311; ends of, 83, 86, 237; gay, 217; good of, 146, 160, 177; goods of 147–48, 238n7; imperfect use of, 185; indissolubility of, 9, 153n5, 200, 208, 214; innovative forms of, 254n19; invalidity of, 225; meaning of, 95; natural, 146; nature of, 96, 312, 353; preparation for, 324; purposes of, 88–89, 149n9, 323; redefinition of, 46; validity of, 225
masturbation, 97, 159, 181, 183–84, 195, 199–200, 207–8, 213–14, 260
Mater et Magistra (encyclical of John XXIII, 1961), 84
May, William E., 180
McAllister, Joseph, 195
McBrien, Fr. Richard, 200
McCarthy, Margaret Harper, 333, 336n27
McCormick, Richard, SJ, 200, 254n8, 280n8
Methodist, 191
methods, artificial: of regulating fertility, 2, 86, 237; of reproduction, 260
MeToo movement, 262–64, 273
misgendering, 339
modesty, 306–07
Moloney, Francis J., 37n36
Montague, George T., SM, 49
morality: biblical, 25, 130; Catholic, 81; Catholic sexual, 3, 180, 201–2, 209, 213–14, 293; Christian, 38, 102, 144; sexual, 1–3, 18, 87, 151, 160, 169, 173–75, 179, 198, 194, 201, 203, 205–6, 214, 254n8, 350, 358
Moses, 24n7, 32, 37, 40, 44
Mother of Fair Love, 218
Mulieris Dignitatem (apostolic letter of John Paul II, 1988), 330n7, 345
Müller, Cardinal Gerhard, 8n3
Muñoz, Domingo León, 35n33
Murphy, William F., 282

INDEX

National Catholic Reporter, 192, 327n1, 351n65
natural family planning (NFP), vi, 177, 226–27, 310, 312–13, 317n23, 318n25, 319nn29–32, 320n36, 321nn37–41, 322n42, 323nn45–46, 324n48, 325, 354–55, 359
natural law, 2–3, 12–15, 54, 57–58, 80, 89–91, 117, 119–20, 129, 142, 145, 183–84, 193–94, 205–7, 209–10, 214, 237, 239n10, 251, 254n10. *See also* law
Nazism, 61, 62n22, 63–64
Neo-Manichaean, 219
neo-vagina, 342
Netflix, 295
neurology, 24
Newman, John Henry, St., 10, 48, 52, 53n71, 55n2, 283–84, 351–52
New York Times, 97, 287n40,
New Zealand, 344
Nicholas I, Pope St., 207
Nicomachean Ethics, 39nn37–38, 103n2, 264, 269n30, 287n41
Nietzsche, Friedrich, 44
non-Christians, 23, 42
non-infallible (magisterial teachings), 196–203, 207, 209, 213
Noonan, John T., 139, 147, 185, 186nn40–41, 189n55, 189n57, 190nn58–59, 191nn67–69, 192n71
norms: exceptionless moral, 142; moral, 1, 8, 12, 16–19, 22, 46, 68n44, 133, 135, 142; negative moral, 17–18; objective moral, 69; specific moral, 134, 150; universal moral, 54, 65, 70

obedience of faith, 289
object, moral, 57, 112, 131, 149
O'Boyle, Cardinal Patrick, 195
Ogino method, 84, 320
Origen, 22n3
Ottaviani, Cardinal Alfredo, 87–88, 94

Paglia, Archbishop Vincenzo, 1–2, 7, 229, 231, 235, 250, 279, 282n24, 289n45
Papal Birth Control Commission: 143, 145, 191–93, 275n51; majority report, 192, 275n51; majority thesis, 88; minority position, 89; minority report, 192. *See also* Pontifical Commission for the Study of Population, Family, and Birth
Paraclete, 36
paradigm: radical change or shift of, 2, 7–17, 45, 48n61, 141, 249–50, 254, 261; technocratic, 275
parents, 33, 90, 92, 147, 171, 233–34, 236, 240, 273, 303–4, 306–8, 322, 335, 337, 338n33, 339, 341, 348, 353, 354; rights of, 352
Parolin, Cardinal Pietro, 45

Paschal Mystery, 37
passion, antecedent, 57
passions, 31, 57, 62n23, 103, 265–66, 270–71, 276; concupisicible, 265–66; disordered, 61, 302; goodness of, 264, 266; irascible, 265n14
paternity, responsible, 88–89, 96
Paul, St., 32, 38, 42, 73, 170, 174, 181, 250
Paul VI Institute, 316n18, 318n25
Paul VI, Pope St., 8, 11n9, 85–87, 95, 98, 129, 140, 143, 145, 147, 149, 180, 190, 192, 195–97, 205, 213, 235, 260, 274, 286–87, 312
Pentecost, 23
Person and Identity Project (of the Ethics and Public Policy Center), vi, 1n1, 327, 330, 353–54, 357
Persona Humana (declaration of the Congregation for the Doctrine of the Faith, 1975), 206
person, human, vi, 69–71, 90, 117–19, 137, 190, 210, 217, 220–21, 228, 241, 249–50, 257–61, 266, 275–76, 278, 280, 289, 329–30, 334, 344, 346, 354
Phan, Peter, 154–55, 158, 161, 165n44
pharmakeia, 148
phronimos, 104
physicalist, accessory, 255; conception of the natural law, 13; way, 18
physics, 24, 222
pill, birth control, 85, 188–89, 313, 316n20
Pincas, Gregory, 188
Pinckaers, Servais-Théodore, OP, 73, 91n28, 255, 259
Pius X, Pope St., 11n9
Pius XI, Pope, 83–84, 134, 138, 140, 186–87, 193
Pius XII, Pope, 84, 90n26, 140, 187–91, 193, 224–26
Planned Parenthood, 314, 340
Plato, 49–50, 299n13; Platonic expression, 41; Platonic sense, 308
Plotinus, 298
Pontifical Academy for Life, 1, 7–8, 13, 17–18, 20–21, 109n15, 161, 203, 231, 249–50, 276n58
Pontifical Biblical Commission, 31
Pontifical Commission for the Study of Population, Family, and Birth, 84–88, 95, 97–98. *See also* Papal Birth Control Commission
population growth, 95
pornography, 74, 169, 260, 295, 297n5
Porter, Jean, 254n10
principles, 10, 14, 39, 45, 56, 59, 73, 81, 101n1, 106, 138, 190, 213, 301; abstract, 9; ahistorical, 14; basic, 3; Christian, 83, 149n9, 286, 325; first, 16, 58, 80; fundamental, 13, 67; natural, 271; of Catholic theology, 213; of interpretation, 45; of moral reasoning, 58, 73–74; of practical reasonableness, 146; of private property, 127; of subsidiarity, 344; of

366

INDEX

Thomistic anthropology, 351; practical, 18; reflex, 75; universal, 15, 65
probabilism, 78
probabiliorism, 59, 75
procreation, 82–84, 88–93, 96, 137–39, 144, 146, 150, 185, 187, 190, 223, 235–36, 239, 252, 255–58; animal, 84; artificial, 8; assisted, 18; responsible, 94
profession of faith, 22, 184n26
prophecy, self-fulfilling, 47
proportion (*proportio*), 298, 301
proportionalism, 91n28, 128, 137
Protestants, 58
Prudence, 78, 143, 301–2
Prümmer, Dominic, OP, 55–61, 75
Pseudo-Dionysius, 301
psychology, 24, 29, 343n43
puberty blockers, 340n37, 341–42
punishment, 50, 71, 72n56, 169, 181, 271
purity, 142, 218
Pythagorean principle, 38

queer theory, 263n2, 333–36, 337n28

radical paradigm change (or shift). *See* paradigm
Rahner, Karl, SJ, 55, 61–62, 65–73, 76, 78–79, 82, 132–35, 144, 150, 194, 200, 270n34
rape, 39, 80, 128, 260
ratio naturalis, 13
Ratzinger, Cardinal Joseph, 17, 21, 26, 27n10, 28nn11–12, 42, 44, 98, 142, 167n48, 184n26, 198–99, 202, 208–9, 213, 288, 289n44, 308, 350, 351n64. *See also* Benedict XVI
reason, 39–40, 59, 73, 89, 93, 116, 121, 129, 177, 220, 241, 267, 268n25, 269–71, 275–76, 279, 281, 287, 290, 302, 330, 344, 346n51, 351; chaste, 302; human, 57, 140; intrinsic, 271; light of, 204, 241, 346n51; natural, 103, 120, 142, 144; nature of, 12; morally sound, 325; practical, 13–14; right, 57; sufficient, 60; use of, 37
reductionism, 109
Regnerus, Mark, 272n42, 273n48, 320, 324, 325n51
relations, conjugal, 89, 138, 187, 287, 312
relativism, 17, 125n54, 241, 346n51; cultural, 109; dictatorship of, 17, moral, 109
Republic, 49–50, 299n13
responsibility, moral, 250, 255, 289n45
Reuss, J. M., Bishop, 190
Revelation, Book of, 30
revelation, divine, 21, 25–28, 37, 47–48, 80, 89, 101, 120, 136, 141–42, 158n21, 178, 206, 213–14; economy of, 210; natural, 120; reductive vision of, 26; sources of, 141

Rhonheimer, Martin, 13n15
right to life, 2, 354
rigorism, 59–60
risibility, 256
Robin, Paul, 93
Rock, John, 188–89
Rockefeller Foundation, 86–87
Rodriguez, Angel, 13n14
Roman Catechism, 185. *See also* Catechism of the Council of Trent
Russian Revolution, 44

sacraments, 23, 159, 181, 243–45, 290, 358
Sacred Penitentiary, 184, 186
Salzman, Todd, 263n2, 232n3
Sandel, Michael, 221–22
Schubert, Franz, 296
Scripture, 2–4, 20–31, 34–35, 45, 75, 81–82, 108, 117, 153, 155, 157, 159–60, 171, 183–84, 204, 206, 209–10, 229, 290; fidelity to, 229; growth of, 30; illegitimate use of, 23; misreading of, 30; Patristic view of, 29
Scruton, Roger, 298
Seifert, Josef, 39, 40n41, 43n50–51, 267n19
self-donation, mutual, 263
self-harm, 341, 344
sensus fidei, 11, 52, 209
Sermon on the Mount, 82, 273
sex: anal, 104, 11; nonmarital, 152; premarital, 97, 183, 199–200, 202, 260, 273n48; oral, 104
sexual activity, 147, 160, 168, 172, 239n10, 253; illicit, 273; nonmarital, 174–75
sexual identity, 81, 331, 333, 344n48; God-given, 327
sexual morality. *See* morality, sexual
sex positivity, 263–64, 277
sexual revolution, 3–4, 44, 220, 263n2, 272, 311, 322
sexual union, 149, 173, 257–58, 260
Shakespeare, 282
shame, 125, 258, 273, 306; sexual, 273
shamelessness, 38, 103
Shehan, Cardinal Lawrence, 192, 195
Shema, 31, 34
Shuster, George, 86
sin, 48, 58–60, 69n45, 72, 76, 114, 170, 172–74, 180, 287, 325, 349; mortal, 112, 140, 168–69, 171, 175; original, 93, 268n26, 271n36; sexual, 169, 171
Sirach, Book of, 49, 218, 269
slavery, 40, 42, 80
Smith, Janet E., 186, 190n59, 191n66, 191n70, 192nn72–78, 194n83, 196n93, 197n100, 274n50
Smith, Msgr. William B., 180, 181n9
sociology, 29, 47, 201, 323

367

INDEX

Socrates, 39, 44
sodomy, 89, 141, 181
sola scriptura, 21, 26
Song of Songs, 218, 235
Southern Methodist University, 194n85, 201
species, animal, 126; classification of, 127; human 251, 257; of a human act, 128, 130–31
Stock, Clemens, 34, 35n31
Suenens, Cardinal Leo Joseph, 192
Sullivan, Francis A., SJ, 140, 154n7, 161–62, 164, 166, 167n48
Sweden, 344
synderesis, 48, 58, 80

Taleb, Nassim Nicholas, 45n54
technocracy, 274–75
temperance, 276, 299, 302
theology of the body, 3, 160, 217–19, 222–23, 231, 263–64, 269, 282, 332, 345, 352n67, 358, 360
The Tablet, 192, 250
Thomasset, Alain, SJ, 12n11
Torah, 31–32, 34–35
torture, 80, 105
tota pulchra es, 218
Tracy, David, 200
tradition, 3–4, 21, 22n3, 27–28, 45, 81, 94, 102, 117, 152n4, 158n21, 184, 186, 199, 202, 207; apostolic, 108, 146, 148, 210; Catholic, 10, 21, 82, 102, 202; Christian 30, 33, 130, 148, 187, 221, 264, 277, 311; Church, 101, 183, 196, 204–5, 208, 250, 260, 301; Greek, 299; humanist, 143, liturgical, 167; manualist, 55; theological, 263, 354
transgenderism, 2, 260, 335, 350
truth, moral, 14, 67, 109
Tuas Libenter (letter of Pope Pius IX, 1863), 182, 202
tutiorism, 59; absolute, 59; moderate, 59

Uecker, Jeremy, 273n48
union: between man and woman, 300; carnal, 206; conjugal, 96, 223, 234–35, 241, 302; "condomistic," 186; inseparable, 260; love-making, 259; marital, 186, 272n42, 286; of body and soul, 250–51, 260; of souls, 259n14; of two bodies, 234; one-flesh, 172, 235; physical, 259; real, 300; same-sex, 254n10; sexual, 149, 173, 257–58, 260; total, 324; with God, 34, 289
United Nations, 94, 317n24, 323n44, 332, 333n14
United States, 46, 64, 86, 97, 189, 195, 198, 212, 295, 297, 314–15, 316n18, 317, 318n25, 322n41, 323–24, 341n40, 344, 350, 354
US Food and Drug Administration, 317
utility, 57, 194n82

Vatican I, 135–36, 152, 193, 204
Vatican II, 26, 51, 55, 135–38, 152, 156, 160, 180, 188, 190n63, 203–4, 209, 210n33
Verbum Domini (apostolic exhortation of Benedict XVI, 2010), 28
Veritatis Gaudium (apostolic constitution of Pope Francis, 2017), 2
Veritatis Splendor (encyclical of John Paul II, 1993), 3, 8, 13, 21 38, 39n40, 42, 49, 51, 55, 73, 81. 102, 106–10, 112, 115, 117, 119, 122, 123n50, 125, 128, 130–31, 141–43, 205, 232, 239, 241, 243, 251, 278, 282n21, 282n23, 284n29, 289n46, 290n47, 332, 345, 346nn51–52
virtue, moral, 14, 16, 18, 276n57
Visser, Jan, CSsR, 192

Welch, Lawrence, 154n7, 161, 164, 166–67, 344n48
Whitehead, Kenneth D., 198
Wicks, Jared, SJ, 21n2
Winnipeg Statement, 97n36, 286, 289
Witham, Larry, 195, 196nn96–99, 201nn114–15, 212n162
Wojtyla, Karol, 98, 217–18, 277–81, 285nn30–31, 288, 300, 306, 359. *See also* John Paul II, Pope St.

Zalba, Marcelino, 192
Zeitgeist, cultural, 82